Finding My Distance

ALSO BY JULIA WENDELL

An Otherwise Perfect History (Ithaca House Press, 1988)
Fires at Yellowstone (Bacchae Press, 1993)
Wheeler Lane (Igneus Press, 1998)
Scared Money Never Wins (Finishing Line Press, 2004)
Dark Track (WordTech Editions, 2005)
Restalrig (Finishing Line Press, 2007)

Finding My Distance

A Year in the Life
of a Three-Day Event Rider

✕

JULIA WENDELL

GALILEO BOOKS

an imprint of The Galileo Press, Ltd.

FIRST EDITION

No part of this book may be reproduced without written permission from
the publisher:

The Galileo Press, Ltd.
3637 Blackrock Road
Upperco, MD 21155
SAN: 240-6543

Library of Congress Cataloging-in-Publication Data

Wendell, Julia, 1955–
    Finding my distance / by Julia Wendell.
        p.   cm.
    ISBN 978-0-9817519-0-0
    I. Title.
    PS3573.E513F56 2008
    818'.5403—dc22
    [B]   2008036426

Cover design by Joe McCourt
Interior design by Charles Casey Martin
Cover photograph: Jerry Henery

Manufactured in Canada
This book is printed on acid-free paper.

Especially for Kim
And for those who've ever kept a secret

WARM-UP

THIS IS A WORK OF PERCEPTION—not fact, not fiction. Most of what occurs within these pages happens in "that purple edge outside most people's vision," as Edna St. Vincent Millay once wrote, where poetry and the imagination watercolor our perceptions of truth. I have tried to be faithful in portraying the characters who come and go. My aim is to illuminate the roles that my friends and acquaintances, professionals and peers, mentors and family members played in the unfolding of what was for me a marvelous and heartbreaking year. No matter the secret or revelation, I admire and am grateful to every person who influenced my year's story. Names have been kept or changed according to the wishes of the individuals mentioned.

I could not have written this book without the unfailing patience and humorous, deft insights of my husband, Barrett, who encouraged me to finish even as he instilled in me the belief that my story was worth telling. My deep gratitude also goes to my children, John and Caitlin, who have put up with my need to write about them—it is always from them that I learn the most about life. Also, my thanks to Sam Schmidt, Mollie Elicker, Caitlin Stephens and Kathleen Achor for their fine copy-editing skills. To Joe McCourt, for his knowledge of cyberspace and for his help broadening the audience for this book. Many thanks also to Chuck Martin, longtime friend and book designer magnifico. Importantly, to my instructors, who have had so much patience with me and my many whims. To the vets and other professionals who have worked tirelessly to help keep my ponies healthy and sound. Especially to Jim Wofford and Lucinda Dyer, who kept the faith. Most of all, enduring thanks to my mentor and friend, Kim Meier, who was seriously hurt in a riding accident during the writing of this book. Her perseverance in the face of unbelievable adversity inspired me to finish. By example, she taught me how to get to the other side.

CONTENTS

Grazing Redmond

Start Box

⁂ This is the only poem I've written in which the words go all the way to the edge of the page. I tip my helmet to Josh Pons. His book (*Country Life Diary: Three Years in the Life of a Horse Farm*, Eclipse Press, 1999) is a model for what follows in my own words and experiences as a three-day event rider.

I'd also like to give a shout to my children. My son John reacquainted me with Jack Kerouac. *Finding My Distance* could have just as easily been called *On the Horse* after *On the Road*, because for both of us, movement is ecstasy. My daughter Caitlin brought back a few things from her summer in Cuba—a little more swing and sway in her salsa and a delight in Che Guevara. The good doctor also kept his diaries of life on the road riding an iron horse, and I cannot look at that cigar-smoking, smiling mug under the black beret without also seeing my horse Redmond.

I spent my childhood galloping bareback on ponies through the dense undergrowth of the Allegheny Forest in northwestern Pennsylvania. I came to the sport of three-day eventing at the age of thirty-eight. Getting such a late start, I had to learn the countless rules of the sport quickly.

Eventing originated in the military, in which the horse needed to demonstrate obedience, boldness, accuracy, endurance, and speed. In a traditional three-day event, each phase is held on a different day, which is how the sport got its name. Horse-and-rider teams qualify for a three-day event by completing various horse trials.

Day one, or dressage, is like ballet for horses, or yoga for horses, in that it requires of the horse strength, relaxation, and flexibility. Dressage demonstrates the quality of the horse's gaits, his suppleness and fluidity of movement, and his obedience and accuracy. The horse undertakes a series of movements, similar to compulsory figures in ice skating. Judges award marks for each movement of the test, which are then entered in a formula to determine the final score, based on penalty points. The lower the overall score, the better the standing. Perfection is represented by zero.

Endurance is considered the heart of eventing. A traditional three-day event has four phases on endurance day. Phase One, or Roads and Tracks, involves a pattern of trotting within a set time span. In Phase Two, or Steeplechase, the horse runs and jumps several brush fences on a turf track within a set period of time at a few ticks below racing speed. Phase Three is another phase of Roads and Tracks. And in Phase Four, Cross Country, the horse-and-rider team run and jump as many as thirty or so immovable obstacles for a couple of miles. The pair is judged on the horse's ability to jump the jumps, as well as on time. A horse trial leading up to a three-day has only the last phase of endurance, cross country, without steeplechase and roads and tracks. Cross-country jumping efforts involve ditches, banks, water, tables, pheasant feeders, narrow fences, fences in combination with other fences, and all manner of wide fences (or oxers) and vertical fences meant to test a horse's boldness and jumping command. The horse runs by himself when he goes cross country, and because he is by nature a pack animal, running and jumping solo over such impressive, stubborn obstacles stack the deck and require bravery with a capital B.

My sport is changing. Many supporters of a modified format for the three-day event are well on their way toward eliminating the roads and tracks and steeplechase aspects of the sport. A few romantics, however, feel that subtracting the endurance phase detracts from one of the principal characteristics of a true event horse: his fitness and conditioning. The jury is still out on the sport's future design, but increasingly, we see a modified endurance phase in the upper-level three-day events without roads and tracks and steeplechase, but with a longer cross-country effort.

Day three, or show jumping, takes place within the confines of a ring and offers the traditional oxers (the height determined by two poles placed parallel to each other), and verticals (the height determined by one pole). These fences are set in combination with other jumps at related distances. Show jumping tests a horse's athleticism, obedience, and accuracy over fences. It is judged both on whether the rails stay up and on time.

In order to be a successful eventer, the horse has to be versatile in all three phases; he must be fluid and brave and fast, obedient and accurate. It is hard to train a horse to be a superior athlete in all phases. It's as hard, if not harder, to train a woman who never competed in anything until she was in her midlife. This book is not just about the sport of eventing or for people who love horses; it is also for all those who've taken up some endeavor with a passion, then committed themselves to becoming the best they could be in the face of many obstacles, real and imagined.

◆◆◆◆◆ *Winter*

"Here is my secret. It's quite simple," said the fox. "One sees clearly only with the heart. Anything essential is invisible to the eyes."

"Anything essential is invisible to the eyes," the little prince repeated, in order to remember.

"It's the time you spent on your rose that makes the rose so important."

"It's the time I spent on my rose...," the little prince repeated, in order to remember.

"People have forgotten this truth," the fox said. "But you mustn't forget it. You become responsible forever for what you've tamed. You're responsible for your rose..."

"I'm responsible for my rose...," the little prince repeated, in order to remember.

—Antoine de Saint-Exupery, *The Little Prince*

First Light

CHAPTER ONE

In the Pasture of Dead Horses

///

⚹ December 1

We wake to torrential rain and wind, which stays with us all morning, until the wind blows the weather to Butler, Essex, the Chesapeake Bay. Clear sky emerges midafternoon. Weather has always been a dramatic aspect of our lives. We took the challenge of planning a farm on unsheltered land rising up from Greenspring Valley. I remember our Maryland neighbors looking askance at our project—they knew how much wind our ground got. We should have, too—there weren't any trees, except for a few crusty relics from the last century whose branches only grew on one side. A dilapidated snow fence encircled the wind-blasted tenant house that served as the property's "big" house. Maybe the farm would have been more aptly named Windhorse Farm, instead of An Otherwise Perfect Farm. But this name works well, too. "What's the Otherwise part?" people ask me. "It's for me to know and for you to find out," I tell them. The deep, dark secret is the allusion to my first book of poems, *An Otherwise Perfect History*—I don't like to admit that I write poems as well as ride horses. Let's just say you didn't hear it from me.

One of my plans for the day is to restart my three-year-old event prospect, Pruitt. The colt has been laid up since he hurt a foreleg six months ago running around his paddock. It took months for him to come sound again. December 1 is as good a date as any to start him up again, with five days of leftover turkey behind us.

One of our first creations at the farm was a huge, high-walled round pen for breaking, turning out fresh horses after layups, and lunging. Lunging is best for a young horse in the round pen—the round high walls prohibit distractions from the outside and, by virtue of their shape, encourage repetitions on a circle. Pruitt, a gangly 17-hand adolescent, is a little slow on the draw. If you want him to trot on Thursday, better ask him on Monday. Needless to say, he needs the structure of the round pen today, which is unusable in the rain and wind, as it has everything but a roof.

When you work outside, the weather you wake to is everything. Small consolation that some Buddhists say that winds carry prayers to Heaven. After a couple of mounts, I hunker down in my office, only to deal with multiple power outages as the prayers get the better of our farm, once again.

December 2

It is dry enough that I can put Pruitt on a rope in the round pen without him slipping and falling on his oversized tush. He remembers how to go in circles about as well as he ever did—which isn't saying much. "What's two plus two?" I say.

"Four," he says.

"What's two plus three?" I say.

"Four," he says.

With size comes laziness. I am exhausted after chasing Pruitt around the round pen with the lunge whip, getting more exercise than he does. I'll have to work on getting his gaits moving forward before I get back on him.

The afternoon brings worry. Huey is lame again. He will be turning seventeen in a few weeks and has come out of retirement three times after two suspensory tears, a pestering ankle chip, and a fractured coffin bone. You name the leg, he's had a problem with it. Huey was my first event horse and seems only to be happy when he's in work—the mark of a true eventer. Each time he's laid up, I worry that it will be the last, and it has been almost the last so many times. Today he is limping behind, on the same leg in which he broke a coffin bone two years ago. Our vet will come in the morning to confirm or relieve our fears. If we have to put him down, I want to bury him some place on the farm where the wind can't get to him.

December 3

Huey crow hops out of his stall. Vet pulls out the x-ray machine, sharing our expectation that he's re-fractured the coffin bone. Seven months pregnant, Vet heaves herself over so she can dig out the hoof and is splattered with blood and pus from the abscess. We hoot with relief.

"Hue-ation Crustacean," she says, using the nickname she herself coined the first time she laid eyes on Huey. "There's my favorite patient," she says, gasping her huge way up to standing. "There's my brave event horse."

Katie, my favorite groom, soaks Huey's ailing foot in the wash stall. Vet watches Pruitt jump shadows in the round pen. "I like him, I really do," she says, giving him her blessing, which I pretend doesn't count but always does. Vet has been with us since the first fence board went up ten years ago. Huey was her first patient at the farm. She gave him a once-over and a jog in the round pen just after we'd claimed him at the Laurel racetrack.

So all is well at Heartbreak Farm, as my mother used to call it.

December 4

My parents both died last year, my mother after a long illness and my father unexpectedly. In October of his eighty-fourth year, my father rode Huey on a trail ride. In November, he was swimming laps with my brother in Miami, then he was off to New Orleans for oysters at Brennan's with John and Barrett. In February he was dead. One of the surprising outcomes of settling my parents' estates is a recommitment to my life in Maryland, after making the decision to sell my parents' 250-acre farm in northwestern Pennsylvania, where I grew up. Baltimore has become home for me in a way it hasn't been in the twenty-five years I've lived here.

My parents' house furniture will arrive next week. I've hoed out my attic and garage, thrown out first-marriage and college furniture I no longer wanted, and relegated pieces to the "pool" barn. This is an old barracks barn we renovated a few years ago for our growing kids, who needed a roomier space in which to stretch their teenage limbs. They promised not to drink and drive. We promised not to look into their condom-stash drawers or to say anything about the hookah. Up in the attic in a dusty box of kids' books, I run across Dad's favorite—*My Father's Dragon*—the copy that he'd bought for me when I was little and that I passed on to John and Caitlin so many years ago.

The cat who sends Elmer Elevator off on his quest to find the dragon in chains on Wild Island is identical to our current house cat, Bitten. When Bitten was a kitten, John and Caitlin's friend Tom, a summer houseguest, showed his trick of putting Bitten's head completely in his mouth. Living in Tom's jaws for an entire summer at a critical period of her growth has affected Bitten in some dark way. Both Elmer's and my cat are striped and miniscule, both neurotic know-it-alls, constantly meowing for attention but never getting enough, longing for the halitosis of the dragon's cave.

December 5

I'm pretty good at taking lessons. First, a dressage lesson at Grace's farm on Surf Guitar. Later in the day, back home, lessons with my event coach on the two five-year-old prospects I'd bought from Peter Gray when my Advanced-level horse, Redmond, bowed a tendon. I wasn't replacing Redmond, but considering Surf Guitar's racing injuries, Huey's fourth retirement, and Pruitt's inability to process basic math, my stable definitely needed a makeover.

I hooked up with Coach in the summer of 2003 at Groton House Horse Trials. Katie and I had just made the nine-hour-plus drive from Baltimore in 90-degree heat with Redmond and Surf. Thirty miles outside of Boston, my father called to say that my mother would probably not last the weekend. I arrived at the show grounds, ran into Coach, whom I wasn't working with yet. "What do you need?" she said.

"Someone to ride my horses?" I said, half jokingly.

"Julia, you've got nice horses," she said, her explanation for why she would agree to compete horses she didn't know.

Less than a year later, I had my horses in Ocala to get a jump start on that season. I got another phone call, this time in the middle of the night, from my brother, telling me that my father had stopped breathing and slipped into a coma after a routine surgery. Coach's husband rounded up my three horses and dog, who were stabled in a barn just outside of Ocala, plus my month's belongings, and hauled them up to Aiken, South Carolina. I rendezvoused with my animals after the funeral. Not only did Coach school my horses, but her pack of hounds schooled Daisy, our yellow Lab, on proper howling technique, which she now performs at small dinner parties. When I finally got to Aiken, still shell-shocked from the funeral and aftermath of my father's death, rendered an automaton by the intensity of the previous weeks, all five dogs were performing the *Sound of Music*, Daisy howling right along. *D, a Dog, a female dog*. It was the first time I'd smiled in weeks. Coach now comes to the farm about once a month to give clinics.

I grew up with horses in Pennsyltucky—what some call Northwest Pennsylvania. I was almost 6 feet tall in the seventh grade, but riding bareback came easier than basketball because I was so uncoordinated. Then came a fifteen-year hiatus from horses as I acquired my undergraduate and graduate degrees in English and creative writing, then a career as an editor and teacher and mom. It wasn't until my four-year-old daughter perked up about wanting to ride a pony that I scheduled a lesson with Louise Halliday. As my little girl circled the ring on a white shaggy school pony, I remembered my own childhood with horses and stories of my mother's extensive showing experiences with saddlebreds. I thought of the poem my mother often shared with me, its author long lost.

> I looked and I looked but I never found
> In the spring sweet grass on the clovery ground,
> Sign of the ring where the ponies ran,
> Lucky and Princess and Ginger and Dan.
>
> Around and around in a circle enchanted,
> We rocked to the canter and rose to the trot,
> While the sun beamed mellow, beat yellow and hot,
> And slid down the sky with its rust rays slanted,
> And the grass was pounded and trampled away.
> But that was another, a happier day.

Oh I looked and I sighed but I could not discover
In the narrowest path in the close green clover
An old rusty horseshoe to prove where they ran,
Lucky and Princess and Ginger and Dan.

And I in my silk dress and flowered hat,
Car keys dangling, a white glove gone,
Waiting for a ghost child to shout, "Rack on!"
Silly in the sunlight crying like that,
Silly to sigh for a vanished spring,
Four lost ponies and a grass-covered ring.

I couldn't remember how the poem ended, so I sat in the car and wrote a rough draft of my own instead. Sometimes you live the poem before you write it. Sometimes you write the poem and then you live it.

I started taking hunt-seat lessons with Jill French at Oldfields School, a boarding school for girls that prides itself on its equestrian facilities. Next came 83 acres and fifteen horses of my own, and a craving to become the best event rider I could. I tend to go whole hog, even when a thin slice off a flank might have been the wiser and happier choice.

My late start in the competition world has meant I've had to play catch-up. I've taken countless lessons and clinics over the last years, and am happy to be a perpetual student in the art of eventing. It took me seven years to earn degrees from Cornell and Boston Universities and the University of Iowa. It has taken almost fifteen to have earned my adult amateur status in eventing. What makes a professional a professional, anyway?

At my first Two-Star, three-day event at Radnor Hunt Club, my husband tried to convince one of the volunteers, assigned to ward off traffic from the stabling area, that since I was an amateur, I needed extra entry badges for a larger support staff. The guard's reply? "Once you make it to Radnor, mister, there's no such thing as an amateur."

I'm proud of my amateur status, whatever it has come to mean beyond its dictionary definition, from the Latin *amator*, lover, or French, *amour*—beyond the passion that it takes to engage in anything that fully. At almost fifty, I want to be a student of eventing for as long as I'm able. I'm nowhere near earning my doctorate in the sport.

December 6

We rearrange my house to make room for my mother's furniture to fit inside. Katie works overtime. She and her boyfriend are also using the tractor bucket to string Christmas lights on the backyard Leyland cypress. Katie hoists Craig up in the bucket so he can reach the tallest branches. This used to be Barrett's and John's Christmas tradition, until John went off to college. Now it's Katie's and Craig's turn to be elves. There's a painter in the house, and the phone is ringing off the hook with angst-ridden worries from both kids, who are anxious to get their school responsibilities over for the semester.

My mother had a spider monkey when she was a little girl. I'm hoping to run across a picture of it in the stacks of photo albums and memorabilia that will accompany the antiques, the armoires and butler's tables, the Limoges and Krizias, the David Robertses and Maritza Morgans. All I've ever wanted for Christmas since I was a little girl was a monkey. "We had to get rid of my monkey because he bit me. Repeatedly." This was my mother's explanation for why I would never receive that gift. As if all monkeys were biters. Barrett doesn't think much more of the critter, nor John.

"All they do is throw their shit at you and masturbate," Vet has told me.

"Can't you geld them?" I said.

"Would you really want to geld something so close to being human?" she replied.

Three-thirty brings my third ride of the day, on Calvin, my five-year-old Irish-shaped horse. My back and shoulder are sore, but we bundle up against the cold and go into the late-afternoon Maryland countryside, where you can still hack for miles and never cross your path. Vibrant blue overhead, lush green underneath, the sun listing and leaning and giving us a wee taste of urgency, our tall shadows growing taller as we go, leading our way. We seek out a neighbor's stream. Calvin plops in up to his knees and stands there, not wanting to move. A great blue heron's pewter mass lifts in slow motion. I wish I could get off and wade up to my own aching back. We step over some rocks, climb up the bank, and canter off, covering ground briskly toward home. Calvin spooks at a few deer trying to hunker down in the woods for the night, hiding from the smell of human beings and black powder this time of year. Every hectic thing in my day is suspended in these moments with Calvin, in which there seems to be no before, no after.

December 7

Grayness all around. A gray, cold sky, the kind of day you don't want to venture out into. A cold alternative is better than the warmer crush of meetings and errands and physical therapy appointments I have ahead of me. I am trying to find the perfect recipe in my baking of a somewhat older athlete. Self-rising flour. Lots of kneading. Hmmm.

Surf Guitar enjoys his hack after two weeks of Pythagorean flatwork: circles, diagonals, serpentines. He doesn't care about the weather. He only cares about showing off his new medium trot to me as we chug our way up hills and down. Daisy runs off again on another scent, deep into the woods across Mount Zion Road. One sense cancels out the other, and she becomes instantly deaf when she's on a deer.

As nighttime comes, so does a phone call from a non-horsy friend, warning me about a woman he's read of in the paper who was thrown from her Arabian and paralyzed. It's clear that he wants to scare me off horses, but could he possibly think this information would have that kind of power? I'm sure the hurt woman would understand my sentiments. A friend of mine, Brenda Herzog, who had her own freak riding accident years ago, teaches riding lessons from her hand pedal-driven golf cart and has initiated her own children, whom she had after her catastrophe, into our marvelous world.

I make a note to send my friend clippings of articles about the dangers of cholesterol.

December 8

It's always nice when a barnful of horses jogs sound, especially around this place. We began this weekly ritual at the farm after Redmond bowed his tendon last summer. We trot the horses on the driveway one by one to check for soundness. It's too easy to talk your way out of a problem when there's only an internal dialogue going on. I'd noticed the ever-so-slight changed profile of Redmond's leg but thought I was imagining it. Of course, I wasn't. I learned the hard way: when you have several horses going, a husband who worries when horses are too sound and therefore not trying hard enough, and a groom who sees lameness that isn't there for fear of not seeing anything at all, it's best to face up to a jog each week, to run your hands up and down the legs, to confer, to trot off. It's also a good time to bring up any training worries or other issues regarding each horse. Above all, it's great practice for the official jogs at the three-day events.

Today, there isn't any cringing at all. Everyone is spot on sound.

December 9

The only horse who didn't jog yesterday was Huey, who is due to get a shoe back on today. Vet shows up to confer with the blacksmith. It's dicey for farriers when vets get involved in foot issues. Vet feels that Huey's infected corn is the result of allowing his heels to grow unevenly—horses get pressure points on their feet just as humans do, and corns can result. Which means that she has something to say about the quality of Bryan's shoeing. Today is a good-mood day for Vet, however. With sugar in her voice, she asks the farrier to float Huey's heel before putting the shoe back on. Bryan pares down the heel so no part of the outside of Huey's foot will rest on the shoe, and thus no pressure point can result. Huey is back in work—one more time. If only it were so easy for the others.

December 10

Katie has to shoo a herd of deer away while out on a hack with Surf Guitar. Surf is unruffled as Katie yells at the does to move out of their path. The time of year is so hard on deer, as they are pursued from every angle. Maybe they've gotten tired of running away. Their instinct wrung out, they'd rather join Surf and follow him back to the cozy barn and the piles of hay.

December 13

I take needles and fluid into my spine. One bee sting for each agony. The pain doctor identifies misshapen facets where needles will work their magic. A digital x-ray machine hovers over my head. I lie on my stomach, my pants pulled down, but otherwise untwitched. I imagine jumps in my future if I can only get rid of the pain. I think of Redmond and Huey and Surf Guitar in the wash stall, the dripping of chalky blood to signify a bad joint's been accurately tapped, the patience with which they've waited, so many times, not knowing why, but trusting.

December 14

I get so distracted jump schooling Houston and Surf Guitar that by the time I realize the dogs are gone, I have to form a posse to find them. I head one way on the golf cart while Katie goes the other on the Gator. They've been gone for well more than an hour. I call through the trees and over the stubble of fields until my voice is all sand-and-gravel sounding. Finally, Noodles, Katie's shepherd mix, slinks toward home from across the far field with Daisy close behind. Our Lab puppy is nowhere in sight. Yet another half hour and nearly frantic in my calling, I spot a brown speck in the distance with something dangling from its jaws. Simon, our MIA puppy, bounds over the corn stubble, delighted to show me his catch. I look on, amazed at the transformation in his seven-month-old body. He now resembles a boa constrictor who has just swallowed a hat. Simon's sealskin body is bulging at the middle from his grotesque meal of deer parts, proof swinging fleshily from his frothing mouth. Some are days for losing dogs and finding dogs, for feasting on the forbidden, a first snow in the air, winter settling in over the cut, tawny bean fields of our Maryland.

December 15

We bought Surf Guitar as a yearling for $1,600 at the Timonium auction in 1996, just as we were falling in love with the quirky sounds of Dick Dale. Barrett had already had a history with the colt, having taken care of Surf's mother, Cynical Gal, at a breeding farm. He had held the mare's leg as she was being bred to Surf's sire. One day she determinedly picked up another groom with her teeth and threw her to the ground, shattering the human's femur. Then of course there was the nipple—Surf Guitar's older half sister had bitten it right off a trainer's chest.

I'd stand at the gate watching Surf Guitar grow—endlessly. I had an agonizing time getting the bridle over his ultrasensitive ears when breaking him and had to take the bridle apart to get the mission accomplished. Everything about him was too big, and slow. He was plumb exhausted all the time, would lay down for hours on end in his stall, with zero energy or patience for my training antics. Only after we caught him rocking back and forth on his haunches in his stall did we realize how he was expending all of his energies. Masturbation. At least fifteen times a day. We promptly had him gelded by Vet, who was awestruck by his package. "Good thing he's a horse," I said. Vet threw his huge Jupiter testicles on our barn roof, for good luck, as if our fortune were tied to something fed upon by crows.

We like to give our young horses some galloping at the track, even if they never run in a race. It helps both their bones and minds to develop and set. But I had my eye on Surf Guitar as an event prospect. I like a tall horse, and this one certainly promised to be that. He grew to 17 feet, 3 inches, a few fists taller than most. I took him to Laurel to gallop for a trainer so he could evaluate him as a racing prospect, but I couldn't get him out of a lumpy, slow canter on the track. Pappy Manuel must have seen something in him he liked, despite my unsuccessful gallop. At Surf's first race, they had trouble finding a girth big enough and had to send the valet back to the jockey room while the rest of the horses were being tacked in the saddling paddock, anxious for the start of the race. No one could believe Surf was a full Thoroughbred. He looked like a Clydesdale on the racetrack beside all the other small-boned, greyhound types.

Surf Guitar had one racing strategy. Because of his size, he wasn't the handiest of racehorses and wasn't agile in a pack. If he was going to win, he had to swing to the outside and run around all the others, which his big moonwalk stride often enabled him to do.

After his first couple of wins and a broken tibia that brought him back to the farm for a respite, we decided to retire him to eventing—that is, if he'd pass a vetting. Which he did not do. According to Vet, the spurs in his hocks were so bad he'd never hold up, a diagnosis confirmed by the track veterinarian. We sent him back to the track and, in order to cut our losses, ran him at a level at which we were pretty sure he would be claimed. And he was. From there on, he changed hands repeatedly, ended up running through all of his allowance conditions, and overall won several hundred thousand. Not bad for a $1,600 yearling, even if we weren't the ones making the money. We'd sent Surf Guitar off to college, and he'd struck it rich. No matter how we looked at it, we were proud parents.

I spent several years missing Surf Guitar, staring dreamily at his portrait that Barrett had commissioned for me one Christmas—if we couldn't have him in the flesh, then at least we'd have him on our wall. We kept up with his progress at the Maryland, then Delaware and New York tracks. When he finally dropped in value, Caitlin suggested to my mother that she buy him back for my forty-sixth birthday. I had hinted that I wanted Surf even more than I wanted a monkey. Barrett donned a suit reserved for weddings and funerals and drove to Penn National to pick him up. We brought the precious cargo back into our barn, took off the leg wraps and ran our hands up and down the tendons, and found a hot and swollen front suspensory. Subsequent ultrasounds confirmed there were bony fragments, multiple avulsions where the suspensory had torn away from the bone. Once again, two vets told us he'd never be good for anything. Vet advised that once we gave him time off and he healed well enough, then we should donate him to a local school as a school horse.

That was just enough ammunition for me to load my big old shotgun of hope.

I worked with him slowly. Surf Guitar would tell me when he wanted to quit. In the meantime, I'd keep riding him. From Huey I'd learned that every day is a gift. From Surf I learned that every hour is a gift as well. Every minute is your birthday and your Christmas if you want it to be.

That was three years ago. Two months ago, Surf completed a One Star at Morven Park. The video from the event just arrived today. Barrett and I sit around the television with glasses of Chardonnay and bowls of popcorn balanced on our knees, marveling at our 18-hand anomaly skipping over the Preliminary obstacles as if they were speed bumps, his massive stride almost convincing us that the tape was in slow motion.

When I think of the soul of this farm, I think of Surf Guitar.

In the Pasture of Dead Horses

Light rain, and I'm carbound,
fiddling with my keys,
watching my helmeted children

repeat themselves on the backs of saddled ponies
circling a weather-worn ring
north of Baltimore.

So around and around the ring I imagine
you must have wheeled,
as the mustached trainer, nervously

cropping his thigh, barked pointers from center ring.
My mother seeming to float above her cut-back saddle
as you racked on.

I'd heard of the ribbons
you sported before the war.
Before your trainer was called to the North Sea

and the groom to the South Pacific. Before my mother,
ambushed by marriage and childbirth, left, too,
and returned to the house of her childhood.

Fifty years of opening the same window
to the usual shadows and drafts.
Daylight struck over & over.

I'd ride over you,
coaxing my pony down the hillside
that cradled your secret of bones.

Impatient in your dark nest,
you'd kick inside the earth, the hillside shimmering.
Though you were not so much as an indentation

your bones lay beneath.
The goldenrod coloring the hillside
late summer, your temperamental monument.

Still, I was told you were there,
Noble Knight, Solid Mahogany, Emerald Future.
The hillside was a mirror

in my mother's life, and then in my own.
We opened our eyes to see into it.
All my young life, I believed you were there.

I'd canter bareback dodging brush & limb,
down the hillside graves to the Sugar Bush,
where Grandfather's sapping shed sank

plank by rotting plank to the earth,
and the maple trees grew huge and unwieldy, left long untapped.
Where the body-stench of crude oil rose from pockets

in the Pennsylvanian marsh,
and the trails that I pretended wound forever
ended. I sensed you were there.

As I sense we are repeated
on the backs of saddled ponies,
my mother, my children, and I——-

carbound, fiddling with my keys,
a young woman revised
in the thunky staccato of small hooves

wearing circles in a ring
each circuit ending
and ending again.

"In the Pasture of Dead Horses" first appeared in *The Journal*, and then again in the 1995 *Pushcart Anthology*, and again in the collection, *Wheeler Lane* (Igneus Press, 1998).

Huey at Loudoun

CHAPTER TWO

Catching Huey

Pull out the long undies, the sock liners, ear muffs, turtle furs. Four horses in lessons with Coach, in 20 degrees. Sweat under my parka. My hands stiffen and freeze into fists around the reins. I have so many layers on, it gives new meaning to not being able to sit up straight or get my shoulders back.

Huey locks his stifles in the cold, which results in stiff high-stepping behind before he's had a chance to warm up—if that's even possible today. I've learned to develop his canter a tick beyond control to make up for his lack of power and scope over fences. He always tries hard, and although he isn't the best mover or most careful of show jumpers, he makes up for his lack of ability with heart. Of the two—ability and heart—I'll choose heart every time. I'm considering taking him Advanced this spring and doing the modified Two Star at Fox Hall in April.

As my first event horse, Huey is also my best friend. We taught each other everything we know. I owned him when he was still racing and lost him in a claiming race, the very race out of which we'd had plans to retire him. That was in 1995. We waited for three races until Dale Capuano dropped him back down in value to the level at which we'd lost him. We found out one Saturday night that he was racing again in a $5,000 claimer the next Sunday afternoon. This would take some doing, as we didn't have funds in our racing account at Pimlico. We had to raise cash fast in order to get him back. I raided every ATM I could find within a hundred miles and begged friends and relatives for a quick loan so I could buy back my wonderful, lovable, mediocre racehorse. It's not all that easy to raise $5,000 cash for this purpose, let alone on a Saturday night—unless you're a thief or a gambler. Would you make that bet? "You know," Barrett said to several people, "his brother was a champion sprinter in France." As if geldings offered much collateral.

Huey finished third in his last race. We turned him out in our biggest field, then were unable to catch him for the next six weeks. He knew the good life when he found it and wasn't about to be claimed. The racing office called us for a month wanting Huey back in a race. Easier said than done, we said, thirty bags of carrots later.

December 18

"Is that one whorl or two?" Vet asks her associate, as she studies Huey's body for distinctive characteristics. "Would you say that hoof is striated?" I feel as though I'm on rounds in a hospital ward with a doctor quizzing her internist.

Vet is filling out a passport for Huey. This is an endearing event for all of us who have seen Huey through so many successes and fabulous returns from retirements and lamenesses—once to be a Preliminary school master for Caitlin. Recently, I've unretired him once more to fill in my upper-level blanks while Redmond is recuperating from his bowed tendon, with the further hope of making Huey a Two-Star horse this May. Hope springs repetitively.

The sport of eventing is not for the weak of heart. You learn to be goal oriented. You learn to make plans, even though so much can happen to upset them along the way. The chances of actually achieving your goals are at best one in three, or "three in nine," as Barrett says, with his penchant for making equations a little bigger than necessary.

A million things can get in the way: soundness, training, qualifying issues, rule changes, eliminations, rider health, family, work, and life issues. You make a plan and work hard toward it, and somewhere in all the fitness and schooling you become so engaged in the process of getting to the event, that you realize the process *is* the event, the end in itself. I'll try to take Huey to Fox Hall for the modified Two Star this spring. Today, I accomplish step one: filling out the passport.

After having paid my steep $300 passport application fee, I find out that the international governing body of eventing, the FEI (*Fédération Equestre Internationale*), has changed its mind. Horses attempting Two Stars no longer need a passport. It's too late for me to save my money—I already have Huey's half-completed passport in hand. I might as well finish the stroke and at least get satisfaction out of the even sweeter irony that Huey is getting his first passport at the age of seventeen. Kind of like waiting till you're sixty to get your first driver's license.

December 20

A predicted high of 27 today; 10 upon waking. A phone call from Barrett in the barn as I'm bundling up: too hard on their lungs. "You'd get your rides in today," he says darkly, "but they'd all be on antibiotics for a week." I jump ship, revise my day. It's black outside as I write this; the brittle wind is yowling against our tin roof. It's hard to change tack when it means turning away from the horses. Christmas is coming, and it's cold outside—maybe I should start my shopping.

December 21

I hack out in a group with Katie, Barrett's old pal Trish, who has also become my pal, and Caitlin. The horses have other ideas. They're a little crazed from being stallbound and coldbound yesterday, on the bitterest day of the year. Caitlin and I joke about how every time we go out on a trail ride together, something goes awry—someone gets bucked off, a horse goes lame, we run into the hunt, a dog falls through ice. Once my horse slipped on some early-morning dew, and the next thing I knew, Caitlin was standing over me. "Mom, are you all right?" I'd blacked out for a solid minute.

Of today's four mounts, not one walks out quiet or sane. Redmond is particularly full of himself, wheeling and snorting and shying at every shadow and snapping branch. He attempts airs above the ground before I realize that the strap on the quarter sheet I'd put on him to ward off the cold is tickling him under his tail. Oh, brother. I get off and leave it on the path, making a mental note to retrieve it on our way home. Then I have to get back on from the ground, a daunting task for my stiffening body with a bad back and a zillion layers on.

The horses settle after an uphill canter. We make our way through chunky footing, the kind that results after weeks of mud, good freeze, and a better thaw. Caitlin, just home for winter break from her freshman year at college, hasn't been on a horse in months. Only reaching 5 foot 2 to my 5 foot 10, she never grew out of her old pony, Sunny Delight, who has been half lame these past months with a niggling stifle issue. Sunny enjoys himself, particularly when we come to his favorite stream, where we have to punch through the ice trying to take hold to wade our way across. No languishing in those cold waters. No slipping off our horses' backs and plopping in for some summer refreshment. Even Daisy and pup Simon only wade in up to their elbows and won't swim a stroke.

This is where Caitlin and I used to come when she was young. Especially during the tensest moments between us, this stream would ease and refresh us, and we'd come home happier with each other. "Let's go to Baden's Stream," we'd decide when things were rough between us, and we'd settle on a ride to try and make things better.

December 24

Today is a heels-down, hands-down, pressed-into-the-withers kind of day. Seven hacks by noon so we can get the rest of our Christmas shopping done and presents wrapped. All the horses are keen, shying at the jangling of the dogs' collars coming up from behind, a patch of ice, a twig breaking. Redmond is especially fresh, once again—off from serious work these past months, he's had about enough of second string. He jigs the whole way as if to prove he's ready for more, his back as tight as a tick. He passes this attitude on to Surf, who is in turn always looking for an excuse to be bad out on the trail, to catch a buddy's behavior like a cold. The footing, alternating chunky and hard, isn't conducive to good behavior anyway. Hands down, heels way down, trot when a spot opens up, keep moving. There's naughty in the air. We sense the horses' excitement as they sense ours, with Santa Claus around the corner and we still haven't greased the chimney.

Christmas Day

The usual rush-hour traffic on our busy commuter Route 88 that runs by the farm, carrying workers between Westminster and Baltimore, is absent. Barely 10 degrees, the fields all have their whiteface on. The horses, just turned out, are quietly grazing whatever edible tidbits they can find. Even the birds have stifled their usual early-morning chatter. Somewhere in this hush is the gift of Christmas, when every little hectic thing stops for a day, and we become reflective and evaluative, rather than busy and alert and doing.

The horses need to be fed and their stalls mucked, as usual. Katie has asked for the first Christmas off in the five years she's been with us. That leaves Barrett and me for the morning chores. It's just us, and the horses, and the blessed quiet.

Surf nickers to me as I pass his paddock, asking for his morning flake of alfalfa, his expected little bit of holiday cheer. As I toss the hay, I watch it arc over the fence line. I am trying not to disturb in any way the soft feeling this day has created.

December 27

Bitter cold again. It's a good day for getting my rides done early and venturing to Pimlico to watch a horse that Barrett owns a piece of. The horse is trained by J. W. Delozier, who also trains our other current racehorse, Carneros. We had named her Apostrophe at birth because of the white mark on her forehead, but the Jockey Club turned it down with an exclamation mark. Her barn name at J. W.'s stable is Julia. Ugh. I hate to think that my name is used for any horse that kicked Barrett's hand off its wrist. Barrett finally settled on Carneros, after a type of grape grown in the region between Monterrey and the Russian River in California. A race tracker once told me that in Spanish the word means meatballs.

We walk into the barn, my favorite place to be at the track. When I'm in the grandstand, I'm too busy watching the array of people, and I feel distanced from the horses—except in the tacking paddock, where you can get a little closer and actually smell the familiar smell of horse, watch them parade by with their colors on. That's the best place to follow your hunches, which is the only way I'll ever bet, and I'm generally wrong. I have an eye for movement and size and elegance, short cannon bones and big shoulders and butts—generally the mark of a jumper, not a runner.

Meatballs was always a customer as a foal, and she was the only homebred horse I chose not to break myself. She was hard to lead and tough to do most any simple thing with as a foal, so we decided to send her out to be broken, to my old coach and pal, Kim Meier. As we were trying—unsuccessfully—to load the filly onto the trailer, with a rope around her butt and three people dragging her on, she went into a kicking frenzy and nailed Barrett's wrist and hand, which he had raised to protect his head. Good thing, the surgeon said, or he wouldn't have had a life to protect or wrist to reconstruct—which they had to do immediately. The result is a partly functional hand and a fused wrist. Now, a year later, the screws have come loose, have backed out of the plate in his wrist. He faces more surgery in a week, which we hope will reduce the constant pain he rarely speaks of, but which I know is there by his all-too-frequent grimaces and nightly tater juice other people call vodka.

As we walk into the shed row at Pimlico, Carneros pins her ears, weaving back and forth, and tries to bite me as I pass her stall. I bop her on the nose. She doesn't scare me, at least not with a stall guard between us. On a piece of twine outside her stall, someone has hung a rubber hand with a fake-bloodied wrist. We pass on by. She's won two races in four starts so far. She'll be at Pimlico with her rubber wrist until she's claimed.

The horse running today is Foolish Groom, by Runaway Groom. Barrett's racing stable, Poetry in Motion, claimed him last month, and J.W. has high hopes for him today. I neglect to tell the trainer that one of the reasons I rarely come to the track is that I bring bad luck. We've had our fair share of wins among homebreds in the years that we've been breeding and racing, all as a result of Barrett's well-studied choices, made with only third-class mares. But I've yet to be in a win photo. I've come today because John, home from college for the holidays, wants to bring his girlfriend Mollie along, and everyone thought it sounded like a fun idea. That was before we woke to 10-degree mercury that managed to stay put through the afternoon's race.

The horses parade in. The rambunctious number 6 horse jigs and rears and wheels with his groom. The owners and trainers in the paddock are understandably leery of the hot horse and back up against any wall they can find when he flings himself by.

We leave the tacking paddock early before the jockeys mount. One of the rail sitters decides that I'm his best friend, and I can't concentrate on the other horses for his comments about the number 2 horse. Bundled up and jigging in our parkas, we walk to the gate to watch them break. Unfazed by the cold in his excitement, Barrett strides on ahead of us in his suit and tie, quite a getup for him, as he is usually in barnwear. Foolish Groom, a closer, stays toward the back of the pack for the first half of the race and makes a play on the turn toward home. He gets up for third, but then tires to finish fifth in this allowance race. Barrett turns to me shrugging. "Your reputation holds," he adds.

I think it is the number 2 horse that outruns the others. We're too busy watching the number 6 horse stumble and go down. The jockey is pitched out of the saddle and hits his head hard on the track surface. He manages to crawl to the rail before he goes limp. Without so much as a heads-up about the accident from the announcer, the ambulance moves down the lane, ominously silent. The backboard comes out while the EMTs manipulate its bulkiness under the hundred-pound jockey. The horses have galloped out and come back around to find their hot walkers and trainers, who will want to find out from the jockeys what went right or wrong. No one seems to pay much attention to the recent tragedy at Pimlico, perhaps so as to ignore the mishap, which in some dark place they know could easily happen to them.

December 28

I have always wanted to make good impressions on my teachers. This is best accomplished by being prepared. Which is impossible with horses and riders, because anything can go wrong. You never know when falling from a horse if your britches will catch on a jump cup and peel right off. So for Stephen Bradley's clinic at the farm today, I wear something lacey under my riding pants. One can only hope for the perfect snafu as I lie half naked on the arena footing. My reverie is undone by back pain. I am in the shed row, straining while bending over to put on my spurs, Las Vegas sexpot disguised as a show jumper, complaining to Katie about my many spinal problems. I am admitting how marijuana alleviates the pain, just as Sir Stephen taps my shoulder to say hello. So much for making a good impression. He's still laughing at my embarrassment after the second, and third, and fourth verticals.

Stephen will be followed by Coach tomorrow. Both could not be more different as instructors, a contrast in styles I find instructive in itself. "The one is a control freak," Barrett says, "the other is an out-of-control freak." Stephen will spend the day teaching his students how to trot a gymnastic, a series of jumps set in a predetermined fashion to help both horse and rider with their jumping form. Coach will focus more on getting both horse and rider forward through a course, on turning and feel, and a basic seat-of-the-pants approach, with lots of smiles and encouragement thrown in. She has also become good at critiquing my position. These winter months between events are a good time to work on form and jumping technique. Stephen, who rode on the U.S. eventing team at the Barcelona Olympics in 1992 and won the Burghley Four Star in 1993, is a master technician. Coach is more of an intuitive rider with a fabulous eye and sense of balance.

You have to be careful in this game, as instructors can get possessive with the students they're teaching. Or maybe it's only that your Spanish teacher would rather you didn't spend all the rest of your time learning French. I've tried to be up front with my various instructors about how I like to shop around and take lessons from different teachers in an attempt to play catch-up. At forty-nine, I like to think I'm beyond having to account for my behavior and role as a student. Other times, I feel just plain promiscuous, like a nun on a nude beach . . . very faithful yet very fascinated by what's out there. It's kind of like going to college. You might have a few favorites, but you end up learning from many different professors. Variety is the spice of my equestrian education, and there is still so much to learn.

Coach doesn't yet know that Stephen has become a part of the crew at the farm. We've invited him for dinner tonight, and he'll be staying over in the pool barn. It may feel like a French farce tomorrow morning as I attempt to get stocking-footed Stephen on the road with his shirttails flying and paddock boots in one hand before Coach shows up. Fortunately, the farm has two driveways, one winding between the front fields north and west, and the other rambling through the trees, heading east.

December 29

Pruitt has his first lesson today. This isn't a lesson as much as an assessment. "How's it going?" Coach says.

"Four," Pruitt says.

We organize his gaits and present him with a canter pole. Funny how much you can tell about a horse's jumping instincts by the way he negotiates a canter pole. Pruitt tends to canter deliberately over the pole with an easy, long, regular stride. "Oh, he'll jump all right," Coach says, after exactly two passes. From the back of my mind I dig up Barrett's comments about racehorses bounding out of the starting gate. He says you can tell if a horse is going to be a good jumper by how quickly and efficiently it breaks out of the gate. I see the analogy at work with the way Pruitt handles his first canter pole. Barrett is in the shed row pretending to sweep but watching this lesson like a hawk. Seeing the colt's good jumping instinct, I can only imagine what he must be groaning to himself . . . "There goes another allowance horse down the drain." Coach gives me some ideas for my youngster's program for the next month and convinces me that I should consider taking him to South Carolina for winter training. The cross-country schooling and Novice eventing opportunities make Aiken a great place to start a young horse. We plan to leave at the end of January, with five horses on board, in hopes of catching several early spring events. We'll have to boot someone if Pruitt gets to go, as we only have room for five on our Eby trailer. As much as I hate to, I'll probably leave Redmond at home, putting off his next competition till the end of spring or early summer, with hopes of getting him to the Fair Hill Three Star in the fall of 2005.

December 30

I hunker down inside to get caught up on house and office work, as well as take a little more time with my writing projects. A luxury—my horses are getting a minivacation while Katie is on hers in Texas. In the meantime, I'll try to use the time wisely to accomplish the myriad of inside chores that have piled up, and spend a little extra time with John and Caitlin. My list turns out to be longer than when I'm riding. I persevere and manage to check off a few items; among them, Redmond's tentative competition schedule for 2005. First a long chat with Vet, who tends to douse my enthusiasm with her pragmatism. Next a call to Stephen, whose horse injured his tendon about the same time Redmond did. Both horses received the ACell injections that promised a speedier recovery. Stephen says to pick a target—Fair Hill, Radnor—and to work backward from the goal rather than work forward from where I am now. Reconsidering the calendar, I decide to slow Redmond's return and perhaps not even think about jumping him till May, with a goal of returning to competition in July. Redmond doesn't have too much left to learn, except how to heal a bowed tendon that will be strong enough to survive Fair Hill in the fall. A seasoned eventer with many miles under his hooves, he won't need much schooling to prepare, just fitness work, which in a conservative way he is already getting. We'll just have to step it up a bit in the spring.

The Fair Hill International Three Star is a pinnacle goal for many upper-level riders in my sport, one I never thought I'd set for myself until I owned a horse like Redmond, who has far exceeded any expectations I ever had for him or for me. I bought Redmond in the fall of 1998, when Huey was having difficulty completing a One-Star three-day event because of soundness issues. My new goal at the time was to complete a One Star with Redmond. Accomplishing this quickly, in 2000, we moved on to complete several Intermediate horse trials, and then the Radnor International Two-Star three-day event in 2001, followed by the Jersey Fresh International Two Star in 2003. When you have a horse that is as eager as Redmond to go all the way, you go all the way. So we tried our hand at Advanced in the spring of 2004 and qualified for the Fair Hill Three Star that year. We were aiming for the big event in the fall of 2004 when Redmond bowed a tendon.

When Redmond tore an origin suspensory two years ago, we decided to let time heal it. He rested an entire year and came back strong. This time, with the bow, we took a more aggressive route and had Dr. Cooper

Williams, one of the vets selected to be part of the ACell pilot study, inject Redmond's injured tendon with the new substance taken from the bladders of pigs. It is mixed into a solution and injected directly into the tendon lesions. This promotes and stimulates the closing and healing of core lesions in bowed tendons, among other things. It also promises to shave about three months off a twelve-month healing time for bows. Looking at Redmond's proposed competition schedule and working backward from Fair Hill, I find another six weeks of downtime for the horse who has already taken me much farther than I'd ever dreamed I'd go as an adult amateur rider. He doesn't owe me a thing. But I owe him a little more time than the time promised, and so I decide to give him more of it and not start him back till summer. Rest, Redmond. And heal thyself.

Catching Huey

She wants him, & he knows it.
So when she walks toward him,
he looks sideways at her, looks off,
then turns on his hocks & walks away.
The field is wide & green
& open as desire.

On the second day, she brings a ditcher
of grain, teases him with a handful.
He watches her trying not to watch him,
pretending she doesn't care.

The third day brings
crinkling pocketfuls of chocolates & mints.
He circles her, like love
hedging the outskirts of her life.

His hazel eyes look through her, take on
the darker hue of the pasture beyond.
He has all the time in the world.

That night, she orders takeout,
goes out to the paddock
with a few pieces of lemon chicken,
feels the blackness move around her.

On the fifth day,
she considers buying a lasso.
She won't feed him until
he decides to come in.
That'll fix his wagon, she thinks on the sixth,
remembering the night
she said no to her lover, don't touch.
Until she got close to him,
saw that his eyes were not hazel, but green.

The seventh day, she lets the gate swing wide
when she brings the others in.
He bolts, then rears, wheels,
jumps the four-foot fence
back into the field, his eyes
a little whiter now.
He'd rather be circumscribed
than caught.
On the ninth, her ex pays
his monthly visit, and she doesn't have time
to bother with the horse.
She'd like to come in,
take her fill, & rest,
but her body memory aches
from too many years
of being cantered the wrong way,

craving a loose rein, long gallop
through the woods.

She decides she has to be eleven again
to catch these horses, running away
from her brother, worrying
her weight, two heads taller
than all the other boys,
so that she's hardly ever asked
to dance. The next day son John
wanders to the gate with a fistful of carrots.
Huey bends his head
to accept the food,
then walks the boy
back to the barn.

"Catching Huey" was first published in *Dark Track* (WordTech Editions, 2005).

Tacking Up

CHAPTER THREE

In the Midst

〰〰

※ New Year's Day

The house still asleep. I edit a few poems, watch the ballerina ornament twirl on her axis. I'll take the tree down tomorrow, put the worn ornaments away for another year. I'm anxious to start packing for Aiken. We pulled all the blankets at night check last night. The temperature went up, and the horses were moist under their layers. We wanted to get our chores done so we could crash even earlier than our 9:30 norm. As long as it's midnight somewhere in the world, that's good enough for us.

Happy Birthday Huey and Surf Guitar, It's My Show and Houston! Happy Birthday R. Isabella and Jerry, Pruitt and Our Ballerina (her baby tucked inside, all cozy for the night, twirling inside his mother's womb).

This is Caitlin's first extended visit since she's been at college. Even Christmas, in all of its abundance, has not made up for the restlessness she feels being near me again, whom she wants to repel as much as she wants to cling to. I know this is normal, and yet my feelings get hurt. Today, a CD of hers is missing. She's sure that I've done something with it. I fail to remind her that I barely know how to work the CD player, let alone share her taste in music. I suggest that we go on a trail ride together, hoping that this will soothe her and repair bad feelings between us. I put her on Huey, who has far more patience than I could ever hope to have and doesn't mind when she leaves him in the cross ties too long or forgets to put on his galloping boots.

Off we go, with Daisy in the lead. The weather has decided to be fickle again; it's 65 if it's a single degree, and we've traded long undies for shirtsleeves. Up and over hill and dale, through the woods and fields till we get to Jackson Hole Farm. Mrs. Jackson used to host the Maryland Combined Training Association's annual training and Preliminary level event, until it was moved down the road to Shawan Downs. Secretly, I have a plan. There aren't too many jumps left standing, but just enough to do the job, what with the addition of a few hunt fences. Suddenly I call over my shoulder, "Follow me!" and Houston and I take off, with my daughter and Huey on our tail, over the split rail, the coop, the table, and up the hill to the bank jump. As Houston and I are galloping away from the coop, I glance back at the girl and Huey, now in midair over a fence. Sure enough, I see the unmistakable facial expression that occurs when a person, no matter the deep-down, is happy about something he or she has done well and is enjoying—even with a bit of tongue in her cheek, she is smiling.

January 2

Our filly, Carneros, runs today. I want her either to win or be claimed, so I decide not to accompany Barrett to the races. I know when the horses have done well. I get the call about ten minutes after the race. Otherwise I wait for a good hour, stewing. We've dropped the filly down to a $16,000 claiming race in the hopes that she will be snagged. The phone call comes about forty-five minutes postrace, with news that they've had to scratch her. The filly has bad ankles plagued by bouts of arthritis, and today she jogs out limping. Normally I would bring her home for a rest, but I warned Barrett after his injury that she was not welcome back. She will have to stay at Pimlico until she's dead. I am a self-proclaimed softy with horses, but this decision emerges from a place deep down that is determined to protect what's left.

Barrett broods all evening, and I can't tell if it's because of the scratch and the ankles or because he is worrying about his second surgery coming up this Friday. The surgeon will remove the screws that have backed out of the plate in his wrist and replace them with a longer plate, larger screws.

January 4

Now the days have a let-down, dreary, after-the-holidays, hurry-up-and-get-caught-up kind of feel. Paying bills, taking down the tree, writing thank-you notes, and turning more attention to the young horses. I resolve to leave Redmond behind and not take him to Aiken and to take either youngster, Jerry or Pruitt, instead. Jerry, aka Suave Rhapsody, though a little back at the knee, has a one-of-a-kind ermine front sock that stops you dead in your tracks. He won about a hundred thousand for us in a single year, running through all of his allowance conditions. Vet didn't like his conformation, and we needed money at the time, so we tried to sell him at the Timonium auction in 2001. Good thing for us he didn't meet our $4,500 reserve price. When he was three, Rainey Andrews and I evaluated his jump. Rushy and flat. Not a good sport-horse prospect. Our plan has always been to send our sport-horse rejects to the track. When Jerry won his debut race, the phone rang off the hook, calls from trainers wanting to know if we had any other horses that couldn't jump.

Jerry's mother, Rhap Danz, once kicked Barrett in the head when he was trying to feed her in the pasture, turning him into a momentary Daffy Duck and earning him his first ambulance ride, his eyes glassy and forgiving even as they were hoisting him onto the backboard. We got the mare for nothing from a friend when a bowed tendon ended the mare's racing career. Barrett liked something he saw in her pedigree and spawned the idea that she'd do well being bred to a freshman stallion in Florida, Suave Prospect, thus inbreeding to the mare Bimlette, Rhap's fourth dam. When you ship a mare farther in miles than the price of the stud fee, you'd better know what you're doing.

That was in the winter of 1998. I happened to be traveling to Florida with Huey to catch some early spring training with Kim Meier and Marty Morani. I must have been one of very few owners who ever came to Farnsworth Farm to visit a broodmare. The barn help looked at me as if I were just another snowbird who'd ventured up their driveway to ask directions to the jumper show. When I identified myself, they pointed to a field of almost two hundred mares. I looked for the biggest mare with the fattest tendon and meanest eye. It didn't take all that long to spot her. Thank God not all mares pass on temperaments to their foals.

In his last race, Jerry was clipped by another horse and pulled up with a cortical fracture of his cannon bone, earning his retirement. After six months of rest and shock-wave therapy, I'm going to give him a shot at a second career and see if his jumping instincts have improved. Both he and Pruitt are focusing on canter poles and cross rails for a month or so, until it becomes ho-hum routine for them. Pruitt, having just turned a big but still growing four, can't decide where to take off to successfully negotiate a cross rail, so I take him outside to see what he'll do in our woods with little logs, where he fares better. I make a note that tomorrow I'll add a take-off rail to the cross rail, so he'll be better guided where to put his feet when attempting to be airborne. Jerry, on the other hand, snaps up his knees like the classy allowance horse he is, every time.

January 5

Rain, rain, and more rain. Katie's back at work, which means I might get all the horses ridden for the first time in a week. Plans for multiple trail rides get thwarted by the rain. Hacks are big in this barn, one of the best ways to break a young horse and to get all of the older horses ready for the cross-country element of eventing.

Last week when Coach was at the farm teaching, I had a friendly argument with her about the benefits of trail riding. No eventer I know does a better job with multiple mounts than Coach, and no rider has a better feel for the jump, or a better eye. She believes her accuracy to fences is a product of jumping so many horses. The repetition of turning and jumping are what educate a rider's eye. She also has a tremendous natural ability. No matter how many jumps I jump, I will still have misses. But I've never once witnessed Coach missing her distance to a fence.

But she doesn't believe in trail rides. "Just go up and down your back hill a few times," she says, "that's plenty to get your horses fit." But will it keep them happy, alert, fresh? Will it introduce them to different kinds of footing, streams, woods, hunt fences, cars, deer? Will it make them brave to the unexpected and train them to deal with anything that happens in their path, like tractors or alpacas? "Alpacas?" Coach says. "How on earth will alpacas make them braver on cross country?"

Our neighbor Tillie owns an alpaca farm. One of my best tests of equine courage is this: Will my horse quietly pass by Tillie's herd of alpacas, protected by two Turkish wolfhounds that come charging and barking over to the fence line? Alpacas are not quite as good as monkeys would be, but they're a pretty good alternative. When I ask my horses to pass through whatever monster's den we encounter, they tend to listen, especially when they find out what's on the other side—the marvelous trails that lie beyond the alpaca fields. They learn that I wouldn't ask them to face up to anything that would kill them.

January 6

With seven horses in training, I have to do more solo jumping. Another way professionals are separated from amateurs: those who have the guts to jump by themselves and those who don't. Jumping alone is now a necessary evil, and I've been experimenting with ways to make it palatable and instructive. Today I decide to take Surf Guitar through a gymnastic in preparation for Coach's visit on Saturday. I am a 140-pound fan of gymnastics. Placing several jumping efforts in sequence, set apart at related distances, teaches the horse to compress his stride and to become elastic over fences, and helps me work on my position. It can also be a creative part of the sport: considering the countless ways to manipulate fences in a single line, varying heights and widths and distances to hone a horse's skill, without the rider having to get in his way. As Kim Meier once said with a wink, "I never leave home without my line of bounces." I've collected all the jump patterns from the lessons I've taken over the last fifteen years. I have a notebook, divided by instructor, as well as by heading: Gymnastics, Lines, and Patterns. If it's ever published, I'll dedicate it to those who jump alone.

I've chosen a pattern from Wofford's new book, *Gymnastics*, that I've modified slightly for big boy Surf Guitar: a single line of four fences, spaced 10, 19, and 30 feet apart. It's designed to teach a horse to trot in quietly to a cross rail, bounce the first combination of fences, then take one short stride, then two medium strides to an oxer out. Surf will learn to be patient, to shorten his stride, to jump around the bounce to the subsequent one stride, then to set up well for the final oxer out. Surf Guitar needs all the bounce work he can get to compress his mammoth crane's body and teach him to wait. He's almost as long as he is tall, and that means a lot of body to compress.

I tend to lose Surf's engine every time I try to turn him. What worked for him at Pimlico isn't working 20 miles to the north. I have a hard time getting him straight to today's gymnastic line. I talk out loud to myself, evaluating my own progress. I comment on the arc of any turn, how with some horses who turn quickly, like Redmond or Huey, I have to be careful to hold them out on a turn. But with horses like Surf, who are slow and argumentative about bending and turning, maybe if I turn a little sooner and cut the arc? . . . I catch his shoulder before it has time to drift, and at last I have a straight horse on my way to the fence. A simple lesson in geometry, and Surf jumps better than ever, hesitating and sinking before he pushes off and rounds himself over the jumps.

January 7

Dr. Wittstadt joins Barrett and me in the green room at Union Memorial Hospital. He draws a diagram of the wrist joint, explaining options for the surgery. He will either have to take the plate and loose screws out and sew my husband back up with bone staples or—more seriously and more likely—re-fuse the wrist, this time in its entirety. I will be in the waiting room either thirty minutes or three hours and will be able to judge the outcome accordingly. The surgeon's explanation takes a literal minute, then he kicks back in his chair, as if at a cocktail party, to ask our recommendation on tractors. Should he buy a John Deere or Massey Ferguson for his 5-acre lawn? This is Dr. Wittstadt's original bedside manner, spawned in his medical beginnings as a nurse, then further nurtured as he went on to become one of the most renowned hand surgeons in the world. Regardless of the context, Barrett always likes to talk about tractors, and he humors the good doctor by saying that it all depends on what color he wants—green or red.

I look up to a poster that boasts, "We saved over four thousand hands last year." And I'm certain Barrett's was one of them.

The operation takes four hours. Any joint bones that could not be nailed shut have been discarded. This will mean a lot more pain during Barrett's longer recovery, but still he gets a good prognosis overall. Dr. Wittstadt joins me in the waiting room two hours after the start of surgery. Though the surgery was a success, what was left of the one remaining joint had deteriorated, so out came the original plate and in went a much larger one. He's happy, his associate is happy, and he's off to yet another surgery though it's almost 6:00 on a Friday night.

The nurse takes me back to the recovery room. Barrett is shaking with cold from the anesthesia, and tears smart the corners of his eyes. He cradles the bandage that runs from the tips of his fingers to his elbow as if it weighed as much as a new foal. "I think I need to find something else to do with my life," he manages to say.

It is the first time I've been in a hospital since my father died. I know enough to know that post-op is no time to change your life. The nurse and I dress my groggy husband, and we get him sitting then standing *tout de suite*, even though he's nauseated from the anesthesia and in obvious pain. When you're used to working with your hands, there's nothing worse than being handless. Barrett expected that the surgeon would tighten up some screws and send him on his way. Back to work the next day. It's hard for him to face the severity of the situation. Recovery is going to take time.

As Barrett is being wheelchaired out, the nurse hands me a baggie that contains the smaller plate and handful of screws the surgeon extracted from my husband's wrist. Just regular screws of various lengths that you could buy at any hardware store. I am fascinated by this mundane detail.

January 8

I'm finishing my third lesson with Coach when Barrett shuffles into the arena barn in sheepskin slippers and with injured wing in a sling to tell us that Foolish Groom came up from behind to win by four lengths in a $25,000 claiming race at Pimlico. Though I know how badly he hurts, and how disappointed he is to have missed the winner's circle, my husband is nonetheless smiling.

January 9

Misbehavior in horses is best dealt with efficiently and swiftly. If Surf Guitar nips as I'm cinching up his girth, I smack him on the nose. If another horse rears while I'm on his back, I rap the crop hard, right between the ears. When a horse stops in front of a fence, again, the crop, right behind the saddle. I never feel guilt for having punished fairly.

Misbehavior in adolescent girls is a shadier realm. My children get the best schools, clothes, vacations and the safest cars. As a parent, I think I'm doing the right thing. But too much fruit in a bowl, and some of it spoils. I try to instill in the kids the value of hard work, and I'm successful, because they see the hard work that I do. I tell them that personal satisfaction is found in the effort and process of trying their best at something they love. This does not prepare them for "no," however, for the times when I find it necessary to remove some of the fruit from the bowl or to make their world smaller.

My daughter wants to do things her way, now that she's had a taste of freedom at school. With my crop poised, I say no to a request to stay out late. She seems startled and unprepared for my swift decision. All hell breaks loose. She does not back down, nor understand that her constant nipping in the cross ties will not curry my favor. I am exhausted and say things I will regret. Our argument leads to hurt on both sides, to her premature return to her father's Tribeca apartment. At these times I worry that she plays me off against him, finds someone who has misplaced a crop or doesn't have the heart to use it on her.

January 10

I'm back on my meds. I have a history of making this decision when the things that bring me the greatest pleasure on earth become chores, items on my list to be checked off. The cloud that surrounds me today has no reason for not lifting. I must weigh a thousand pounds, without the energy to walk up to the barn. This has been coming on for a few weeks, and at last I'm able to face it, head on.

"Bye-bye, poetry," I say to Barrett. This is common knowledge in our household, and the chief reason why I decide to go off the antidepressant at least once a year in the first place. I fear that the medication interferes with my creativity, as demonstrated by the sheer amount that I write medication-free.

"Bye-bye, dressage," he adds. This stops me.

"What do you mean?" I say, perplexed.

"I think it has something to do with details," he explains. Here's a comment that lifts the cloud for me, if only momentarily. At least it's something to chew on. If God is in the details, then maybe he rode dressage, too. I think of the minuscule thoughts that go through my brain in order to do a correct shoulder in. I disagree with my well-meaning husband who loves to make associations between contrary ideas. The rational part of my brain actually gets in the way and is the reason I'm not that good at dressage. I think, but don't feel, when I ride that never-quite-perfect shoulder in.

Bye-bye, thinking. Hello, Lexapro.

January 11

Vet joins us for our weekly jog to get a read on each horse's soundness before the season starts up, as well as to meet the new horses, Houston and Calvin. She has only seen them from a distance grazing in the field since their arrival in October, neither horse having needed any vet care yet, thank God.

Pruitt is the first victim. "This one needs a pasternectomy," Vet says, eyeing his long, four-year-old pasterns. Oh-oh. Not a good-mood day.

Hue-ation Crustacean's right front is a little swollen because of a scratch. Vet predicts that he will blow his right front suspensory before the year is out. I bite my tongue and manage to refrain from asking, "Is that because it's the only one he's got left?" I also stop myself from reminding her how she also predicted that Surf would not make it through the Morven One Star. Nor would Huey make it out of his last retirement. Nor Surf come sound again after his devastating suspensory injury. I bite my tongue until I taste iron.

She won't let Surf trot on our asphalt jogging pad that doubles as driveway because of the severe rotation in his hocks. Jerry comes out ouchy and is a little off at the trot. She mocks his head-bobbing lameness by chanting, "Sellhim-sellhim-sellhim," then manages to criticize pup Simon for needing an eyelid tuck when she passes him snarfing spilled grain in the back of the golf cart. "They're called trash-can eyes," I say, defensively but with certainty about the name I give to the big, droopy lower lids of our chocolate puppy.

She calls Redmond an overgrown pony yet admits that he trots well within his package. She's not at all convinced that the ACell we allowed Cooper to inject in his bowed tendon will accelerate the healing process. As far as she's concerned, the jury is still out on anything that doesn't fit in the basket between the handlebars of her vetmobile.

We pull Calvin and Houston out of their stalls. Two whistle-clean vettings just two months ago would indicate there can't be anything wrong with them. Wrong again. After a six-hundred-mile phone call with the pre-purchase vet, Vet was convinced that Houston would become a head shaker. When Barrett, playing the role of Iago, reminds her of the prognosis, I blow like my father's cat cracker, saying that he's not shown any sign of it. "It's not summertime yet. Just wait till fly season," she quips. She finds him to be back sensitive just in front of the croup and traveling wide behind, making him a candidate for acupuncture. Calvin apparently has midget feet on a giant's body and doesn't land evenly behind when he turns around.

After the sixth horse, Vet wiggles her chin, takes a deep breath, and remarks on what a wide range of horses we've got in our barn. "No one could accuse you of going after a certain type," she says. She smiles in a way that tells me despite everything, she approves and will always support, no matter our differences, no matter what.

I take a minute to review my stock. There's the 15.3-hand overgrown pony Redmond. The 18-hand monster Surf Guitar. The sleek, beautiful, very-average-in-talent-but-not-in-heart Huey. The poor-moving, back-at-the-knee homebred Jerry. Pruitt, whose only reason for not riding the little school bus is that he wouldn't fit on it. The tall, floaty, yet somehow also waddle-gaited Houston. And the big-boned, lovable, weight-lifting-but-ballerina-footed Calvin. I feel as though I'm introducing the talented members of a rock band midgig, all of whom come from radically different backgrounds and walks of life, all of whom are heroin addicts. That Lexapro? Better make it a double.

But Vet is wrong. All you have to do is to look in their eyes to realize that all seven horses are exactly the same, between the ears and between the shoulders, which is where it counts.

We end the session by injecting Huey and Surf's hocks. Vet takes a lot of time explaining how it's to be done, the divots and bumps that are the best entry into the joint, how long to scrub, how to pull the caps off the syringes, the pop that the needle should make as it enters the joint capsule or, when the joint's too worn, how the needle feels like it's entering an orange. I realize she's talking to herself the way I do when I jump by myself. When she starts humming an unnamable tune, I file away the stress reliever as another option for myself.

My day ends with a phone call from my ex's apartment in New York City. "Hey, Mom," Caitlin says to me casually, as if things were just hunky-dory between us. "I was wondering. . . would you like to come to New York next weekend for that show you got me tickets to?" I glance down at my calendar, paging to that day, which is already filled, including a commitment to be part of a Jimmy Wofford demonstration at the World Horse Expo in Timonium. "You bet," I say anyway, "Thought you'd never ask."

January 12
Hacking horses in pea soup fog—a little luck, a lot of feel, and trust. Mush underneath. Steady. Lean back in the saddle. Take a feel of your horse's mouth downhill, but only a little. Then let go. This is how you enter dreams.

Trish on Calvin, Julia on Houston, Simon leading the way. He runs off on the other side of Mount Zion Road. Our voices, amplified in the dense, quiet air, call after the dog. We wait for what will come back to us: a dark brown shape moving and materializing out of the underbrush.

January 13
For ten years, we ran the farm as a boarding facility. We were always as full as we wanted to be; for a time, we had almost fifty horses stabled. It is nearly impossible to run a boarding operation and keep everyone happy, especially ourselves. We were able to cut our business in half a few years ago by selling our development rights and creating a conservation easement on the property, which enabled us to pay off our mortgage. We can now rest assured that our farm will remain farmland in perpetuity— and the bank won't ever come after us. Just last year, after Barrett's

accident and the deaths of my parents, we cut back again, deciding that we needed at least an eighteen-month sabbatical from boarding. We nudged almost everyone out.

We kept just two boarders: Connie Bison's weanling Nifty and another event horse, Smarty, owned by Chandler Willett. In the meantime, I've been focusing on my event horses, my writing, and being the executor of my parents' estates, as well as trying to get caught up on farm business we'd put off because we were always too busy with the boarders. Our sabbatical has been not so much a reduction in work as a reduction in noise. No longer do we have to face a steady stream of traffic each day in and out of our driveway or the constant interruptions by boarders with questions and complaints.

I'm an adult amateur eventer—I don't teach, I don't train or ride for others. I've only sold a couple of horses over the years. Barrett is best at seeing mares through their pregnancies and taking care of the babies. He enjoys bringing those young horses to the track and seeing what they can do. But there's too much work at the farm for him to be a full-time trainer. So that leaves us with few options, as far as how we can make money, which we must do again soon if we are going to stay put. Mom and Pop have this discussion too late at night. We go back and forth with our options, breaking the cardinal rule of never talking about the farm on the second floor of the house.

January 15

Barrett and I carpool with neighbors, Walter and Linda Reynolds, to the Maryland Combined Training Association's annual banquet and awards ceremony, where we listen to Gretchen Butts and Kim Meier speak about their experiences at the Burghley Four Star last fall. Gretchen's horse Zydeco is related to my Redmond. Both horses were born on Doug Dean's farm in Canada, as was their cousin, John Williams's Olympic horse, Carrick. Gretchen has been at this game a lot longer than I have but still considers herself an adult amateur. Kim is my good friend and event mentor. I spent several of my formative years in the sport under her passionate tutelage. I cannot hope at this point to ever get to a Burghley, though I suppose on my better days I have dreams of one day earning a trip to Kentucky Rolex, or, more realistically, to the prestigious Three Star at Fair Hill. Perhaps it would be easier if Redmond were not so hard on himself and did not hurt himself so often. Of the six years since we've been together, he will have spent a full two on layup because of serious tendon and ligament injuries. If there ever was a horse to get an adult amateur like myself to places she never thought she could go, it is Redmond. As Marty Morani once said, I could drink a martini on my way to a fence, and Redmond would still get the job done well. He sleeps on my pillow most nights, to borrow another phrase, this one coined by Jimmy Wofford.

Both Kim and Gretchen fell at Burghley in horrendous conditions. Kim remounted and finished after landing in a ditch at the coffin jump. She developed a blinding migraine from the fall and later said that the only thing she wanted to do less than get back on was not get back on. She did, and finished, by riding on feel and trust in her horse Merle to get them the rest of the way home. Gretchen fell at the second water and got back on, but was sopped and fell again three fences from home. They both plan on returning to the Rolex Four-Star International event in Kentucky next spring. With fingers crossed, Kim will be off to Badminton next fall, where we hope the weather will be on her side.

January 16

Gretchen Butts calls today. What horses do I have for sale? I'm caught off guard. I don't get enough practice with such phone calls. I couldn't sell a hundred dollar bill for ten bucks. I stutter, say that I don't know if I'm ready to sell the horses she's most interested in, Calvin and Houston. I equivocate, then put a price on them I hope will be out of her ballpark. I sigh with relief when she admits that my figures are more than what she wants to spend. I direct her instead to Katie's young horse, priced exactly where he should sell well.

I awake violently ill in the middle of the night with "female trouble." Six o'clock on a Sunday morning I'm wiped out from losing so much blood, nauseated, and lightheaded. I still make my way up to the barn and start loading the trailer. Trish arrives to accompany me to Jimmy Wofford's for lessons. Trish is a critical-care nurse when she's not having fun at my barn. When I almost faint in her arms, she convinces me that the only thing I better jump is ship. I wake up my gynecologist, who groggily tells me to take aspirin and go to bed—and stay there. I spend the morning tossing and turning and stewing about the passage of time and the many ways my body manages to sabotage my plans, now with menopause looming, and all that that might mean for my riding "career." The phone rings. What do I have for sale? Nothing today.

January 18

Everything slows down in the cold. It takes me all day to get my rides in. The situation is not helped by my nagging female complaint, and I don't finish babies Jerry and Pruitt till 5:30, when it is almost dark. The sunsets lag till 5:45, so poignant on these clear, cold days.

Grace comes to ride my horse on the flat, to prepare Huey and me for our proposed Advanced ride at Pine Top Farm in Georgia late next month. I watch her not move a muscle, though I know she is working hard. She makes dressage seem fluid and effortless. Huey is a good boy, though I can tell he is strained by her requests. I can hear him grinding his teeth as they trot by. She works him until he relaxes, until he carries himself higher and lighter in front and is able to push through with his hind legs more effectively to make the most of his movement. His whole body lights up, becoming expressive and alive. Huey is a tall, rich chestnut with sleek, classic Thoroughbred lines and an endless, swanlike neck. He looks a little like those English paintings of Thoroughbreds from the late nineteenth century. The horses are usually at a steeplechase meet or the racetrack. They are either jumping or running or arcing through the air. They look more like the idea of horses than actual horses. Huey is obedient and quick to respond to Grace's aids, even in the difficult downward transition from canter to walk and back into the canter again—the simple change—which I have had a devil of a time with. Huey likes to load his front end to get any job asked of him done, until a master like Grace is on his back to encourage him that it is indeed possible for an old dog to learn new tricks.

January 19

Coach cancels her lessons at the farm because of illness. Maybe female trouble is contagious. I decide to have Katie set up an old well-loved Jimmy pattern that includes a triple and a couple of bending lines, as well as a corner on a short side of the arena, so I can get Surf and Huey jumped today. I used to help Katie with all of the jump setups, but since the disk degeneration in my lower back set in, I've been advised by my physical therapist to give it up. Katie has also had to water by hand the 200-by-80-foot interior space. It's been well below 30 degrees all week, and the sprinkler system cannot be turned on or the lines will freeze.

Surf reacts quickly off my leg, particularly coming out of corners. He snaps his knees up and rounds his body over the fences, hardly touching a rail. I end, as we often do at Jimmy's, by practicing square turns to the corner jump setup on the short side—which is exactly what it sounds like, a jump in the shape of a corner, or a triangle, coming to a point on one side and widening on the opposite side, enticing the horse to refuse or run out at the point because of its irregular shape. Even in a ring that is 80 feet across, the turn after the corner, particularly on an 18-hand horse who is still green and does not turn well, can be a challenge. Katie lowers the jump for us, and he jumps it well both ways. But when she puts it back up, he is sluggish coming out of the corner and gets to the fence on a short stride. He pecks the ground before jumping, his arc just awkward enough to pop me out of the tack so I lose my right stirrup. We land, and though I'm discombobulated in the tack, for a split second I think I can right my balance. He careens around the left turn, and the centrifugal force sails me off the right side of the horse and down to the ground—hitting my bad side.

When I fall, there's a moment of no return, an awareness that I'm losing my balance and just how bad it's going to be. Nine times out of ten, I sense that I'm not going to hurt myself. Then I relax so that I don't get hurt, after all. I know it before I even land. This was easier to judge when I was younger and my body was a hundred percent. Now when I fall, I feel myself protecting my back, worrying that I'm going to land on it, which I invariably do because I'm no longer as relaxed. In other words, if you're nervous and anticipate something about to happen, those very fears can contribute to bringing that something on. Scared money never wins.

I've not been significantly hurt from falls beyond a broken ankle, a few broken fingers, and some stitches—unlike so many of my unluckier colleagues, like Grace or Kim or Coach, who've had to nurture themselves back from major injuries. But when I have taken more serious falls, I always know it on the way down.

This is not one of those times, though I feel myself bracing my right lower back against my plummet. Fortunately, the footing is soft in my indoor arena, despite the 72-inch height I've fallen from. I get knocked a little silly. I sit there a moment reciting the alphabet. Surf stands over me with a worried look in his eye as if to say, "What are you doing down there?" When I finally get to Z, I get back on and finish the jump school, ending with a left-hand corner. Surf Guitar is not the least bit flustered by our little mishap. I then have a terrific jump school on my schoolmaster Huey, who shows both Surf and me how the corner should be jumped successfully and fluidly on the first pass.

When I show up for my physical therapy appointment, I inform Dr. Frankenstein that I've fallen today. "From a horse?" he says, aghast. I feel a little like a reformed smoker who's fallen off the wagon and is reporting her lapse to the doctor: "I swear, I only swiped two!" My therapist's eyebrows go way up.

"Did you hit your back?" he asks. When I reassure him that the fall was soft, he nonetheless pulls me off my exercise routine and orders heat and electrical stimulation again for my newest problem. I don't complain, looking forward to the heretofore relaxing twenty minutes of soothing heat and lightning bolts.

Assistant Igor comes into the treatment room with all of her gidgets and gadgets.

"I mean, aren't you scared to death that you're going to fall off and get hurt? I mean, all I can think of is Christopher Reeve."

"Aren't you just terrified," I say right back to her, "every morning when you get in your car that you're going to have an accident and die on your way to work?" Her eyes turn into slits. She cranks up the machine, turns out the light, leaves me alone.

Ten minutes into the treatment, I shift on the table and get a jolt of electricity throughout my body equal to grabbing a hot fence wire. I jump up off the table, rip off the pads, throw on my jeans, and hightail it out of there, way before my time is up.

Inauguration Day

I watch Grace ride Huey, making him look like a dressage horse. Then she helps me jump the new horses. Calvin is her obvious favorite, because he's the type she herself wants in a good horse—you can ride him softly and just keep coming to a fence in a naturally regular rhythm. Houston is like riding a slinky. He's got enormous scope but tends to expand over his fences, and he needs to learn that jumping is not such a big deal. It's a matter of education, and I'm up to the challenge because I like the horse. But there's also a female/male thing going on—Coach and Grace love Calvin; Jimmy and Stephen and a few steeplechase trainers love Houston. It's fun to watch the people I admire most in the horse world pick their favorites when I have both of them.

The afternoon brings a sore throat and a prediction of more snow. We watch the same old president with the slitty, sunken eyes take another oath.

In the Midst

—for John

of rush hour traffic, twin fawns sprawled
on the road like toys
tossed over a balcony.
On the shoulder of the two-lane
where grazed land meets housing developments
and the dangers of proximity,
their injured mother
struggled to stand
in the whirling strobe of so many headlamps.

Cars slowed and veered;
one stopped by the side.
We didn't have a shovel or a pistol.
My son was twenty and still
had his spots. I couldn't ask him to take
the tire iron to the doe's
wringing head, could I?

We slowed, we looked from our closed windows
as if looking were enough.
And passed on, making our way home
to the awful
even now: hooves clattering
on blacktop, teeth bared
for her young
laid out like little crooked saints
on the road
that shouldn't even be a road,
not in our wilder imaginings.

Baden's Knee Tub

The Interstate in Aiken

CHAPTER FOUR

Man Overboard

✕ January 21

Gretchen Butts comes to the farm to look at Boy Wonder. Katie is a nervous wreck. If there is prestige and dedication in the sport of eventing, then Gretchen has it. She is a licensed judge and technical delegate, internationally and nationally, and has ridden her marvelous horse Zydeco through the Four-Star level. Today she tells us she doesn't want to spend a lot of money on a new horse. Moreover, her situation has changed since she made arrangements to look at Boy. Zydeco has been injured and is out for the spring.

Gretchen and her daughter ride Boy for a long time. No matter how they place him at a jump, he tries to jump it well, without ever getting flustered or revved up. Boy, whom Katie bought from Kim Meier and Marty Morani, is a nice young Novice horse, with lovely correct gaits and a big, powerful jump. Katie's competition hands have been tied by her lack of solvency. Boy hasn't gotten the mileage he would have had if Katie had the money to compete him, which is the main reason she is selling him. She has too much tied up in him, and she needs to get out.

Gretchen suggests that she might want a more experienced horse to keep her eye sharp while her Advanced horse is out of the picture. I can relate to that. You either use it or lose it after forty. I sense that Gretchen will not choose Boy even as she is climbing out of her truck. "I'd like to see more neck," she says. Buying horses is a funny business. Someone once told me to always pay attention to my first impression of a horse, as it will be what will stick. Does Boy have a short neck? I hope I am wrong, but I don't think Boy will be experienced or long necked enough for Gretchen to make an offer.

January 22

A blizzard forecast up and down the East Coast, from south of D.C. all the way through Maine: 12 to 24 inches of snow, winds gusting to 50 miles per hour and paralyzing windchill. I am determined to make it to New York via Amtrak. The snow starts somewhere in Jersey. By the time I meet up with Caitlin in a coffee shop next to the theater, a foot has already fallen. We dash next door to *A Number*, Caryl Churchill's play about cloning and a father's strained relationship with his original son and two of the clones. The acting is a bit of a letdown, as is the contrived plot. Caitlin is also disappointed. She's a first-year acting student at Sarah Lawrence College and has high performance hopes for herself. Unlike her mother, she loves the city. She even considers herself a New Yorker now, which is what she tells our cabby when he asks where she's from.

We smear our way through the snowy streets of Manhattan to the Hudson Hotel. The blizzard continues through our early dinner at the Hudson and through the night as Caitlin and I toss and turn on our scanty mattress in the art deco room that is no bigger than a large box stall. I check the windows several times in the night, but they will not open. Caitlin has asked to stay with me, and I offer to share the tiny space with my insomniac daughter who will have to read and watch TV till 3:00 A.M. before she can at last fall asleep. When she finally does, she talks and carries on with the imaginary characters in her dreams, as she has since she was little. Not a good setup for a country bumpkin claustrophobic like myself. Sleepless in Manhattan, I start worrying about how Barrett must be faring back at the farm, with his casted wrist and hand. A blizzard fifteen stories up—there's a kind of beauty in it, for those whose imagination stops there. I try not to let my daughter see how my mind has wandered back to Maryland. Even over our penne pasta, in front of a raging fire in the great dining hall at the Hudson, my heart is kicking drifts away from the barn door.

January 23

The New York airports are closed because of blizzard conditions. The New Jersey Turnpike is reportedly impassable, but the train schedules don't blink, and the cars on my train are stuffed with determined passengers who've found a seat on the only way home. A snow squall is created outside my window by the wheels of the train stirring up the snow, a blinding blizzard on one side, bright sun and fields and cities of snow on the other. Drifts and ice sculptures are forming in the gangway connections between cars. I hunker down under one of my mother's minks, thinking of Dr. Zhivago, counting the miles until we pull into Baltimore Penn Station, right on time. *Dasvedanya!*

January 24

Suave Rhapsody gets the green light from Cooper to be a part of the Aiken caravan. He stands patiently for the digital x-ray—probably at least his tenth since fracturing his cannon bone eight months ago. His eye is soft and relaxed. He trusts that he is home from the track for good and likes his new role as event horse. I can count on Suave Rhapsody, or Jerry, to try his best every day. He's aided by an unusual intelligence: he picks things up quickly, with a good attitude and work ethic. I'm delighted that he'll be joining our Aiken gang. With good weather, perfect footing, and lots of schooling opportunities, it's a terrific place to introduce young horses to the eventing world. Or so they say. I, on the other hand, have my misgivings about southern horsey zip codes. The footing is consistently good, but there aren't enough hills. The upper-level horses get their screws tightened, but without the benefit of uphill and downhill runs that are the signature difficulty in Area I and Area II courses. Plus, it will be a long six weeks without either Whole Foods or my Tempur-Pedic mattress. Or early-morning sunrises over the farm's far hill, the distant wending whistle of the B&O freight line.

January 25

I'm down with a bad head flu. Katie jogs all of the horses while I flounder in my sickbed. It is not looking good only 72 hours from departure. I struggle up to the barn around 2:00 P.M. to let my crew know of my change of plans. Katie is tacking up Calvin, her last ride of seven. "Just looking at him is enough to make you feel better, isn't it?" she says. His huge dark Irish head nuzzles into my arms like an overgrown Lab. She is anxious for Barrett and me to leave, anxious for all of her hard work to pay off. And probably anxious to have the farm to herself. I have a wave of energy, and I recommit to our Friday launch.

I could only do it with Katie's and Barrett's help—Katie to pack the trailer with tack and sheets and blankets and coolers and buckets and feed tubs enough for five horses. Snaps and wraps, studs and pads, boots and more boots, towels and sponges, and a myriad of products from shampoo to WD-40. Enough hay and grain for a week times five, and finally, yes, my exercise bike will have to find enough room in the stuffed gooseneck to also make the journey so my heart can stay sound and fit enough to ride all five every day and to compete every weekend while we're away.

Barrett spends the day running "Aiken errands"—getting the truck and trailer tweaked and tightened and filled, picking up meds and equine passports and vet reports, cases of wine, making trips to Southern States and True Value hardware, and, most importantly, having the satellite radio Santa brought installed to make our ten-hour trip to Aiken more pleasantly jet fueled. Such ardor, while I languish on the runway. How could I not feel better? By six, I'm revving up my engines with my first tall glass of Chardonnay.

January 28

We roll down the icy driveway at about 5:30 A.M. with our fifteen-thousand-pound load. We gun the motor and almost run smack-dab into the electronic gates at the back entrance, which have seized up in the 7-degree cold, only opening partway. Barrett gets out to jimmy the one side open. The trailer starts to rock and roll with the horses' impatience. I get out to check on them, skate my way to the back hatch. Trying to duck away from Surf's nippiness, Calvin has gotten his head caught behind one of the partition bars. We spend the next half hour taking apart the trailer from the inside with the horses loaded in order to free Calvin's head. Mission accomplished, we tie him shorter, prop the full hay net between the warring horses, keep our fingers crossed, and slam the trap door shut. Barrett pushes the gate open as far as he can while I jockey the truck and trailer through the inadequate opening. In the process of attempting to squeeze through, I slam the gate with the trailer, mangling it and throwing Barrett onto the snow-covered icy driveway. He wrenches his back and leg in the process. In the collision with the gate, the satellite radio comes tumbling out of its dash-board holster. "Don't worry," says Barrett, "I'll fix it"—the sentence of doom around the farm. Barrett can't even fix a bowl of cereal. I glance at my watch. We've been up for five hours and have only traveled six tenths of a mile. I reverse and try again, and succeed this time, but barely. I have a sickening feeling in the pit of my stomach. Bye-bye, electronic gate; hello, good old-fashioned pipe gate. The neighbors will just have to smile.

We've barely gone 20 miles when I cajole Barrett into calling Bill, who has been doing handyman work for us since the farm's inception. He dug almost every post of our 4 miles of fencing and can be called on for anything, from helping Vet put down our beloved farm dog to helping us get the hay in under darkening skies on a moment's notice. A horse goes through the fence, and Bill will be there in a matter of hours to repair it. "Julia ran into the gate," Barrett tells him this morning. "We're thinking maybe you could take it apart and put up a pipe gate instead, or something like that," he continues. It's about seven in the morning; Bill's apparently not had his third cup of coffee.

"Wait a minute, I'm confused. What did you say happened to the gate?" I cringe, feeling like the epitome of a woman driver.

The farther south we go, the later everyone goes to work, so that we catch Baltimore, Washington and Richmond rush hours as we make our tedious way down I-95 with our heavy load. The new satellite radio weather channel informs us of a major ice storm about to hit the Southeast. We arrive in Aiken under dark, threatening skies. The owner of the farm where our horses are staying is filling up bins of water in the event of a blackout. Great. We've left our indoor arena for this? "Look at it this way," says Barrett, "most any place is going to feel warmer than home." We unload the horses and get them settled for the night, then head over to the cabin across the pond where we'll be staying for the next six weeks. Our hosts, Frank and Kay Chew, greet and show us around, then ask us over for a dinner of lamb and Merlot, ice cream and cognac. There's nothing like southern hospitality.

January 29

Rain, rain, and more rain. Of the freezing variety. No one gets ridden today. Not even the sandy South Carolina soil can handle this kind of weather. The satellite weather channel tells us that it's colder in Aiken than at home. I'm reassured by our barn landlord David that nothing lasts long in these parts. Tomorrow promises to be rideable. I knock the receiver off the dash again and break it for good. "A blessing in disguise," I say, fumbling with radio parts. After the eleven-hour trip, the horses need to settle into their new environment. Barrett is tickled pink about the weather making my decision for me.

We are freezing. Neither one of us brought enough layers from Maryland, sure we wouldn't need our long undies and down parkas in a southern version of winter. David keeps driving the four hundred yards from house to pole barn in his burgundy Ford Dually to make sure we're settled in and have everything we need. He's got on his Aussie raincoat and hat and looks as dry as a bone under there. I stand out in the raining icicles with a bare head and no gloves, answering his questions and trying my best to match his pleasantries. I'm towering over him with my 5-foot-10-inch frame, my teeth beginning to chatter. His wife Paula, the spitting image of Laura Bush, pulls up in her identical silver Dually to ask us in her roomy drawl if we'd like to join them for Saturday morning pancakes. I review the long list of barn chores. I decline her kind offer, then get back to my wet work. Down at the big house, Paula cracks a window so we can at least smell the bacon.

We spend the soggy day taking care of the horses, turning them out in installments in the pine-cluttered paddock. Our curious steeds, not used to sharing their paddock with conifers, spend their icy turnout time in a huddle around the juiciest, nibbling on its sap-sweetened bark and fighting over whose turn it is. After the barn chores are finally completed, we spend the rest of our time getting settled into our cabin and huddling around a roaring fire sipping Chardonnay and nibbling on cheese and crackers—and each other—all evening.

January 30

One-two-three-four-five, all the horses get hacked today, and each one—with the exception of Jerry the Racehorse—is a ding-a-ling. Surf jigs and whinnies frantically for his buddies the entire ride, Calvin pulls on the bridle and spooks at every twig, Huey thinks he's back at Pimlico when I trot him onto a weed-strewn quarter-mile track where he tries to run off with me, and Houston puffs himself up and practices his airs above the ground. But Jerry, instantly relaxed, takes in the new scenery and happily does the job I'm asking of him. Go figure. Just eight months off the track, where he ran his heart out, he has more excuse than any of the others to be naughty. Maybe I won't sell this one, after all.

January 31

My lesson on Houston with Coach reminds me of the ironic twist that occurs in the training of horses. Houston has a huge stride, and one of my jobs in training him over stadium fences is to keep his canter as regular and as packaged as I can. I must give him a lot of support and guidance and encourage him with my aids to add another step before each jump. In other words, I must encourage him to go against his natural tendency to leave the stride out. This is to maximize safety and success when jumping and to encourage a better, rounder jumping technique.

With Redmond, it is just the opposite: he has a natural 11-foot stride to Houston's 13, and his tendency is to dribble his tight little body like a basketball down to each jump and chip in another stride whenever possible—until one day Coach encouraged me to open up his canter and go faster with more impulsion so as to better negotiate the Advanced heights and widths. Redmond's bouncing-ball package worked well through Intermediate level because he is such an outstanding jumper, but I probably would have run into trouble at the Advanced level if I'd not been able to show him that it is possible to lengthen his natural canter stride, thereby training him counter to his own instincts.

Maybe the analogy holds for artists as well. Robert Bly thinks that if a poet's natural tendency is to write longer narrative poems, then her best effort will probably be a lyric poem, because she will have to develop within her poetic nature a trait that runs counter to what comes easiest and work harder to produce the result of that trait. I know that my natural tendency is to overwrite, and so I am constantly cutting and honing and trying to find the crystal of the poem within the first-draft mass of words. Writing is rewriting. Maybe my best poem—as yet unwritten—will be a haiku, in the way that Houston's best jump will happen when I'm able to package his long body into an 11-foot stride and successfully ask him to wait to the base of the fence—against his natural tendency.

Perhaps the metaphor extends beyond the realm of jumping and poetry—that our best, most enduring efforts are produced from what we have to work hardest at, and we have to work hardest at things that do not come naturally to us.

February 1

The days in Aiken take on a rhythm: feed, turn out, barn chores, hack up the mile-long bright clay road to Jumping Branch Farm, where I school the horses myself or hook up with Coach for a lesson. The road is soft on the edges, almost the consistency of a sand ring, and perfect for a warm-up trot. There's no traffic, and the tall long leaf pines that line the road add a sense of serenity.

The road is also the exact color of Huey, and my favorite times on it are with him, glancing down at his mane and neck, and then to the chestnut road. This is my seamless painting, my horizon of sky and sea with only a thin shadow between.

Jerry has a cross-country school today. He is patient and quiet and doesn't back off any of the Beginner Novice fences I introduce him to. He's in a group of horses that take turns trotting and cantering fences. There's a lot of commotion, including a colicky horse of Coach's that her colleague is walking. We're all on edge for the horse, who several times tries to throw himself to the ground in his discomfort—plenty of excuses for my ex-racehorse to be bad. Jerry impresses Coach, particularly with his jump. "Too bad he's not better with his front end," she says ironically. "You're going to have to stock up on chin guards!" she exclaims, after the next jumping effort. I beam and hack him back down the road when we're finished, which is secretly the thing that I'm happiest about—that I could separate him from the herd and hack him by himself without a fuss.

I wake in the middle of the night with the first line of this entry in my head and have composed most of it before I get myself out of bed at 5:45, eager for yet another day in Aiken. My days have taken on the quality of poems: their lines weave in my head while I'm dreaming.

February 2

Huey's right front leg is the size of a tree stump. His temperature is 104. Barrett runs for a vet. I'm hoping that it's from an old cut that has become reinfected. I imagine twenty new billboards posted around our South Carolinian digs, with Vet's face on each. She is saying over and over, "Suspensory, suspensory, suspensory."

Misery loves company. Surf Guitar has rubbed both hocks raw getting up and down in his stall. We noticed it yesterday on one side only. Barrett dumped several new loads of shavings in his stall, thinking he was hitting bare floor when he got up. Everything is exaggerated with big horses—even the effort of getting their bodies up from a reclining position. Now he's got about ten loads of shavings in his stall, enough to stuff several mattresses. Still, he's opened up the other hock and made the first hock worse. I can only think one thing: that he's up to his old tricks rocking back and forth on his haunches, rubbing his hocks raw when he spanks his monkey. Barrett lights up when he hears my theory, wishing he'd thought of it first. Masturbation is not the first thing you think of for causing horses—or anyone—injury, unless you're a Victorian. I give Surf the benefit of my analysis: it's probably because his sheath is dirty. The cold winter weather at home pressures us to let slide the horses' hygiene—they don't get baths for months, and they certainly don't get their penises cleaned from November to March. It'll have to wait a while longer, though—it's raining again today in sunny Aiken, and the temperature's not supposed to go above 45 degrees.

The vet confirms my diagnosis of Huey, which brings a huge sigh of relief—he's got cellulitis, or a localized infection from the newly inflamed cut, probably aggravated by our jump school yesterday. He should be all right in a couple of days, with meds and some R and R. As for Surf's johnson—I have put it on my to-do list: post office, grocery store, penis.

I'm two for two today. It has to be bad news for me to be right about something.

February 3

A dreary day. Huey no better. Rain, rain, and more rain. The mercury no higher than 40. But at least Huey's temp is down to 100.8. He's walking like he's got a massive wedgy. Barrett and I start brainstorming, wanting to add something into the mix like Isoxsuprine or Azium to increase his circulation, but our southern vet advises us to wait it out. His blood results come back clean. It's a localized infection, so we need to remain local with our remedies.

I'm not a patient sort, except when rehabilitating horses that I know are out of the game. But before the lameness flags have dropped, I get event drunk and tend to push things. I start counting down the days till I'm fifty, as if I'm going to turn into a pumpkin when that happens. I remind myself that Huey is seventeen, that we have brought him out of retirement three times, that every ride on him is a gift. I still have time for him to heal before his first scheduled event. There is more to this game than the sport itself. When I walk into the barn and he's bobbing his head up and down in anticipation of dinner, I revel in the magic of dailiness, the special attention paid to the littlest thing that can make my day—Daisy snoozing on her new blanket on the backseat of the truck, her chin propped up on the back dash, looking out the window as we bring in the rest of the horses for the evening. Huey turns his head to take a small chunk out of Jerry—he wants his dinner first—and I know he's feeling better. He'll be back.

Thompson, Georgia

We load Calvin and Houston and head to our first horse trial of the spring season at Pine Top Farm, an exciting and often disorganized occasion, largely because it's hard to find the necessities that have been hiding since last November. Where are the boot pulls, the galloping boots, the Vetrolin and Show Sheen, the hoof oil, hair nets, stock tie and pin?

Calvin and Houston put in respectable dressage tests. Both have quite a bit of potential. They have lovely innate movement and are more naturally in a dressage frame than my other horses. Most horses carry about 60 percent of their weight up front, 40 percent behind. Racehorses travel more like 80/20—like the weighted front ends of darts. These two horses are natural 60/40s, or maybe even 50/50s, and in that more even balance, better built for dressage.

The horses put in fluid rounds in show jumping, too—clean, clean. I'm hesitant about the cross-country course, having walked it the day before. It's big for Training level, and I share my concerns with Coach, who walks the course with me before my first ride on Calvin. The course is intestinal. I'll have to negotiate the twisting and turning on young horses that don't steer well. The course designer has used round bales as decoration on several of the jumps, and both horses are easily spooked. We will have to jump through a narrow 8-foot opening with round bales as the frame, hemming horse and rider in. Perhaps this course is not an appropriate first for my two new ones, but Coach reassures me that they've both been schooling well and can handle it. She's confident that we can get the job done. That makes one of us.

I tack up Calvin, but cannot find my Saddle Tite—a sticky substance that you roll on your saddle to help you do just that—stick. Calvin warms up well and comes out of the start box with lots of Irish, ticks off the first four jumps. The fifth is a bank complex. We're supposed to jump up, take one stride, then jump a log on top to get us off the other side. It's a pretty straightforward question for Training level, and this is not one of the jumps that I've been worried about. I come at it briskly—maybe a scooch north of where I should be—and at the last second, Calvin exits stage left and runs out. I'm pissed, let him know it with a growl. I don't dare do more because of a runaway-bride experience I had with him two months ago when he spooked at my use of the whip. I still haven't broken him to the disciplinary tool like I should have. I circle and come at the jump again. He jumps up, veers left, chests the white flag, stops, and I somersault off the bank, landing like a boulder on my right shoulder. The air is knocked out of me, and I can't move. The jump judges radio the EMTs and the start box. There's a frenzy to catch my horse and make sure I won't be drooling for the rest of my life. I'm finally able to sit and then stand and then breathe before I experience a raging pain in my neck and shoulder. All my event buddies come running, except Barrett, who is anchored to the start box, holding my second mount, Houston. Calvin's caught, Coach shows up, and I retire from the course and walk home.

I spend hours in the Aiken hospital getting x-rayed and MRIed. Nothing is broken, although the radiologist does find a suspicious shadow at the top of my spine, suggesting that I fractured a vertebra in the past. This time I've got a strained shoulder and a stoved neck, as well as a blow to my ego. I conclude that I'm all washed up and had better find something else to do with my life. Barrett shows up after having seen to the horses. I reveal to him my doubts. "Well, if it's an out you're looking for, then this is a good one," he says.

"My pride gets in the way," I admit.

"Like most poets, you tend to be an egomaniac with low self-esteem, a fatal mix of pride and lack of self-confidence," he explains. I'm shocked by the astuteness of this new analysis from my well-meaning husband. "And they are completely contradictory. So much so, that you'll never be happy with both of them warring inside you."

He's right. The wake-up call is not about the fact that I'm engaged in a dangerous sport from which I should back off, but that I need to do a better job of listening to my instincts. When I sense that a course is inappropriate for my horse, I'd better go with my own judgment.

The doctor writes a prescription for Percocet before shooing me out the door. He doesn't even bother to warn me not to ride for a while. I'm still dressed in my boots and britches, with my medical armband strapped to my biceps and my stopwatch on, beeping reassuringly as each minute passes.

This is horse country. He knows I won't listen. The best advice he could give me would be to remember my Saddle Tite next time, and don't just put it on the saddle but paint it on my britches, too.

February 6

Barrett recommends that we grind the Percocets in a coffee mill and roll the powder into joints. Instead I take the painkillers the conventional way. Which have made me nauseated. I try to get some small chores done in the cabin and don't even make it to the barn until eleven. I hack Calvin over to Coach's barn and get him situated there, as we've decided to pawn him off on her professional care at least through Sporting Days Horse Trials. Huey's leg has gone from trunk to sapling, but it's still far larger than a horse's leg should be. I commiserate with him—my head feels about three times its normal size and weight, from pain, not pride. The pride factor would make it about pea-sized right now.

Last year I tried to winter in Florida with the horses. Upon arrival in Ocala, we turned Redmond out, and he immediately lost his cool galloping around in his paddock and splatted on the slippery sand footing. The fall produced a massive hematoma on one stifle that put him out of commission. Which hardly mattered, as the next day I had to abandon the horses and Daisy to fly north so I could make the decision to let my father die by removing life support. He had plunged into an irreversible coma after routine surgery. Now, a year later, with a lame Huey and a concussed Julia, my latest southern working vacation is once again not off to an auspicious start.

As I hack Calvin down the orange road to Coach's, I note our silhouette on the clay surface. The sun is brightly shining. I am used to checking the mirrors in my indoor arena back home to note my position and my horse's frame and step. I've not seen anything resembling a barn mirror since coming south, until now, trotting my naughty horse up the road to reform school.

When the sun is shining in Aiken, who needs a mirror? Calvin's shadow tells me his ears are pricked, his step is bright, his movement forward and obedient. He doesn't know that anything's wrong, doesn't check in the shadow mirror to see that my shoulders are somewhat slumped, my heels are too far up, my aching head is slightly cocked to one side. I study my depressed frame in the shadow that precedes me. Perhaps Calvin feels a change in my looser contact on the reins, the way I slip so easily out of the saddle, latch the stall door at Coach's barn, and turn away from him.

February 7

I can't cry, because when I do, my head begins to throb. I want to go home.

I ride, and that makes me feel a bit better. A dressage lesson on Surf increases the better. My head is killing me. I can only turn it by turning my whole body. I spend some time dreading the upcoming event this weekend. Huey's leg is better, but he's still quite off. Huey and me, Huey and me: I carry the rhythm in my head when I trot him up a hill on his hack today. I hit damn hard, I hit damn hard. The beat changes for Jerry. I want to sell, I want to sell and hunker down at my desk. The sun is shining, maddeningly, like a ball of electricity and shame. My head is hurting, my head is hurting. I finish my rides, clean my tack, think about Calvin. Coach tells me he was perfect for her this morning, though she could feel the crankiness in his stiff green body to the left. She will fix him, she will fix him. I carry that rhythm back down the hill toward home, knowing that a week is not enough time to fix anything. I fill a bucket with warm water, get out the leather cleaner, line up the dirty bridles and my bruised ego, and get down to business.

February 8

Our day begins with a long talk in the wee hours, and then a Percocet omelet when I finally wake up hurting. We are trying to plan our day and the rest of the week, as well as the rest of our lives. Barrett is on a roll. It's like being married to Winston Churchill.

"The true test of passion is this sort of adversity," he says. "The difference with you and eventing," he adds, "is that, unlike everything else in your life, where you tend to withdraw when there's a problem, you love the sport so much that you become more aggressive and committed when there's trouble." Well, we'll just see about that. Another siren wails through the dawn and more bombs fall on London.

A few hours later, our Ford Dually breaks down on the way to the barn. Barrett has to cancel his flight back to Baltimore. Just as well—the plane would've probably crashed. I school Surf and Houston cross country while Barrett attends to the truck. I screw up my courage and head out on the cross-country course at Hopeland Farm on Surf, my most reliable mount except Huey. I get the job done thanks to Surf's patience, though my head is still pounding and all the turning and looking for the next fence dial up the pain a notch or three. My ride on Houston goes well, too, despite his greenness and what must be a dim awareness on his part that I am not quite whole. I feel more grim determination than love of the sport. How do you back down and go home when there's a group of riders cheering you on and also secretly wondering just what kind of metal you're made of?

This is not a good trait: my desire to please and to make a good impression, my concern for what other people think. There must be a marvelous freedom for those who simply don't care—they are free agents, those who don't do anything motivated by the opinions of others. How can I achieve that freedom for myself when my whole existence has been geared toward pleasing my parents to make up for my older siblings' failures? As the baby of the family, I was the only one left to get the job done—to earn my parents' respect and approval. Even after their deaths, that legacy lives on. I would cut that umbilical cord right now if I could figure out how to start the chain saw.

We rent a car for the day, get the fuel sensor in the truck fixed, put up the horses, make some dinner. Barrett will try to leave again tomorrow. We go to check on the horses later that night. It's been mild enough that we've been able to leave them out pretty much 24/7. Surf and Jerry stroll up to the fence when they sense us approaching. Surf nuzzles my sore shoulder with his big Roman nose and Bullwinkle head. He has to be the tough guy, has to sneak in his affection when it's dark and he thinks no one's looking. Thanks for today, Surf.

February 9

It's raining again. Pouring, in fact. At least it's a warmer rain. I try to keep my spirits up, though I still have a stiff neck and raging headache. I'm soaked from head to toe before I even get on my first horse. My barnmate Kris tells me that the extended headache part is not normal. I need to get it looked at again. I yes her continuing kindness and concern, then bury the recommendation in a little hole no one will notice. In the year I've known Kris, her kindness and generosity have gone a long way in times of need, and in times when I need a good time—pass the Chardonnay, please.

I flat Huey in the rain to determine his degree of improvement after his bout with cellulitis, then take Barrett to the Columbia Airport so he can finally make it home to take care of our abandoned farm. Katie is on her way to Aiken with our sole boarder, Chandler, and her horse, Smarty, and all three are due in tonight. After dropping Barrett curbside, I return to the barn to get the other horses schooled on the flat, then stop off at Coach's barn to check in on Calvin before cashing in my chips for the day. One chest bar has grown to three across his stall front. He's gotten good at snatching the blankets hung on his stall door. "I may send you home with someone else," Coach tells me. "He was perfect over fences today." We talk about rumors circulating through the barn, from her having bought a farm in Aiken to my having bought a bad horse in Calvin, which leads us to a discussion of my inherent self-doubt that leaves me fair game for such rumors. "Why don't you just call it an analytical mind instead of a self-doubting one?" she suggests. An analytical mind for a poet is a must. It's what discerns wheat from chaff and asks the hard questions. But self-doubt in an event rider is all too often a career and sometimes even a neck breaker. You can't question yourself as you come at 550 meters a minute into a 4-foot oxer that is more than twice as wide. You have to have the determination of a kamikaze pilot without the kamikaze part. The gutsiness the sport demands is what keeps my self-doubting mind at bay. A little more sake, please.

In the evening, I pop a couple of muscle relaxants and get loopy and groggy by nine, my head pounding away in rhythm to the rain's soft Chopin on the cabin's tin roof.

February 10

The headache hasn't subsided. Surely I'm about to croak from an aneurysm. I return to the hospital. Midafternoon on a weekday at Aiken General can't be too bad an idea. Wrong again. Twenty ahead of me: some bandaged, some wheelchaired, some reeking of whiskey, mothers swaddling pink sleepers and even pinker-cheeked babies. One toddler is wearing miniature Ariat riding boots. I write my name on the sign-in sheet, hunker down with my latest cheesy novel. I'm 90 feet under on a treasure-hunting expedition, somewhere off the coast of the Turks and Caicos looking for pieces of eight. I want one of the other divers to fall in love with my amphibious voluptuousness. The bends . . . the bends. What a great word for what happens when you come up too soon. I want to stay down forever.

My name is called. Luckily, my records are at ready disposal from the other day, so I don't have to review my medical history for yet another doctor I don't know. This one, a tall, swarthy South American, doesn't even blink when I remind him how I got my throbbing headache. He brushes me off, identifies the perispinal muscle that runs from brain to pelvis as my problem: it's strained and causing the headaches. "I'd recommend a shot of Turbitol," he says.

"What's that?" I ask.

"It's like a megadose of ibuprofen, steroid free."

"Sure," I say, eager for relief from the megapain in my head. "Just don't tell me I can't ride."

"I wouldn't," he says, another doc well accustomed to the tunnel vision of snowbird event riders in wintertime Aiken. I begin to roll up my sleeve, when the drop-dead gorgeous doctor returns to my cubicle with a needle the size of a balling gun for horses. "You wouldn't want this one in your arm," he says. "It has to go in your hip." I drop trou, turn the sweet spot to my beautiful doctor. First comes the alcohol kiss, the steadying hand, the sting of the poke, the delicious burn. Goodness.

My new goal with Calvin: fall off as much as possible.

Sporting Days Farm

The swelling in Huey's leg has disappeared. He is sound and ready to rock. I steel myself and decide to run all three horses: Houston, Surf, and Huey. Houston is first to go in dressage and cross country. I've entered him in the PT division, a move-up division you occasionally see at events that has the horse do a Preliminary dressage and show jump test and a Training cross country. It is our first Preliminary test as a team. Houston puts in a respectable effort. He is a bit of a wiggle worm down center line, but performs all the movements with a reasonable amount of focus. Coach is on Calvin and beats me easily in dressage.

I'm nervous as hell cross country, shuddering at the memory of my last trip out of the box when I bit the dust, hard. The only way to get over my inner hysteria is to get in the start box and go. The only way out of self-doubt is to turn it around myself.

I ride aggressively to each fence. My fancy five-year-old gawks and shies at everything the first thousand meters. He finally settles in, and we put in a solid run. I'm beaming, mostly from relief, when I gallop through the finish flags. Coach is double clear on Calvin, as well. I pack up Houston and all my stuff with Kris's help, stash him on the trailer, and head back to the barn to pick up Surf and Huey, who still have to perform their dressage tests this afternoon.

Both horses put in good efforts in dressage. Huey stays focused and doesn't shy, Surf tries his heart out, which he does not always do. I'm happy as a clam. Until Katie asks if I know why I was eliminated cross country on Houston. I'm flummoxed as I review the round in my head: Did I miss a flag? False start? Not wear my armband? Jump all the jumps?

The scorers tell me that I jumped a Preliminary jump 13 instead of the Training one. The jumps were side by side and looked almost identical except a few inches and differently colored numbers. I went whizzing over the Prelim fence and didn't even know it.

February 13

Superstitious nut that I am, now the date is the worry. Today is cross country on Surf and Huey, and show jumping on all three. The technical delegate has decided out of the kindness of his heart to let me show jump Houston despite our technical elimination.

Huey is an ass on the trailer. He doesn't like the new configuration of three horses side by side. He suffers from claustrophobia like I do. *Imagine*, he says. *Fifteen floors up in a New York blizzard. Trapped.* The trailer rocks and rolls with Huey's anger the whole 2 miles to the grounds. When we open up the back, we find Surf pressed up against the far side of the trailer, a quivering mess, having been savaged by Huey on the trip over. His face looks like someone started peeling it like an orange. He's okay, though— the bites are superficial.

Both horses—thank you, dear Huey, thank you, Surf Guitar—are clean cross country. Neither misses a beat. Show jumping will be much harder, as it's a step up for all three horses, and it's a crowded, twisty course. If I'm going to go off my form, my record would indicate that it will be in show jumping.

I do have a serious directional deficit. My nearest and dearest call me

Wrong-Way Wendell because I've gone off course so many times: missed a jump, jumped the wrong one, or jumped a fence backward. In other words, what happened yesterday on Houston is par for the course. You can count on me to come out of a building I've just gone into and turn the wrong way. It often takes me hours to find my car in a parking lot. I had painted diamonds on the doors of the truck so I could find it at horse trial. My problem makes the sport of eventing all that much harder. Most riders walk a course once or twice, but I have to walk the same course three or four times to feel prepared and know where I'm going.

As Houston canters into the ring, he comes unglued. He's looking every which way except where we're headed, and his lack of focus stays through the entire round. I haven't been jumping him this high at home. Three rails come down, but at least we finish. It's hard for Surf, too, but I can count on him to stay focused, as he's had a lot more miles than Houston. The twisty-turny, technical nature of this course and the new heights get him, too. Two rails.

I never look at scoreboards. As an amateur in this sport, I can't hope to compete with the professionals. Rarely do you see any amateur divisions in eventing, so at all levels, they lump amateurs and professionals together. Eventing is the first competitive endeavor of my life. Before that, I always shied away from situations that pitted me against other people, in which my efforts would be evaluated and measured. But love of horses and the sport compelled me to go against my own nature. The result?—I'm a better rider than I am a competitor. I'm still learning how to improve my competition skills and have made headway in recent years. But I never look at scoreboards. It's too much like making love with the lights on.

We're show jumping in order of standing, which means that the horses that are at the top of the ladder jump last. I'm surprised Huey is sixth in a division of thirty going into show jumping, with a dressage score of 39 and no cross-country time penalties. He knocks down fence 3, but when I put him in overdrive, he jumps the rest of the course without another fault. We finish seventh and are part of the victory gallop with our pretty purple ribbon.

Huey celebrates by savaging Houston on the way home. The blood pouring from the gray's scalp when we open the trailer doors is all that more shocking on his pale coat. All superficial, but the poor horse seems dazed. I put some salve on the wounds, turn them out, and despite his behavior in the trailer, think glowing thoughts of dear old Huey and how he saved this lucky day. Kris has left a bottle of Clicquot for me in the barn aisle, as if I'd just won Rolex, the note signed by "Charlie," as if I were one of his angels. The one who could shout. The one who could kick. The one who was good with knives.

February 15

Some nights, South Carolina seems like the end of the earth. I'm looking for something, but I don't know what, as I drive from my cabin to the barn for night check up the mile-long sandy driveway lined with tall southern pines standing at attention. I've left the dogs in the cabin; there's not a soul in sight. The driveway goes on forever.

Huey had a colic scare today, was pawing after dinner, not accepting a carrot, then lying down in his paddock when I turned him out. We gave him 20cc of Banamine, and he seemed to settle, but I'll have to keep a close eye on him tonight. My truck headlights make their path up the drive. When I clamber over the fence, I find Huey quietly grazing next to Surf and Jerry. All is calm.

February 16

Katie walks Huey, who is blowing hard and has broken out in a sweat with his veins popped out, pawing every chance he gets and desperate to go down. I call the vet, whose associate arrives within minutes. She gives Huey more Banamine, then threads the long snaky plastic tube through his nose and esophagus to administer a gallon of oil into his gut to help things along. She warns me of the dangers of introducing coastal hay to horses not from the area and not accustomed to Bermuda grass. I look out guiltily at the round bales of coastal I just asked David to spear into the paddocks. I ought to have known better. Round bales, even made from the choicest grasses, are suspect. Left to ferment in the elements, it's hard to say what modulations the grasses go through before they get to the horses' mouths and stomachs. I'm reminded of my first instructor as an adult rider who admonished me when I pulled a horse out of his paddock, leaving his buddy stranded and upset: "You don't know anything about horses!" I feel that again now, bearing the blame for not doing my research on this local hay and ordering the cheaper version in the form of 800-pound round bales for my trusting, hungry horses.

I spend the night checking on Huey every couple of hours. Kris, whose cabin is right next to Huey's barn, has offered to help with the night watches. At 8:30, Huey blinks sleepily when I turn on the barn light, vaguely curious that I haven't given him any hay for the night ahead. Drive up the long driveway, turn on the light, and drive back down. I repeat this three or four times before daybreak, the long leaf pines along the drive standing guard, throwing their confetti of pinecones at my rumbling tires. Nothing to celebrate tonight.

February 17

Huey is better in the morning, but apparently my social status isn't. A couple of rumors circulate that I'm dissatisfied with Coach. It goes something like this: every few days, another two-horse trailer arrives with a half-dozen suitcases and someone's twelve-hundred-pound Hitler whose halter is cats-cradled into a hay net. One hand graze leads to another, and pretty soon the stories start. "I see Julia is keeping some distance. . . . Someone said she brought her own jumps. . . . I hear that she's writing a kiss-and-tell about all of us."

Coach is a great rider and teacher, though she's not been a professional or in the teaching business for long. She is an active woman with many horses to ride and compete. Her days are pressed, to say the least. When you're that busy, something necessarily must go by the wayside. She knows what makes a good jump, she rides countless different types of horses, and she has three or four patterns that will get the job done and prepare her for the events. This is usually not enough for the Novice likes of us, who need variety in our lessons to feel prepared for the technical courses in both show jumping and cross country that we are encountering in competitions these days. Coach is trying to teach us the great eye she has developed and the perfect balance. When a teacher is gifted with both of these traits, technique is not so important. When a rider isn't so blessed, like myself, technique means everything.

I should talk to Coach about these things, but don't yet have the heart to bring up the subject. Something of my dissatisfaction gets back to Coach. Chandler has a few problems of her own schooling with Coach, who keeps her at 2-foot fences when her quite scopey little horse Smarty keeps running out at his fences. Like any good Dostoyevsky character, Smarty would rather be bad than be unchallenged. We're probably all better off that Fyodor wrote novels rather than sold popcorn for a living. So, Chandler turns to me, in hopes that I will help her with her problem and test her a little more.

After running Smarty through a sizable gymnastic built from standards and poles we brought from home, I help Chandler through a cross-country school at Sporting Days Farm, where I encourage her to jump the Training trakkener, a cross-country fence that involves a log hung over a ditch. Smarty gets it done the first time, albeit a little sticky. When I ask her to come again to smooth it out, he stops dead in front of the ditch, gapes down into the abyss, and Chandler goes tumbling. She's as pissed as she's unhurt, gets right back on, digs in and comes again, and jumps it well, then proceeds to jump the rest of the Training level fences on the course. I'm impressed by her grit and feel confident that she's ready for more. She just needs someone to tell her that, like so many of us when we're unsure of attempting the unknown. She doesn't need a kick in the pants so much as a pat on the rump. Today, I school her through a gymnastic that's the same size as the one I jumped with Smarty two days ago. "This is what I came to Aiken for," she says. I get a glimpse of my old days as an English teacher, when I would encourage my more talented creative writing students to submit their best work to literary journals.

"You should aim for the Training three-day event at Waredaca in the fall," I tell Chandler, and her face lights up.

"I'll have to tell my fiancé that the babies will have to wait," she says. I have a few brief thoughts of ruining a happy union.

Word has gotten back to Coach that Chandler is unhappy, which I hear in my first lesson on Calvin since my spill at Pine Top. I'm self-conscious as hell, and not riding well, and then Peyton Place hits me in the face. I act dumb, keep riding. I know nothing except the bones underneath me, and even those feel foreign to me today. "Do you mind if I get on him?" Coach asks. I say no, but she reads my face. "Julia, I'm considered one of the best jump riders in the country," she explains. She is normally a humble person, and I am taken aback by her statement.

Chandler and Katie, who've come up on Huey and Smarty to watch my lesson, laugh, out of nervousness or surprise. Coach rides Calvin beautifully, and when it's my turn again, I turn to Katie and Chandler, and ask in my most polite voice if they would mind . . . and Chandler says without missing a beat, "if we leave." Bless her. I can't stand yet another humiliation right now. As soon as they wander off down the sand track, Calvin and I settle, and I get that butter feel back when I'm not pulling and he's not pulling and the jumps happen like smooth magic.

"Did you catch them laughing?" Coach asks. I want to defend my friends, but I can't blame Coach either, because I know it took a lot to take a deep breath and call herself what she is, one of the best jump riders in the country. I wish I could do the same. If only I had the talent to call myself that, or whatever else would make me that self-confident and special and secure in what I did. Most days, it's enough to say I take lessons from one of the best jump riders.

Thompson, Georgia

Surf Guitar's first Intermediate go. The scene of my debacle on Calvin. I bring Huey along for the ride, to show Surf how to do it. Huey's back to his cranky self, yanking my arm off to get onto the trailer, biting at Surf's head in the cross ties. Surf pins himself against the wall to get as far away as possible from the savage, looks sideways at the enemy who is also his friend. I am reminded of our family's awful trip to the West Coast in the station wagon . . . brother Stephen's nacho-flavored flatulence, brother John's angry glare, Mother's disgust with everything west of Lexington, Kentucky, Father's hand-wringing.

Both horses put in good efforts in dressage. Surf is feeling sluggish today and is consequently well mannered. Something must be up. I warm him up for show jumping, and he jumps the practice fences well and is seemingly ready to go. As I enter the ring, I feel his eyes triple in size. He instantly loses focus and drops a mile behind my leg when I ask for the canter.

It's a tough, complicated course. It feels like I left my horse in Timbuktu and I'm jumping the fences by myself. Surf decides the object of the game is to chip in and clunk the fences. Who knows how many rails drop? I've lost count. When we make our turn to the triple, he chips in to the first element, lands like a boulder, puts two strides in where there should only be one, can't jump out when the fence is that close, and crashes into the second element of the combination. The whole fence tumbles like a tower of pickup sticks. The judge blows the ominous whistle while the jump crew dashes in to rebuild the fence, which takes an eternity.

Pine Top is a pretty big deal. Forty-five of the top hundred U.S. event riders are here, including John Williams, Kim Severson, Stephen Bradley, Sally Cousins, Peter Gray, and many of the professionals I've met and admired over the years. They are all at the side of the show jumping ring, watching my disaster on Surf Guitar and comparing notes on what a bad student I am, while Surf and I kick dust, waiting for permission to finish our awful round. The whistle blows again. We manage to climb over the triple combination and finish the course. I want to go hide under a rock. What is the matter with my horse? Maybe I need Turbitol between my ears instead of between my cheeks.

I have to turn my attention to Huey. The last thing on the planet I want to do is to go back into that ring with all eyes watching the woman who just put in the worst show jump round of her life. Huey warms up well. I take ten deep breaths and go back into the ring, imagining, as my mother once told me when I'd get nervous for piano recitals, that all the heads watching are merely pumpkins. Huey jumps all of the fences with his usual *joie de vivre* and ends by pulling only one rail, the first element of the triple, the result of my overriding the fence to be sure that we get the job done the first time this second time through.

I scratch Surf from cross country, probably the wisest decision of the day. No sense attempting his first Intermediate cross country on a day like today. Something is up with him, though I'm not sure what. Maybe he's just tired or a little under the weather. Maybe I didn't get after him enough when I felt him sluggish and make the appropriate adjustment when I entered the ring. Or maybe we haven't seen enough variety in our jump schools with Coach. Probably it's a combination of all of the above.

Huey skips around the cross-country course like it is child's play, handles all the tough elements: 90-degree turns to fences, narrows, massive oxers, skinnies in water, scary jumps involving round bales, keyholes, you name it, and comes back hardly breathing and jigging for more. I feel confident in calling him an Intermediate horse now.

February 20

I mosey on over for a powwow with Coach. "It doesn't surprise me that you've come to me today after your round on Surf yesterday," she says, all steely faced. She's got me wrong. She thinks I'm trying to put my bad round back on her. But no—I've been trying to have this discussion with her for weeks.

Coach has about twenty horses here. For her to get them all jumped in the course of a day, she's on their backs for maybe twenty minutes each and uses the same pattern day after day. While her simple combination of jumps might work for her, for an amateur rider at the upper levels who is not as gifted as her coach, it's not enough to jump the same pattern time after time. She does not agree with me, suggests I come up with different patterns that will work better. Now would not be a good time to add that the repetition has gotten boring.

Like any self-respecting power tripper, I like to have as many options as possible. Making choices lets me feel in charge. That's why I bring seven pairs of shoes to a sock hop. Have two vets. Two farriers. Four coaches. I'd have three husbands if Barrett didn't have so many personalities. I can't be in charge and learn at the same time without having options. And I can't ride if I can't be in charge. So how do I learn to ride? Or maybe it's all the Waffle Houses down south. Every few miles you see one. Plenty of auto supply stores, double-wide dealers, Wal-Marts, Taco Bells. Captain D's. Fewer Olive Gardens or Chili's, where I can at least get a drink or two. Liquor stores that sell lots of cheap bourbon and screw-top wines. No Anthropologie or J.Crew. Scant bookstores and libraries and movie theaters. Beam me up, Scottie.

I come back to my barn down the red clay road to find Houston lame on the left front. Katie and I pack and wrap the foot in Forshners, wrap his fronts, and put him away for the night while crossing our fingers that he's only wrenched an ankle at worst or shifted a nail to a soft spot. I say my goodbyes to Katie and Chandler, who are leaving tomorrow. Fighting the urge to throw my things in the trailer and pack up my own horses to caravan home with them, I hug them both, with a sinking sensation. I'm even a little teary-eyed, as if I were going off to war, sensing that I should stay put and live this life, and fight the fight, and then come home to write about it.

February 21

The vet has to bring out the x-ray machine for Houston's left fore when the foot isn't sensitive to hoof testers, thereby throwing out the welcome possibility of a hoof abscess. "Nice horse," the nice vet says, as I'm lunging him on his good, left side where you can't see the lameness at all.

"Thanks," I say, flatly, "I've only had him since October," as if I deserve a break for this fact. I flip him over to the other side where he's head-bobbing lame.

The vet opts not to take off the shoe to take the pictures. He doesn't see any fracture on the x-rays, I find out a few hours later. Sure enough, the shoe is covering the wings of the coffin bone. He'll have to come back tomorrow to pull the shoe and take more shots. With some confidence, I tell the friendly old-time vet, still working hard when most are resting in their easy chairs, that it couldn't possibly be a fracture—coffin bone fractures are rare, and he admits that he hasn't seen one in years. In my short eventing career of ten years, I've already had not one, but two coffin bone fractures within two weeks of each other—one, a front, done galloping out in the paddock by a horse who never came sound enough again for me to compete, and the other—by dear old Huey—a hind, done at the end of a jump school in Jimmy Wofford's ring. The vet's eyes grow large. The odds are long for anyone to have two horses with coffin bone fractures within that time frame. To have a third in one's career would be pretty much unheard of and enough to indicate that someone were trying to tell me something. Apparently, that someone will have to scream if I'm going to hear it.

I struggle to get my rides and all of the barn chores done by cocktail hour, which will have some significance for me today after the worry over Houston. The heavens open up with thunder, lightning, and torrential rain as I'm finishing up, aping my mood and confirming that I'll have to keep the horses in tonight, resulting in more work for my bad back tomorrow.

February 22

I feel like a successful gambler with chance on my side: Houston's foot x-rays are clean. We have gone from a possible fracture to treating the injury like a bruise. With a little more luck and a couple days of soaking, poulticing, and bute, he should come sound and be back to work. He'll still miss the event this weekend at Paradise Farm, and who knows exactly what else?

It's funny what happens when a horse is sick and you end up spending the early morning with just him munching hay in his stall while you clean the rest of the barn. You become buddies like nothing else. Houston occasionally stops chewing, glances out from his chest bar to check my mucking, hoping for a reassuring pat or maybe even a carrot if he's lucky, then resumes his munching. He's got an irresistible gray muzzle, made grayer and fuzzier by his winter coat. He's a stunning big dapple gray with tons of suspension and movement. But his head, quite honestly, is a little homely: flea-bitten and freckly like the rest of him is not, and his eye is small, but trusting nonetheless. His head is so unlike the rest of his body that it has become endearing to me. I take a few moments for my Aiken version of a coffee break: give the gray muzzle a kiss, exactly in the indentation above the left side of his lip, where horses must be kissed for the greatest satisfaction. With a little time and a lot of kisses, he'll be okay; that is today's mantra. I vow to not gamble any more, but to call the insurance company as soon as I get home to insure my two new horses, Houston and Calvin, which I have yet to do.

February 23

I take Calvin and Surf to a schooling combined test at Sporting Days Farm, and they are both obedient and level. Particularly Calvin. The dressage judge even leans out of her car window to tell me *what a nice test* after my finishing salute. This is a first for me. Usually my judges scowl at me as if to say *better luck next time,* then glance back down to write their cryptic, critical notes on my test.

Surf is strong and a little cranky, so I put on bigger spurs, pull out the dressage whip, and ride more firmly, and he manages to hold it together through the test. Calvin jumps clean and wiggles only once to a fence, and Surf pulls one rail. I go back in the ring to try again for a clean round—the beauty of schooling shows—and he leaves that one up but pulls another. Oh, well. He's feeling like his old self, perky and aggressive to his fences without being rude. Both horses manage to earn second place in their respective divisions. Time to cash in all my two-dollar win tickets and bet the fifty-dollar triple: a cross-country school with Coach's team—my first on Calvin since I tumbled from his back two-and-a-half weeks ago at Pine Top and took a trip to the hospital. The only bad fence we have today is—not surprisingly—the bank. "Oh-oh, here comes my nemesis," I say when it's my turn to canter up the bank. We stumble up the bank the first time through because I've chased him there on a long stride. The second time through's a charm, when I'm more relaxed and I wait for Calvin to get to the base of the bank.

"He's got so much power, you never have to chase him anywhere," Coach reminds me.

My sport is a demanding one. After a bad fall, you have to talk yourself into building up enough nerve to come back and jump the same type of jump again. "The bravest thing I ever did," Coach has told me, "is to go back and jump the same jump I broke my leg at." And so we face our demons, pulling out the sword, even on the days when we know the sword is made of cardboard.

I come back to the barn glowing and exhausted, and guess who's waiting for me besides hungry horses? Hungry Barrett. Our dinner of Mastodon ribs is interrupted by my cell phone.

It's Caitlin calling again. We've been here before. Freshman year in college. The big move up. The inherent disappointments. I tell her about my demon, how red his eyes were, glowing at me from the top of the bank jump. How good it felt to jump right over him and canter away.

February 24

Kris, Barrett, and I end up at the local Mexican dive clinking our fishbowl margaritas drenched with salt and tequila to yet another good day:

dressage headway on Calvin, and Surf and Huey's first jump school after Pine Top. Huey came out like a tiger, and I could hardly hold him to the jumps—he was feeling that aggressive and excited to do his job. Not bad for seventeen. I hope someone somewhere says this about me: "Not bad for forty-nine." And that they will say it again in ten years, and then again in twenty. Still looking good and happily doing my job well.

As the chips and guacamole arrive at our table, I glance up at the wall festively painted with beach scenes in Mazatlán, where I see a real live cucaracha the size of a date scampering across a pink sombrero. Kris takes up a napkin, takes its sad life in her hand. Pass the chips, please.

We had hoped to have Trish with us tonight. She's joining us to help out at Paradise Farm Horse Trials this weekend, but she got stuck in Northern Virginia traffic. It will be a long night on the road for her.

After my early bedtime, Caitlin calls to report that she feels much better after a slam-dunk audition for a summer theater program in Amsterdam. Not bad for almost nineteen. Happily doing her job. I tell her, *See, told ya so*, and take a deep breath.

My tomorrow starts at 3:00 A.M. with a tequila insomnia. As I head to the computer, I step in a present left by pup Simon and have to pull out the Resolve and paper towels and scoldings before I go further with my early day. Pass the keyboard, please.

February 26

Dinner at a local Aiken tapas bar with John Williams and his wife Ellen, along with my pal, Trish, who finally made it to Aiken. John is both an internationally experienced eventer and a recognized Combined Training course designer. John and Ellen and Barrett and I have become close friends over the years, since we bought Redmond from the couple seven years ago.

The five of us order enough hors d'oeuvres to choke an elephant, which is all we'll be able to order at a tapas bar—an entire meal sampling tiny portions of spinach gnocchi and fried artichoke, carpaccio and eggplant tapenade, bruschetta and snails. You end up nibbling like a goat, sampling every flower, every weed. Have I mentioned that Trish is 6 feet tall, with porcelain skin and chiseled cheekbones? It is impossible to sit across from her at the dinner table and not want to sample her, too, as she brags to John and Barrett in her silky voice, "Perhaps I should tell you I'm trained in how to cope with a biological weapons attack."

I have a heart-to-heart with John Williams, admitting how full my plate is. Maybe he would like to take a bite or two, perhaps consider taking the ride on Houston? John is a cautious person and seems more interested in developing his own horses than in following another's attempts. When I query him about Houston, he admits that the horse's back is longer than he likes and his height north of noteworthy. He's more interested in Jerry the Racehorse. Aside from twenty starts with our jockey, Charlie Forrest, Jerry is raw material, unmarred by anyone else's influence. I talk myself out of being offended. I still believe that Houston is a special horse, perhaps best appreciated by the likes of John and poorly represented by the likes of me.

Paradise Farm

I get the news that Houston is bleeding from the hoof and not able to move. Barrett takes off to the barn while I try to finish my rides. The hoof must have finally abscessed; thus the blood. I get Calvin ready for show jumping. Just as I'm ready to put a foot in the stirrup, Barrett pulls up. "You have to come now," he says.

We ride the 2 miles back to the barn in silence. A grim huddle of humans surrounds the horse. David's wife is holding Houston, who is violently tossing his head and trying to inch his way back to the barn but is unable to do so. His left leg has been bandaged from hoof to shoulder by David's vet, who was called when his wife found the injured horse in the pasture. I hold him while the vet tells me how serious it is, that there is an open wound from the fracture. The bones of the pastern have shattered into countless pieces. There is little hope. She runs to get her x-ray machine so we can be sure of the damage, while I count to a thousand several times over. I stroke my horse's neck and tell him it will be all right even as I sense it won't be, sliding my hands under his blanket so his warm body will warm up my icy hands. It has been rainy and blustery all day, hovering around 40, in sunny southern Aiken. After an eon, the vet returns and snaps the x-rays, then positions a breakdown cast on the horse so that he can walk on his toe and put all his weight there rather than on the demolished pastern. We maneuver Houston into his stall, then follow the vet to the clinic. My horse has plenty of painkillers on board, so he should be comfortable for a short while.

The x-rays confirm what we thought: the pastern is shattered. There is no hope of recovery. I have Dr. Handy call our vet back home, who assures me that the diagnosis is correct. What the vet I just met an hour ago is saying to me is true. We have no other option but to put the horse down.

My mind races to what I did or did not do and what responsibility I hold in the matter. Our southern vet blocked the problem to the foot, but I'm reminded by Barrett that sometimes that block will also affect part of the pastern area. Most likely a hairline fracture in the pastern was overlooked. We treated it like a bruise, the horse got better on bute, and so we turned him out. He took a wrong step on a tiny fracture, and the pastern shattered.

I want to be there when they put him down, but on the way back to the barn I realize that I can't handle it. I ask Barrett whether he would mind if I went back to the cabin. Barrett is my rock: there's only a little rust on his ironclad nerves. He says he wants me to *not* be there. Trish offers a Valium, which I gladly accept. Time is happening way too quickly, and I want to slow it down.

Life throws us curves, and we either react or miss the ball. A year ago my father had to be put on life support when he slipped suddenly into a coma after undergoing minor surgery. Three days later, I had to make the decision to turn off the machines, according to his wishes. I stood by his hospital bed, my hand on his thin leg, and watched him die within minutes. I am still trying to steady myself from the responsibility of that decision and find my distance to all the countless choices I've had to make since then. I've been in search of some good luck, only to find that there really isn't any luck to find. There is only good, hard work. Goodbye, Houston, with your amazing potential that I will never have an opportunity to tap. I hope you will learn your flying changes and find the courage to jump 4-foot walls and bounces into water, wherever you are.

February 28

Walking by the empty stall of a horse you have had to put down—no one is home or ever will be. Later in the day, I find tucked under a towel a shock of the luxurious white tail Barrett decided to cut and save. Blink, blink.

Man Overboard

It was only for an hour,
before a Royal destroyer
happened to come by,
spotted him, and picked him up.

How surprised must the Brits have been
to find a man
bobbing up & down,
as they scanned the horizon of whitecaps,

beaconing in the middle of the night.
Just one among a million possibilities.
The expression on my father's face,
ecstatic & dreadful,

as if searching for—& finding—me,
and making me entire
years later in my mother's womb.

Page 51

He began a book of 2000 pages
on the Duke of Marlborough
& put it down when his stomach
began to hurt.

That's how he died—
He began his future with another's past
& put it down
when the present interrupted.

He wasn't worn by pain or time.
That's how I know he wasn't ready,
because he was only on page 50 of 2000
in a book about the fascinating Duke.

———————

His Suits Were All Hung Neatly in a Row

When I opened the closet door,
my father ducked his head & walked out,
all dressed up & ready for my wedding.

But it was just his smell,
a mix of Vitalis & shoe polish, linen & old silk,
the scent of my father taking shape.

For how long would the suits
have to hang there without him

before they'd lose the smell of him
or get fed up waiting & walk out?
Something tells me my father will live forever,
insubstantial in that musty closet air,
its thick oak door opening & closing
with a satisfying *thwump*.

———————

Every Valentine's Day

He would send us
several cards, unsigned.
A family joke, this excess of sentiment
from a stoic who wouldn't sign his name
to how he felt.
Our mailboxes would fill up.

After his sudden death
on his favorite holiday,
I returned home to the usual cards
which I stuffed unopened
into my bottom dresser drawer.

I opened them one hot July afternoon
when time gave me courage,
when an excess of dragonflies
skimmed across my backyard pool,
each one offering in its signature touchdown,
"Love Dad," in nearly illegible blue.

These poems first appeared in my chapbook, *Restalrig* (Finishing Line Press, 2007).

◆◆◆◆◆◆ *Spring*

Saddle the bay mare, there's a long ride ahead.
—William Augustus,
   Duke of Cumberland, at his death

Lucky Calvin

CHAPTER FIVE

Mediocratus

✕ March 1

Speed, torque, concussion. Horses are intricate puzzles constructed in heaven that we can only be poor guardians of.

I receive cards, phone calls, and e-mails. Word travels fast about the gray one who now lies in Eddie Coward's graveyard for horses. "We bury our horses here," Dr. Handy said, like she was used to saying it.

I hook up in the afternoon with Hans Gerling at Full Gallop Farm to jump Calvin and to condition Surf Guitar alongside one of Hans's horses. Hans got his start with Jimmy Wofford, and now, at twenty-one, he's running around Two Stars with his horse Leap and has his whole eventing life ahead of him. Lucky duck.

We trot around the sandy fields for a timed thirty minutes. I'm missing home. I'm missing the trails. I'm missing the streams to cross and woods to penetrate. I'm missing the unplanned fun of riding for the sake of riding not geared toward any competition. And I'm missing Houston.

Now that I miss her most and need her voice, Caitlin has decided to boycott nightly telephone calls in an effort to work things out herself and not to rely on me for daily answers to the endless questions of her life. I feel as though I weigh one thousand pounds, as if I were a horse who's gotten into the feed bin and can't stop eating until I colic on the profound heaviness of absence.

March 2

Jerry and Surf and I make ourselves busy at another schooling show. Loneliness sets in. Sadness loves solitude, cracked hearts, silence. You drink your own tears when your world is a desert. Who else besides Barrett understands finding Houston in the paddock, frantically tossing his head up and down with his hoof at an obscene angle to his leg? Vet was right—he did become a head tosser in his final hours.

Part of my loneliness is the fact that I am removed from Coach's inner circle. As her trailer pulls up at Sporting Days for a cross-country school, I feel like a middle schooler leaning up against the gym wall, waiting to be asked to dance. Coach's staff and students unload their "babies," hoot and holler as they tack up, while Suave Rhapsody and I wait near the bleachers, Jerry jigging and a little revved up for whatever he senses is coming. I feel a walnut grow to the size of a grapefruit in my throat. I am a good head taller than the other middle school boys, which translates that I'll be passed over.

Jerry is a star cross country, as he had been for his first stadium show jump round earlier in the morning. This is what I take away from my day—the sad shock of Houston, balanced by the surprise of our little homebred Suave Rhapsody, who ran so well for us and now puts A-plus-B-plus-C together as he computes a new career. I don't know what else to do but to keep riding.

March 3

We invite Kris over for dinner at the cabin, who insists all night, through several vodkas and glasses of St. Francis Chardonnay, that Barrett is married to an angel. There's nothing that makes a forty-nine-year-old woman more uncomfortable than to be flattered by a way-more-beautiful younger woman. Kris brings her "pet-quality" dachshund along, who's about the size of pup Simon's head and has an exaggerated breast bone that sticks out like a chicken's. Simon and Hattie spend the night tearing around the cabin while Daisy mopes in a corner, disgusted by the other dogs' immature antics. Kris, bless her effusive heart, tells me repeatedly how gorgeous and talented I am and how she's read each of my poetry books six times.

I sense that Kris's sugar springs from some insecurity as dark as my

own that I may never be privy to. I squirm in my dinner chair, keep trying
to change the subject. Barrett proposes a rafting trip for her and her
husband with the two of us. "Come on," Barrett says, ever encouraging.
"We all didn't end up in our forties for nothing." Big wild river.
Overhanging rocks. Wild rhododendrons. Kris and I in bikini tops and
cutoffs. Barrett and Kris's husband beshirted and beer-bellied, slugging
away at their Schlitzes. It's endless.

I am in the barn, drunk on irony, beauty, the working hard at something I
love, no matter my degree of success. I am thinking of Mediocratus and
the poem my ex-husband wrote years ago, which felt like a signature
statement for me at the time and still does. The truth is that I always
wanted to be great at one thing. I'm still working toward that goal. I think
of Simon and Hattie barking, barking, barking and wagging their tails with
glee. Just perfect at what they do.

Our barn landlord, David, joins me in the barn. I'm braiding Huey's
mane for dressage. He tells me that he and his wife are proud of me for
sticking it out after Houston's death. I don't mind this acknowledgment of
my stubbornness, which is one of my only attributes that will keep me at
least on the perimeter of the circle of The Great Ones.

We talk about parents dying, and he, of his time as platoon leader in
the Mekong Delta. I see how he has earned his happiness, why he loves life
so much on his 150-acre farm in Aiken, South Carolina. He has suddenly
earned his fatuousness in my eyes. "Look at my life," he says, beaming and
gesturing toward his small herd of Santa Gertrudis and then toward the
big log house where his wife is probably cooking something yummy for
dinner. I imagine that satisfaction is balanced in the context of the
unimaginable. David stuck it out, got lucky, and was able to find peace.

Thompson, Georgia

Warming up for dressage, Pine Top Farm. I feel the fish-in-the-fishbowl
syndrome. I've gotten somewhat better in the few years I've been
eventing, am able to focus more and keep riding, but it's still a pressure
cooker. As I put Huey through his paces, I spy Peter Gray at the fence line
watching some rides. Maybe he's going to say hello, or inquire how

Houston and Calvin are doing. "Quick," I say to Barrett, "go over and tell him what's happened. I can't talk to him until after I'm done with my ride."

I try to find my center and the mental energy to put in a decent test. Huey draws himself up and sucks in his breath, ready to explode as we're about to trot into the ring. I dig even deeper and manage to pull off a respectable test with my average-moving ex-claimer who tries his heart out, once again.

I exit the ring. Sure enough, Peter is waiting for me. "I'm so sorry," he says. And I repeat the painful phrase, bending over to give him a hug from Huey's back. I go even deeper, pull myself up, take my horse back to the trailer to untack him, and give him several carrots as reward for his efforts today.

March 5

I wake up, dreading the run, am nauseated with nerves in warm-up and shaking in my stirrups. Surely I'm asking too much of my seventeen-year-old, particularly in the context of the week we've had. But after Huey clocks around the cross-country course, I spend the rest of the day making plans for his Two Star this spring and am eager for the next run. What a head game.

One jump on the course is worrisome to Coach. It requires us to run up a steep mound and jump a 3-foot-6-inch log pile at the top to a blind landing that catapults horse and rider down off the mound. Huey skips over it like a six-year-old. "He was terrific at the mound," Coach tells me later.

"Maybe the old boy has more scope than we thought," I say.

"And the old girl," Barrett says.

We get Huey iced and lasered and Vetrolined and poulticed and buted and fed and tucked in for the night, then call Coach to find out show jump times for tomorrow. She's on her way to the University of Georgia vet school with the horse who just had colic surgery four weeks ago and is colicking badly once again. "I fell off one of mine today," she reports, "which wouldn't even have registered on the Richter scale without this bad news again about the colic." It takes a lot for Coach to ever sound down, but there she is.

Barrett and I run out for coffee and sugar and muffins for Coach's morning, replay Huey's run again, then cross our fingers that he'll have an uneventful night and will jog sound tomorrow.

March 6

Day Three of Pine Top Horse Trial. In my division of thirty, seven were eliminated cross country, and several others had stops and lots of time, moving Huey and me into the ribbons. I hate this setup, when show jumping is last and jumping is in reverse order of standing. When I'm balanced on the precipice of the ribbon cliff, I tend to get vertigo.

In warm-up, I start Huey off quietly, feeling him out after his big run yesterday. Coach, who's warming up her own horse, encourages me to build more canter. I press him forward, and we come more briskly to a warm-up fence. I miss my takeoff and ram poor Huey through the jump, which tumbles like a tower of pickup sticks. I am thrown out of the saddle and up his neck and almost come off. Sideline spectators run to rebuild the fence, while other competitors waiting to go into the ring impatiently circle around, anxious to jump another jump and probably annoyed that they have to wait so long while the bad rider's mistake gets fixed.

I'm rattled and never get my focus back. I try to replay our good round of two weeks ago. But this week Huey's coming off the biggest cross-country run of his long life as he enters the show jumping ring, and he's a little tired and strung out. The last thing I need to do is hurry a tired horse to his fences.

Six rails come tumbling down as Huey gets faster and increasingly flatter and begins charging his fences. I leave the ring, tail between my legs. "That's twenty-four jump penalties," the cagey announcer informs the audience, "but certainly no time."

I know how to ride this horse. I've ridden him for ten years, taken countless lessons from good people, brought him along from nothing after his racing career, and yet something within me freezes when the chips are down.

It is only a sport. My ride today will not matter at all in a week or a month. The pumpkin heads watching me won't remember the woman who rammed her struggling-to-be-good Intermediate horse at all the show jump fences, nor should I care if they do.

But I do.

I make a promise to listen to myself. I put the promise in a big box of promises and haul it up to the second floor of a whole big house of promises. Look around and you'll see something about inner connection with the outside thing. To listen to and synthesize someone else's criticism, you have to be a little disconnected from your internal mechanisms and that feeling part. But when you go out on course or into the ring, you've got to crank up that internal part again and feel more than you think.

As I'm watching the Advanced riders show jump, Peter Gray comes up to me and puts his arm around me, producing from behind his back two dozen roses: "With fond memories of our dear friend."

March 7

I hack Surf Guitar around the perimeter at Jumping Branch Farm, Daisy and Simon leading the way. We scoot by the cabin where the dogs make good use of Frank and Kay's pond, then gallop up the sand driveway and down the clay road to David's, duck in through the open top gate, then wend our way, taking the woods path that leads back to the barn. The path is carpeted with pine needles and strewn with pinecones, the smallest the size of Acadian Oysters. The dogs, noses to the ground, search for the biggest ones, as if we were on the beach looking for specimen seashells. Surf is alert and happy to make good use of another 45 minutes of soundness. I take my time admiring this gift, the ribbons tied with old memories of Surf, the wrapping paper fastened with the skill it has taken both Barrett and me to keep this horse going strong.

Over our nightly bottle of vodka-chased Chardonnay, we're fascinated by an article in *Chronicle of the Horse* by show jumper George Morris. The Maestro breaks down the qualities it takes to make a good rider great—ambition, emotion, management, selection, and talent, in that order—then asks his readers to be deadly honest with themselves and score each category from 1 to 100. I give myself respectable scores for ambition, management, selection, and even talent, but I honestly can't rate myself higher than a 50 for emotion. When the rails started to fly at Pine Top, instead of making the necessary adjustments that may have saved the round from catastrophe, I froze, let this fish get swallowed by the eyes of the barracuda peering into the bowl. The best riders are the cold ones, Morris goes on to say, who go into the ring so many times they learn how to manage their nerves, put their game face on, and not let stage jitters interfere with their performance.

"Everyone gets butterflies," Jimmy Wofford used to say, "but those butterflies have got to fly in formation."

So much for riders, but what makes a good horse great? We brainstorm the categories: heart, work ethic, soundness, brains, and talent, then rate the categories for each of our event horses, from 1 to 100. Redmond comes out on top, ranging from a 110 on brains down to a respectable 80 on soundness, even though he's had two years off recuperating from injuries. He's a good healer, and I hope he'll be ready and waiting for me when we get home, eager to start jumping again.

The good news is that all of my horses score better than I do. The bad news is that I have my work cut out for me. The major challenge is headwork if I want to be more competitive in this game. How does a middle-aged woman develop the mindset and focus to become a better competitor, when by nature and for most of her life she has avoided just that?

March 8

I fall off Jerry in a jump school over at David's barn. It's the first time I've ever come off him. That's the first thing I think when, not quite midair, I know I'm going down. Kris is setting jumps for me. Jerry shies, and I hit a standard and tumble from his back. "Oh no, your neck!" she says, but I'm thinking more about my lumbar region. Thank God for the soft sandy soil of South Carolina. I pick myself up, brush myself off, get back on, and keep riding. It wasn't Jerry's fault. I rushed the school. He was surprised by the second fence in a line off a turn, which I should have presented at a trot first. He's a baby, after all. From here on out, he snaps his knees over the fences like he's been jumping forever. Besides a bruise to my right leg and a little stiffness added to an already stiff body, it's reassuring to know that I can fall off and not get hurt. I cross my fingers that my fabulous luck will continue.

March 9

Jerry earns his first ribbon at Sporting Days Schooling Show at Beginner Novice. He's a giraffe in dressage, but who cares? I'm able to keep him in the ring and complete the movements. He jumps around the stadium course without looking at a thing. He can learn to keep his head down later. Calvin has wrenched a front shoe, which we discover when picking his feet before dressage, so he gets to stand on the trailer all day munching hay while we wait for a farrier. No problem, as far as Calvin's concerned.

I ask Hans to help warm me up for stadium on Surf Guitar. When I start jumping, I see nothing but long spots to the fences and start to flatten out my horse. "You're trying to see your spot too far out," he says to me. "Just come around the corner and keep your rhythm and try to get closer to the base. He jumps way better if he gets closer to the fence."

Hans's advice is familiar—it might as well be Jimmy standing there with his shock of red hair and green ball cap, looking like Christmas. I come around the next corner, sink into my seat, and try my best to wait to the base of the jump. Surf gets to the bottom and lifts his long, blue-heron body and folds himself over the fence.

My first round isn't perfect, with two rails down, but it's an improvement over Sporting Days and Pine Top. I keep my canter slow and rhythmic, try not to look for a distance, and wait to the base of each fence. I go in for a second round—again, the beauty of this little schooling show with the possibility of do-overs. The second time's a charm. I get off Surf and give Hans a big embarrassing hug for a twenty-one-year-old. Pinch, pinch, pinch go my fingers to his face. Wrap, wrap, wrap go my arms around his body. "You've given me such a good surprise today," I tell him. He replies that he didn't really give me anything. He just encouraged me to ride the old way.

Jerry schools cross country with Coach's team. "Too bad you didn't run him over hurdles," one of Coach's students says. I tell her to hush, and to be sure she doesn't say this to Barrett, who has been saying it for years. No way am I going to let this one go again. The other horses are schooling at a higher level, but Jerry doesn't seem to mind jumping different jumps, and then, at the end of his school, jumping two fences that take him away from the group who are still not finished with their work and back to the trailer where Barrett is waiting for us. I brag to my husband what a good job Jerry did, especially the part where he had to canter away from the group over two fences and leave his new buddies behind. "Doesn't surprise me," Barrett says, "he made a whole career of galloping away from other horses."

March 11

I wake up hurting everywhere, my body screaming from constantly being on the go with the horses for the past six weeks.

With only one more event to go before we're homeward bound, I decide to take Calvin to Full Gallop Farm, where Hans is keeping his horses, to see what else he has to say about my deteriorating eye for show jumping.

I first knew Hans when he was just a kid in pony club, riding at Training level, which was an impressive accomplishment at eleven. He was eager to move up to the Preliminary level as soon as he turned the minimum age. Hans's parents opted not to buy made horses for him, but picked out youngsters with eventing potential that he learned to bring up through the levels himself. This made things more challenging for him. Without fancy, polished horses and without an utterly natural ability for the sport, he would have to work hard at it, which he has done.

I confess to him that I am seeing all of my jumping spots from a long way off and consequently running my horses off their feet to the fences. They either get there on a long stride and have to take off too far back or chip in a last-minute stride and labor over the fence. I remind myself of Coach's maxim: a horse can jump either short or long, but a horse can't jump weak.

Hans encourages me to go back to a basic we both learned at Jimmy Wofford's—to count to the base of each jump, thus keeping the canter rhythm regular, in order to avoid chasing the horse to the fence. Jimmy's principle of jumping: if you keep things simple and the canter stride regular and don't rush things, then the jump will happen naturally. *Danke*, Hans.

We walk the dogs up to Jumping Branch Farm to pick up my competition packets. I stop by Coach's RV to ask what time she's walking the Preliminary cross-country course. We engage in a conversation about making money in the sport. At one barn she teaches beginners how to post at the trot. She calls them "up-down" lessons and wishes she didn't have to teach them. You do what you have to do to make things work.

Our way home is lit by a cloud of tiny light bulbs around my head. Of course, one of the best jump riders in the country doesn't think, she feels. Perhaps it follows that the best teachers are not necessarily the naturals, but the ones who have to think through what they do and break their art down into articulated parts that, once clear to themselves, they can pass on to others.

Jumping Branch Farm

I coordinate dressage on Calvin, Surf, and Jerry, who is making his debut at a recognized event. I manage to pull off the day pretty well, especially considering that this is my first time riding three horses at the same event. I also have to work in the walking of three different cross-country courses.

Somewhere on the Beginner Novice course, waves of illness engulf me, and I realize the fatigue and muscle soreness that I was feeling yesterday are not just that.

March 13

I toss and turn in a feverish blur. I am not going to be able to ride. I spend the day glued to the couch, first listening to the cabin's wind chimes responding to a vibrant spring wind, then to the announcer on the loud-speaker just across the way at Jumping Branch. I hear reports of every completed or refused jump on course. I stew and second-guess my decision not to compete. I long to be out there, visualizing the ups and downs of the terrain I am missing. Meanwhile, Barrett takes care of the horses and me, makes me a fire and homemade chicken soup to sip beside it.

March 15

The trip home makes my health lapse into what is probably pneumonia. Vet offers up shipping fever as a diagnosis. Barrett is sure I have tuberculosis or consumption. At least I can die in the relative peace and obscurity of Upperco.

I unpack six weeks' worth of horse stuff, then retreat indoors to spend time with John and Caitlin, who are home on spring break. Barrett turns out Redmond with Huey and Surf Guitar, and I nervously watch them play racehorse in the paddock, then advise Barrett to turn Redmond out by himself tomorrow and henceforth until we are reassured by another clean scan that he can handle hearty play.

I am at sixes and sevens all day, in that shadowy transition period of being home but not quite settled in, reflecting on Barrett's and my business decisions that took every hour of the eleven-hour trip to make. We will take in a few more boarders in an effort to make ends meet, and I will start teaching riding, something that I said I'd never do. I figured that if I were to teach anything again, it would be literature and creative writing. But that is not my life now, and if we are going to keep the farm, we need to bring more money in. Barrett is inclined toward mare care, but because it is late in the year, mare care won't be a possibility until next winter. He will turn his attention instead to the racing syndicate, Poetry in Motion, while I'll use the knowledge I've bought and earned, and begin teaching. This will put a kibosh on my amateur status, though I'm not sure it will make all that much difference in the long run. I am resigned to doing whatever in order to keep the farm and my eventing stable alive.

March 16

Fits of coughing lead me to sip prescription cough medicine throughout the night as if it were juice. I wake in a near comatose state unable to move. When I attempt to get up, the room lurches and spins. Vertigo overwhelms me. I call Barrett down from the barn, then I wake the doctor at 6:00 A.M. to list my symptoms. He says I've most likely overdosed on cough medicine. "You just have to let it work its way out of your system," he says. The kids and Barrett come and go, busy and productive, while I languish on the couch, ashamed for having poisoned myself with my own medicine. I add this last insult to the constant injuries of the last six weeks. Katie rides the horses for me, while I wait for the nausea to pass.

March 17

I pull myself up and out the door to get on Surf and Huey, with hopes of running them both through a gymnastic exercise. I am still lightheaded from the dope, and from so far up, I have a bit of an out-of-body experience, as if the woman riding Huey were some other two-bit woozy drug addict. Jumping fences when you're feeling dizzy is not recommended. Two horses down and I'm pooped, must return to the house to lie down for a while. I head back up to the barn, armed with a second wind, to ride Surf Guitar on the flat. I run into Trish, who's come out to hack Pruitt and Redmond. She's saving up for a new horse and in the meantime helps out with whatever rides I can throw her way. There have been a lot of meantimes in the eleven years I've known Trish. She is always here, and always helping out. She has become a constant in my life.

How much we take our health for granted and how we miss it when we don't have it. For my mother in her waning months, the slightest gesture was too much effort. With every day, another little task was taken from her—brushing her hair, dressing, feeding herself, waving goodbye. She wasted away in stillness and silence. I think of her when moving and doing are conscious efforts for me. The heart digs in and tries and does.

In the afternoon I feel well enough to take John and Caitlin to see *Million Dollar Baby*. Substitute boxing for tennis or archery, dancing or painting or eventing. It's the passion and drive that matter. That's what we go to the big screen for, what we spend our own lives attempting to recreate.

March 18

Grace stops by for a powwow. We review the horses' tentative competition schedules, which do not include any three-day event in the spring. Jersey Fresh is running a traditional Two Star after all, which means that Huey would have to run steeplechase and roads and tracks. This would be too hard on his aging body and not worth the risk of injury. Surf will not be ready for a Two Star this spring, and Redmond will not have recovered from his bowed tendon in time. Calvin and Jerry have miles and months of turning combinations to go before they sleep. I'll have to live without a three-day in my immediate future. With the pressure off, maybe I'll be able to focus more on the horses' educations and less on qualifying and conditioning for a three-day.

Grace feels as though I should focus on Huey while waiting for Redmond to come back and possibly consider running a couple of

Advanced horse trials with him. I'm not sure either one of us is up to that challenge, but I tuck it away in my Pandora's box of possible outcomes.

Grace is all gung-ho to help me sort out my show jump fiasco. She leaves, and I take a deep breath, already feeling back on track.

March 19

Simon scares up an owl while I'm on a hack with Calvin. The bird exerts his wingspan and lands high on a bare branch in a neighboring maple, where he sits, inquisitive and quiet and apparently at ease with our own startling presence in his world. I look for signs of illness, but I can't see any. There's nothing out of whack, except for his presence at this time of day. Just a stone's throw away, he is watching when he would otherwise be sleeping, drilling holes in Calvin and me with his big, round, slow-blinking eyes, his head swiveling on its axis as we pass, so he'll be sure not to miss a thing.

March 20

Brenda Herzog comes this afternoon with her entourage to set fences for the Jimmy Wofford clinic. Brenda brings along her youngest, who scampers around the farm, entertaining Huey, who longingly watches her from his paddock. Huey has always been in love with little girls, but it has been years since he had one of his own. Brenda's little one tries with all her might to close the end door of the indoor. As Jerry the Racehorse and I attempt beginner flatwork in the outdoor ring, I have visions of Atlas holding up the world. The girl grunts and strains and can't budge the door an inch. Huey watches and watches as she runs to her mother and climbs aboard her mother's John Deere wheelchair.

March 21

There aren't many signs of spring. We are still having 20-degree nights, and the mercury is not reaching much past 45 or 50 during the day. It's bundle-up weather, and we're all sick of it.

My days take an uninspired turn. I can't seem to shake this flu bug, which lingers and morphs into a head cold, nor can I shake the flashes of dying horses. I tag along with Katie and Caitlin on a trail ride. Pruitt has developed some bad trail manners while I was in Aiken. My daughter is on

Redmond, and I note how perfectly she fits him in her 5-foot-2 frame, and how well he goes for her. She's in the lead, which she tends to choose on trail rides, always wanting to do things her way, and pops him over a couple of logs on the woods trail—his first jump in nine months. I warn her to slow down. Redmond is not used to jumping and probably shouldn't do too much of it. Boo-hiss, Redmond says. He swishes his tail at me. I make a note to turn my attention back to Pruitt in the next few weeks and to make some adjustments. That's one thing you can count on in farm life. Things are rarely static, and you have to learn to be flexible and make constant tweaks and changes when dealing with living things, each of whom is a 1200-pound individual with specific, modulating needs.

We are also waiting on one of our broodmares to foal—R. Isabella, or affectionately, Cherie. There's a lot of the watched-pot syndrome at play when waiting for a mare to foal, especially when you don't have a barnful. Most mares display early signs for weeks—restlessness in their stalls, getting up and down, going off their grain, blowing their winter coats, waxing from their nipples. We were getting worried calls from Katie while we were still in Aiken, even though Cherie was a couple weeks out from her due date. I've become cavalier about the process and don't believe the barometer of these early signs. Just like spring, there are a lot of false warnings and hedgings and warm-ups. But then again, unlike Barrett, I'm usually not the one doing the checking and watching. Ninety-five percent of the time, there's not much to do when a mare foals, and they're better left alone. There's the other 5 percent when a human presence can save a life, or even two. We've definitely had our share of those 5-percent situations, which is why we can't stop watching the pot.

Cherie is a maiden mare, meaning she's never had a foal before. She's a homebred and didn't seem to want any career we offered her—neither racing nor eventing—even though she was fast and could jump the moon. She didn't want to work that hard, insisted on doing things her way, and couldn't seem to find her niche. I think of my daughter, blasting ahead on the trail, irritable and restless on her spring break, as she waits for her own life to open up and to find her path. Cherie comes from a nice family, although she is far from its best representative. Without another athletic career to offer her that was up our alley, Barrett found a match for her in Mighty Forum, so we thought we'd let her give motherhood a whirl. When Barrett contacted the sire's owner, she wrote back, "I've been looking for this mare for so long." Something tells me Cherie's not going to be fond of our presence in her stall when it comes time to foal, will probably intentionally choose solitude and quiet.

March 22

I have a smashing day with my horses at the Jimmy Wofford clinic, introducing the Maestro to Jerry the Racehorse and Calvin, and reacquainting him with Surf Guitar. I am impressed by Jerry's calm in the midst of a chaotic eight-horse class. He stays focused, does everything I ask of him with a good attitude, and jumps well. Jimmy asks what he's done. "Nine furlongs in one fifty-two," I say.

"How long has he been jumping?" Jimmy inquires, a little surprised at being surprised.

"About two months," I say. Three cheers for Jerry-Bear. I'm hoping that Jimmy will see his win photos that Barrett just hung in the tack room of the indoor—the ones in which I am, predictably, not present.

Jimmy asks if he can have Calvin, wink-wink. It's with Calvin that the first light turns on and illuminates my recent problem in show jumping. "Wait to put your leg on," Jimmy instructs as we canter to our first oxer. "That horse can and will jump from about anywhere," he says. "You don't need a whole lot of leg, and you definitely don't need to put it on that far back." Most instructors emphasize using a lot of leg at all times, as if you can never put too much leg on a horse that's approaching a jump. But with Jimmy, it's more a matter of timing, particularly with a going, eager horse, which my horses tend to be. If I put too much leg on too far back, I end up pushing them past their point of balance and running them at the fence, and then the striding gets fouled up. "Leg on farther back translates to speed; leg on at the base of the jump affects the arc and height of the jump," Jimmy says.

Bingo. I think of my rides on Surf and Huey at Pine Top, and how I blasted them around the show jump course, my spurs gouging into their sides in an effort to produce more canter. Jimmy encourages me to wait to the base of each fence to apply my heel. It's all about rhythm and timing; just like dancing. Or boxing.

I take Surf into the 3-foot-6 class. "Oh, I already know you. You're wonderful," he says to Surf.

"Not lately," I admit. "I seem to have lost my ability to show jump him." Halfway into the class, after Surf has executed the gymnastic patterns with ease, Jimmy says he doesn't see what I'm talking about. Then, at the end of the clinic: "Just as I said two hours ago, you're wonderful." So nice to learn something old that feels new.

March 23

More sessions with Jimmy, this time with course work that includes lines of related distances. Today's lesson: I can hold my forward horses, or those that tend to rush their fences, with the backs of my knees, rather than my reins. Too much rein, and the horse will brace against my restraint and rush more, stand off and launch his fences; soften the reins, and the horse will want to get to the base of each fence before leaving the ground. Jimmy reminds me that when horses are put in a jumping chute without the influence of the rider, or if they're lunged over fences, they always get to the base of each fence, naturally and instinctually. It's only when the rider interferes with harsh or confusing aides that the horse gets diverted from his natural jumping instincts. Less is usually more. Which is why my omelets tend to look like scrambled eggs.

Huey plays around the course, shaking his head and bopping up and down between efforts, as if he's a six-year-old. Jimmy remembers him as the first horse I brought to him for guidance several years ago. "Too easy," Jimmy says, as Huey executes the last exercise: an oxer, two strides, skinny, two strides to another oxer. "I should have made it a lot bigger for him."

March 24

Barrett arrives home past midnight smelling of gambling and greasy chicken and poultice. Foolish Groom brings home a third-place ribbon in a Charles Town allowance race.

Mediocratus: His Phobia

I have climbed half-way up the mountain
this far down the mountain chain, which is
my life half-lived. I have also been in the lab
with its vapors of vanilla and onion and its
crystalline circus of fluids and forces. I have

been called many things, some half-rightly; genius
was one of these. As a child, I wore it like a name
tag on my blazer's red felt lapel. . . .

Renaissance man, Jack of all trades, these
schoolroom phrases impregnated me before my shell
could harden. Now I can do many things: I climb, I sail,
I extend my night vision with long tubes and mirrors;
I can name for you that bright blue dwarf over there,
or brew iridescent pigments & bitter tinctures
from beetle carapaces and the saprophytic plants
most feet pass over.

My fear: that one day my vision lased and flew
beyond my horizon
where there is no known way to capture
or reflect it.
And my memory of resonance and meaning flew with it.

And here, my dream: I have been into dense woods
where no one has been
and run into myself in there.

—Jack Stephens

This poem originally appeared in *Vector Love* (Haw River Books).

Cherie and Ditto

CHAPTER SIX

A Rat Has Bones

✖ March 25

Cooper gives Redmond a clean ultrasound scan and advises me to step up his work but postpone jumping for a month or so. I'm in no rush, because I don't plan to compete him until July. It's not like this one needs a lot of schooling.

Calvin and Katie and Redmond and I have a romp through the woods. Redmond revs himself up, as if he's also heard the vet's clean bill of health and can feel me let my guard down. I let him out a bit. Calvin is huffing and puffing and dying to call it quits, can't believe the energy of the twelve-year-old cantering beside him. This is way too much work for my lazy Cavalier. I have a lot of work ahead of me if I'm going to put the fire in him.

On the trail, Katie and I amuse ourselves by imagining what the horses would be like if they were human beings. Huey, in his long and lanky, drop-dead classy chestnut frame, is the Fred Astaire of the bunch. Surf is the pot-smoking, guitar-playing, tall, dark college kid whom everyone has a crush on. Pruitt, the 6-foot-2 twelve-year-old with size-14 feet who keeps tripping over himself. Jerry, the punk skateboarder with piercings and tattoos whom no one can catch. Calvin, the lopey-dopey big kid on the block who plays amazing football but who's nonetheless scared of his shadow. And Redmond, the gum-chewing, cigar-smoking gambler, who's got everyone's number, especially mine. "Five gets you ten that Wendell won't have the guts to take me to Fair Hill."

Grace comes later in the day to coach Huey and Surf through a couple of gymnastics. I raise my eyebrows when I note the tight distances, but am even more surprised when she instructs me to canter, not trot, through them. Moreover, she presents the gymnastics as a line of four fences right off the bat and doesn't build them up, jump by jump, as is Wofford's style. Surf is rattled by the demand. He stops the first time through, which in turn rattles me because he's never done this before. But to his credit, he does it right the second time and henceforth puts in good efforts to fit his huge body into such tight spaces. "I've always thought of Surf as shy," Grace says. "He shouldn't be rushed through any exercise. He needs to take a good look at what you're asking him to do to fully process the question." The canter she has me develop on both horses to execute this tough series of jumps is more of a collected dressage canter, about a quarter of the Mach speed I was using at Pine Top. Grace wants to give these big ex-racehorses the opportunity to rock back, gather themselves, and push from behind when jumping instead of using speed to get the job done. Her aim is to encourage a rounder bascule and improve the overall form of my horses' jumps. Huey pulls a few rails in his eagerness to get the job over with, but he's thinking about it and trying hard. We give Surf the gold star for the day—he hardly touches a rail once he works through his initial mistake.

Grace had a bad fall at a horse trial last year. She shattered her scapula, punctured her lung, and broke several ribs. She has months of rehab and recuperation behind her and is back to riding and competing. She is a pro at coming back from serious injuries, and I admire her stamina and determination to make it back to the sport, which she has done repeatedly over a long career of riding and competing.

I tell her news of a young rider recently falling at the same Advanced tables where Grace fell last year. The girl is in ICU with a multiply fractured pelvis and broken vertebrae. We share our mutual disgust that changes weren't made to jumps that had already caused such a bad accident the year before. Or that the jumps wouldn't have been taken off the course altogether after wreaking such havoc. Though my teacher is generally quiet and not a complainer, she will now make her voice heard in the matter.

March 26

Flatwork times four. Which is just as well, as the weather is cranky, overcast, and cold. Spring doesn't seem to want to come this year. I zip through my rides and am done at the barn by one. My thoughts turn toward Easter, an odd holiday for me, particularly now that my parents are gone. I shop for a little something for Caitlin and then spend the rest of the day cooking a ham and pineapple upside-down cake for my family— my own answer to every holiday.

It's been years since the day had any religious significance for me. Still, on Good Friday, I check my watch and then the sky, to see if it becomes overcast between twelve and three, which it is supposed to do during the hours Christ hung on the cross. No trouble fulfilling that myth this year; it's been completely gray all week. Each year my parents would send a lily, as well as a ham. The house would fill up for days with the rich scent of the flower. Come to think of it, I wish I'd thought to get a lily this year—the multicolored crocuses outside my office French doors will have to do, reminding me of what comes back again and again.

Easter Sunday

We celebrate Easter on a trail ride—Barrett on Calvin, Lady Lazarus on Jerry the Racehorse. It's Barrett's idea, one he doesn't have often—about once a year, to be exact. He's asked to do this on a holiday, a day when he can be assured no one will come to the farm to see him ride a horse. He suggests Calvin, whom he hasn't ridden yet. Calvin's a pretty good choice. Dead quiet until he spooks at something, he's big enough to give my 220-pound husband a sense of security and vice versa. This will be a walking trail ride, and both horses cope well with the reduced speed. Calvin doesn't put a foot wrong, and Barrett comes back smiling.

In the afternoon, we go to our old friends' annual party for eggs and champagne, with the emphasis on champagne. I spy two bottles of Snapple lemonade hidden behind a porch beam, as if my friends were hiding more than eggs today. Though it's got to be five o'clock somewhere in the world, it's too early to start drinking, even for me. I've come to this party for the last twenty years, and besides the host and hostess, I don't see any of the other guests during the year unless I happen to run into them at a bar. We're all getting older—that's the first thing you notice when you only see a person once a year.

Caitlin was a tot when we first started coming to this annual Easter party. I'd dress her in extravagant Easter dresses and bonnets. She'd trudge around with her Easter basket over an arm, madly searching for enough eggs to stuff it full. And now here she is beside me at nineteen, in jeans and red cowboy boots, chatting up her plans for an acting career. This is as close to church as I'll get—the trail ride and the annual Easter egg hunt that has less to do with our search for eggs than with our hopes for another spring and ensuing year. Though it's a dreary day, our host's crocuses are popping out all over. This year our friends have repainted their house for the occasion—it's trimmed with florescent pinks, yellows, and blues, and looks exactly like an Easter egg itself.

Later in the evening, I take my daughter a rainy 40 miles away to meet a school friend whom she will hitch a ride with to Sarah Lawrence. She doesn't want to go back to school, which I take as a compliment. It has been so nice to have her home. Hello, spring and solitude and having the house to myself again. But goodbye, little girl and big girl Caitlin. It's a tough trade.

March 28

It's Barrett's and my anniversary today—only our third, though we've been together for eleven years, while I hemmed and hawed and postponed getting married again. Before that, I was living in Baltimore suburbia, getting back into horses after my fifteen-year hiatus from them and living with my children's dad, an intellectual who had no interest in horses or moving to a farm, which was exactly what I wanted to do. The writing was on the wall. It had been a volatile, intense marriage, probably doomed early on exactly because of that and because we were too much alike: a high-strung, volatile person myself, I need a steady Eddy to keep me on the straight and narrow, the winding and wide.

Before we can celebrate, I have five horses to ride and will have to cope with horrendous, pelting rain once again. As I tack up each horse, I keep an eye on Cherie in the back field, who has still not decided to foal, though she's now surpassed her due date. She romps in the rain with her buddy, Carneros's mother, Our Ballerina, enjoying her last taste of freedom for a while, despite the rain. When it decides not to stop well into the afternoon, she and Ballerina finally retreat into the run-in shed. "What's up with Cherie?" I ask my husband at one point in this miserable day.

"She's waiting for Ballerina to foal," he replies.

"Well then, she's going to have to wait a long time," I say. Ballerina is not due for another month.

Thank God for the indoor arena on days like today. I've scratched all hopes for the horses I'd intended on hacking, and everyone gets flatted in the indoor instead. It's still raining on my fifth and last ride: Huey. I throw caution to the wind and head for the blinding rain and the outdoor ring in order to practice this weekend's dressage test. Hoss trainer J. W. Delozier pulls up to visit his two racehorses at the farm on layup. "You're a die-hard," he says, and then pauses before he asks the million-dollar question, "What are you doing riding outside on a day like today when you've got an indoor?"

"Because it's my anniversary," I reply. Oh. Well, that certainly makes sense.

"Happy anniversary!" he congratulates, without missing a beat.

March 29

Everyone jogs sound today, and I think of Houston.

Katie and I venture outside with the horses for an unusual taste of fresh air. All the horses slip and slide in the mud, except sure-footed Calvin. I imagine he'd make a mudder, if they raced Irish sport horses. And if he had any speed. He and little goat-footed Jerry are the only two we dare let canter in this slop. We head toward home, neck and neck. They pick up a wee taste of pace, and I feel Calvin kick into a higher gear, competing with the racehorse. Jerry pulls away at an easy lope, not even testing his own ability. But I still have hope that somewhere deep down Calvin might have a desire to be more than just a rocking horse.

March 30

Grace comes to help put Surf and Huey through their paces in preparation for Morven Park Horse Trials this weekend. We begin outside on the flat, then move inside to jump. Katie has set up another tight canter-in gymnastic and then a couple of lines, including a bounce and a skinny and a corner. Huey is eager without being rude, and although the gymnastic is tough for him to negotiate, it does provoke his jump to become rounder by session's end. Once again, Grace has me jumping him out of a dressagy collected canter, which forces him to jump out of power and rhythm, not speed, which is his custom.

The exercise is harder on Surf, because of his greenness and size, although he makes an effort and handles the jumps quite well, initially. The jump I'm waiting for—the one when he backs himself off, gets behind my leg, and barfs over the fence, enticing me to hustle him too forward, thereby running him past his distance at the next fence so he crashes through that one—happens when he starts to get tired and the jumps go up to Intermediate height. I should be grateful that Grace gets to see the problem, which is exactly what happened in competition at Pine Top. Surf's eyes get big and he backs off—his error. I overcompensate and rush him forward and flat—mine. We egg each other on to disaster. Seeing the iceberg in the distance, we run our ship right for it.

"The first pukey fence isn't really the problem, Julia," Grace says. "He's so big he hasn't figured out how to recoil his body when he gets in tight like that and jump out of that distance. You just have to support it, and then get busy on landing to recreate a decent canter to jump the next fence without running him off his feet." Easier said than done. All in all, the session ends well for Surf, and I'm confident that we have both learned from Grace's expertise. Less confident that the weekend will go well.

March 31

The footing is still mucky, but I'm determined to get Surf and Huey outside. I wouldn't mind getting Surf's toes wet either when I realize he hasn't had a cross-country school since we were down south, and this weekend will be his first Intermediate run. I take him on a loop over to

Jackson Hole Farm. I trot Surf over a board fence that will take me into a Jackson Hole pasture. Surf gets bogged down in the muck on takeoff, twists over the fence, slips on landing, and goes down to his knees. I come off, bonking my head and nose on God knows what. Thanks to the voluminous rain we've had, it's a muddy, soft landing that greets me. Surf, angel that he is, stands and waits for me to right myself when he has every opportunity to run off. It's a long way down from a 17-foot-3-inch horse— and it's an even longer way up when mounting from the ground. My nose is throbbing, and I think it may be broken, until I run into neighbor Cindy Halle on my much slower retreat home. "Is my nose straight?" I ask her. What a question. She can't help but laugh.

"Yeah, but you've got more mud on you than Surf does," she replies.

The afternoon brings a conference call with my family estate's lawyers and my two brothers. We try to decide whether to sue the local hospital for what appears to be negligent care at the time of my father's death. We have been unanimously given a certificate of merit to proceed with the case— a requirement in the state in order to file a lawsuit. Both lawyers are advising us to proceed with the case, but my brothers balk. I'm glad I don't have to compete them . . . eventing means you're obsessed with getting to the other side.

I have never sued anyone in my life, but I feel confident that it is the right move. I'm convinced that my father would still be among us enjoying the rest of his life had he been given normal postoperative care. Someone might have noticed that his oxygen level was dropping and not left him in his room to suffocate himself into a coma. When the ER doctor subsequently intubated him, he did it incorrectly and had to call in an anesthesiologist to redo the procedure forty-five minutes later, which by that time was too late to save my father's life. By conference call's end, my brothers have more or less slipped over to my side, but even so, I feel sick at heart, reliving the details of my father's premature death and then trying to convince my brothers that suing the hospital is the right thing to do, even if I'm not wholeheartedly committed to this path myself. I try to explain to them that our goal should not be to gain financially but to take a principled stand in an effort to get the hospital to change its procedures so that such an occurrence doesn't happen again—a point that I have never before had to impress upon myself, let alone two fence-sitters.

I turn and toss all night from a screaming sore nose and neck, and sorer heart.

April 1

Living in a world of complicated horses makes it all the nicer to share it with a man of uncomplicated needs. This year for his birthday, Barrett wants homemade macaroni and cheese and pork barbecue. I add a salad, so as to hide the pork I will not eat under lettuce leaves. "Isn't there anything else you want?" I ask, enjoying how a forty-three-year-old man can still blush. Afterward, he says he wishes we could have birthdays once a week.

Goodness. That's an awful lot of macaroni.

Leesburg, Virginia

I brave the elements and haul Surf and Huey to Morven Park Spring Horse Trials. Dressage and show jumping are scheduled for today. Grace has offered to coach me this weekend, despite the dire forecast. It begins to rain torrentially on the trip to Leesburg in the early A.M. I barely recognize my other coach when she walks up to the trailer hidden in her many layers of rain pants, parka and hood, as if she wants to appear incognito. I am already soaked, and the trailer is a swamp. I contemplate scratching, but the horses and I are here, and so is Grace It won't hurt to ride a couple of dressage tests in the pouring rain.

Surf goes first, and he's one of the lucky Intermediate horses that gets to do his test in the indoor and out of the rain. Grace is helpful when Surf and I start to unravel in the overcrowded warm-up space. She encourages me to let him stretch, then put him on a counterbend, to a leg yield across the diagonal. We're both able to recapture our focus and put in a respectable effort, which shows improvement from the last test that Grace had seen. Midway through, the skies split with a huge crack of lightning and thunder. Surf, bless his heart, keeps his head down and finishes his job, right before they put a hold on dressage proceedings until the storm clears, as well as postpone all show jumping until tomorrow.

Two hours later, after the worst of the thunder and lightning pass, the tests resume. When it's Huey's turn, he's all fired up. I'm going to have to ride well to keep him on track. I'm fairly pleased with the results, as is Grace She says it's the first time she's seen me ride every stride of a test with such determination.

Both horses score only passably, in the low to mid-40s, which puts them low to middling on an impressive list of riders that includes some top event professionals. Because amateurs and professionals are lumped in the same divisions, as an amateur myself, I'm forced to come up with my own set of personal goals that have nothing to do with winning or placing.

I'm awakened in the middle of the night by a ringing phone. It's Barrett from the barn, and Cherie is at long last foaling. Or rather, she has already foaled, and her new one is standing and dry when Barrett finds them, only one-and-a-half hours after he last checked the mare to find her peacefully snoozing with no indication that she was on the verge of anything special. "I'm looking at your 2011 event champion," Barrett tells me.

"It's a colt!" I say, relieved and enthusiastic all at once. I throw my winter parka over my pj's, pull my paddock boots over my bare feet, and head up to the barn. The first thing that strikes me is that the foal is identical to his mother—bay, with a star in the shape of a pie with a piece cut out from the bottom right corner. "Identical, that's a good name," I say. Barrett's now stooping over the foal, armed with a flashlight and a cup of iodine, in an effort to find his umbilical cord.

"Oh-oh," he says, looking perplexed. "I'm afraid it's a filly, after all."

"She's all yours," I say, referring to our agreement that the colts will become event prospects and the fillies will race.

She's a cutie, nonetheless—very correct and feistily nursing—and Cherie is handling her new situation with ease and aplomb. "How about Carbon Copy?" I ask.

"Or Ditto," he adds.

"Maybe Spitting Image," I offer. "Or Identical. Then her barn name could be Ditto." With the stallion's name Mighty Forum, and the mother's R. Isabella, there's not much hope of combining the two into anything catchy. "We could always try 'A Funny Thing Happened,'" I go for broke, knowing that we will play this game of naming for days, until something strikes us just right.

April 3

I return to Morven Park, without Grace, to show jump Huey and Surf Guitar. Because of high winds, they've decided to move the jumps to the indoor, and we're all asked to come and help with the setup. It's a free-for-all. Dozens of competitors and grooms mill around the indoor kicking footing, as the course designer runs around trying to stuff his C-cup course into the indoor's B cup. A couple of disorganized hours later, they're ready to get show jumping under way. I return to the trailer to get Surf tacked. My first mistake.

Grace has advised me not to jump Surf if the jumps move inside, as this indoor backs horses off so they don't jump well. Surf needs a good positive go to build his confidence, as well as mine.

I've asked Rainey Andrews to be my eye in Grace's absence. Rainey encourages me to give the indoor a try, as Surf seems to be handling the claustrophobia of the warm-up area. Plus, he's used to jumping inside at home. Mistake number seven hundred.

Surf backs off from the jumps badly. I compensate by overriding him and make a mess of the round. He comes around each corner with eyes the size of Mars, chips in, and barfs over the fences. I try to reorganize him for the next fence a hair's breadth away but end up running him off his feet. To Surf's credit, he keeps trying to get the job done and never stops out on me, but keeps crashing through each and every miserable spot we keep finding. I head for the exit after we demolish the last fence.

They practically have to call out the Army Corps of Engineers to rebuild the course for the next rider. Rainey tells me what went wrong from her perspective, and right behind her is the president of the ground jury, who's come to admonish me for not pulling up midway through the course. This is a first for me, having such a miserable go and then being corrected by an official. I am mortified. Rainey blames the round on my overriding. I know it wasn't pretty, but I'm not so sure of her assessment. I spend the rest of the day recreating the stickiness I felt underneath me and the ways in which I attempted to respond to that ride. There's never an excuse for bad riding, and perhaps my reaction wasn't the best, but it still doesn't answer the question at the heart of the problem, which is why Surf backs off in the first place. I respond in the ways I do because I feel something undesirable going on underneath me, and I want to fix it. I may not choose the right ways, but there's a problem with my horse to begin with.

I opt not to jump Huey—probably my only good decision of the day—pack up as quickly as possible, and drive home with my tail between my legs.

Shame is such a physical feeling. It makes your insides contract and your eyes well up. It makes you want to talk to no one and then to talk to everyone. It makes you want to avoid, and then it makes you terribly needy. It reduces you to about five years old. It also makes you want to give it all up, even though you know deep down that given time you'll feel differently. You've been through this process of humiliation before. As with grief, time and distance are the only things that are able to ease it. In the meantime, it makes you unable to sleep.

I can't help but think of Huey's father   Time For a Change—and how his name applies to my life right now. In a few short months, I've gone from planning four three-days for the spring and the momentous Fair Hill Three Star with Redmond in the fall, eager to write this chronicle as an account of those accomplishments, to no three-days in the near future at all, as well as stinking up the joint with my riding. Even with this stickiness in my heart, I do feel compelled to keep going for the sake of the horses. This chronicle has become a kind of lifeline for me, transformed in four short months from an *account* of the reason for my being to *the* reason for my being.

Maybe I've bitten off more than I can chew. Now I'm compelled to spit something back out. The problem is, the food is delicious. Which two horses of the six would I possibly choose to refocus my attention on, when I love all of them as individuals and have worked so hard to bring each of them along? Huey and Surf are my two favorites, but realistically, Huey is seventeen with lots of physical issues, and Surf is, well, Surf—huge and still green, and sometimes a bit of a customer, come to eventing from his long term at the track with a lot of emotional baggage and physical issues to boot. The writing is on the wall, and perhaps it's time to think about putting these two on the shelf, to turn my attention to Redmond and Calvin, and to work a little harder at getting Jerry sold.

I have one more practical realization—that Surf's bad jumping form has something to do with his overreacting to his bit—a Waterford Baucher—which is a strong bit, but has worked quite well up to now. Maybe it might be worth it to jump him in his dressage bridle tomorrow to see if he is less backed off and more willing to go. A possible solution is the best medicine—my one accomplishment today. And with this hope in mind, I am at last able to sleep.

April 4

I get up, go up to the barn, throw a saddle on Surf without so much as taking a brush to his sides, and put on his dressage bridle. It takes him about one third of the jump school to realize he's got a softer bit in his mouth, but by session's end, he's starting to take me to the fences. I know the answer couldn't possibly be as easy as two plus two, but it's a start. Same school for Huey, with the jumps a little higher, and then a long hack on Calvin with Trish on Jerry.

Though I feel confident in my decision to cut back, I still agonize over the situation. This is an unfortunate part of my personality: to make a decision and then to second-guess myself, over and over, scratching my head over the solution when the equation's already been solved. Making a decision to cross a bridge means I've made a hundred decisions not to cross a hundred other bridges.

The afternoon brings a business meeting with Barrett. We review the farm budget yet again, trying to balance the lopsided equation of expenses outweighing income while trying to figure ways to make the most out of the least. Barrett proposes we put Jerry into steeplechase training with Jeremy Gillam, our neighbor. He's already spoken to Jeremy about it, who is delighted by the prospect. As much as it pains me to think of putting Jerry back into race training, it's an outstanding idea. Jerry's a runner, through and through—he proved that over and over again at the track—and in recent months he's also proven to be a talented jumper. Two plus two.

April 5

I set up the identical show jump course I ruined in Morven's indoor in my own and give myself three lessons on Surf, Calvin, and Huey. It's obvious that in my indoor arena, Surf's dressage bridle is plenty enough bit in his mouth. He tries to stall out on me around turns to a fence. If I think about coming forward around the turn and not pulling back on the reins to check him, then the spots open up better. Keep coming around the turns, don't touch his mouth, I tell myself.

I keep Huey in a collected canter. He jumps well until he opens up his stride and gets strung out and the rails start coming down. I reestablish a softer canter, then try a new tactic: every time he hits a rail, I stop him and back him up. We repeat the fence he knocked until he gets it right. This pisses him off, particularly when I have to use my new strategy several times at the skinny, which he has always loved to pull. I feel a light bulb go on in Huey's head, too, when he finally balloons over the skinny, not touching it by a mile, and clears the rest of the course.

Katie invites me to join Chandler and her on a several mile "Rambo" trail ride to a course of timber race logs set several miles away behind the Dulin's farm. This will be perfect for Jerry. The weather is lovely—it's one of those cool-building-to-warm, clear spring days, one of our first sunny ones, which feel like such a gift when they first happen.

This used to be one of Caitlin's haunts on Sunny and one of my favorite memories of our time spent together. There are three or four separate lines of logs, with maybe ten logs in each line, ranging from 2 feet, 6 inches to 4 feet tall. I remember Sunny, who's no more than 13.2 hands high, bombing through the line of "big" logs, with Caitlin, whooping it up on a spring day much like today, maybe eight years ago, when we first realized that little Sunny could jump the moon if he wanted to.

Jerry jumps everything I put in front of him, long or short, it doesn't matter, first in line or waiting till last, it doesn't matter, calm as could be. Focused. Attentive. A horse with a clear grasp of the task at hand.

I come up with the name Likewise for Cherie's foal with the look-alike star, who's an overall carbon copy of her mother, and Ditto for her barn name. Redmond does a lot of standing in the corner of his paddock, as close as he can get to mama's and baby's, staring at the antics of the newborn in the next paddock over. I bet Calvin's never seen a baby horse before—he seems almost scared of her but excited by her appearance, too—does a lot of stopping and staring, his heart beating through his skin when I walk him by their paddock. It's always fun to see how the newborns perk up the event horses. They genuinely seem to enjoy having the babies in their barn.

April 6

I luxuriate in only having two rides—the lyric of my day—first a hack on Redmond, then flatwork on Calvin. I take my time and don't even wear a watch on the trail ride. Redmond and I meander over to Jackson Hole Farm, explore a new trail, then trot and gallop toward home to get our hearts pumping. Everyone gets bubble baths on our second serious spring day. Hurry up, there's more rain in the forecast for the weekend. Katie hauls out the Orvus and leaves it in the wash stall as one by one the horses all get bathed. I like this idea of being able to spend more time on each horse without so many to ride in a given day. I am feeling things out.

Barrett informs me that Jerry is to leave next week for Camden, South Carolina, with Jeremy, and Cherie will go to the stallion Parker's Storm Cat at Country Life Farm. We get the suds going for her while Barrett throws his arms around Ditto to keep her in the aisle as her mother turns a different color in the adjacent wash stall. *What a funny life this is turning out to be.* She's right about that.

A first-class second-guesser, I am stewing over my recent decisions regarding my cutbacks, my plans for Jerry and lack of them for Surf, my decision to pare down and refocus. I still haven't spoken to Grace about my show jumping debacle last weekend. I call her, leave a message, nestle into my own hot bubble bath with a new read for the night, my tried-and-true remedy for what ails me. My feelings are as fickle as the spring weather that surrounds me.

April 7

I hack over to Grace's farm on Calvin. She's hand grazing her Advanced mare, who recently damaged a tendon on their trip south. I begin to fill her in on what went wrong in show jumping last weekend at Morven. She patiently listens to me, despite the fact that I went against her advice and jumped Surf in Morven's indoor. She is interested to hear how I came home and set up Morven's exact course in my indoor, and what I learned when I jumped both Huey and Surf again on my own turf. She reassures me that I have the knowledge and tools to figure things out for myself. I tell her of my decision to cut back on the horses I'm competing and focus on her as my sole trainer for a while. Too many horses, too many cooks in the kitchen, and I feel overwhelmed with work and information. Not enough horses and not enough cooks, then I feel claustrophobic. She is glad to be of help.

Three horses come charging down Grace's country road. We recognize them as belonging to our neighbors, Walter and Linda Reynolds. I'm used to loose horses being easily caught at my farm because of the splits that run between paddocks and lots of horses left inside to draw the unencumbered ones like magnets. But Walter and Linda's three horses are the only ones on their farm, so now that they're loose, they become runaway bandits, with no intention of being caught. We almost nab them as they pass through Grace's place, but they're determined to slip by the four of us—Grace, Linda, and me on Calvin—when we try to corner them. Off they go, and Calvin and I go galloping after them, with Linda in her Subaru and Grace on foot. "I guess I won't have to get on the treadmill today, after all," Grace calls out to me. Calvin is thrilled to be introduced to his new role as quarter horse. He knows that the other horses are being naughty, so he gets quivery with excitement while the Upperco bandits maraud the countryside. It takes a couple of near misses—galloping down farm roads and across cornfields—before Calvin and I find the three in a neighbor's alfalfa field, chowing down. We wait for Linda, who comes armed this time with a feed bucket and halters. She tempts the spotted one into captivity, but the chestnut and gray charge off again. A half hour later, I corner the chestnut in a split, and the gray follows resignedly back to their rightful paddock. Whew. That's more exercise than Calvin's seen in a while. I make a note to let him have tomorrow off. "Calvin gets a gold star," Grace reminds me. "There aren't many horses who wouldn't lose their cool, given the circumstances."

April 8

I've come to New York by train to spend the weekend with Caitlin, who has gotten us tickets to see *The Glass Menagerie*.

I'm a big fan of Jessica Lange. She is vibrant and appropriately strained in the role of the fading southern belle and jilted wife and mother, Amanda. I am distracted by extraneous hand and arm movements of actors on stage, and even Jessica gets a bit carried away. In the cinema there are a lot of partial shots in the filming of a scene, but on stage we get the whole actor—no subtractions—who must act with her entire body and can't hide a thing; retakes and zooming are not options. And what to do with the hands? The hands in the process become as constant and evident as facial gestures. Christian Slater, in the role of the unhappy dreamer son, Tom, seems comfortable on stage, perhaps because the director has given him something to do with his hands at all times: smoking. Ms. Lange puts her hands to her heart a lot, which is a poignant gesture for this unhappy, hysterical belle, but she's less effective when her arms go flying about in more awkward, pained moments. I think of my own pained moments, pushing and pulling Surf Guitar unsuccessfully around Morven's show jumping course last weekend, way too noisy with my hands, distracting my horse away from his jumps and his job. Lange's role would have been more effective if she'd been stiller in her demeanor and movement. The best art is when there's a lot going on but it doesn't look like it. The sleight of hand, the quiet ride, the ballerina seemingly effortless in her difficult leaps and arabesques. Quiet the hands, Julia.

April 9

Saturday in New York City. Not a cloud in the brilliant blue sky that I see up there between the skyscrapers. Shop till you drop. Get as close to Caitlin as I can. Soak in the short time with her. We're on our way from Betsey Johnson to Barneys when Barrett calls to tell me that he got Cherie and her foal to Country Life Farm without a hitch. How impressed the manager at the breeding farm was with Ditto. How calm and composed Cherie was when she walked off the trailer, spic and span at long last with a job that she loves, soaking in the short time with her little one, and preparing herself for what's next: breeding until you drop.

April 10

I kiss Caitlin goodbye as I wait for a cab, watch her back and unpulled mane of dark, wild hair recede down the bustling Sunday streets and still-brilliant skies of the Upper East Side on her way back to Grand Central, and back to school. We've seen it in films galore, people walking toward us and away on crowded city streets, the camera's eye singling out the one out of hundreds. But when my little one is now grown enough to be sent off into the belly of New York City, my chest constricts, something rises within it, and I want to reach out and pluck her back, my own camera's eye swelling and burning. I reflect on our weekend together, feeling myself grow fond of the city I've detested in recent memory, ever since my ex moved here eleven years ago and the city became central to John and Caitlin, who visited it and their long-distant father every couple of months. "Don't forget to take hold of your father's hand when you cross those busy streets," I remember warning ten-year-old Caitlin, as I now give her a kiss and let her go and watch her walk away to negotiate Seventh Avenue all by herself.

April 11

Dear Caitlin,

When you called last night, twisting and turning over your chosen path as an acting major, I wanted to tell you a little story of happenstance. When I'd moved to Arizona for my first teaching job I was unhappy and lonely. I missed home and my first big love who had moved to Mexico. Your grandmother made a suggestion to me: Why not join the church choir? It was a logical thought coming from my mother— she was a good Episcopalian, and an even better musician. But for me? Although I could harmonize a bit and sang in the choir as a kid, we all know what my voice sounds like. But I was pretty miserable in my job and life at the time. I took her up on it and joined St. Barnabas Choir in Phoenix.

I met a boy in the choir whom I dated. Unfortunately, he was ninety percent gay, which didn't leave much room for me. He introduced me to his friend who was only seventy percent gay. After a few months I took up with a contralto—a woman—and we all moved in together. These were all graduate students at Arizona and they gave me the bug to go back to the piano. The rub was that I needed a music undergraduate degree but I could apply to the poetry program and sneak in some ivories on the side. All I had to do was dig around the closet to find some poems. They accepted me, and a few days later my doctor found a large cyst on my ovary. I had to go home for three weeks of surgery and recuperation. The university wanted to let me go, but the resident poet insisted they let me stay in the program. The English Department would hire a temporary Teaching Assistant until I could come back to Phoenix. That was how I met your father who was a graduate student in the creative writing program. From Arizona, we moved to Iowa, then Baltimore, where we settled and taught and wrote and ran our small publishing company, and eventually had you and your brother. Because I joined the church choir, I stumbled into a program in creative writing and a writing career . . . and the rest of my life just happened.

So, does Sarah Lawrence have a choir?
All my love,
Mom

April 12

Word from Country Life Farm is that Cherie has an enlarged uterus and won't be a good candidate for foal heat breeding. They will wait another five to seven days and try again, with Prostin on board. Poor Uncle Redmond. He gets turned out in his paddock, which is adjacent to Cherie's and little Ditto's, runs to its farthest corner in search of his new friend, whinnies, and then canters back to me at the gate as if I might have the answer as to her whereabouts.

I can relate. I gallop out into my day as if in search of some distinct feeling of absence I can't quite put my finger on. I get my rides done, put in time at my desk, have dinner with an old friend who owns part of the racehorse Foolish Groom, but I never find it. The formlessness of melancholy, the looking for something that's not quite there, the lacking and loneliness of an uncentered day. Maybe Redmond has the answer as to her whereabouts. I'll ask him tomorrow.

April 13

Chandler on Smarty, Katie on Boy, and Julia on Calvin go cross-country schooling at Weave a Dream Farm. It's my first stab at my official capacity as instructor, although this may not be crystal clear to Chandler, who gets smoldery quiet when I give her a hard time about the crusted state of her bit. I'm neurotic about keeping clean tack, particularly what the horses have to put in their mouths, a concern I picked up from my old teacher, Jill French. I figure it's not a bad neurosis to have. But it always amazes me how many riders don't take care of their tack. And Chandler, apparently, is one of them.

Smarty jumps great, but Chandler feels as though she's being run off with between jumps. This is not apparent to Katie and me. At least 75 percent of the sport is a head trip. I know this too well from my own experiences. I encourage Chandler to circle or halt every time she feels out of control between fences, then to reestablish the canter and softness before continuing. She circles only once on her next execution of about eight jumps. She still feels uncomfortable, and I hope it's not my teaching style that's getting to her. "Why was it more fun in Aiken?" she asks, which is not the conclusion I'd come to. Meanwhile, I experiment with bits on Calvin. I've bought about ten new ones in an effort to find perfection. But the bit I like the best is one I already had—Huey's two-ring lever.

Kim Meier comes for dinner, and we stuff ourselves with salmon teriyaki and spring veggie pasta, spinach dip and popovers, ice cream and chocolate sauce. Oh, and lots of Chardonnay. And when that's gone, Cabernet Sauvignon. We talk about horses and books and food, about her experience last year at Burghley, and about everything else under the sun. I am smiling for a change.

April 14

I've got Grace and Kim intersecting today. Kim hangs out for the morning, while Grace comes to give me a couple of lessons on Calvin and Huey to prepare for Plantation Field Horse Trials. Several years ago, when I was still taking lessons from Kim, she helped me design some cross-country fences to build on the farm. I ask her if she'll take a look at the course to see what else it needs and be a fly on the wall for my lessons. It's good practice, having an audience, and it's even better practice with Kim as my eye. Kim's a tough cookie to please, and it's odd having her watch me take a lesson from someone else after all the time I spent under her guidance. She has become a close friend and understands my need to move on and absorb as much as I can from as many people as I can. The lesson for the day is learned on Huey. Grace reminds me to make my adjustments early and then to soften and leave him alone in front of the fences. It's tough to accomplish on Huey, who is eager to the jumps; he lures me into taking more of a hold. But when I'm able to soften, the quality of his jump improves, and he's less likely to touch the rails, his favorite game. I turn to Kim, who's leaning on the fence. I tell her how I've heard this before, remembering her constant instructions to "Let go!" in front of the fences.

It's nice to be jumping outside. Last weekend, Katie's boyfriend, Craig, hauled all the standards and poles from the indoor up the long hill to our outdoor jump ring, which is situated on top of one of the several hills at the farm, about a five-minute hack from the barns. In the spring and fall, it can be breezy and cool up top, and too often we're righting fences that have blown over. But in the dead of summer, there's always a welcome breeze on top of the hill.

Chandler wants my help jumping Smarty over some stadium fences, so I put her through Grace's gymnastic and show jump lines. I note some positional issues that Chandler could work on, and Smarty becomes softer and happier to his fences as a result of the changes. She is eager to schedule her next lesson.

April 15

The exterminator comes for his every-six-week inspection and application to keep the rodent population at the farm under control. I am terrified of mice and rats, and one of the first things I did when buying the farm was sign a rodent-killing contract. At the time the house had rats living in the attic. Had I known this fact before buying, I probably wouldn't have. We remained rodent-free until, a few months after moving in, a rat came up from the dirt-floor basement through a heat-duct vent and alarm-clocked our household early one morning with its scurrying and scratching. That was years ago. Now the hit man comes periodically to keep the rats and mice at bay. Unlike other horse farms, you're hard-pressed to see a rat here, with only the occasional mouse scurrying by. Our cats help out some, too.

Now the rats have wings. Countless starlings have taken over the indoor arena and are nesting in the insulation, pulling it out in huge chunks and scattering it all over the barn. The birds' activity in the indoor has been a problem for years, but this spring they are particularly numerous and destructive. It's more like an aviary than a barn. We've taken to closing up the barn doors, but that doesn't work. Barrett has even started shooting at the birds with John's old BB gun (he hasn't hit one yet), but the busy birds could not care less about the gun. Nah-nanny-boo-boo. We are thinking of hanging nets when Barrett pulls the exterminator aside. He runs through the list of available bird poisons that might be the most effective considering the structure, the type of bird, the problem with the insulation, not to mention the presence of the other animals. An hour of possibilities goes by. "I'll have to think about it and talk to my boss," he says, "but I'll get 'em. I got a 1200 on my SATs, and birds are the dumbest mammal known to man."

This could be a long, noisy spring.

Unionville, Pennsylvania

Plantation Field Horse Trials. I'm a nervous wreck. I've got Calvin and Huey with me, plus memories of my last show jump rounds. It's cool, with sunny skies, so nothing in the show schedule should be rearranged this time. Dressage on both is okay, despite the fact that as we're trotting down center line, Huey spooks at a white horse coming toward him as if he sees a ghost. He tenses up, and the progress we made in warm-up shrivels. I manage to ride through it and get some good work from him. I'm pleased I can keep my focus when things aren't going well. Years of practice. Years of learning to feel every off-key nuance. The judge, after my final salute, leans out her car window to ask if I have any concerns about my horse's unevenness behind. Not a good sign. I run through the catalog in my head of Huey's numerous old hind-end issues, although I'm pretty sure this time what she's seeing is a function of tension. "Not really," I say as casually as possible, throwing out a good score for this test. What do those racetrackers say? . . . "Just his way of going."

Calvin stays relaxed and steady and obedient throughout his test. How easy for some and what a struggle for others. I stand by my belief that I'm a better dressage rider because of the struggle. Well, still in the making, anyway.

Grace encourages me to soften the reins in front of the jumps during the warm-up for show jumping. Though the course is tough, with lots of turns on rough terrain, Huey only takes one rail. Rainey Andrews comes up to me afterward and gives me a hug. "Well, at least it's an improvement over Morven," I say. She's quick to say it's the best she's ever seen me ride. To Rainey, when it's good, it's fabulous. When it's not quite right, it's awful. She's still learning from her mentor, Jimmy, about the gray areas in between. Calvin puts in a good round, too, at Training level. Maybe there's hope yet.

April 18

I'm nervous going out of the box on Huey. He jumps around clean, but slow. I never get my mojo going, and although I feel good about the round, I know it's subpar and nowhere near as decisive as our run at Pine Top. Can't have everything. Huey is aggressive to his fences, never backs off, so I'm not able to recreate the softness I had in stadium. I start pulling to get him back before the fences, and he starts fussing with his head.

It's a sport of making adjustments. I slow down and stay soft for show jumping, and then I lose some of my aggressiveness on cross country but end up getting in my horse's face.

Calvin's a different matter. He's a young Training horse who's still unsure of himself. I take him slow intentionally, let him get a good look at the fences before he has to jump them. He lopes around and jumps everything beautifully. Slow, but clean.

Huey earns a silver ribbon, and since Calvin finishes his run barely before dark and cocktail hour, we head out before his scores are posted.

April 19

My yum gets yucked. I check online for Calvin's time cross country, only to see that the scorers have given Huey twenty jump penalties. He didn't stop anywhere, and we even got a ribbon, so how can this be? When I query Barrett, he tells me that the placings for Huey's division were posted, but the time and jump penalties weren't, when he last looked and collected our prize. That'll teach me to get better about watching the scoreboard myself, something that I detest doing—a leftover from my youthful aversion to competition. Or, let me put it another way: I haven't gotten on scales since I was pregnant with Caitlin, as a way of overcoming an old battle with anorexia. If I don't know, then I can't feel bad about myself. Good thing the sport no longer requires weighing out. It's past the protest period, so there's nothing official to be done about the wrongful jump penalty, anyway. I replay our run several times in my head to make sure I didn't do anything stupid. I call the event secretary, who sounds exhausted from what must have been a grueling weekend of long days and late nights. And cranky, complaining competitors. She promises to look into it and get back to me. It's been a hard morning of putting on my glasses and getting on those damn scales.

I teach Chandler, then critique some poems of a friend and feel the sense of satisfaction of giving back a little, which takes me gratefully away from the more painful process of watching my weight.

Tomorrow I must decide whether to take Huey to the CIC Two Star, an international event at the Intermediate level, this upcoming weekend at Fair Hill.

April 20

Huey jogs sound. The cherry tree outside my office window is vivid with bloom, the tulips underneath its canopy are having their say, too, and my brother John comes up from Miami for a couple days' visit. I use Surf Guitar as the guinea pig to learn the CIC Two Star dressage test, which I'll have to ride this weekend, as Huey gets a hack day today. I piddle around in my office editing poetry and paying bills, watching pinkness explode outside my window, before I roll up my sleeves to start cooking. Deep into supper's preparation, I hear from course designer Denis Glaccum. He's reviewed the score sheets, and I'm right—Huey jumped a clean round, and they had mistakenly transposed the jump penalty for the horse and rider after me, who earned it. They have erased Huey's penalty, at least on the records they send to the United States Eventing Association (USEA) and the United States Equestrian Federation (USEF), although they can't do anything about the placings. We stuff ourselves on prime rib and roasted potatoes, feta cheese and orange and pecan salad, followed by homemade coconut ice cream, and then hunker down for a long night watching *Blue Velvet*. Wouldn't have been my choice, but my brother and Barrett are mesmerized, the dark vision of David Lynch contrasting with the cherry tree and tulips, sound horse, and satisfying meal, and the rest of my warm spring day. Hours later, the two boys, age forty-three and sixty, are still cracking each other up, talking in fake munchkin voices, "Mommy, Mommy."

April 21

I run through the elements of the CIC Two Star test. Grace emphasizes accuracy and exaggeration of Huey's bend through his body in the lateral work, and once again I realize what a challenge I have working with the Crustacean and how far the two of us have come over the years—Huey, who is an average mover by nature and who is also battling the inevitable stiffness that comes from having achieved the overripe age of seventeen. Barrett says of the many Fuji persimmons that line our driveway and that don't ripen until Thanksgiving: the bad-looking ones taste the best.

I spend time in the afternoon with my brother, and then he and Barrett and I head out to eat at my favorite local restaurant. My brother is a body builder and thinks nothing of ordering multiple, high-protein entrees, which embarrasses the rest of us at the table. A mountain of Thai calamari, followed by a Caesar salad, then seared tuna with rice and the works, topped off by half of a broiled chicken with more works. I stick with salad and Barrett with crab cakes. My brother admits he's never sampled crab cakes before. Barrett offers John half of one of his two crab cakes, though they're barely the size of small biscuits. As Barrett is balancing the forkful with his bad hand, it plops in his water glass, another case of the dropsies we're accustomed to since his hand got kicked off his wrist. I fish hunks of crab out of the glass, but the soggy meat is beyond salvaging or tasting. I turn my attention back to the conversation, which has been about what is currently wrong with John's life and what to do about it. Should he pursue a new acting career at the age of almost sixty, should he move to L.A., or get married?

Since my parents' deaths, my sisterly role has become more maternal, even though I am the youngest of three and might take more advantage of the excuses that often accompany that placing. I am the one who has more often than not pretended to have my shit together, and therefore my brother comes to me for advice. I am tired and preoccupied tonight, and my ability to focus on my brother's problems has plopped in right alongside the hunks of crab in the glass of cloudy seltzer water. Barrett tries to fish out my advice, but he has no better luck than I had with his crab.

Fair Hill, Maryland

Grace makes the hour-and-a-half drive to Fair Hill on each of the three days to help me as well as another student, Sue Ward, who's riding her red mare at the Preliminary level this weekend. Dressage is on Friday. Huey gives me a wonderful warm-up; I'm psyched about how far he's come and how much progress we've made on the flat in recent months, despite the fact that he's an old dog trying to learn new tricks. As soon as we go into the ring, I feel him tense up. The good news is, I don't. This ability to focus in the dressage ring no matter what's going on between my knees has taken me 11 years and 125 days to develop.

I'm riding the Two-Star test for the first time, and there's a lot of walk work in it, followed by all the canter work. Huey's never been able to settle well in the walk. Dressage is full of oxymorons, and it takes firm relaxation on the rider's part to get through the walking. Huey tries to jig through the entire walk. I sit there. Keep asking. He gets strong through the canter work, and I keep riding what I have and trying to make it softer. I'm not displeased. Huey's still a different horse than he was, though he's been difficult today.

Barrett joins me for dinner with good news: Foolish Groom won another race today. He's all smiles and energy. We eat Chateaubriand for two at the local Fair Hill Inn so I can get my red-meat fix before cross-country day, toasting to Foolish Groom with a nice, rich Merlot.

―――――――――

Torrential rain and thunderstorms pummel the Motel 6 in Elkton, Maryland. Come dawn, it slackens, having accomplished its job of sweetening and softening the hard ground.

Huey is a star on cross country. He's bold to his fences without being rude, we're a lot quicker than we were at Plantation, and I'm able to give the hands forward at the fences, so Huey fusses less with his head and is overall softer and more rhythmic. We only have four time penalties and are tied for the third-fastest time in the CIC Two Star division.

I wake Sunday in the dark for the jog and show jump. I walk Huey, hose off the poultice, ice him, walk him again, put in studs, clean him up, get myself dressed for the jog, and lunge him, just in enough time for the inspection at 8:00 A.M. This is the scariest moment of the weekend, as Huey with his age and issues is not always the soundest-looking horse, nor the best jogger. And we've gotten spun in jogs several times in his long career. But the ground jury doesn't bat an eye today.

My nerves continue to mount for show jumping. This is a big pressure-cooker event, reminding me of Pine Top, with an impressive audience at the side of the stone dust ring about to watch me have yet another disaster.

Huey warms up sluggishly, but becomes wired as soon as we enter the ring. Though he starts hauling me to the fences, I fight the urge to take back coming into the jumps and instead give the hands forward. It's not as smooth as last week's round at Plantation, but we manage to bust only two rails. I almost go off course only once—after the triple bar that Huey gets deep to but nonetheless clears so well that I'm popped out of the tack. I wobble for a few strides afterward and take too sweeping a turn to the next roll back before I regain my seat and focus. Huey is jumping better than ever. Though he's tough and strong, I let go when I need to so he's able to better use his body over the fences. Sometimes, when everything is telling you to pull, you need to soften and let go. Sometimes you have to react contrary to your desires to have the best outcome. Despite the rails, Huey finishes seventh in the CIC Two Star division, gets a pretty purple ribbon and is part of the victory gallop, during which he takes off with me, pissed that he has to follow six other horses.

———————

On my way home, a phone call from Caitlin. She wants to stay in New York this summer to take a Spanish course at NYU and sublet an apartment in the city. She tells me how much it's going to cost, sheepish as she always is when it comes to spending my money. To her surprise, I encourage her to go for it, though deep down I want her home. She is grateful for my support, and now she's hedging. She's just not sure, maybe it's not such a good idea after all. Whether she comes home or not isn't the point. It's how I give the reins forward after the request, allowing her to better use herself in the making of her own life.

"If she wants to learn Spanish that bad, why doesn't she just hang out with the weed wackers?" Barrett says, ever the unromantic. He leaves out the part about being one of the wackers himself, or that he used to live in Barcelona, or that what he really wants is for her to come home and spend time with him.

I'm now qualified for the CIC Two Star at Jersey Fresh in three weeks. It's a long format, including steeplechase, and with Huey's issues, I worry if it's the best idea. "Why not?" Grace says. "You'll never know unless you try." Right there.

"But he's not been on a serious conditioning program," I hedge. "And we only have three weeks."

"Just look at him," Barrett offers from the sidelines. "Huey doesn't need it." Grace shakes her head in agreement. Huey practically stays race fit standing in his stall. Plus, I know deep down that if I don't at least try, I'll be plagued with regret. It happened years ago when Huey qualified for a One Star his first season at Preliminary, and I decided to wait till he became more seasoned at the level. The following year he got hurt, and then it took me five years before he was able to complete his first One Star at Morven in 2002. From that disappointment, I learned that when you qualify, you go.

On the way home I call up Jersey's secretary. "Might it be possible at this late date? . . ." I ask.

"Send it in," she replies.

April 25

Caitlin is conflicted about her summer plans: whether to stay in New York, sublet an apartment in Brooklyn, or take a dorm room at NYU. Take a Spanish class, but where? Get a job, but where? Or, the big obvious: come home to fold underwear and sell Angel credit cards at Victoria's Secret. She thinks I want her home, but I stand firm in my support of her independence. I'll agree to whatever she decides. John's having tensions with his girlfriend and is stressed over the amount of work ahead of him to finish his semester. Mollie goes to school at Cornell, and with John in Boston, they've spent more time away from each other than together. I advise him to smooth things out as best he can, focus on finishing his semester, and then hightail it to Cornell. Some things are impossible to do long distance. John turns twenty-one next month, and I am flattered he feels so easy with me that I'm still the one he seeks for comfort and advice when clouds darken.

Brother John's partner Mark has sent me a copy of his furious letter to John's therapist, written in his best ninth-grade-education rhetoric and acute native intelligence, blasting the man for unprofessional behavior in coaxing John to move to L.A. to pursue an acting career. *Why don't you come and pack up all the boxes and call the movers and find a new home and make new friends for John, because he won't do it?* That sort of thing. *Why don't you encourage John to find other interests besides acting so he has something else to fall back on? I think telephone therapy is a scam to take people's money because you can't see their faces and their reactions to what you're saying, which is so important.*

That's exactly what I've done with John and Caitlin today, and I make a note not to try to advise too much long distance, remembering that you can't say you're sorry to a telephone receiver and make a difference.

April 26

I accompany Katie and her young event horse, Boy Wonder, to Boy's vetting, which takes place at a farmette in suburban Washington, D.C. Today's vetting is supposed to start at 3:30, so we muscle our way through two beltways' worth of traffic to get there on time, only to have to shuffle our feet for an hour and a half, making small talk with the bubbly teenage pony clubber and her mother, who are to buy the horse, and the owners of the farmette, a retired foxhunter and his shuffly wife, who live in what was once the old schoolhouse for the neighborhood but is now the sole structure in the area built before 1975. Boy is to live on this 3-acre piece, with a paddock about a twentieth the size of the one he's used to back home.

Highway traffic zooming by. A neighbor's backyard of eight rottweilers carefully trained to bark at women and horses. Pools and rooftops and swing sets visible from every angle. My truck and trailer camped out on the edge of the tiny side road, too long to make the turn into the narrow driveway. I have an attack of claustrophobia. I learn everything there is to know about the mother while waiting for the tardy vet, including the loss of her sixty-year-old husband to a massive heart attack while he was on the operating table for a hip transplant, her hysterectomy at forty-two and subsequent change of life at forty-four, the embarrassment of hot flashes in the middle of executive meetings, and so on. She's my best friend by the time the vet finally pulls up at five.

I know we're in trouble when it takes fifteen minutes to examine Boy's eyes. "They're brown," I say, trying to move things along. Ten more to read his tattoo. By six, I'm starving and salivating for the glass of Chardonnay the girl's mother brings down to the barn for herself only. The vet takes the mother and daughter aside for a whispered conference during Boy's lunging. The vet finally informs Katie that she's detected a class-three heart murmur, which she feels needs further examination, and recommends a sonogram to determine its severity and prognosis. The mother, who knows nothing about horses but quite a bit about heart problems, becomes silent and strained, and the girl starts sobbing—she'd already bought halters and girths and bridles for her new horse and was all ready to hop on and go. Katie is shocked herself—three other vets have listened to the horse's heart in the two years she's owned him, including a surgical vet who performed splint-bone surgery a year ago, and no one ever picked up an irregularity.

It takes another hour or so to take tons of x-rays. Katie expected to go home with a $15,000 check in her pocket, but now has to load the horse back on the trailer and face the prospect of finding out where in the hell to get a heart sonogram for a horse. She's sick that she may have lost this sale and that the horse she has her future solvency banked on just might have become worthless.

We pull back into the farm around ten. Through the dark, I feel the expanse of pastures and barns with their roomy box stalls. I feel the trails that go on for miles and the cross-country fences just over the ridge. I feel the dressage and jump ring and even the indoor that we had to mortgage our life for with all the insulation being plucked out and used for another kind of home. I feel the luxury of this life we built with space to explore and move and graze welcoming me home, along with Daisy and Simon galumphing up the driveway, tails and bodies madly wagging. The dance of doggies.

April 27

Emily Dickinson described her poetic efforts as "my letter to the world / That never wrote to me." The description fits the poet as snug as a new riding glove. In contrast, I reflect on how I am constantly receiving a return response from the world I am writing to. I walk up the driveway after dinner to find Huey and Redmond quietly grazing in their adjacent paddocks. They hear Barrett's and my murmurs in the assessment of our day, the padding of our tired footsteps. They hear the retrievers duck under the lowest fence boards and run off to the woods in search of Mr. and Mrs. Rabbit. They lift their heads momentarily to write their brief postcard back to me that says something like, "Glad you're here."

April 28

I dream of a Siamese horse joined in the middle with one head in the front and the other in the back. A few hours later, I school Huey with Grace, and he jumps like that Siamese horse might jump, not knowing or caring which end's up. He leans on the reins and takes the rails with him. Plus, my timing is off today. I half halt too close to the jumps. Huey grabs hold when he feels the correction and braces against me. I remind myself to play chicken with the half halt after I turn a corner to a jump and soften no matter what.

Calvin, on the other hand, jumps like a charm. "Calvin's your future," Grace tells me. "He's the one you could win on. If you take your time with him."

"You mean *you* could," I say, reminding her of my weakness in the competition world.

"No, *you* could," she corrects.

As soon as you send in a $600 entry fee to a three-day event, things inevitably start to go wrong. When Huey comes in with a puffy eye, I panic, although with a couple of squeezes of triple antibiotic ointment, the eye goes down in a few hours. Then he gives me a questionable jump school, and my doubt blows up and swells my own eyes shut.

The Two-Star three-day is a long, long shot for Huey because of his soundness issues and age. Each day that we get closer without a hitch is an accomplishment. I hope I am learning to be a better rider along the way. The finish line isn't the goal, anyway. It never is.

Barrett brings Cherie and Ditto home from Country Life Farm. Seems like Ditto has grown feet in the three weeks they've been gone while Cherie got rebred. They trot around the paddock, and little Ditto gallops circles around her mom. Huey sticks his head out his back-stall window to watch the television show. He has always loved the babies, just like Redmond, just like any seasoned event horse who cares about the future and likes to be entertained. I wonder if Huey's other head is sticking out the stall guard, his other end pawing for supper.

Leesburg, Virginia

Another rainy Morven Park. Huey is tenser than ever in dressage but manages to have a decent show jump round at Loudoun Horse Trials, with only two rails this time—both my doing. He's attentive and bold without being fussy and rude, and I remember to forward my hands so he stays soft to his jumps. I'm not planning on running him cross country tomorrow because Jersey Fresh is too close, so the pressure is off, and that helps my nerves entering the ring. Exiting, it's the first time in a long while I wish I could go right back in and correct my errors, and I am excited about our next round—because it's the first time in a while I've not been ashamed of my efforts.

I run into Yvonne Lucas, who just finished her round before I went in on Huey. "How'd it go?" she asks casually. I must have something in my face that belies my mixture of emotion.

"Better," I say. "We're definitely on the upswing."

"I know what you mean," she says. "It's so bad, sometimes, I feel like my head's going to explode before I go into the ring."

"Really?" I say. I'm surprised. Yvonne has studied for years with Jimmy. She does a nice, consistent job with her horses, particularly in dressage. It's news to me that her nerves get the better of her, too.

"It happens to all of us at one time or another," she says.

"Really?" I ask again, wanting to hear more about her misery, as if it will lessen my own, just knowing that it's there.

"Yep," she says. "Sometimes I think I should just give it all up and focus on my babies . . . but then, here I am."

I've got Stephen Bradley parked next to me. "Sounds like your chestnut went well today," he compliments.

"Yeah, I think we're on the upswing," I say.

"What's made the difference?" he asks.

I want to tell him I wormed the horse—Barrett's pat response anytime someone wants to know our secrets. But Stephen is so sincere that I decide to meet him halfway. "Her name starts with G.," I reply. Grace never says "Don't pull back," but rather "give." She tells me what to do rather than what *not* to do. This has got to be the mark of a good teacher, who instructs with positive reinforcement and advice for further action.

Stephen mentions the teacher certification program he's currently engaged in, in hopes of raising the quality of eventing instruction in this country and creating a uniform standard of instruction like they have in England. In the United States, anyone who rides can teach if they can muster up the clients. All they have to do is hang up a sign. Few "professionals" want to pay out in time and money to get certified in something they've already been permitted to do for years. I've heard more than one eventer bitch about the program, calling it unnecessary and a waste of time. Of course, they probably don't pay insurance premiums, either. "It's a pain in the butt to find the time to do it . . . but it's a good thing," Stephen concludes.

"Just because you can ride doesn't mean you can teach," I say, ending our conversation for now. He's nice for not adding the ironic twist, that just because you can teach doesn't mean you can ride. Which is probably a truer description of me than I care to know.

Calvin does his own good job—is obedient and steady in dressage, and clean in stadium at Training level, and tacks on only two time penalties this go. He's got to be the slowest rocking horse in the world. But he's jumping well, albeit in slow motion. It's okay, I tell myself, it's okay if he's slow until he gains more confidence at this level. I remind myself that he's a young five. I just have to remember to bring enough quarters to put into the coin slot.

I come back home to find the wisteria trees in full bloom outside my office window. And news from Caitlin of a summer job offer in a dress shop in Soho and a possible sublet in the Bronx. As I fix a long vodka tonic, I think how it's not my idea of summer fun, staying in hot, stinky New York City, helping sweaty shoppers, but she's determined to stretch those new wings. She sounds bright and happy. Definitely on the upswing.

Ten days till we ship to Jersey Fresh.

May Day

Calvin jumps clean around Loudoun's cross-country Training course, and it feels like Easy Street. He finishes seventh in his division with just two show jump time penalties tacked onto his 38.5 dressage score. I find out these details after I'm done, when I finally check the score board.

The bummer is Huey's dressage score of 51, which isn't qualifying. It hardly matters this weekend, as we weren't planning to run cross country. Huey is using the event as a combined test with just the dressage and show jumping elements, to clear his throat for the three-day. Still, it's disappointing. Okay, so he was tense . . . but a 51? The same judge gave Calvin a 38.5. This one's obviously into big Warmbloods, whose fluid gaits disguise both greenness and disobedience, as opposed to the feisty Thoroughbred masters like Huey.

For most of my life I avoided competition—hated taking tests, hated performing the years I played the piano, hated being judged in any way, particularly in comparison with others. It's odd that I took to eventing, because its nature runs counter to my own. Passion for horses gave me the courage to confront my internal fears, including the larger-than-life ones.

Not to mention the countless rules I've had to learn to abide by. I'm a child of the sixties, grew up thumbing my nose at the establishment du jour. Twenty years later, I refused to send my kids to any school that dictated a dress code. I'm now engaged in a way of life in which, if I don't follow the rules, I'll get eliminated—if I forget my stock tie or my spurs, or jump the wrong jump, or get assistance from the sidelines in show jumping, or carry too long a whip, or jump a practice fence the wrong way, or forget my medical armband, to name only a few of the ways I've gotten bumped over the years. But this is something I love enough to override my fear of judgment and my unease with strictures.

My drive home from Morven Park is plagued by self-doubt and second-guessing my decision to attempt the Two Star at Jersey Fresh. Huey's dressage test presses into the truck seat, burns a hole in my back pocket. Mediocratus pokes his head from behind our backyard stand of Leylands as I pull into the driveway, curls his finger for me to come to him. "Fuck off!" I shout, "I can't be bothered with you right now."

May 2

Some heat in Huey's right hind. I try not to overreact. I'm bad about this sort of thing. In an effort to will it's nothing, I tend not to mention issues when I first discover them. Sort of like my mother not wanting to talk about my brother's being gay or my partying too much with boys and highballs in the library, right under Dickens's watchful gaze. I thought I detected a change in Redmond's tendon at least two weeks before his bow was diagnosed last summer but said nothing in the false hope that it was only my imagination. From then on, I promised myself that the minute I noticed a change in my horses, I would bring it to Barrett's attention. But still, today I say nothing.

Vet is scheduled to inject Crustacean's hocks with hyaluronic acid, which we hope will augment his performance at Jersey Fresh. So odd that we can inject joints with substances like steroid or acid and yet are not permitted to give our horses so much as a bute at FEI competitions, which can be detected through a simple blood or urine test. It says something about the many ironies and contradictions in our sport. I jog Huey for Vet before the injection. "He'd like to have his hocks done," she says, "but he's sound." The subsequent injections go well. Now Huey will have a couple days of rest ahead of him before going back to work.

The afternoon brings an 8-mile trail ride on Redmond, the kind only possible when I have the luxury of extra time and am willing to surrender to the woods, wanting to be lost again. After years of cruising the trails and fields in the north country just above the Worthington Valley, it is still possible to discover a new route. I've only scratched the surface of our riding country, but I need more time to dig down deeper. Out there, the boys and I are Mohicans of the lost variety.

It's as easy as turning right at a fork in the trail where we have always turned left. The trees begin to change in limb and leaf, so that it feels like Maine. We follow a ridge, try to keep that stream on our left. Redmond perks up when we enter unfamiliar territory—ears pricked, observant, trot bold and forward—he loves newness, too, and the sad shudder of loons calling. We come out on a farm we've never seen before. The horses in one paddock startle from their graze when they hear our hoofbeats and race over to the fence line to see who's come to visit. We hope the trail will allow us to make a loop and come back around so we won't have to retrace our steps. That's one motto of a diehard trail rider: never retrace your steps. It's a cool, crisp spring day. It starts sprinkling midway through, but we don't care. We pick our way through the mushy spots and trot on better ground, giving ourselves a pipe opener when we come back to a familiar trail and the big field with a gentle grade that leads to home. Redmond plays racehorse for a furlong or so, as I play Edgar Prado. He's happy and sound and feeling good. And so am I. Eight days till we ship.

May 3

The heat's still there in Huey's hind. I muster up the courage and call Barrett on his cell. "What took you so long?" he says. He's on the road to Boston to pick up all of John's belongings from school. He recommends I take Huey's temperature to make sure nothing is brewing. Normal. Something tells me I'll be taking his temperature quite a lot over the next few days.

Huey can't be ridden because of the recent injections, so I spend part of my day hand grazing and walking him. He shakes his head at us and pins his ears when we walk by his stall, pissed off at having to relax, occasionally even pawing to get our attention and dragging me around the farm when I try to let him graze. I get my other rides done early, then plug myself into my computer and vibrating car seat to get caught up on myriad projects and errands. Before I know it, it's midnight. I'm almost exhausted enough to fall asleep even without the great, comforting mass of Barrett's body yawning beside mine.

May 4

Blood hits the shed row. Pruitt pops an abscess in his swollen leg. Vet comes to culture and clean and probe and flush the wound, and pull out huge chunks of clots and tissue that repeatedly clog the wash-stall drain. She tells me it's a hoof abscess that came out the knee rather than the coronary band.

Katie hears from the equine cardiologist that Boy Wonder has not one but two heart irregularities and is therefore unsellable. It is a dire day for Katie, as she has her small inheritance wrapped up in this horse.

I find Bill the handyman having a heated conversation with Bryan the farrier about how we've allowed our babysitter mule's feet to grow too long. In his opinion, "Jenny" needs immediate farrier attention. Jennifer Johnson was my birthday present from Barrett last year. Somehow monkey got mixed up with mule, and Barrett figured a mule would be a better babysitter than a monkey, which is what Surf needed at the time. And she wouldn't be able to throw shit at us. Surf dislikes Jenny almost as much as I do. She basically hangs out and waits for the less discerning to need her company. "Well, at least I got the first letter right," Barrett said, after a feeble "Happy Birthday."

I pull Bill aside, tell him that we've had the vet as well as our other farrier watching the mule for some time—that is, when she'll allow us to catch her. I find this human encounter the most disturbing element of my day, which speaks to a lack of faith on Bill's part that I never knew existed until now. Katie, in tears, comes to fetch me. Bill, using his own belt, has dragged Jenny up to the barn with a bleeding wound from a front leg. Two rare leg abscesses in one day? What are the odds of this? Now Vet's Associate comes to probe and flush the mule's shoe boil, then shoot her full of the same good old-fashioned penicillin Pruitt has recently been switched to after the more expensive Baytril and Gentocin and Naxcell wouldn't influence his infection. Vet's Associate issues a warning that the cultures will determine if there's a dangerous bacteria on the loose at the farm causing the systemic infections we've now seen in two of our animals. It's sure to be a sleepless night for me, with only six days till we supposedly ship out to the Two Star at Jersey Fresh.

Barrett calls me from the road. Carneros, the wrist breaker, won again and was claimed. I have never before been so delighted to sell a horse. This is a milestone for us. Sayonara, Sophie.

May 5

I'm not the best jogger of my own horses. My problem back makes me lame. Last year, at the Morven Park One Star, I asked Coach to jog Surf Guitar at the vet inspections, which is permissible if the rider has a medical excuse. Huey's not the best jogger either. He likes to shuffle rather than trot and needs all the support he can get from someone who can actually run and present him well. I ask Grace if she might be able to jog Huey for me at the initial vet inspection at Jersey. Grace has not been competing much since a bad fall at Southern Pines last spring and is currently living in a trailer while her new house is being built. She welcomes the opportunity to get away for a few days and keep her hand in the sport by being a good observer. "Do you have room for me?" she asks, as she offers to come up with me not just for the jog and dressage, but for the entire week, as well.

"You really want to help two old farts get through a Two Star?" I tease.

She pooh-poohs my comment, says she'd be happy to come along for whatever I need.

Shawan Downs

Two hundred acres of prime real estate that would otherwise have been cut up into quarter-acre lots if a group of Greenspring Valley folks didn't pass the hat. Now it hosts steeplechase races, as well as the Maryland Combined Training Association's Annual Horse Trials. I competed at Shawan Downs two years ago at the inaugural event at this site, as well as last year, but have decided to donate my services instead of riding this year. My job is to help set up and host the contributors' party. I'm not much for parties, but still it's fun to drink some wine and chat with neighbors about what geniuses their horses and kids are as we all huddle under the tent on a 45-degree "spring" evening, drinking a little more wine than we should to stay warm. Dinner is melon balls speared with toothpicks and small bulbs of cauliflower raked through smeary artichoke dip. A few glances at Barrett, and it's clear he should have become a bartender. He keeps a crescent-shaped band of riders and grooms cracking up over his one-handed wine bottle opening tricks. For bottles of beer, he uses his right armpit to snap off the caps. Barrett's got one of the strongest armpits in the world.

May 7

I jump judge for the Novice cross country at Shawan Downs. It's a perfect day to sit down by the water jump in a folding chair, clipboard perched on my lap, and watch about a hundred horse-and-rider teams negotiate a 2-foot-6-inch log, then trot through the puddle of the water jump. It doesn't sound like such a big deal, except that the other jumps for Training and Preliminary are there, too, and the "puddle" is lavishly decorated with plants and flowers and surrounded by a white picket fence. There's a lot to look at for the Novice horses, many of whom are certain the Loch Ness monster lives in the puddle and is going to eat them. Some stop and pop the log. Some veer and choose to jump the plants instead. Some will not turn left in their approach to the log but run sideways back to their trailer waiting somewhere over their right shoulder. Others plant their feet and absolutely will not go forward. A few are brave enough to jump right through the complex and beyond.

Volunteers are what all of the events could not run without. The organizer, Hans's mom, needs her friends and neighbors to help out and pull the whole thing together. So I'm glad to be volunteering and not riding at this one. It's a little too close to home, anyway. I know too many people affiliated with the event—friends, neighbors, and the usual traveling circus of my fellow competitors. The last two years when I've drawn into this event, I've ended up doing more socializing than riding.

Last year, my 18-hand Canadian sport horse, Corin—Redmond's cousin—went lame in show jumping warm up. I parted the waters of the spectators and horses and riders with my rig and drove down through the warm-up area to pick up my three-legged lame Adonis. It's nice when you can shine in your own backyard. But it's fairly tortuous when your horse goes lame in front of all those friendly eyes. I wish I didn't care what other people think, because this fear of judgment still guides me to action or inaction more than it should. If you grow up under judging eyes, you carry them with you for the rest of your life. Maybe this is the competitive nut I can't crack and what ironically makes a good competitor: she cares so much about competing that she doesn't give a damn about what other people think. Corin was never a hundred percent sound again, at least for the purposes of upper-level eventing. I donated him to the riding program at Garrison Forrest School, where they love him and are able to keep him sound at the lower levels.

May 8

I've swapped Huey's full cheek snaffle for a double bridle, with two bits, which better enables me to keep his poll up in dressage and therefore keep my strong, eager horse off his forehand. He's light as a feather in my hands and carrying himself. Why didn't I think of this before? It seems like a logical move for an upper-level horse who is still tending toward heavy on the forehand and who doesn't want to take the weight into his hind legs. The difference in Huey is startling. I'm able to ride my partner forward and softly, and his power can no longer run out the front door because I now have more influence on his mouth. The double bridle is a barrier of sorts, so that all the power stays underneath me rather than escaping. This also makes him more flexible in his body. With the double bridle, it feels like I've given Huey his first pointe shoes.

I opt not to go back for Day Two at Shawan Downs and stay home so I can get my horses ridden and start packing for Jersey Fresh. We ship in two days.

It's not often that I'm the only one on the farm besides the animals. I slow down and look around. The lilacs are full blast in the backyard— when did that happen? After calling and searching for the orange cat, Pie, who's been missing all morning, I see her at the sliding door, frantic for breakfast. There's a fence board off in the steep paddock. Ballerina's belly has dropped, and her milk is coming in. Surf's knee is up, Pruitt's leg is down. The bleary-eyed mule is stallbound quiet. She even stands politely in the wash stall when I hose her wound. Spring is busting out, the sun is shining, shining, and I should be packing, but I'm too busy waltzing with the humanless world around me.

May 9

Huey jump schools before we ship to Jersey Fresh. He stays soft and attentive for the most part, jumping with his newfound roundness. "Just like we can change at fifty, I guess horses can change their way of going at seventeen," I say to Grace. She agrees with me. Barrett, on the other hand, walks inside a cloud of lazy procrastination.

"You can change at fifty?" he says. "Good, that gives me five more years."

John arrives home from the end of his semester at Berklee College of Music, after a weekend visiting Mollie at Cornell. He plays us the music he's composed for his final projects at Berklee, ranging from a Bach-like invention to jazz to an Eastern-influenced rock piece, which is my favorite. Not for the first time I see a connection between his art form and my sport. How varied my rides must be among my very different horses if I'm going to win a Grammy with my Bach invention, my jazz piece, my Sufi chant, my Pete Townshend.

The New Jersey Horse Park

Huey's last hack before we ship out coincides with the honeysuckles blooming. We take several deep whiffs of their rich perfume as we trot by.

We load Huey on the trailer, take an inventory of the hundreds of items we've already packed, and head out, Grace and Daisy in the truck with me, Katie following behind in our beat-up, errand-hopping sedan. We make the three-hour drive in moderate traffic up the New Jersey turnpike, then get Huey settled into his temporary digs. We practice jogging Julia in preparation for tomorrow's first vet inspection. I'm a lot lamer than my horse, who's sounder and fitter and more regular than he's ever looked on a jog in his life. Grace has brought along some jogging duds just in case this picture of me jogging Huey isn't too pretty. Katie and Grace and I decide that I'll be sound enough to jog my own horse tomorrow. So far, so good. We're here, we're unloaded, and we get through the in-barn inspection and the practice jog. We tuck Huey in and head to our motel—the only one in Jersey that allows dogs, apparently. It's on the seedy side of Hightstown. A bare-bones affair, with not enough soap or lights and bath towels the size of hankies. Daisy doesn't mind, though—the stained carpeting is comfortable enough. We head out to a local pub where we whoop it up over pasta and margaritas, then back to the Jersey Horse Park to night check Huey, who is resting comfortably in his stall. "Maybe we should also night check each other later tonight," Katie says, referring to our plush accommodations back at the MGM Grand.

A Rat Has Bones

Mice, the exterminator tells me,
can scrunch themselves through holes
the size of pencils, but a rat, now a rat has bones,
he says, his eyes growing large
with a lifetime of experience. This should
be reassuring. All I have to do

is parge the holes in the farmhouse's
old foundation, and I'll have it.
I'm still cringing from the squeal
when the cat was on it at 4 this morning, the rat
tearing under the fridge, then leaping
out beyond Barrett's broomstick

as he tried to flush it out, beyond
one 8-pound Jack Russell & 6 awaiting tabbies,
& down the heat duct vent
left screenless by the glassy-eyed heating man
who never properly finished the job.
Barrett recommended we crank up the heat.

The exterminator places rat hotels
at strategic points around the farm,
baits them with poison, delicious but deadly,
that will send them out into the woods,
parched & hemorrhaging, in search of water.
He shrugs when I ask what might have happened

to the one lost in the funhouse
of my heat-duct system.
"It's not there now," he says, adding to my list
of the inexplicable. I think of my

compulsion for work since you've been gone,
making myself small as I can

to get through the necessary passages. Lately,
I've been confusing the rats,
getting up at 4 in the morning,
re-entering night's maze
as I scavenge the kitchen floor
for poems to write.

Or stalking the fridge,
not knowing what I long for.
Or I hide right under it
till Barrett brings the flashlight,
shines it in my eyes, till they get so small
I can stare right back. Next visit,

the service man tells me
the bait's all gone.
That's good news, he adds.

This poem first appeared in *Southern Poetry Review* and then again in my collection,
Dark Track (WordTech Editions, 2005).

Jogging Huey

CHAPTER SEVEN

Names of Horses

※ May 11

The honeysuckles have followed us to New Jersey. I inhale deeply on my first hack around Phase A of roads and tracks. We ice Huey and braid him and rub on him until we can see our reflections in his coppery flank. I dress in black pants, purple tank, and black jacket that get splattered with gooey stone dust as I'm practicing how not to appear lame in the recently watered warm-up ring. I shrug off the ridiculousness of our having to dress for the jog. Contrary to the hopes of some of the young female riders who attempt to jog in dresses and high heels, the ground jury won't be paying much attention to the riders' hemlines.

The jury is a formidable group—mostly women in pantsuits and Panama hats, a token male judge or vet in their funeral best, all carrying clipboards and wearing dark glasses and darker frowns, as if they were distant cousins of Truman Capote. You can bet they're not thinking pleasant thoughts. Just because they let you pass doesn't mean they haven't made a note to watch your horse closely throughout the weekend. I do my best to give them a big smile as Huey and I march up to the flowers surrounding the stern group. We trot, they hesitate for twenty interminable seconds, we pass, and I take my first deep breath. At Huey's last three-day—and the only one he's completed so far—he was held for reinspection at both formal jogs. Not here, not today.

Nothing like a cross-country course walk with Grace to settle my stomach after the inspection. Just as my pancreas returns to its small nest against my liver, we arrive at the second water—a new complex that involves a bounce out of water up onto an island, then three strides to a bounce back in and a turn to a corner. I'll have to walk that line about a million times over the next few days before I'll feel comfortable enough to ride it.

May 12

We arrive at the park in enough time to give Huey a practice ride, then ice him, put him away, and braid and shine him up before I get back on to warm up for the dressage test. Because of his tension in recent tests, our strategy is to keep him as relaxed as possible by riding him in different areas of the park in the hopes that he'll be more ho-hum about his surroundings and not lose it when he trots down center line. I'm dressed in my shadbelly and new top hat for the test. Huey looks like a million dollars, resembling his grandsire Damascus more than ever in his long chestnut elegance. I trot down the 1000-mile center line. We halt straight and square, I take a deep breath, and we're off to the best dressage test of Huey's career. He stays calm and focused, he does the movements well, we work together as a team, and I keep riding every stride to produce a test that I can feel proud of. Before I know it, I'm saluting again. Huey's ears are pricked, but he's calm, and his eyes are shining. He knows what a good job he's done in dressage at the Two-Star three-day event he never thought he'd see.

May 14

Number 9 and I trot early on roads and tracks. The day is crisp and cool. Huey is positive and alert—he knows what's coming. Unfortunately, the event officials never got the rain they'd predicted, so the ground is rock hard underneath. What was that old Joni Mitchell tune: They paved paradise, put up a steeplechase course? I'm leery of the group of officials who are huddled by the lane at the end of Phase A. It doesn't occur to me that they may be watching Huey until they move down to the steeplechase box and watch us gallop out. I hear the unforgiving pounding that sounds like we're galloping on cement. It's only one swing around this course placed in a newly planted field, with grass whose roots haven't had the chance to take hold and capture enough moisture to make a difference to my horse's hooves. Usually, I think steeplechase is a blast. I allow my horse to gallop as fast as we dare and don't have to set up for the fences. Each hoofbeat today makes me cringe, and I can't wait till we gallop through the finish. It's an interminable and brutal three minutes to my horse's legs. Nonetheless, Huey feels fine to me on Phase C and trotting into the vet box. His statistics are good, and he is ready to rock and roll. Barrett trots him for the vets so they can check for soundness, and they ask him to trot again. They've seen a lameness in the right front, and they won't let us continue.

"This is a final decision," the vet says.

My heart falls to my feet, remembering the officials at Steeplechase and the hesitation at the jog, and all the other times at three-days in the past when Huey was spun. Tails between our legs, we pack up our equipment and take Huey back to his stall. Months of hard work fizzle, a week's worth of teamwork between Katie, Grace, and me up in smoke. I do my best to chin up, get my horse situated, and head out on the cross-country course to cheer on my fellow competitors who've been given the green light I didn't get.

We station ourselves at the new water complex. One horse flips over the bounce bank and his rider, barely missing her. I throw my hands up to my face and turn away when the next horse comes through, as do several other spectators. We head out onto the main course and see elimination after stop after fall—only one half of the Two-Star division makes it through without withdrawing or getting eliminated.

The statistics on the Three-Star course are even worse. The second water complex involves a bridge that the horses have to bounce back into water. The distance is long on top of the bridge, so the riders have to push on top to make the distance and get their horses to bounce back down into the water. The drop is huge. Graham Thom is the first to come through. He pushes and the horse drops back in, and both horse and rider fall—mandatory retirement. Buck Davidson almost does the same, but after getting thrown up on the horse's neck, manages to hold on for dear life, right himself, and go on. The third rider does nearly the same. The officials initiate a hold as the course designer and other event honchos have an impromptu conference and decide to take the bridge off the course. The next rider, who's been held on course, is given an alternate route through the water. She negotiates the convoluted path as best she can quickly understand, but it isn't what the officials meant. She jumps off the wrong bank—and is eliminated.

The officials and riders finally get the route sorted out, and it rides reasonably well the rest of the afternoon. There are lots of spills and stops elsewhere, horse-and-rider teams that were expected to do well not even finishing. The rides have become too painful to watch, and we decide to leave before the end of the Three Star. We do a crazed job of packing up, getting Huey ready to ship, throwing all of our stuff in the trailer tack room, and hightailing it out of Jersey Fresh. We're not alone—the stable is emptying out with disgruntled competitors, and only a few are walking around the stabling area with smiles on their faces. It's bound to be a dead competitor party tonight. Grace wonders out loud how many horses will jog lame at tomorrow's vet inspection.

Grace and I drive in relative silence, with Katie following behind. Three hours later, we're home. I walk Huey down to the paddock where Surf and Calvin are prancing around, excited to see their buddy home with tales of the great sea of eventing. Huey takes off out of the gate, extending his trot to show off and greet them, sound as can be.

May 15

Today is a shuffle-around, try-to-get-motivated-and-figure-out-what-went-wrong-at-Jersey sort of day. I take a stab at unpacking, let Barrett take care of the horses, and spend some time with John, who clearly wants to spend some time with me. He's got a hundred dollars to his name, no job, and a portion of rent on a summer sublet to pay for. Barrett gives him mowing work for a few days until he can find work elsewhere. He takes various breaks throughout the day and comes in search of me. I make him grilled cheese sandwiches for lunch—his little-boy favorite. In the afternoon, we break for a run to TCBY and the nursery to pick up my summer supply of tomato and basil plants, and then I cook a meal for my family—my recipe for nesting and giving back to them. Barrett wants me to come up to the barn to check out the summer *Omnibus*, a publication of the United States Eventing Association which lists upcoming events. "How come?" I ask. "I've already entered who I need to enter," meaning Surf and Calvin for their four events in May and June.

"What about Huey?" Barrett asks.

"What about him?" I say. He tells me I'm crazy if I don't take advantage of his fitness, his readiness, not to mention about a grand of pharmaceuticals roiling around in his system. I retreat to my cooking. Caitlin calls. More secret disappointments, unmentionable rejections. I give her a pep talk. If she really loves what she does, she'll keep doing it. The process matters most. All this is hard to hear for a nineteen-year-old with stars in her eyes. As it is apparently hard for an almost-fifty-year-old who has just gotten spun in the vet box.

"Oh my God, Mom," she asks, with panic in her voice, "you aren't writing down this conversation, are you?"

I can't help myself—I pick up the *Omnibus* after a meal of grilled burgers, orzo pasta, broiled tomatoes, and homemade ice cream cake to discover that Waredaca and CDCTA (Commonwealth Dressage and Combined Training Association) are offering Intermediate divisions next month.

May 16

Barrett and I go out to the field to wake up Surf, Calvin, and Huey, who are lying down and snoozing side by side. Huey heaves himself up to lameness. The vets were right—he's got a definite problem in that right front. Barrett suspects a foot abscess, but I'm more inclined to worry about the tendon. In any event, he needs some time, maybe a little, maybe a lot. We'll baby him for a few days and see what happens. My plan to enter him in a couple of Intermediate events goes up in smoke. A three-alarm burn.

May 17

Barrett leaves for Camden with Jeremy and a half dozen yearlings to watch Jerry the Racehorse gallop fences. That leaves me in charge for a couple of days. The relief of the day is that when Katie and I trot Huey up the driveway, he is 50 percent better. It's possible his injury is minor, after all. I cross my fingers and make a mental note to schedule an appointment with Vet for an ultrasound of that right front so we can rule out or face a tendon tear. Katie next leads in Ballerina, now 330 days into her pregnancy according to the whiteboard. "This is the hugest udder I've ever seen! Definitely an EE cup," she says.

"What do you mean?" I say. Could she be that close to foaling, with Barrett gone?

Barrett calls later in the day with glowing reports of Jerry. He lives and works on a ten-thousand-acre farm and has a daily schedule fit for kings: a snack at 4:30 A.M., work at ten o'clock, turnout with fly sheet and bonneted fly mask, turn in and lunch at noon, snooze, snack at five, dinner at nine. "How much weight has he gained?" I venture.

"They adore him," Barrett says. "They've never had a green steeplechase horse learn so quickly."

"No-brainer," I say.

"He brushes his toes through the fence beautifully. Now all he has to learn is to brush his pasterns, and we'll be set." I imagine the seconds gained over a steeplechase course by getting infinitesimally closer to the fence.

I head up to the barn for my first of many reinspections of Ballerina, with her huge and waxy udder. I struggle to stay awake until Caitlin's arrival around eleven, armed with cupcakes from the bakery where she works in Manhattan and tales of the city and the life she has chosen over this one. I listen with detached interest, because it's way past my bedtime. I crave the undulations of my Tempur-Pedic mattress, and I'm already making lists in my head of tomorrow's activities with the horses. Caitlin loves the farm and her family, her pony and her cats, but she now lives in the next field over with the other yearlings, having grown huge with a life of her own.

May 18

I return a call from John Williams, who has left a message about a young horse he has for sale, the last get from Redmond's father, out of the mother of his Olympic horse, Carrick. He wants me to have this horse. John is the only person, besides Peter Gray, with whom I've had smooth dealings when buying a horse, and I'm flattered that he's matched me with this youngster. I'm tempted as well. The horse is in Southern Pines, North Carolina, where John Williams currently lives. Coincidentally, Barrett is close by with Jeremy, on their way back from Camden and dragging a trailer behind them with a couple of two-year-olds. John offers that I take the horse for a week and see if I like him. "Why don't we swing by and pick him up?" Barrett says. Barrett pulls off I-95 toward Southern Pines and calls John himself.

"Okay," John says, "but I won't be here when you arrive."

"No problem," my well-meaning husband says. "What color is he?"

"Same as Carrick," John says with his characteristic hesitancy, but this time for good reason: better not take the wrong horse! I hem and haw before I pull the mental plug, resolved to stay on my reduced track of focusing on two or three horses at a time. If I wanted another wonderful youngster to work with, I wouldn't have sent Jerry away. I call Barrett, tell him to turn around and come home. I later learn that Barrett and Jeremy were nowhere near Southern Pines, but a solid two hundred miles already farther north. This is Barrett's and Jeremy's characteristic, unrealistic zeal that people used to call gamesmanship.

May 19

Huey jogs sound, and I allow myself a glimmer. Vet will haul out her ultrasound machine for him tomorrow. I'll know then whether to continue with him or put him on the back burner. I spend some time pondering my stubbornness with horses. With the exception of Calvin, none of them are good bets, as all three of them—Redmond, Huey, and Surf Guitar—have physical issues that we must carefully manage to keep them sound enough to continue training and competing. Even our steeplechase prospect is coming off a broken leg. Maybe I'm fighting a losing battle. Why continue to compete a seventeen-year-old? That's the impression I got from John Williams when I spoke to him about his young horse. It may look like I have a lot of horses going, but—Huey's almost over the hill, Surf Guitar has terrible hocks and a front suspensory that could blow back apart at any moment, and it's unclear whether Redmond will make it back from his bowed tendon. Although he's apparently healed beautifully, I won't know until I start testing the tendon under the stress of competition. But the hearts on these three are bigger than their problems, and so I find myself feeling responsible to keep them doing what they love for as long as they can do it.

I spend time with Caitlin before she has to leave again. Nothing I say sits well with her, and we end our trip to the train station in tears. She's got two years on Huey, which means that she has to reject a lot about me to separate herself and learn to live apart. I know this rationally, but it still hurts.

Back home I meet up with the rest of my family, as well as Barrett's friend, Jerry, also partner in the Poetry in Motion racing syndicate, who has flown in from Texas for the Preakness and to see Foolish Groom run on Preakness Day. My day ends well with Barrett's shrimp pad Thai and lots of Anapamu, and reruns of our eventing and racing videos. There goes Foolish Groom from the back of a twelve-horse pack, picking off his contenders in the last quarter mile, winning again by a good 10 lengths. He's no stakes horse, but he's a Great One nonetheless in this $16,000 claiming race, demonstrating a heart almost as big as R. Huey's, but with wheels to match.

May 20

With the exception of a few strained fibers that have been a long time in the straining, Huey's ultrasound is within normal limits, and Vet gives the go-ahead to continue on with him. Mine is a reserved happiness, because no matter how clean Huey's legs are, I know that his competitive future is limited. After fifty-five race starts and almost one hundred horse trials, Huey's legs have run a lot of miles. He doesn't owe me another furlong. Still, I look forward to climbing up on his back tomorrow—the place in the world where I feel rightest. I wish Caitlin had a place like this to climb when the chips are down. I'd like to think the stage was her Huey, but when you're nineteen, it's the end, not the means, that you set your sights on.

May 21

Preakness Day. Foolish Groom is substituted by Winged Sumac, a race-horse Barrett and I own with J. W. Delozier. My racing luck stays true to form when Sumac comes home a disappointing fourth in the second race, although he is still driving at the wire, beating ten other horses in a big field. Yours truly is sitting in the grandstand, cheering him on. No winner's circle for me—yet again. He earns $2,500 for his effort.

"Not bad for a parking pass," one of the syndicate members says.

It is a long day of crowds and races. Barrett and I have come to Pimlico with our out-of-town guests, a couple of Poetry in Motion partners, plus John and Mollie. We do some mild betting throughout the day, waiting for the Preakness race. We get up and down from our seats periodically and attempt to sneak outside to the glorious spring day and a closer view of the horses, where we might be able to smell them, see the dirt fly as they gallop toward the finish line and not be protected by the barrier of grandstand glass. But our grandstand tickets will not allow us to go outside to the preferred box seats, so unless we can make it past an inattentive guard, we're stuck behind glass. It becomes a kind of game for me, finding one unguarded door among the hundred patrolled by yellow T-shirts and bossy ball caps.

Waiting for the Preakness race, I lose some money making hunch bets on horses that attract my notice when I make it to the tacking paddock to see the prepost parade. On horses whose numbers in the program, it turns out, don't clue me in to any revelations that bring good luck. And on horses whose names I like, such as Ougamon or Takeachanceonme. I want Giacomo to win the Preakness, which is not good news for him. Everyone wants another Triple Crown winner. The favorite is Afleet Alex, perhaps because his owner has decided to donate some of his earnings to finding a cure for pediatric cancer. Alex's lemonade stand—or a version of it—is at Pimlico, and the donation jar is stuffed. The lemonade's not bad, either.

The infield party at the Preakness has a Woodstock feel to it, and for those who tend to suffer from claustrophobia, the jammed infield is a worst-case scenario. I turn to Chandler. "If I gave you twenty dollars, would you walk through the infield right now?" Her eyes get big.

"You'd have to put a couple more zeroes on it," she says. "You mean a walk-through or a stay-all-day?" she qualifies.

"A walk-through," I specify.

"Two hundred minimum," she says.

"Ten grand for me," I say. "How about you, John?" I turn to son John: "Twenty dollars for a walk-through?"

"Sure!" he says, without blinking. That would leave him only $480 short of his first month's rent.

This is my first Preakness and may well be my last. It's smoky in here. Guys wearing aprons—and carrying trays of black-eyed Susans of the alcoholic variety—are screaming at us, "Suzies, get your cold Suzies!" as if we were at a baseball game and they were selling hotdogs. I would rather be back at the barn. Or at least on the backside, peeling off mint wrappers for Foolish Groom and Winged Sumac and Giacomo.

Before the big race, our party slips out en masse into the sunshine and goes behind the grandstand to the stakes barn area, where we meet up with the parade of kings marching to their respective guillotine start boxes. The Preakness organizers have laid out the red carpet of wood chips, and the path is bordered with gobs of real black-eyed Susans. Except for a few savvy reporters who've guessed where the action is, we're the only ones there, the rest of the crowd sweating in their glassed-in seats or throwing frantic, last-minute bets. I want to reach out and touch Giacomo as his groom leads him by. I am struck by how small he seems up close in the flesh, how tiny the lightning bones and speed-tuned mind. The idea of tremendous speed in a small package, like the best Christmas gifts—the diamond tennis bracelet in its tiny wrapper my mother placed on the fireplace mantle so it wouldn't get lost in the mass of lesser but larger gifts underneath the tree.

The Preakness finally goes off around six-thirty. There's excitement when Afleet Alex, driving toward home, gets clipped by Scrappy T. and nearly goes down. The jockey almost comes off, and still the horse manages to rally and win the race. An amazing show of heart.

We head back to the car, then through bumper-to-bumper traffic in a sea of infielders making their way on foot, hoisting empty coolers. Corner barbeques still raging. Shopping carts empty. College kids in tank tops with lobster-red skin, clearly wasted and exhausted, though they probably never even saw a horse today.

May 22

David Bomba is visiting from Vancouver, where he's working on a
DreamWorks movie about a young soccer player. Both David and Jerry
Henery have come for the Preakness and the two-year-old-in-training sale
at the Timonium auction, and to visit us. Jerry first came to our farm as a
boarder when he was in Maryland building sets for the movie *Runaway
Bride*. Jerry brings along his horse, Hillbilly Rock, wherever he goes to
work on a movie,. When Hillbilly stayed at the farm for a few months
several years ago, Jerry struck up a close friendship with Barrett that has
lasted through the years and miles. Like Barrett, Jerry is in love with
racing, and also with photographing racehorses. Jerry and Barrett are both
enamored of the lesser-known full brothers to fabulous sires. Surf Guitar's
dad, Vaal Reef, now standing in India, was Mr. Prospector's brother, and
Hillbilly Rock's dad, Ragtime Band, now standing in Sweden, was a
brother to Dixieland Band. Jerry brought David to us on a Preakness
weekend a couple of years ago, and since then, David and I have become
buddies. Our farm got famous for about thirty seconds when it appeared
in a cameo shot in *Runaway Bride*, as did the kids' ponies. Jerry the
Racehorse is named after Jerry the Photographer, Jerry the Movie Set
Builder, Jerry the Best Friend. When Barrett found a gangly giant turned
out in a field of Connemaras and zebra-mustang crosses, he didn't call
me—he called Jerry. Two years later they had a racehorse in the making
worth every bit of ten thousand. I sent Jerry a check for five and brought
Pruitt home before such a fine beast got injured. Barrett held out his hand
for his half of the sale. "Congratulations," I told him, "you now own half of
an event prospect." Oh, the grim look on his face.

I have a jump school on Surf Guitar while David sets fences. I talk to
David about my tendency to interfere with the horse too close in to the
jumps. I comment on each effort and give myself suggestions for improving
the jump and the balance of the canter. It seems to work. My little bit of
teaching has helped me be more self-analytical. Teaching is its own education. I learned this years ago when I taught literature and creative writing.
Verbalizing a process to someone else helps put the subject into sharper
focus, and I am discovering that I can teach myself by teaching others.

In the afternoon, Jerry on Surf, David on Calvin, and Julia on Redmond go on a hack. David appears to be in seventh heaven and doesn't want to go in after a couple of hours when I suggest it might be time. He's like a kid playing soccer out in the streets long after dusk has fallen and his dinner's cold on the family table. Jerry keeps his feelings closer to the vest, but I later find out he's thrilled to be on top of Surf Guitar. He's watched the horse for years from afar when he was racing and can tell you more than I can about his galloping style, his various wins and owners after we'd lost him, his speed figures, and so on. Now Jerry gets a chance to feel the hugeness of Surf's trot and canter from the closest perspective of all. "His gaits feel like an exaggeration of equine movement," Jerry finally says, as we finish a gallop up the side of a long, slow hill. It is an interesting comment from an ex–bull rider from Terrell, Texas, who must know a thing or two about exaggerated motion.

"Everything about Surf is an exaggeration," I reply, reflecting on my 17.3-hand monster. I take Redmond in a little early when David begs to stay out longer. I admit my overprotectiveness of Redmond's injury since his recent return to work. A full fretful hour later, I see the figures of Surf and Calvin on the farm's far hill, with a bounce in their step toward home.

We come inside for lemonade and SunChips and to watch reruns of the Preakness race. There it is again—Afleet Alex clips heels with Scrappy T. and almost goes down at the top of the stretch. When Scrappy T.'s jockey switches his whip to the left side, his horse veers out and bumps Afleet Alex, who's driving on the outside. Afleet Alex's nose goes down to the dirt. The jockey, Jeremy Rose, goes up on his neck but is able to right himself. The horse's ears go back, and he digs in and passes Scrappy T. to win what will probably be one of the most famous Preaknesses. The racing network replays the race over and over, and we watch the near fall in slow motion, mesmerized by this display of perseverance and recovery.

May 23

Barrett and I head to the Timonium horse auction. Barrett's got his eye on a colt by Snuck In and is hopeful that he'll fall into Poetry in Motion's price range, not to exceed $14,000. We visit the bay colt in his stall. I turn a critical eye on him when they bring him out to walk up and down the aisle.

He's slightly back at the knee and a little butt high. He's got a nice sturdy body and neck, I'll give him that—but the real problem is not one, but two white eyes. "Don't ask me to ride him," I say, having long ago bought into the myth of white-eyed horses. In my experience, they are a handful: untrusting and untrustworthy. And that's only with one. Maybe like a double negative, two white eyes are a sign of kindness and nobility. Barrett is hopeful that the little horse won't go for big dollars because his pedigree isn't special. Barrett likes him because of what he calls a Seabiscuit moment when meeting him. He had his eyes on another colt in the next stall over, and having gotten his back close to White Eyes's stall, the colt playfully nipped at his sleeve: *What about me?* Barrett turned to the nibbler and fell in love.

We look at a couple of others, and I feel my own excitement growing. There's nothing like a horse auction to get your blood up. It's like browsing in a bakery when you've got a food fetish, shopping at Saks when you're a shopaholic. Then we sit down in the amphitheater to watch the show. Afleet Alex was sold at this auction a year ago for $85,000, and everyone wants to buy another Preakness winner. The prices have sky-rocketed: $50,000, $75,000, $150,000—very few horses go for less than $20,000.

When White Eyes is led into the ring, Barrett changes his mind, says he'll go as high as $16,000. "I'd go eighteen," trainer Delozier nudges. Barrett is the only one I know who can turn $1,500 a year in wages into a $25,000 line of credit with the auction company. One horseman can always trust another. Within ten seconds, the little gelding is out of Barrett's inflated price range and in another blink sells for $49,500. Barrett tries not to seem crestfallen, but I can tell he is. "Now I know how you felt when I got spun in the vet box," I say.

We leave the high-stepping bidders and head home to prepare a din-ner of filet mignon and Anapamu. John is hungrily waiting for us, with a jar of peanut butter half consumed in the waiting. No more mouths to feed besides our own, at least for now.

May 24

Barrett calls me from the second day of the Timonium auction. "I got Surf's sister for ten," he tells me, out of the blue. What? Surf's half sister?

He explains that both were out of a mare named Cynical Gal. Yesterday the filly sold way out of the racing syndicate's price range. Barrett goes on to say she was an RNA (reserve not attained), and when he approached the consignor, she in turn approached the owner. She proposed Barrett's offer, and the man agreed to let the filly go for $10,000. Barrett takes a stab at explaining why. "You've got to figure he made at least $25,000 in breeder's bonuses from Surf's racing."

"Talk about your Poetry in Motion," I say, thinking of the aptness of the racing syndicate's name in this case and how things have a funny way of coming back around.

We help John move into his new summer digs, carting all his belongings up a hundred eroding front steps to a weedy townhouse, perched on the side of a hill with thirty others just like it, situated off one of Baltimore's artery interstates and across from a park that is littered with countless wrappers and beer cans. Then, we stop in at the auction. We find our new filly munching away on oats. I'm eager to go in her stall, but Barrett warns me to wait till she's done with her dinner. One of the handlers comes by, asking us if she's our horse and warning us to be careful, as she kicks. Good going, Barrett of the only one fully functional hand.

But she's a beauty. Four white socks, a light, shiny bay coat, jet-black mane and tail, pencil-thin white blaze on her face, and a nose just Roman enough to be reminiscent of her brother's. There's nothing like the excitement and promise of a new horse. Unless you're an almost-of-age young man, sleeping on a new mattress the first night in your very first apartment. A world of possibility opens up. "You wouldn't think of bringing her home for a couple of days, would you, before she goes to Pimlico?" I request tentatively, as if I'm asking if I could please peek in my stocking on Christmas Eve. I'm dying to see this one move. Worry lines spring between my husband's eyes. He thought he was safe with this one. Never in a million years did he think I'd take to a filly.

"I wasn't planning on it," he says.

I start pleading for some candy. "But a little turnout would do her some good after the sale. It's got to have fried her."

Barrett hesitates. He's worried that if she comes home I'll fall in love with her. Too late; I already have.

May 25

Huey jogs lame again on that right front. I'm still banking on a heel bruise. At the very least, he'll need back-burner time.

Barrett brings Surf's sister home for a few days, after all, with the condition that I'll get on her. What sort of a condition is that? She marches off the trailer and out to the square paddock filled with the luscious green stuff she hasn't seen in a while. And off she goes, trotting and galloping back and forth from one side of the paddock (the one closest to Redmond's) to the other (adjacent to Surf and Pruitt): "Surfie, is that you?" She sure picks the geldings' heads up. She's even more gorgeous here than she was at the sale. And she can move, too.

May 26

We put the new cutie patootie on a lunge line, and although it's clear she hasn't been lunged before, she seems willing to learn. Within minutes, she gets the hang of going around in circles. Trish, Barrett, and Katie sit at the gate, all three drooling as she picks up a trot, then an easy canter. I get on her, and she offers up all three gaits soft and sweet as you please. "She doesn't look much like a racehorse," I offer.

"That's the look of a stakes horse," Barrett says. "You're just not used to the really nice ones." We table the discussion of Sylvia, short for Sylvia Plath, Barrett's new name for the filly in his attempt to combine her father's name (Composer) and her and Surf's mother's (Cynical Gal). Yesterday, Chandler vetoed the poet's name: "She committed suicide, for God's sake." But Sylvia has already stuck. Big hugs to Trish, who is leaving the farm for a year, exchanging her small kingdom for a horse. She's off to seek her nursing fortune in California, where they will pay her living expenses and triple her salary, so she can pay off her student loans and buy her dream creature.

We head to Annapolis to meet my Aunt Kay for dinner at Cantler's Riverside Inn, where we introduce her to a slice of Maryland she's not partaken of before: platters of crabs brought steaming to our table. Barrett shows her how to crack open and hammer and peel, and before we know it, several mountains of spent legs and shells litter our brown-papered table, along with empty plastic containers of cole slaw and straggler fries and rings. Crab parts go flying, Aunt Kay busily wipes her white shirt, the clientele whoop it up at the tables and bar behind us, dusk starts to fall, and the Magothy River starts to sparkle behind us. We order another round of beers, another half-dozen crabs, and more slaw. After we've consumed our very last crab, we still have room for more and order key lime pies all around. Our server doesn't even bother to clear away the mess before bringing out dessert, and now we've got a Vesuvius on our table. Aunt Kay lives in nearby Alexandria, Virginia, and my family gets together with her for dinner a couple of times a year. "I've never seen you eat with such gusto, Julia," she says.

"You've never seen me eat crabs before," I reply. She's amazed by the mess.

"I wish I'd brought my camera," she repeats. We decide that enough is almost enough, say our goodbyes, and head home, satisfied with the meal you can only get in a couple parts of the world.

Fair Hill, Maryland

I've moved Surf two levels down in hopes of reconnecting with him and piecing together his self-confidence, which I pretty well shattered when I last had him out at Morven Park. Apparently, the break has brought back his worst habit. He is completely herdbound to Calvin and has a nervous breakdown when I take either him or Calvin away from the trailer. Dressage suffers as a consequence. His mind is not on his game. I get his attention for a while in warm-up, but as soon as I move him to the dressage ring, he loses it, tenses up, and the test becomes a tug of war rather than a test of obedience and fluidity. I just sit up there on Mount Everest, try to set up camp as best I can as the blizzard hits. "Tactful ride on a tense, difficult horse," the judge writes on Surf's test. On the other hand, Calvin stays relaxed and attentive throughout his dressage test and performs the movements well.

We ride stadium in cross-country gear, then go immediately to cross country. Logistically, it makes sense and should be a real time-saver, even if it undermines the point of eventing: to deliver an artful, composed stadium round after going hell-bent for leather on cross country. Surf and I head the mile down the road from trailer parking to stadium and cross country. Surf delivers his first clean show jumping round in about a year, mainly because I stay out of his way.

They're already behind on cross country from all the falls and loose horses on course when the dark clouds roll in and the wind picks up and the skies start rumbling. Horses are still going out of the box as the rain is pelting sideways. The announcer informs us that there's a hold on course until the storm passes. Twenty of us who'd been milling about trot back up the mile-long road, anxious to reach the safety of our trailers before the lightning hits. Surf uses this part as an excuse to lose his cool. He is caught in the back of the pack and is dying to stick his nose out front. We are soaked to the bone when we make it back. We huddle inside my spacious Eby trailer, taking shelter from a raging storm.

The trailers leave, but we stick it out. In about an hour, the weather clears enough for us to start up again. We trot back down the road. Surf is completely confused now. It's still raining lightly. Shivering from the dramatic change in weather, I've thrown an extra layer over my soaking clothes. Surf goes out on the training course in his dressage bridle so he'll stay forward to his fences, and between the Band-Aid in his mouth and the smaller jumps, he's a runaway freight train. He's used to bigger fences, and on this course there's nothing to make him so much as wiggle an ear. It's unsettling, and I have to haul on his mouth to get him back before the fences. My reins are wet and slippery, and they keep slipping through my fingers, which doesn't help matters any. We get around, but it's not a pleasant ride. Surf rams the last fence, chips in at the last millisecond, and catches a leg. I get thrown halfway out of the saddle just as I'm galloping across the finish line, hanging on for dear life, wet reins and stirrups flapping. I'll need something else in his mouth if I'm to take him Training again next week at Waredaca. Like a chainsaw.

Calvin puts in solid stadium and cross-country rides—is soft yet eager to go forward when I ask—and we make it to the finish well under the time. Foolish Groom also finishes well today and is claimed for

$12,500 to boot, allowing Barrett to cover the check he gave Fasig Tipton Auction Company a few days ago, having signed it with the fingers of his good hand crossed behind his back.

May 29

Today's alarm clock: Barrett from the bottom of the stairway: "Bay colt!"

"Is he standing?" I mumble from half-sleep. I yank on my jeans, slip on some sandals, and dash up to the barn to see the new one. By the time I get there, he's standing as well as nursing. He's big and beautiful, with a star plus a snip and a pencil-thin white line that connects the two running from his forehead to his nose. Plus he's a he. Ballerina, true to form, waited until the wee hours when the barn was dark and still, except for Barrett's hurricane snoring emanating from the tack room, which doubles as Barrett's bedroom during the foaling months. I wouldn't doubt that Barrett's heavy breathing makes the mares believe he is having a foal, which starts a chain reaction. The colt was dry by the time Barrett found him.

When I come close to the stall bars, Ballerina bares her teeth and lunges at me. I act unfazed and back away. I'm used to this protective behavior from her for at least the first few days of her foals' lives. "She's a great mother for the first three weeks," Barrett comments. "After that, she's rolling her eyes and shooing them out the door toward college."

"Who's the father again?" I ask, my mind already starting the process of naming. Pedigrees and breeding selections are Barrett's territory, and he knows a lot about both, is able to find clever matches for our midstream mares that make the managers of breeding farms take notice.

"Silic," he says, "by Sillary, who's by Sadlers Wells. They have an S thing going."

"What's a Sillary?" I ask.

"Some sort of French saddlery," Barrett informs me. Or is that *sellier*?

"Sounds like celery. How about Celery, at least for a barn name? Or maybe Celery Salt. Or rather, Selery Salt." And bingo, there it is.

By the time he has a name, Selery is napping, plopped down on his side, his front legs tucked up tight underneath him the way they were for eleven long months *in utero*, a position he will take for the next few days, until that dark, watery memory fades and he grows enough and becomes acquainted enough with the outside world to realize that he has to stretch his limbs to be a part of it, even in sleep.

Names of Horses

I wanted to name her Apostrophe
for the white squiggle on her forehead.

I didn't care what she was called
after she kicked Barrett and went to the track.

So he named her himself, sometime after the surgery
when feeling came back in his fingers:

Carneros, after the wine
and its mean sound.

The filly born by the sire Fred Astaire
out of the French mare, Busserole,

I named Cyd Charisse,
hoping for speed and motion with a twist.

When the Jockey Club rejected it
Barrett pulled Isabella out of his hat of second-choices.

We never called her that.
Like after the second and third and fourth

titles of poems, you tend to go back to the first:
she'd always be Cherie to me.

Even my kids tweaked theirs
revising what I'd given them.

Caitlin clipped hers to Caite,
then threw it out altogether

in exchange for her middle name, Saylor,
the latter having more of a Broadway ring.

John Logan halved his so he might
meld with all the other Johns. Not guessing

what you throw away
you eventually want back.

The way I dip my fingers into the trash,
smooth out the crinkled & illegible,

that might better suit
my ever-doubting nature.

Shed Row at Pimlico

Sylvia Plath at the 8th Pole

CHAPTER EIGHT

Why I Love to Drink

We've planned a Memorial Day barn enema that consists of power washing the aisle of the indoor arena barn aided by lots of beer and chips. Katie and Chandler have brought the chips and salsa. I've brought the beer. This power washing is the final step in an all-out attack against the barn sparrows and starlings who've taken over the indoor this year and wreaked havoc by tearing out the overhead insulation for nesting material and shitting all over the stalls and aisle. The other day, Katie hoisted our summer barn help, Gregory, up in the bucket of the tractor. With a veiled bee hat and gloves, he cut away the shredded insulation and bashed dozens of nests—a grisly, though necessary, task. Step two involved purchasing a noise box that squawks the call of barn sparrows' and starlings' predators. Its continuous ear-piercing screeches make humans want to run for cover, too. But still it's better than being dive-bombed and shat upon.

Step three is power washing. We take turns with the wand, satisfying our cravings to clean by running the jet of water over ten years of grime and making a visible difference in the floor. It's repetitious work, mesmerizing in the way that mucking stalls is. As I take a turn, my thoughts turn to the season's first cantaloupe that Barrett and I dug into this morning—my father's favorite. As I sweep the wand back and forth across the aisle, a rhythm of words begins to happen in my head.

Cantaloupe

Memorial Day, 2005

I stand at the kitchen sink,
slice my knife into the flesh,
halving, quartering,
scooping innards,
sprinkling salt liberally.

My father would buy four or five routinely
from Big Joe's Fruit Stand,
slice open each, take one bite,
then throw the rest away
if it wasn't perfect.

My father was a frugal man
& not much of an eater—
except when it came to melons,
his one terrific indulgence,
which I remember

as I put the morsel in my mouth,
digging down to the tart rind
to get as close as I can
to my father in his Sunday suit & tie
standing at the kitchen window,
looking out to the pool & the larches,

to the pasture & the Alleghenies beyond,
spoon in one hand,
salt shaker in the other,

clogged with all the years
he wouldn't have before him
without the foresight
of a grain of rice.

This poem first appeared in *Attic* and then again in my chapbook, *Restalrig* (Finishing Line Press, 2007).

May 31

John's twenty-first birthday. I get my barn work and rides done early so I can spend the afternoon cooking for the birthday bash. John pulls up in his blue Volkswagen Beetle around eleven, excited about the day ahead. I pull his ears—a ritual in our family begun by my father—twenty-one times with one to grow on—then I get down to business in the kitchen. Everything goes into a carrot cake except the sink, and I calculate that it will take several hours to pull it off, from eggs to icing. Barrett's still not home from the grocery store, so I sneak up to the barn to steal what's left of the horses' carrots in order to get the cake in the oven. A little limp, but they'll do. I ceremoniously send John out with my Visa card to find beer and whatever dangerous other substances he can now officially buy for the party, and he comes back cracking up. "Nothing like going whole hog," he says, having spent more than a hundred dollars at the local Butler Liquors. He offered his ID, but Pat, the owner, frowned at the credit card.

"Whose card is this?" she asked.

"My mother's," John sheepishly replied.

"You look like her," Pat said, with a wide grin, then, "Happy Birthday!" God knows, she's seen enough of my face in her store.

John's friends start to pull in, Barrett revs up the grill, and I throw some pasta and a salad together. Sylvia Plath wonders why all the cars have parked outside her paddock. After dark, when we walk by on our way to the mare barn to show John's more inquisitive friends the farm's new addition, little Selery, Sylvia uses the opportunity of an audience to pick up a gallop and fly around the paddock a few turns. "A lot of carrot cake went into that one's night vision," I tell our guests, with a wink. There is a kind of light created by speed. We see flashes of it all around us as the filly tears across darkness.

June 1

I pick my way through the litter of passed-out bodies, dirty plates, wrapping paper, mounds of opened presents, empty shot glasses, beer bottles, half-consumed fifths of Jack Daniels and cases of Heineken. Daisy is nosing around the coffee table snarfing up leftover carrot cake. I head straight for the coffeepot. "Automatic drip." That's an appealing idea after my own Chardonnay excesses last night. I mosey up to the barn and curl up in the tack room for a few.

Maybe I'm half dreaming when Katie, Calvin, and I take Sylvia Plath on her first trail ride. The filly wants to be up front, and I let her, as we practice effective half halts. She crosses her first stream, without blinking. "I sure hope you can find a way to buy her from Poetry in Motion," Katie says. I have mixed feelings about that prospect, resolved to focus on two or three horses until I can get my own problems sorted out and not get in over my head like what happened last spring. Plus, there's the little issue of dinero.

Daisy's feeling punk, is all quiet and curled up in a corner. This time, it's carrot cake that comes up, not hoof clippings. Barrett hauls her off to the vet. The bank, the post office, the doggy vet, the florist, the frame shop . . . they all look forward to Barrett's *Deliverance*-mucking costume and Einstein hairstyle, partly because he always has a story to tell them and partly because he *is* the story. If he didn't smell like manure, you might think he was a bad guy. When he walks into the flower shop and the flower keeper is surrounded by flowers and says, "What can I do for you?" and Barrett says, "Well, I could do with some flowers," the obviousness of his plainspeak and the complexity in his gaze can be quite disarming. After they get to know him, they can't get enough.

   Dr. Goode and the receptionist raise eyebrows over the carrot-cake explanation, which Barrett is eager to give them. The vet decides to keep

Daisy for the day for observation and blood work. When I pick her up later, the vet on call greets me disapprovingly. "I hear Daisy went to a party last night," Dr. Steele says.

I feel like a mother picking up her teenager at the hospital when she has been ambulanced for alcohol poisoning. I write another extravagant check to the animal hospital. Dr. Steele in turn arms me with syringes of Carafate and Pepcid, which I'm instructed to administer several times over the next twenty-four hours for Daisy's gastritis and apparent new ulcer. Still a bit woozy myself, I down a couple of the Pepcid on my way home.

June 2

Cooper does an ultrasound on Redmond's tendon before giving the thumbs-up to start jumping and competing him. The fibers are strong; the horse is healed. He injects his hocks for good measure with hyaluronic acid to relieve his old spur and make him as comfortable as possible when I start jumping him next week. A whole other world of possibilities opens up. Redmond is back.

In the afternoon Vet comes to evaluate Huey's ongoing right front lameness. After a period of negative hoof testing and lunging and trotting up and down the macadam driveway, Huey blocks sound to the foot. Once, this was good news. If the pain was in the foot, then most likely it was a hoof abscess and easy to fix. But Houston's shattered pastern throws up a red flag. Vet hauls out the x-ray machine, and I don rubber gloves and hold the plates as still as possible while she shoots the pictures. We've been doing this routine for eleven years. Instead of asking if I'm pregnant, she asks if I'm still having sex.

Vet does not yet have a digital x-ray machine, which means that I'll have to wait and wonder for hours while she goes back to her office and develops the film. I beat her to the punch and call her from the road as Barrett and I head out for another liquid dinner with old friends who love their Chardonnay even more than I love mine. She tells me the x-rays of his foot are whistle clean and that everything points to a deep bruise, probably from the hard ground on steeplechase at Jersey. Huey needs time, as much as a couple of months, she tells me, which is often not great news for an older horse with back-end problems. Being out of work will give his arthritis a ripe chance to seize him up and make it that much tougher to get him back. He *is* seventeen, I remind her. Vet outlines my choices: I can either go for some fancy shoeing—bar shoes and pads—inject his hocks again, manage him with bute, and try to keep him in training. Or I can pull his shoes and turn him out for a couple of months. "What would you do?" I ask the question I always ask of professionals when I'm on the fence.

"With the year of frustration you've had, I don't think I'd ask for more. Turn him out," she says.

We walk past a queue of lawn jockeys lighting our path to the cigar bar at Oregon Grille. Dinner is grisly, with so many dark thoughts about Huey and how one by one our backs are failing us. And then, of course, there's The War. Our friends ask to see Barrett's hand. He starts with the long smiling scar and bends his arm to show the ridges and folds of unattached ligaments where the bones were discarded. Last comes a large triangular pocketed area on the bottom of his wrist where slices of his thigh skin were whizzed in a blender and poured into the open spaces that would not heal, where his hand attaches to his arm. "We call it the French Tickler," Barrett says, chasing our friends' nausea with a little laughter. We drink to this one, and that one, until vacuum cleaners begin to appear at the edges of the dining room.

In the car, I ask Barrett if we ought to try the natural way, let time do what it will to Huey. "We'll turn him out with Surf," says Barrett. "That'll keep him moving." Ever since we first got Surf as a yearling, the two have been off-and-on pasture buddies, having spent endless hours playing grabby halter and tug of war with sticks.

One door opens, another closes. I leave it cracked, though.

June 3

It pours, then pours some more. By the time I get to the Waredaca cross-country course to swim it, the rain has stopped. I get my walking done and am back home in time for a tall glass of Anapamu and chicken Parmesan, compliments of Barrett, then an early tuck-in with our latest read, as is our norm. Barrett is currently on a Sylvia Plath kick, not so much for obvious equine reasons, but because he has agreed to deliver a paper on the poet to my hometown literary club. My father had committed to the project but never got a chance to write and share it with the group before his death. When Barrett isn't mucking stalls, he's writing poems . . . *his* best-kept secret. Sylvia Plath, the poet, has always been one of his favorites, because she hated her father so beautifully. Barrett is tucked somewhere between the covers of *Ariel* when I turn out my light.

Laytonsville, Maryland

Surf is not a whole lot better this week than he was last time out. He whinnies hysterically for Calvin whenever the Irish one is out of his sight. In dressage warm-up, when I put my outside leg on at the walk, Surf pins his ears and pushes into that leg, rather than away. The test goes downhill from the first disobedience. The judge gives him a deservedly insufficient score of 51.5. I'm surprised the judge doesn't include the advice: "This one should be separated from all field buddies and needs to go alone on the trailer next time out."

Calvin has to do his test in the terrifying indoor arena at Waredaca, where there's only a 3-foot warm-up lane between the walls and the dressage ring chain to thread my giant bay marshmallow before the judge blows the whistle, signaling the beginning of the test. Calvin shies at the viewing window, at the judge's table, and even at himself in the mirror. It's a less-than-perfect test, but it still scores well, with a 38. Given the right dressage type, which Calvin is—a good-moving, relaxed, obedient horse—he will score better than my other horses—the tighter, more nervous Thoroughbreds—even on a bad day.

I get what I came for when Surf jumps a clean show jumping round. It's a hard course for Training level, involving bending lines, an in-and-out with a rolltop, a Liverpool with planks over it, and all with tight turns involved. Calvin does a good job, too, though I override the Liverpool, and the top plank comes down.

I scratch Surf from cross country as I'd intended. Calvin goes out and puts in a solid cross-country round—forward but polite, rateable, with balloony efforts over the fences—and he finishes seventh in a large field. Before leaving the show grounds, Grace suggests the "P" word for Calvin. To the long list of Grace's talents, add mind reader. Maybe I will consider moving him up to Preliminary level at CDCTA in a few weeks.

June 5

Chandler and I head back down to Waredaca for her Novice rounds on Smarty. She's nervous, and part of my job as coach is to soothe the savage beating in her breast. She warms up well for dressage and puts in a good test. But she's less confident of her efforts. Show jumping is not as smooth. She has a rail and a stop, while displaying a remarkable verbal enthusiasm, calling encouragements to Smarty at each fence. I tell her what others have told me: if she were as strong with her other aids as with her mouth, she probably wouldn't have had her problems.

Chandler heads down to cross country, and just as she's about to go out of the box, there's a hold on course. A Novice rider has fallen at fence 3 and has to be ambulanced out. This does nothing for Chandler's morale. "Maybe I'm not cut out for this," she confides, as she tries her best to cool Smarty's heels as she waits. And waits.

When it's finally her turn, I head out on course to watch. I hear from the announcer that after one stop at fence 5—the second element in a bending table combination—Smarty clears it and goes on. Chandler tells me later that was the point she dug down and started riding, calling out commands to herself. I've stationed myself at the more difficult Novice elements to hear her screaming at herself as she rides by, "Sit up! Sit up! Left leg, left leg! Look at the fence!" She has a smashing second half of the course, with all of her noisy self-coaching, and comes across the finish line beaming. "I'm pretty pumped," she says. She gets even more pumped when she discovers that she's received a 30.5 dressage score and was fourth after dressage.

I tell Chandler that it's as much about keeping her focus as anything else. Eventing is a head game. She admits that this is a problem in other areas of her life, her tendency to zone out. "Conquer this in your riding," I say, "and maybe greater focus will infiltrate your life in other ways. I've learned so much about myself that has nothing to do with riding by riding." I could go on but decide not to admit my tendency toward self-doubt. Might be good for poetry, not advised when heading into 4-foot immovable obstacles at 27 mph on 1,200-pound animals. There's an element of trust and self-confidence in myself and my horse that I have to have cross country like in no other area of my life. This need to dig in and overcome fear has helped me become more confident in general. It's a gift from the sport that I didn't foresee or ask for when I started competing twelve years ago, but one that I've come to depend on to help make me stronger as a person.

We get back to the farm in enough time to take Redmond for a hack. Daisy and Simon are thrilled and run up ahead, noses to the ground. We walk down the split between the front field and the big field. The mallards are back—each year one couple takes up residence in our water jump. Romeo and Juliet are sunning themselves on the bank. I'm never sure they're the same ducks, but I choose to believe in that kind of loyalty and constancy, and return.

June 6

When I was a young woman, I looked forward to visiting my brother as often as possible in his digs in Chelsea and later in the West Village. But New York long ago lost its allure for me. I take my verve and excitement elsewhere. My daughter, however, has now adopted the city and has decided to spend her first summer there in a determined effort to exert her independence. She is working at a happenin' bakery. Jerry and David have heard of it. Our friend Mag, who has a fondness for racing and Italy, has heard of it. My dentist has even heard of it. Barrett and I, country bumpkins that we are, have not. Caitlin is subletting an apartment whose cost she shares with me as well as with my brother, who plans on staying there a couple weekends over the summer. I've pitched in a third, with the thought that a monthly visit will cover the cost of a hotel room.

I take the train up to New York to spend the night, get a feel for the sublet and a tour of Magnolia Bakery in Soho, where if I linger long enough I might run into Nicole Kidman or Claire Danes. The current kitschy kind of restaurant or shop in the Village seems to be the kind with a down-home, fifties flair, and Magnolia is no exception—they boast of baking everything the old-fashioned way without the aid of new-fangled kitchen utensils, including frosting cupcakes by hand with specific swirls of a butter knife. They've become famous for these cupcakes, the way anyone can with the right twist.

Caitlin barely knew how to scramble an egg until a month ago. She now boasts of the various cheesecakes and exotic cookies she has learned to bake as part of her job, as well as the gourmet urban dishes—from pasta primavera to arugula and goat cheese salad with toasted walnuts and warm pears—that she's put together for friends in her new apartment. For years I could never get her to so much as stir a pot on the stove, and I often think about what we missed in the kitchen as a mother/daughter duo because she never wanted my help or to help. Or maybe I rarely called for her help in the kitchen because I didn't want her counting the glasses of Chardonnay I liberally poured for myself before dinner, which she disapproved of. Some of my fondest memories of my own mother are those spent stirring for the karma of a soufflé, or years later calling her on Thanksgiving morning to ask whether the turkey should be covered and with what—tinfoil? Straw?

I find my weird claustrophobic-slash-agoraphobic tendencies exacerbated by the city, with its crowds and smells and expanses of buildings and blocks. Add stifling summer heat to the mix—a heat you can't seem to escape, as none of the restaurants or shops or apartments has sufficient air-conditioning—and my agoraphobia morphs into paranoia. Caitlin is unfazed by the dirt and the noise and the heat, is thrilled to be able to show off her comfort level with all of the above, as well as her new knowledge of the city. I suck it up, try to seem enthusiastic about the warm sushi at lunch, the fried trout at dinner, the miles of walking in flip-flops on dirty hot streets to the next subway stop, the broken air-conditioning in the dress shop, whose inescapable heat causes us to sweat through the expensive, ill-fitting dresses we try on. My mind wanders to the horses and the farm. I try and talk to Caitlin about what's going on at home, but there's a new distance that has opened up between us. Her heart is in New York, and mine is in Maryland, with the horses and Barrett, the farm and the dogs, and even with the cats that she has always adored but speaks of now only in passing. I am eager to leave the city, but I don't dare show it. I am not eager to leave my daughter, however, and this inner conflict produces a splitting headache and a slight queasiness for the twenty-four hours of my visit. I want to slip her in my pocket and take her away from this. But what I say is, "So long, Caitlin. Thanks for the wonderful weekend." New York's Penn Station never looked so good. And hey, it's even blessed with Mach-4 air-conditioning.

June 7

It's not much cooler at home, but when you're looking at green, there's at least a pretense of cooler. Caitlin's cat, Fuzzy, is hanging out in the mare barn when I pull in, rubbing her body on the stall jambs and looking longingly at me as if to say, "Okay, where is she?" Caitlin's long gone, I tell her, seeking her fame and fortune in that stifling cement wonderland.

Katie tells me that all the horses were good while I was away and that Surf's canter never felt better. I'm pleased to hear this, but I'm maddened, too. How can Surf produce such good work at home but then fall apart at the shows?

Broodmare Rhap Danz has returned home and is successfully bred to Unbridled Jet standing at Country Life Farm, although Cherie and little Ditto have had to stay behind. Country Life missed Cherie's ovulation, and she will have to be rebred. It's disappointing, as it's getting late in the breeding season, and before we know it, it will be too late.

Son John is going great guns at the track with his summer job, hot walking for J. W. Delozier. John was a natural rider as a kid, far more so than either his sister or me, but gave up the sport years ago when his fear got the better of him, though he wouldn't admit this in public. He never got over getting run off with and bucked off a horse when our old family was vacationing on a dude ranch in Montana. He rode and took lessons for several years after that, but his heart was never in it. He worked for the farm off and on through high school and during summer vacations from college, mainly mucking and mowing and painting fences. When given the option, he stayed clear of putting his hands on the horses. It is deeply ironic to me that he is now hot walking and rubbing and giving baths to racehorses at Pimlico. It makes a kind of sense, too. John is a sweet, mild-mannered sort, and these characteristics translate well to horses and can have the effect of calming down the hot, nervous types at the racetrack. He caught Huey, after all.

It also makes sense on an artistic level. The same poetry that's in jazz guitar is found at the racetrack. It is a fast-paced, colorful life, filled with characters who live on the edge, but love what they do and wouldn't trade their hard lives of big hearts and busted veins for anything else in the world.

June 8

Dressage in 90 degrees. Sitting trot in a sauna with a thousand half halts peels the skin right off my derriere. I've tried baby powder, I've tried Monkey Butt Powder—whose name aptly describes what happens to a rider's ass, over time. I've tried Body Glide, which you can also use in the bedroom. There's seamless underwear, a hot item in equestrian catalogs. Or washcloths placed right under the butt bones. There's triple antibiotic ointment or Neosporin after the fact. But the best prevention for butt sores is the thong. Thank you, Victoria's Secret. I'd guess that all who've ridden seriously suffer from this plague of riding, even though few ever talk about it. Needless to say, all my thongs were in the wash. It's a long soak in the tub at the end of the day.

June 9

Redmond is surprised that I've chosen a 95-degree steam bath in which to jump him for the first time in almost a year. His eyes get as big as Mars when we round the corner to his first set of trot poles. Sitting on Redmond is like balancing on a bouncing ball. It's hard when you're a long 5 feet, 10 inches to find a good, secure place to sit on his exuberant back. After the other tall rocking chairs I've been riding all year, I am reminded of how I can't sit down on Redmond's back before a fence but have to perch in two point or get bounced right out of the tack. With Grace's eye, I work on his obedience in the trotting of low fences. It's a challenge to keep my Advanced horse in a trot all the way to the base of a cross rail. He believes it's beneath him to trot fences and wants to scurry into a canter and power off the ground over the tiny jumps.

John comes for a dinner of sushi takeout with good news from Pimlico and his first win as a groom's deputy. Delozier had two fillies in the same race, and John was responsible for walking Marley Hart over to the tacking paddock. Barrett tells me that J.W.'s strategy was to sacrifice John's horse as a rabbit, the front-runner speedball who would tire everyone out and enable his second horse, Hillflower Grace, the favorite and long-distance closer, to come up from behind and take an easy lead from her stablemate. But John's horse fought to keep her position in the stretch and won by a couple of noses over the good horse. John is as thrilled with his day as Redmond.

Unionville, Pennsylvania

I've scratched Calvin from Plantation Field Horse Trials just so Surf has the opportunity to redeem himself alone. This is also his first go back at the Preliminary level, so I want to give him every chance. It's nice to have the time with him, too, one on one, and he couldn't be better behaved. Until Surf, I'd never given much thought to being herdbound as a vice. There's not much that can be done about it, except to separate the horse from the pack.

Surf is a different horse today. He stands politely on the trailer, waits for me to mount before walking off, doesn't push back when I put my leg on, doesn't pin his ears resentfully when I ask for the canter. He puts his head down and focuses, improving his dressage score by 14 points—I am stunned by his good score of 37.5. I don't think he has ever scored below 40 in his eventing career, until today.

Show jumping still needs work, though. He pulls two rails, both off tight turns when he's cross cantering, which has the effect of unbalancing him. His canter loses power, and most importantly, I start picking at the reins when I feel the loss of power and don't see any take-off spot. I suspect that the answer is to fix his canter. No small task. For my jolly green Surf Guitar, tight turns are even tighter. Everything gets exaggerated when you're on a big horse, including the effects of an unbalanced canter and an overly anxious rider. I increase the problem by fussing with the reins too close in to the fences. Maybe we should tie my hands together while we're at it. Maybe I should try riding bulls.

Surf clicks right along on cross country, despite the heat. He has plenty of energy to finish, but it takes him an excessive amount of time to cool down and stop blowing.

I'm no scoreboard watcher, which is one reason I'm not a good competitor. I hate placing myself and my horse in relation to others. I'd rather avoid the comparisons altogether and focus on personal goals. Even so, it's nice to come home with a ribbon. But I'm anxious to get out of the heat, so I hit the highway before the final results are posted—a typical move for me. I've got my glowing dressage test right beside me on the seat. I got what I came for.

Once home, it's cocktails and popcorn and the Belmont on our TV screen to cheer Afleet Alex on to another amazing win, this time without being bumped and almost going down in the stretch. He wins by an easy seven lengths. "Did you see the horse who finished third?" Barrett says. "He beat Winged Sumac on Preakness Day. We were good enough to be fourth to a horse good enough to be third in the Belmont!" His excitement eludes me. I turn my attention to sesame noodles and steamed shrimp and more Anapamu to celebrate this day.

June 12

Surf's long legs are cool and tight and ready for more action. In the evening, we turn him out with Huey, sound again after blowing out a hind abscess from yet another infected corn. He's barefoot, too, the first time in I can't remember when. Huey's ripening age strikes us again as the pair wander off in search of the sweetest patch of grass to share, side by side.

June 13

I walk up to the barn in the early A.M. to find Barrett stuffing Sylvia Plath onto the trailer. She's got her big butt and hind legs off the ramp and camped out as far as possible. Her front half is on the trailer, and her neck and nose are stretching forward to reach the bucket of grain Barrett's dangling before her. It wouldn't surprise me all that much if she sprouted another head from her ass end and walked back off the trailer and into the barn. But in short order, she's fully on and loaded. She's a good girl.

Just yesterday, Barrett and I decided that she needs to go to the track. She's only two. I can't do anything with her for another couple of years. In the meantime, she might as well return to the track to see if she can earn some corn. Even so, I didn't expect to see her leave the farm so soon. I suspect Barrett wants to get her gone before I change my mind. I open the hatch and pat her nose, thinking about all the times I've done just this in the ten years since we've owned the farm.

I get the remaining horses ridden and bathed. Surf Guitar is in the wash stall when the trailers start pulling up. Yesterday, we got a call from Goucher College, in need of a large pasture for nine school ponies for the summer. We've got just the field.

Out of the corner of a soapy eye, I see the parade of nine school horses, and then a buckskin pinto whom I would recognize anywhere. I shoot out of the barn, soap suds flying. "Who's that?" I ask the woman leading the pony.

"It's Al," she says, "Aladdin."

John's pony. The one we reluctantly sold four years ago. Sunny's pasture pal, star in *Runaway Bride* and one of the farm originals. I couldn't be more delighted to see him. "You're welcome to ride him while he's here," the woman says, eyeing his huge belly. "He could use the exercise."

"I may take you up on that," I say, giving Al a big welcoming pat.

I think of the horses that have come back to us and the ones that haven't. There's Huey and Surf Guitar, most notably, but also Jerry and Rhap Danz, Jerry's mother; and Cherie. And now Aladdin. I also remember the ones who haven't—that list is longer—and whom I would love to see again. Beth, who was struck by lightning in our field but still went on to be a two-time winner at the track before she was claimed. Corin, a marvelous jumper who never fully recovered from a coffin bone fracture and who is now a school horse at Garrison Forrest School. Little Red and Mona, homebreds who've gone on to be event horses. Mecke, a yearling we lost to a spinal abnormality. Homebreds Jig and Rosie, claimed at the track. Diamond Mesa, whom we had to put down after she left her ankle at the 3/8th's pole. Suzie Cutely and her dam, Absalutely Cutely. . . Hall of Games, Little Currency, Gilded Key, Cherokee News . . . but not Carneros. She can stay away. She's the only one I wouldn't offer a field to for the summer, or for the rest of her life.

June 14

The horses whinny for me as I enter the barn, anxious for space and green, and unhappy about having to stay in till 8:00 P.M. because of the oppressive heat. When I put their halters on, they toss their heads and practically put their hats on themselves, diving their noses into the leather pieces they know so well. Then it's a forward, marching walk to the gates, the quality of which I'd love to get in a dressage test. I unsnap the shanks and they're off—with a couple of bucks and playful twists of their big bodies until they get down to the business of grazing. Calvin and his new pasture buddy Pruitt play a little longer, and they're fun to watch together. They would work well as a driving team, both more than 17 hands and plain bays, though *plain* is the last adjective I'd choose to describe either one's movement. Pruitt, now that he's sound again, moves like a giant ballerina—light and floaty and ground covering—while the power and grace of Calvin's hindquarters are riveting. I stay at the gate a long time, until the dark gets the better of my watching. These quiet moments fill out my life, give it shape, perspective, and deep satisfaction.

June 15

From my early-morning bed, I can look out my loft picture window and see the fence line at the far edge of our property. That's the good news about building a farm on a hill: you can see it all at a glance. If I stretch and yawn and wait long enough, the yearlings come into view, 83 acres away, and then a few minutes later, glints of gold in the rising sun that I first sleepily mistake for fireflies but then realize must be the brass fixtures on the horses' halters catching the light and signaling me to hurry up and get out of bed—I've got horses to ride and stories to tell.

Grace shakes her head—she wants to try to get Redmond to develop more of a rhythm to his canter on the way to his jumps. I, on the other hand, don't want to change him. I agree with Coach: Redmond is a freak of nature. So what if his rhythm is irregular, if he never touches the fences and maintains his form over them? Why fix it if it isn't broken? It crosses my mind that Grace might not be the best ground person for bringing Redmond back. I don't want to curb Redmond's enthusiasm for jumping, even if his erratic pace and speed-of-lightning stride and take-off spot make it harder on me, as well as on him. "I don't want him to get hurt again," Grace says. I can't argue with that. Nor the fact that it took my tall frame a long time to find a place to sit comfortably on Redmond's tight little wrestler's body. After riding the monsters Surf and Calvin all year, on whom I feel inherently more comfortable, I realize it is going to take some time to readjust my ride and comfort zone. Part of riding Redmond is sitting still and being patient, and part of it is surrender. I rode him at Mach speed the year before he got hurt. Coach used to say that the faster he goes, the better he jumps. Today, that ride is exactly what he recalls and gives me.

The afternoon brings lots of giggling. While mowing, Gregory has found several volunteer marijuana plants growing along the fence lines. Katie presses a few leaves of one plant between the pages of our farm daybook, eager to show me what's been found when I'm done with my rides. I've seen enough pot plants to know what it is. Beneath the leaves is a heart with a note: "Love, Redmond."

I call up Caitlin. "Nice 'gourds' your friend David planted," I say.

"What do you mean?" she asks.

I tell her what we've found growing on the farm. She's genuinely baffled and a little defensive.

"I helped plant David's plants, and they weren't marijuana," she says.

I call John, leave a message that gives me some fun and I hope will bring hysterics when he shares its weirdness with his roommates. By the end of the day, no one fesses up; the planter of the pot remains a mystery. I have a friend who loves to grow his own and who may have snuck out to the far reaches of the farm after his last dinner with us to smoke a J and throw some seeds out to see what might happen. If he did, he never shared either the blunt or the gardening experiment with me. Or maybe it *was* Redmond. "Now I know why our horses are so lopey-dopey," says Barrett. "They've been getting stoned off their asses."

"That'll teach you to be better about weed-eating our fences," I say, ever the slave driver. And then, "I hope marijuana doesn't test," fearful as I am of the vets who randomly test for illegal substances at the events. I check Redmond's paddock, but I can't find any telltale plants growing along *his* fence line. It might not be a bad idea if we switched his paddock with Calvin's and Pruitt's, where most of the pot plants were found. Cannabis seems to produce fabulous movement.

June 16

I take off my spurs, put on Redmond's jumping bridle with the twisted Dr. Bristol bit to give me more brakes, and put the jumps down to about 10 inches to try to encourage a ho-hum, relaxed attitude in my rabid kangaroo. I do my best to lope him around the course, and the fences are so small he doesn't treat them as jumps but as pimples in his canter stride. Which is exactly how I want him to respond before we head out into the countryside. The air has turned a tad cooler, and a breeze has come up that's reminiscent of the Caribbean. The ground is dry, and the new corn plants in the fields are only about as tall as the fences Redmond jumped today. Hundreds of rows of little green soldiers toss their heads in unison in the delicious, bossy wind. So much movement without going anywhere, acres and acres of it. We skirt its edges on our hack, a route intended to relax Redmond even further. Pup Simon, as usual, uses our walk as an excuse to go for a swim in the neighbor's pond. On our way home we scare up a hawk, who catches a draft overhead, taking his own advantage of the welcoming new breeze.

The night brings John home with Mollie and her best pal from Cornell. Rebecca is studying literature there, which was my major at Cornell. I mention my favorite professors, but she draws a blank at the names. It was, after all, thirty years ago that I haunted those halls; I'm sure my mentors are long gone. We stuff ourselves on crab cakes, homemade potato salad, and fresh tomatoes and mozzarella. I've finally found my mother's ice cream maker in one of the last in a mountain of boxes that have been crammed into my garage, and I try my hand at chocolate ice cream. It's as easy as making bread in a bread machine: you dump in the ingredients and the machine does the rest, with Freon as its secret weapon. We end our meal sitting around the back patio dreamily spooning into our mouths silky smooth ice cream that would rival all of Baskin-Robbins' 31 flavors.

June 17

Barrett leaves early for Colonial Downs Race Track in Virginia, where Winged Sumac will be running in his first turf race late in the day. This race is the cornerstone of his and Delozier's plan, code named "Sumac Attack." Sumac is by Dynaformer, the leading grass sire in the country. Barrett and J. W. claimed him three months ago to make their fortune on this seasonal surface. I get my work done early so I can get down to Seneca Valley Horse Trials to walk the cross-country course and then get back up to Baltimore in time to pick up Caitlin at the train station. As I hop in the car, I glance out the window to see our exterminator heading up to the top of the hill in the Gator with an "assistant" sitting beside him, brandishing a long metal pole about the length of a javelin stick. That must be one helluva bird they're after. I stop at the barn on my way out, only to find out from Katie that Surf threw a hind shoe on a trail ride and ripped up his foot, and no, she did not tell the Atlas guy that he could use the Gator. "I hate to leave you to do the dirty work, but I've gotta go," I say. "Pull Atlas off the Gator and get a farrier in here before you leave for the day," I add. I hope I won't come home to find a Katie-Kabob.

It takes three hours to make an hour-and-a-half trip from Seneca to the train station, thanks to three bumper-to-bumpers, including a bad accident that involves a tarp draped over a wrecked VW Bug and the closing of I-70 in the opposite direction, with cars crossing over the median strip and heading the wrong way on the deserted interstate to escape the 5-mile-long jam on my side. The cops are too busy with the accident to worry about impatient motorists' infractions. Just as the traffic starts moving, I get stuck in an even worse mess from the Orioles' game traffic as I'm approaching the city. Caught in a caterpillar procession, I call Barrett to see how Winged Sumac did, though I already guess from his silence that the news will not be good. "Still running," he says to me. "Never got out of a canter. Looks like we own the only Dynaformer colt in North America who doesn't like to run on grass." Must be in the stars today. I nervously glance at my watch for the gazillionth time, with no way to thread my way through the traffic to cross this finish line. I finally arrive at the train station, frazzled and more than an hour late to pick up Caitlin, who's tapping her toes on the curb when I pull up, with a gigantic smile on her face.

June 19

We're invited to a wedding Saturday night in Frederick, Maryland, which means I have no sleep before Seneca Valley Horse Trials. I see midnight, and I see 3:30 A.M., and neither is pretty. But I'm up and at 'em, and I hit the road with only Surf Guitar on board. A friend has volunteered to bring Calvin later in the morning in hopes that we'll trick Surf into being good if he thinks he's alone. Fat chance at Seneca. Dressage at this horse trial is set smack-dab in the middle of the cross-country field so that, as we're trying to execute our dressage test and display Surf's obedience and fluidity, horses are tearing across the field right in front of us at 550 meters per minute on their way to the next fence.

When I put my leg on Surf in warm-up, he pins his ears and leans into it and toward the horse galloping past. His behavior in the test itself is worse. When I ask for the canter, Surf spooks at the ghost of Houston, standing next to our ring. He crabs sideways across the arena to its center, refusing to pick up the left lead canter. So much for our trailering experiment and the kindness of friends.

Surf is terrific on cross country, though, despite smacking his already abused timber knee on a table. He earns the second-fastest cross-country time in our Preliminary division.

As we're on our way to show jumping, a stranger runs up to me. "Is that Surf Guitar?" she asks. "I heard the name over the loudspeaker when you were running cross country, and I figured it had to be him. I used to hot walk him as a two-year-old in Pappy Manuel's barn. I'm Lisa Richardson." I chat for a few with Surf's old fan. She is surprised to find Surf doing well so many years later—not the fate of most racehorses. I condense his long history with us and then excuse myself to get Surf ready for show jumping.

His knee has blown up, but he's sound, so I decide to jump him. In the ring, he's forward, a leftover from his cross-country run, and he jumps well, only pulling one rail. He moves from bottom of the pack up to tenth because of his clean cross-country run and time.

We pack Surf's knee in ice, just as Calvin shows up in my friend's two-horse trailer. Surf is a little too delighted to see his buddy, whereas Calvin looks plain confused to see Surf and the familiar trailer—*Where did you come from?* Calvin is distracted in his dressage test, so I'm surprised by his solid score of 35. Barrett says there are horses that look better than they feel, and those that feel better than they look. Calvin is so far consistently the former, and dressage judges love him. He remains distracted on cross country, and I have to ride him harder than usual to get the job done. I'm guessing that the inconsistency of the course has something to do with the rougher feeling. On the Training course, there are maximum heights intermingled with softer fences against which there is little to ride. Even so, it's not a bad run for him.

Craving sleep and regretting my late night, I have to bolster myself to finish the day. A couple of deep breaths and stretches, some pretzels and Gatorade. Stadium on Calvin is very twisty-turny, and at one point, when Calvin jumps too big over an oxer placed perpendicular to the middle of the ring, I have trouble negotiating a smooth turn to the next close fence, and we have that rail down. I'm disappointed by that, but I have little to complain about for the day. Surf will get a small vacation while we nurse that knee, and then it's dressage and jumper shows for him during the month of July before his next event in August. As for Calvin, it's a move up to Preliminary next weekend at CDCTA. Gulp.

On the way home, Barrett calls me with news from Colonial Downs and Jerry's first hurdles races. "Sixth out of thirteen!" he brags. I must not sound disappointed. Barrett defends Jerry's first effort at almost 2 miles. He was setting the pace for the first mile and a quarter before he tired, and he was up against some of the best steeplechase maidens in the country. "He needed this first race," Barrett explains further. Jeremy Gillam's daughter and Jerry's new jockey, Diana, speaks glowingly of Jerry Bear's jumping effort in the race and compares notes in the jocks' room with Charlie Forrest, who rode Jerry on the flat in numerous races. Both are obvious fans of Suave Rhapsody, and Barrett sounds psyched about his debut race as a steeplechase owner. I sound, I suppose, like I always do when I hear news from the racetrack: politely interested but obviously detached. I'm a rider—I have to be on their backs and feel the race between my knees to get excited.

Why I Love to Drink

Driving through a suddenness
of March snow, listening to a radio talk

show about parents who let their children
drink at home, I winced. Kept driving,

loving the snow, the feel
of the road in the snow.

I grew up drinking because my parents drank.
Wine with dinner, Mother insisted,

pouring her fourth, turning her cheek
the other way if I mixed a little gin

with my juice, said nothing about my late-night cruises
as a teen, my sloe gin with cranberry, vodka & ginger ale

behind the high school football field
along with Sharon & Kris & Larry

& a slew of others whose names
have slipped away.

My parents pretended not to know,
though they must have recognized

the smells & postures when I reeled home.
Maybe they thought I was in love.

They were the sort
who hoped if problems weren't addressed

they would just go away. My brother's
homosexuality, for instance. And my drinking.

Not a day goes by I don't at least think
about having a drink, in passing throughout

the afternoon, as one might long for their children.
My mouth waters as I glance at my watch.

Though I've not admitted this to a soul, until now;
somehow, over time, my compulsion to tell the truth

has become as strong as my compulsion to conceal.
The need to drink, almost sexual,

the way I crave it after a long day,
the alarm clock of ice cubes rattling into their glass,

the first cool sips of Chardonnay,
color of figs, the first

dialed-up sensation as the smoothness
slips down the chute of my throat,

& with it all the day's
anxieties & glitches.

Now my daughter looks away,
my son wants a sip.

And for at least a few moments
until the dulled repetitions

of the second drink set in,
I am swallowing the world.

This poem first appeared in *Southern Indiana Review*.

 *Summer*

Winning is overcoming obstacles to reach a goal, but the value in winning is only as great as the value of the goal reached. Reaching the goal itself may not be as valuable as the experience that can come in making a supreme effort to overcome the obstacles involved. The process can be more rewarding than the victory itself.

— W. Timothy Gallwey, *The Inner Game of Tennis*

Surf Guitar at Plantation

CHAPTER NINE

Choices

///

✕ June 20

Redmond and I gambol about the farm, picking off smaller jumps, while
I try to keep him from busting an artery. We pass the aging—though still
fragrant—honeysuckle that has taken over our fence line between the big
and front pastures; we pass the mallards in the water jump, colorful papa
and now not one but two mates; and we pass our back field with the hay
down and drying nicely in its neat wind rows, still not having been rained
on, though the skies have threatened it since the field was cut two days
ago. We spy a fox, who runs across the neighbors' field, darting away from
Simon and Daisy and back to his den; we pass the young corn struggling
to grow in dry soil; and we pass the streams that a couple of us dive into.
We absorb as much as we can on our hack that seems to fuel and feed all
four of us. Daisy trails us at the end, quite sore with her persistent elbow
lameness. I'm worried for her worsening limp that the vets can neither
seem to get to the bottom of nor ease with pain medication.

I cook a big dinner, as John will be coming home. It will be the first
time our family has sat down together in weeks. We have mounds of
steamed shrimp, a sun-dried tomato and basil pasta, and Caesar salad at
our table tonight. But first, a poem, as was our family custom every night
before lifting our forks. John chooses one by Frances Cornford.

"You'll like this one, Caitlin," he says.

The Watch

I awakened on my hot, hard bed,
Upon the pillow lay my head;
Beneath the pillow I could hear
My little watch was ticking clear.
I thought the throbbing of it went
Like my continual discontent;
I thought it said in every tick:
I am so sick, so sick, so sick;
O death, come quick, come quick, come quick,
Come quick, come quick, come quick, come quick.

He says he likes the way the words and sounds in the poem match the ticking of the watch. We talk for a minute more about onomatopoeia, ignoring the dig to his sister about her discontent before we dig in to our meal. Oh shrimp, come quick, come quick, come quick.

Hay Day

I'm so glad when this day finally arrives each year. We depend on our neighbors, the Prices, to cut and bale, and we depend on the weather to be on our side. It is always a stressor. If we're lucky, we can pull in enough hay from our fields to feed our horses and then some for an entire year, with a few hundred left over to sell here and there. But if the timing isn't right and it rains on the cut hay, then we're out of luck, at least for this cutting. Our crew is small but sturdy: John, his friend Andy, farmers and neighbors Frank and Ed Price, Gregory, his buddy Mike from the liquor store, Barrett, and even me, though my back will only take a couple of loads. Two in the hay wagon to pitch the hay onto the elevator, the rest in the mow to lift and stack. It's satisfying to watch the wall of sweet, delicious new hay get built, bale on bale, until one side of the bank barn is half filled and reeking of the sweet fields. We work until dark, pulling in about 850 bales, with a thousand left lying raked in the fields. That will be tomorrow's work.

It's a various day: dressage on Calvin with Grace, jumping Redmond, sending Caitlin back to Gotham City. Gregory takes Mike around the farm to show him all the weed he's found in 4 miles of paddock fence lines. If the bank barn ever catches fire, Baltimore will be stoned for a week.

June 22

Katie, Chandler, and I hightail it back to Seneca Valley's cross-country schooling day, leaving behind Barrett and Gregory and John and whomever else they can muster to finish bringing in the rest of the hay.

My plan is to test Calvin over the Preliminary jumps to see if he is ready for the move up this weekend. My Irish one doesn't bat an eye at anything. Boy Wonder, on the other hand, will barely jump a stick. My job as Katie's coach is to get her to dig deep, not back off when the horse stops, and learn to ride him through his resistances. The most unathletic horse can practically jump Beginner Novice and some Novice fences from a standstill, but Boy finds a way not to. Boy had a scary cross-country experience at his last event, getting his hind end hung up on a log, and apparently he has not forgotten this. Katie has some fixing to do.

Chandler and Smarty jump all of the Novice and some of the Training fences. Smarty is happy and forward to his fences.

As a new riding instructor, I'm learning how to deal with a cross-country school of multiple rides when some of the horses go well and some don't. I want to jump up and down for the ones who are stars, but I can't, because I have to play down the contrast between the disaster and the success. I don't want anyone feeling too discouraged. The psychological aspect of encouraging everyone is my new game.

On our way home, dark clouds build and break, and it rains torrentially for about two seconds. "Oh no, there goes the hay," I say, feeling guilty I'm not back at the farm, helping to hurry the threatened bales under the dry cover of the bank barn.

"Maybe it's not raining at home," perky Chandler says. Sure enough, we spy patches of blue sky up ahead—the rain stops and the sun comes out. But more dark clouds accumulate as we pull in the farm driveway. They bring in the last wagonload of hay just as the heavens open up again.

"Eighteen hundred square bales, eighteen round ones," Barrett says. Not a bad two days' work. That's the most we've ever gotten in a single cutting.

"What's the difference?" I ask.

"We didn't fertilize," he says. I'd like to think this is my husband's way of saying less is definitely more. But what he means is that fertilizer can put a little burn on a plant for a week or so before it starts to benefit. Combine that burn with a drought, and you stress out the sugar and the starch. When the rains came back, we were lucky enough to have plants still healthy enough to drink.

June 23

Calvin is keen beans in a stadium jumping school, having learned forward thinking from his cross-country school. Afterward, I venture down to Hampden, in the heart of Baltimore, to visit John in his summer digs and to take him grocery shopping. I'm armed with a packet of info recently come in our mail about his upcoming semester in India. We sit on his couch with a sheet thrown over it, hiding God knows what, perusing timetables and inoculations and supplies needed for my son's big adventure across the world, while roommate Andy sips from a can of National Bohemian and plays video games on the tiny TV screen that the boys have placed within the bombed-out shell of a much larger screen. Ranger Dave comes home from work and tells us about his job at Fort McHenry. As a recent graduate of the University of Maryland and a history major, Dave considers giving spiels to tourists about Francis Scott Key and "The Star Spangled Banner" a perfect summer job. Plus the wind across the bay is great for Frisbee golf. The fourth roommate, Pete, is off working his construction job. They all have early hours, though John's are the earliest, as he has to be at Pimlico at 6:30 A.M. six days a week to walk the hot racehorses. It's fun to sit on the ratty couch while Baltimore is going on outside in 75-degree sunshine, spending time with these young men who are happy to be doing what they're doing, keen beans for their summer, independent of us oldsters in their Baltimore row house, working hard at their blue-collar jobs and proud to be working.

"Have you seen any rats yet?" I ask John, on our way out the door to the grocery store. I'm not sure why I ask this, but I do, fearful of the answer. He knows how I feel about rats. His eyebrows go way up and his eyes get big.

"About one a minute," he says, "and they're huge."

"Uh-uh," I say, "not one a minute."

"Well, maybe every five minutes," he revises. "Do you want to know where they live?" Long pause.

"Tell me."

"You don't want to know." But I do. I beg him to tell me, though it's the last fact I want to know.

"They live under the rubber mats at the front of the horses' stalls," he says, eyeing me for my reaction. I shudder with my aversion to the news.

"You've got to be kidding." Those poor horses.

"They don't really do anything," he explains. "They mostly just hang out." And eat. And grow.

Onward to SuperFresh.

Culpeper, Virginia

Calvin works hard in his first Preliminary dressage test. He actually gives me a couple of reinback steps before freezing up, although I just introduced the movement to him yesterday. One of the secrets to developing young horses is preparation. Don't be too last minute with the schooling, but allow some room for spontaneity. We've never worked on counter canter either, and this test calls for that, too. We do our best and still manage to pull a 39.5 score.

Show jumping is in the polo arena. Though it's twisty-turny, Calvin puts in a clear round, despite the fact that I almost miss a roll-back turn and end up turning wide and accruing time penalties because of it. The horse does everything I ask of him and jumps well, is even willing to go off course when I ask him. Big kisses. Wet ones.

I negotiate the Manassas and Dulles traffic, the Washington and Baltimore beltways, and struggle home, looking forward to a nice swim in the pool and a huge steak-and-potato dinner, my recipe for a good cross-country run, which is tomorrow. Home brings a visit from Hans, who wants to take five years to make it in the horse business, and would like to rent out our bank barn and go into business with me. Much talk over a mile-high vodka tonic. Barrett and I consider his offer, say that we'll talk about it, and shoo him out the door so I can get down to the real business of swimming and eating. I dive my grimy, naked body into the water, but next thing I know, Barrett is bringing the phone out to me. It's Grace, wanting to ride to the event with me in the A.M. "What's that? I can't hear you very well. You sound like you're underwater." Almost. I haul myself out of the pool, toss a towel over my shoulder to finish our conversation. Damn these "long-range" portable phones.

Barrett turns his attention to me. "Aren't you worried about the neighbors seeing you?"

"Serves them right for looking," I say, and turn my attention to dinner and a T-shirt. Barrett fries up some peppers to go with the steak, not realizing that they're of the firecracker variety with millions of potent little seeds which he pours all over the meat, rendering the dinner inedible unless you're a dragon. It's solitude at last as I curl up with my latest novel. Wrong again. John pulls up with an arsenal of guitars. He needs a change of scenery, he says. His housemates want to party tonight, and he'd rather practice. Guitar sounds infiltrate my much-sought-after silence. At least it's jazz and not heavy metal. And it is son John, after all, whom I'm always grateful to have around.

Cross-country day dawns hot, humid, and overcast. I make it down to Great Meadows just as the Intermediates are coming out of the box. Grace and I watch their runs as we walk the Preliminary course. I find moving horses up to Preliminary especially nerve-wracking, more so than the other levels, because for the first time in a horse's career, the jump combinations get technical and speed becomes a factor. I have high expectations that my horses will jump clean, despite newness, and today this eager nervousness on my part causes me to override and start shoving Calvin at his warm-up fences, throwing him off his rhythm in the process. I miss badly twice and almost come off him once.

When I gallop out of the box, I settle into a more forward pace, and Calvin ticks off the jumps, one by one. Never backs off, never gets crooked or cranky or rank, comes back to me when I ask, gallops on when I let him out, and we both cross the finish line smiling. What a good boy. I am thrilled with this first clean Preliminary go for Calvin.

I head back home through beltway traffic, only to find trailerfuls of people and horses back at the ranch. Student Dan and his wife have brought over some pals to cross-country school with. I chat with them for a while. Another friend stops by. I've got John and Mollie down at the house, and all I long for is a quiet drink by the pool. It's eight or nine o'clock by the time my barn chores are done and the kids and trailers have left. Three cheers for Calvin, I say to the quiet, dark waters of our back-yard lagoon. The fireflies respond with their multiple bright cheers above the steaming water, then higher in the butterfly bushes, the weeping beech, the crepe myrtle and Leylands. Farther up in the hot, almost-Fourth-of-July sky, Mr. and Mrs. Bat perform their blind acrobatics in the brilliant sunshine of radar. It's what I need: built-in motion detectors to feel my way over jumps and horses and husbands without having to see or think about them.

June 27

Five rides today, and five baths. I'm more impressed by the number of baths. By the end of the day, I've had several myself. The big ones always get you, as they use their height to evade the sponge around the face. I have to stand on my tiptoes to get my hand on the front of Surf's nose for leverage when he throws his massive head up almost to the wash-stall ceiling so as not to get his face wet. Yet he'll play with the hose for hours, ducking his head right toward the nozzle when it's time to rinse. Just like a little kid—don't let him see the washcloth, yet he'll dash naked toward the hose whooping and laughing on a hot summer day.

Redmond's hind legs have been stocking up in the heat the last couple of days. He's been a little quiet too, not his normal perky, Canadian self. We sweat the legs and turn him out with Pruitt in hopes that he'll play the swelling down. I pull his salt. Redmond is the kind of horse who'll lick his salt block for hours—must take after his mom. Popcorn is one of my five favorite foods, and I'm not sure what the other four are. I know I've eaten too much when I wake up in the morning with swollen fingers or a hang-over on one glass of wine. Or maybe it was two glasses and I hopped on Huey bareback in the dark. I go for broke and pull Redmond's popcorn. This morning his legs are almost back to normal.

Vet's Associate pulls blood anyway, to be sure nothing else is going on. She has come to the farm to palpate Ballerina, who might need surgery after big Selery tore and bruised her cervix during his birth.

"What have you been up to?" she asks, eyeing my drenched appearance.

"I just gave my fifth bath," I say. It's one way to keep cool in the heat. Selery comes over to say hi while Associate is busy with his mom. He is surprisingly friendly, considering his mother only recently stopped trying to take my head off when I attempted to interact with her new colt. And his sister is the wrist killer Carneros. Ballerina's getting bored with mother-hood, which slowly happens to the mares. They allow a little more dis-tance between themselves and their colts each day out in the paddock, until the boundary of the fence line sets the limits. When it's time to wean, the seasoned mares barely fuss. Humans, unfortunately, don't have this built-in mechanism. We question every decision when it comes to our teenagers' increasing need for independence.

Caitlin calls from New York. She started her movie internship today. Maybe she won't come home for that weeklong visit after all. The movie people need as much of her as they can get. "That's fine, whatever's good for you," I say, a little dashed, but thinking of Ballerina grazing in one corner of the paddock and letting Selery gallop over to the fence to say goodnight to me. I give his star and snip a pat, rub his forehead and then his butt, and he leans into my rubbing the way the babies always do.

June 28

Surf's timber knee is up, but he's sound at the jog. I ride him on the flat, cold-water hose the knee when it's no smaller after riding, then put him away. An hour later when I check on him, he's standing morosely in a corner of his stall. The swelling has started to creep up the leg, which he's clearly favoring now. I call Vet, then tack up my next victim, Pruitt. I ask

Katie to join us on pony Sunny for a mini–trail ride around the farm. Pruitt is a brat and can't handle any downhill grades. When there's a semblance of a slope, he starts tossing his head and rearing. When I raise my crop and smack him between the ears—my tried-and-true remedy for rearing—he gets pissed off and goes up all over again, this time in succession while striking and plunging sideways at the same time, and all as we're trying to make our way downhill and back to the barn. I manage to stay on until I get him to the round pen, where I work him to exhaustion. It's the scariest ride I've had in ages. I have it in my mind to send Pruitt back to the track. But first, I'll give him a month of serious and intense ring work and see what happens. Which I hope does not include my getting hurt.

Barrett arrives home from Country Life Farm with Cherie and little Ditto, who isn't quite so little anymore. She a beauty, too, with a refined head and eye, classically outlined with a thin black line that extends beyond the eye's border at the far corner, which gives the impression that she's got a smidge of eyeliner on. Cleopatra's mother is teaching her the important things in life. "Is Cherie pregnant?" I ask.

"We won't know till Tuesday," Barrett says. She's been rebred several times unsuccessfully while at Country Life. If she doesn't take this time, that's it for the year, as it's getting late in the season.

Surf's knee is as big as a bowling ball, and he's lame. Vet's pretty sure it's lymphangitis and not a fracture, but she pulls out the x-ray machine anyway, just as dark clouds are building and closing in on the farm. We apron and glove up, and Vet plugs the cord in as the thunder and lightning hit. Surf stands in the cross ties, waiting for whatever we are about to do to him. Just as she's shooting the third or fourth picture, there's a lightning strike that would wake the dead horses resting peacefully in our back field. The lights go out, and Vet drops the machine and leaps backward. The lightning has come through the socket and zapped her. She's visibly shaken, and her hand stings. The lights come back on, the storm passes, and we finish taking the pictures of Surf, who's unfazed by all the goings-on. You want storms, we've got them, like nowhere else. "I think it's because you're on a hill," Gregory says, as if this were a new revelation. That's college for you.

"Who would ever build a farm on a hill and not a dell? Or is it dale?" I ask my audience.

"Over hill and dale, I think," says Katie.

"But it's the farmer in the dell," I say. "Well anyway, you're looking at the farmer on the hill. What morons. We get more snow, cold, wind, storms of any sort, and lightning strikes," I catalog, thinking of the two poor horses who got struck in our field, years ago.

"And more of a sure summer breeze, fewer mosquitoes, fewer flies, and gorgeous sunsets," Barrett says. My husband is the type who could find a way to make Hell passable, whereas I'm the one who could find too many pearls in the Pearly Gates.

Vet loads Surf up with massive antibiotics and returns to her office to develop the x-rays. She calls back a couple of hours later to say the x-rays are clean. It's lymphangitis after all. He'll need a few days off and will be back to work in no time.

We wait till after dinner to turn out the horses, till after our new boarder Alex arrives from Massachusetts and we get her settled in. We lead the mares and foals first. It's the first time they've met, and they all run around, researching the field's boundaries, using their mothers as shields. Curious Selery is dying to come closer, keeps looking over his shoulder at Ditto. "Hey, you're my size!" he seems to be saying. Then they all start to graze, still keeping their distance. "They'll be on top of each other by morning," I say to Barrett, as we walk back down the driveway to get on top of each other before tomorrow hits.

June 29

Pruitt is mannerly in the ring, but when I take him for a walk in the woods, he starts rearing again. I jump off to hit him a good one, within the five-second window of a horse's memory, but in my rush I forget to take the reins over his head. He rears and strikes at me, lunges out of my grip, and gallops back to the barn. Everyone comes running. Gregory's eyes are huge and dilated as he catches the renegade and brings him back to me at my insistence. It's the round pen again, circle after circle until Pruitt's tongue is dragging.

Surf's leg looks like a tree stump. We cold-water hose him at intervals and pump him full of bute and antibiotics, and on the hour I walk by his stall in hopes that there will be a noticeable decrease in the swelling. But there isn't. The good news is that he clearly feels more like his old self, is alert and eating.

Barrett's off with a horse to the Charles Town racetrack in the afternoon, to help our neighbor Baden, who trained Suave Rhapsody on the flat. I'm exhausted from my last event and from the hairy week I've had, with too many horses to ride and no rest in sight, so I plan a solitary night of swimming and eating and bathing and reading. John calls—would I like to go out to dinner with him?—and as much as I hate to say no to his request, I do. I need this night to myself.

The skies rumble and open, lightning is followed by a power outage. These are the days of the afternoon summer thunderstorm, violent and insistent, and mercifully brief. Tonight, the storm comes in waves and doesn't seem to want to resolve, as insistent as Pruitt's insurrections the last couple of days. I watch the skies for a couple of hours and wait till my best guess says it's over for now and quiet enough to turn out the horses. After a quick dinner of artichoke pasta and green salad with mango slices, I take the dogs on their nightly constitutional. A fog hovers in patches over the farm, as does a sense that all is quiet but not quite over—an in-betweenness that is beautiful and ominous all at once, as if a painter had her hand in this landscape, or like a poet on the verge of tears.

Sometime in the middle of the night, I feel Barrett crawl in bed beside me, having arrived home from Charles Town. I turn toward him, in between sleep and waking, put my leg over his hip, and now we are both wide awake but still dreaming.

June 30

I have a whiz-bang jump school on Redmond. It's a bit like trying to ride popcorn with his boxy, bouncy, quick-as-lightning stride, and he jumps with such power, often popping all of my two yards straight up out of the saddle. He's the best jumper I'll ever have the privilege to ride. Though he'll take some getting reused to, he's still the one. And he's back.

My goal today with Pruitt is to teach him to pony off Huey. I start by taking my old boyfriend on his first hack in six weeks. He's delighted to be back in work. Back at the barn, Katie has Pruitt all tacked up and ready to go. We head for one of the smaller paddocks, Katie hands me the lunge, and I pull Pruitt as close as I dare to Huey's side. Barrett's on the other side of the youngster, leading him with a regular shank, and Katie's behind us with a lunge whip. Pruitt likes none of it, however, plants his feet, and refuses to go forward before lunging back and rearing. We sort it out, and eventually Pruitt is mindfully marching beside Huey. Then I turn to Katie and ask her if she'd mind hopping on Pruitt while I pony him. She runs to get her hard hat and climbs aboard. Pruitt butts Huey and tries to push us over, I swat him to get him to mind his own space, he lunges back and up—with Katie on his back—and flips over backward. Katie deftly bails and manages to scoot out of the dumb ass's way, now on his back and flailing. Katie's okay, but she's visibly shaken, as if she's just taken a lightning strike. We hope that Pruitt has scared himself and won't attempt that again. I try to pony him without a rider, without success. He's got it in his head that all he has to do is lunge back and he'll give me enough of a rope burn that I'll have to let go. What I need is the pommel of a western saddle to wrap the shank around and give me more leverage. Good ol' Huey is a trooper through all of these shenanigans and only once spooks at the lunge line whipping around the legs of the stupid four-year-old galloping across the pasture. Huey does seem perplexed, though—"You brought me out of retirement for this?"

I bag the ponying idea and go back to what I know will work. I put Pruitt in the round pen on the lunge and work him till he nearly drops, then get back on him in the safety of the round walls and ride him till he can barely stand. Then I ask Barrett to lead us back to the paddock that was the scene of today's crime. I trot him through the gate, go around the paddock both directions, then pick up a canter and do the same. After we execute a few turns, I hop off while the hopping's good. There's no way he can rear if he's trotting and cantering, so we'll have to bypass the walk for a while. I don't know if I want to take the risk of continuing to work with the horse or send him to someone more knowledgeable in dealing with difficult horses. I'm not as spry as I used to be, couldn't have dodged disaster the way Katie did. I go the hard-ass road. I turn him out by himself 24/7. He is not to eat any grain. Perhaps isolation from the company of his own kind will make me his best friend. The only kindness and company he'll get is from me, so he'd better be good. I'll give it a week's whirl, see if I can make a difference. And be sure to wear my safety vest when I'm on his back next time.

John comes for dinner distraught over troubles with Mollie. He's the attentive, giving type, and she's the quiet, more withholding type, and lately these differences have been getting in the way. We talk for hours about his dilemma. I think of advice that my father would give: "Why don't you try playing it cool for a while?"

"Cool? What do you mean, cool?" my son asks. Before I have time to answer, he lights up with understanding and a seeming appreciation of the advice. He joins me in the barn before he leaves as I'm bringing Surf Guitar in for the night. "He looks a lot like his sister," John says. "You can really see it in his face." I'm moved by John's newfound appreciation of Surf Guitar and his renewed connection with horses in general since he's been working with them at Pimlico. "I can't break up with her," he says, through the quasi-dark of the barn, his voice catching. I hug him and hold him close. He's still not too old for that.

This is what my mother would say: "Don't forget to walk up the stairs backward!" It's the last day of the month, and my mother was full of old superstitions like this assurance of good luck. On the last day of each month, you're supposed to walk up the stairs backward so that all of your next month's dreams will come true. Apparently, Pruitt would have no problem with this backward task, the lucky bastard. But I better think forward thoughts as I fall asleep tonight, heading into July and my continuing work with Pruitt, as well as Redmond's debut.

Choices

Gregory asks if he should shoot the sparrows
in the mare barn, too—tear down the clay nests
fastened high up to the door runners.
I have nothing against these birds
that can do no damage over here.

I've asked him, however, to shoot at will
the starlings that have infiltrated the insulation
in the arena barn, tearing it out in huge gobs,
causing thousands of dollars of damage,
as well as shitting all over the barn, dive-bombing

the horses & humans, with Hitchcock as their inspiration.
We hoist Gregory up in the bucket of the tractor
to bash the nests of eggs and baby birds.
A new machine squawks
high-pitched versions of the sparrows' predators:
starlings, crows, blue jays, even monkeys.

The actuals become manic,
attacking each other, swooping down
from the rafters, scaring up clouds
of loose insulation that rain down
on the humans and rile up the horses
before escaping through the barn doors into the wide

& much more silent night.
For weeks we keep ear-plugged
until the smartest figure out the ruse
& fly back into the racket
to nest once more in the luscious insulation.

Too soon again I hear the chirpings of newborns
tucked high up behind steel beams.
I ask Gregory to go fetch the B-B gun
and have another go at nonexistence.

"The babies are flying," he says, one morning,
surprising me in the calm of the mare barn,
looking up to the nests I've allowed to exist
where tiny dinosaurs are bursting from the seams

of overstuffed pastry,
lifting and ruffling their tiny wings.
Gravity looks up with me —
It's now or never —
& coaxes them over the edge.

Suave Rhapsody

CHAPTER TEN

Rhapsody

✕ July 1

Even Pruitt goes well today. My isolation tactic may just be the ticket—and my lunge-line-in-the-round-pen drill followed by mounted sprints around the mare barn paddock. It's too early to tell, but I'm hopeful.

Even so, a nameless melancholy has hold of me. Midday when I come in for my daily tomato sandwich—my summer staple—I realize that it's the second anniversary of my mother's death. Not a day goes by that I don't think of her at least twenty times, and yet it is lunchtime before I remember that she died two years ago to this day.

I go upstairs before heading back out in the heat. I hear the thumping at Caitlin's bedroom window. The cardinal that my daughter would always complain about is bashing into her window and flapping away. Seconds later, he's at it again. He is beautiful and sad, and obviously frustrated when he can't get to the striking rival he sees in Caitlin's window. From all my years of writing poems, and tending house, and caring for absent children's rooms, and not being able to get to the beautiful just beyond reach, I know what to do: I close her purple curtains, and the persistent thumping immediately stops.

July 2

I have to get re-accustomed to bustling days like today, which is how it used to be at the farm when we were full for all those years: lots of horses to ride and lessons to teach, plus every time I turn around, some new person showing up with a question. A mother and her plump, horse-hungry daughter ask, *Do we have any horses for sale?* having pulled up to the barn without forewarning in their Chevy wagon. *Do I know where Katie is?* the accountant's secretary asks, as she arrives in SUV with grandkids for lessons.

Where would I like them? Dave Wisner says. He's armed with presents: the Maryland Combined Training Association's jumps on loan. I hand him the map Katie's drawn, which indicates where we want the jumps to go in our back field, with sketches of each. "Julia, you've got way too much time on your hands," Dave says. What he doesn't know is that what might have taken him a month only took gifted Katie an hour or so.

We head out to the back field, and Dave picks up the jumps with his Bobcat as if they weighed no more than air. All afternoon the little dinosaur runs back and forth across our hay field, carrying cross-country fences as if they were dinner. When I come back from my hack on Surf, Dave's still at it. Surf is curious about the goings-on. Having lived in the inner city at Pimlico for years, he's broke to gunplay, sirens, pit-bull fighting, and heavy machinery. At two o'clock, Dan and his wife arrive to help Barrett clean up our woods and chop some firewood. I feel like Larry King presiding over a big natural disaster.

I watch the mares and foals through the wash-stall door as I'm bathing Surf. Selery is trying to engage Ditto in play. She'll have none of it. The colt runs up to her and rears, then wheels his butt on her and bucks and kicks out, but the filly won't budge from her quiet mode. Then he's off to bug Rhap Danz, the boarder mare in foal, dying to have one of her own at her side, having bonded with the foals in lieu. Into the run-in shed Selery goes, to see what's going on with Rhap, while his mother is grazing clear across the big field, not bothering to wonder where her baby is. It occurs to me that Selery just might try to nurse from Rhap, and if he does, I bet she'll let him. We had one mare like that years ago, Cherie's mother, Busserole, a veteran French broodmare who took on another's foal who had been ignored by his mother and nursed him as well as her own.

I'm looking forward to a quiet night at home. The phone rings. "Could Mollie and I and Ariel and Dan come for dinner tonight?" John asks. Sure, why not?

Caitlin calls from the city: "I'm about to get on a train home."

"You're coming today?"

I'm excited at the prospect of having the kids close again, though unprepared. Barrett runs out for teenage supplies—chips and beer—while I finish my rides. Then it's shrimp and pasta and beer for all of us, and goodies from Magnolia Bakery, followed by a night swim. Pup Simon enjoys the pool, too, though Daisy mopes on the deck—she prefers the cooler, scummier neighborhood ponds—too much chlorine in a pool, not good for the coat.

July 3

Surf's left stifle has locked up, and when I back him up—the age-old remedy for his locked stifles—he doesn't work out of it. I repeat the rein back, then walk him forward, and he's only slightly better. I tack him up with hopes that he'll work out of it. He's still hitchy on the leg when I get on, and it isn't until I canter him that he comes sound. I call Barrett, who's on his way to Colonial Downs for Jerry's second hurdles race, and he makes an appointment with Dr. Meittinis at Pimlico to have Surf's stifles injected.

The highlight of my day arrives: Kim Meier with a vanload of horses and students and daughter Kelly for a cross-country school. I join them on Redmond, who will see his first cross-country fence in almost a year. Kim's a little worried. Her big horse, Test Run, who ran her around the Four Star at Burghley and strained a tendon in the process, still isn't one hundred percent. I talk to her about the benefits of ACell injections.

Kim discusses ways I can alter my aids to discourage the bid Redmond likes to make before he jumps. She reminds me to soften after my half halts and to be lighter with my hands in general in front of the fences. I tend to hold eager-beaver Redmond to his fences, and I need to give more than take so that he won't lean or pull against me and quicken to his jumps. Riding is all about contradictions. If you do the opposite of what logic tells you, it's the right thing for the desired result. It's a wonder that more riders aren't dyslexic. You want to come down from a trot to a walk, you put your leg on. You want to turn left, you don't pull on the left rein, you push with the right rein and leg. You want your horse to slow down and stop pulling, you let go of his head so he has nothing to lean against. You want your daughter to come visit you, you tell her what a busy schedule you have.

Barrett calls with frustrating news: Jerry was in the lead when his jockey fell after the last fence. Diana explains that the horse accelerated when she wasn't ready for the push, and she lost her balance. She's unhurt, though disappointed. So are Barrett and trainer Jeremy Gillam. But I'm not. "Should we bring him home?" I ask a little hopefully.

"Oh, no," my husband says quickly. I'm always looking for an excuse to bring our horses back home. Maybe if I hadn't said anything. . .

We head out for dinner at Bertha's Mussels in Fells Point. In between picking tiny pearls from our teeth, both Caitlin and I notice how quiet John is. Something must be bothering him. The perky sister turns to her brother, whom she adores but from whom she's been alienated ever since his ten-thousand-year-long relationship with Mollie. "So, what's happening?" she asks brightly. She has learned a lot in her summer away from home. She loosens the reins and waits for him to respond. And he begins to talk.

The Fourth of July

Today's Main Street parade is a trail ride with Caitlin on Huey, me on Redmond. We make our way over to Baden's Stream, which is deep enough for the horses to wade in up to their knees, and the dogs can swim happily in the refreshing water on this hot, hot day. The horses know the way, and we feel their excitement on the last part of the mucky trail before the stream. They plunge down the rocky slope and dive into the water, making a beeline for the deepest spot, to stand, for as long as we'll let them, with the canopy of trees over us and Daisy and Simon swimming circles slow motion around us.

When I was a kid, my father and I would polish the horses till we could read our futures in their coppery flanks, dress up in our finest western gear (fringed leather jackets, chaps, cowboy boots and hats), and hack the interminable 5 miles to downtown Warren to take part in the annual Fourth of July parade. We'd always get the tail end of the parade, so the high school band members and town politicians wouldn't have to dodge the land mines of manure. But I didn't care. It was the highlight of my year, because for those 5 miles, my father was all mine. I remember having to soak for hours afterward in the bathtub, the skin on my little girl's butt so chafed and sore from so many hours in the saddle. Usually I'd take my brown spotted pony, Tommy. But one year I borrowed my brother's black pony, Billy, who, when he wasn't bucking me off or running away with me, would also pull a pony cart. I spent days decorating the blue, rusty cart with streamers and pom-poms, and talked my mother into transporting the cart into town in her station wagon while I brought the pony the long way. That day, it rained on our parade, and by the time my father and I marched the 10 blocks through town, the streamers had all been torn or rained off, my own Scarlett O'Hara outfit was drenched, and my father, on Jim Horse, was left waving his soggy cowboy hat to the parade diehards. Everyone knew my father. He was a big man in our small town, vice president of the local oil refinery, the most knowledgeable man in Warren on most any subject from Shakespeare to crude oil. So to the locals it was a joke: Jack Wendell can ride a horse! And has a sense of humor, too! And dares to be part of a parade! But to me, it was a matter of ownership and pride. Riding alongside my father, the center of the town's attention for those few blocks, I puffed up with my small importance and beamed.

I teach a lesson, then hurry to help Barrett with the late-afternoon feeding in time to leave for Katie's Fourth of July party in Fells Point. I'm looking forward to the Inner Harbor fireworks display, my second favorite part of any Fourth of July celebration. Little did I expect that my fireworks would begin in the car with Caitlin, who has taken issue with all of us having to drive together to the party. My daughter suffers, as does her mother, from claustrophobia, which for her manifests itself in cramped driving situations during which her schedule and freedom to come and go as she pleases are hampered by the wishes of other passengers. Our ground fireworks blossom into skyworks as the argument progresses to sensitive issues like money and her chosen summer path in New York. I press her buttons and she presses back, and by the time we get to John's digs, we're screaming at each other, while Barrett sits silently in the passenger seat like Ben Franklin, having given up any hope of productive diplomacy. Smart man. Caitlin doesn't want me in the car anymore, so John and I end up driving separately to the party. I weep quietly from Hampden to Fells Point. John takes the opportunity to tell me about his plans to go on a two-week backpacking trip to Europe at the end of the summer, sponsored by his best friend Andy's parents. I look sideways at him. "Can I come, too?" I say.

Both Caitlin and I are pretty good social actresses, and at the party, you'd hardly guess we'd had a problem. I don't think she has any more fun than I do, but we laugh and joke with other guests and talk as if life were hunky-dory. An hour or so later, after John has already exited stage left to join his real friends, Caitlin and Barrett and I make a hasty retreat, long before the fireworks at the Inner Harbor even begin. We stop off at our favorite sushi place and pig out on nigiri and rolls, ordering way more than our stomachs, even Barrett's, can handle. It's as if nothing has happened between us, and we're pleasant over dinner. The three of us are exhausted from our day and decide that bed is the best place to be. We fight lines of traffic at Oregon Ridge, hatchbacks and sedans and trucks on their way to the northern Baltimore County skies: cars stacked up along the sides of the back road we duck onto off the main clogged drag, children and coolers perched on roofs, families lugging blankets and chairs to get a little closer to the magic. "Fireworks are so fucking dumb," Caitlin says.

"I wish you wouldn't use that word so much," I say.

"Which one?" she asks. "You mean fireworks?"

We negotiate this long, unhappy day and return home. It's upstairs for me for a long soak in the tub and bed. "If I open the window, do you think we could hear them?" I ask my drowsy husband. Without waiting for an answer, I crack the window, and sure enough, I hear the distant thunder of blooming skies. I imagine the ones we missed, blossoming over the water at the Inner Harbor. I think of the hordes of people, heads tilted up, arms around each other, waiting expectantly. I see them against the black sky of my closed eyes, big and full and startling with various colors, filling the entire span of my imagination.

July 5

We make one more attempt at a good time together before Caitlin goes back to New York, this time over Maryland crabs. John joins us, and we roll up our sleeves, get the crackers ready, and start hammering away on the shells to get to some of the sweetest crab meat we've had in a long time. An hour later, we're still working at it, and eating, and laughing now, our hands and shorts and T-shirts smeared with Old Bay, old racing forms spread over the backyard table, piled high with crab debris, the dogs at our feet, eagerly awaiting any spare tidbits of backfin or a stray claw scuttling across the patio.

Owings Mills, Maryland

Surf Guitar's first jumper show. Hot as blazes. I'd forgotten how much standing around there is at jumper shows while you wait for your two-minute turn to jump. They're also a challenge for the directionally challenged, because they require memorizing several different courses and sometimes riding them without the benefit of walking the course beforehand and without sequential numbers on the jumps, as in eventing.

Surf is quiet and patient, not at all like his usual high-strung self. He jumps well for the first two classes—clean rounds for both!—though it's only a 3-foot division. I almost go off course only once in the second class and have to circle to the next jump, but I'm still pretty happy with the round, despite my minor memory failure.

As I'm waiting around for the speed class, I start to feel a little woozy and realize that I haven't eaten or drunk enough water today. I enter the ring, jump the first five jumps, and as I'm jumping the fifth, the world ahead of me—meaning the last three jumps—goes completely blank. I have no idea where to go next, and so I excuse myself from the class. I'd simply forgotten where I was going, and yet when I come out of the ring, I pretend I'm sick. I sit down, put my head between my knees, pour a bottle of water down my back—which it's true, I need to do—and drink two more that someone produces for me, while yet another neighbor takes Surf to walk him until I feel better. I do a pretty good job of covering up my senior moment. At the same time, I'm embarrassed and irritated that I haven't taken proper care of myself, especially considering the extreme heat.

Once again, I've crumbled when I have to perform too close to home. I know too many people standing at the sides of the ring, and I let the pressure of familiarity, combined with poor personal habits, get the better of me. At least Surf Guitar has done a good job today. Now, if I can just find the trail of bread crumbs to follow home . . .

July 7

Both Calvin and Redmond feel like a million bucks in a jump school with Grace. I play up my "illness" a little more: I tell her that I'm still not feeling too well from my heatstroke episode of yesterday. It's true, I'm not, but it has more to do with the gigantic vodka tonic I fixed for myself last night than any heat exhaustion—not exactly the best remedy for dehydration. On the other hand, given all the quinine I've had over the years, I'll probably never get malaria. We all keep self-defining secrets. My drive to write about them reveals a compulsion to get to the bottom of things, when I might otherwise lie—and therefore unearth those secrets I've buried so well over the years I'm not even sure where to find them. It's true: the person who hides an eating disorder for her entire adolescence— that would be me—is the same person who still can't admit to the world when she blanks out from memory loss on a show jump course, in much the same way that it's impossible to admit to a problem with food when the compulsion to keep the secret is as much a part of the problem as the problem itself.

Later in the day, Barrett takes Surf to Pimlico to have his creaky stifles injected. A year ago, when Barrett brought Carneros to the racetrack, she was the fourth horse in Delozier's small stable. Now J.W. has nineteen divided between Dickie Small's barn and the Preakness barn. Barrett asks J.W. for another stall for the day and an hour later walks Surf Guitar off the trailer. J.W. and Tony, his groom, remember the horse from his Scott Lake days, but they've never seen him so muscled up. Tony lets out an 18-hand whistle as the boys scramble to direct the big horse to his temporary digs and shut the door before Surf can step over the webbing. Dr. Dan Dreyfus comes calling. "What's the basic complaint?" he says, staring at the biggest knee in Baltimore.

"Well, he seems kind of stiflely and hockey," Barrett says. "We'd like you to inject him." Dreyfus stoops to massage and flex the knee.

"How long has he had a problem with his stifles?"

"Since he was a yearling," Barrett says. "And when he was three, he broke his tibia." But Dan won't leave the knee alone. Barrett tells him it's just a timber knee. He explains that in eventing, not all of the jumps come apart. "He'll pick up those knees higher next time," Barrett adds.

"I get it," Dan says. "The idea of the sport is basically to run over your dog a few times to teach it not to chase cars."

Fire Island

Even before Hurricane Dennis hits, a few hundred miles to the south of us, I'm fretting over the mushy state of the footing in our outdoor jumping arena from all the rain we've had in the past few weeks. Yikes. The John Williams clinic at the farm will happen this weekend. I call Dave Wisner, and he assures me that he will take care of it and do what he can to make the ring jumpable.

The rains begin, and all night I keep waking and listening to the thundering on our tin roof. The storm worsens in the early hours and becomes ferocious right before Barrett and I hit the messy roads for Fire Island and my brother's commitment ceremony. We leave Katie to oversee the farm and the footing disaster in our absence, as well as to get everything in order for the clinic. I would never have left the farm with a clinic going on if it weren't for my brother's wedding.

We battle our way up the messy New Jersey Turnpike with nearly zero visibility, then veer off on the Southern Parkway, which will take us out onto Long Island toward Sayville, where we will catch the ferry to Fire

Island. Today is no day to be out on the water if you tend to get seasick, as Barrett does, and the wide hull of the ferry rocks and rolls through the dark waters punctuated by roiling whitecaps and even darker skies. Thank the merciful Buddha it's only a twenty-minute trip to the island. There are more dogs than women on the packed ferry—specifically six dogs and three women—and so our weekend on Fire Island begins, Barrett getting greener by the moment beside me. I keep my fingers crossed that we will make it there before he loses his lunch, and breakfast, and last night's fettucine alfredo.

The harbor comes into view and the ferry captain throttles down. The first building is a grocery store. Barrett is perking up already. The second a florist. The third a discotheque. The fourth a liquor store. Now I'm interested. All along the wharf are dozens of beautiful tanned men with perfect hair and teeth and fingernails. All their attention is focused on Barrett, the new kid in town, as far as anyone around here is concerned. Next, we see my 6-foot-4-inch brother John, in shorts and tank top, with arms wrapped around himself and tucked under his armpits, hugging his massive bodybuilder's frame against the wet cold, and his partner Mark, standing under the cloud of a black umbrella. Both are waiting for us on the other side of their kind of love, smiling, expectant, anticipating their wedding ceremony, which is only possible for my brother after the deaths of our parents, who would have so strongly disapproved of this commitment between two men.

July 9

No vehicles are permitted, including bicycles, on Fire Island. Small red wagons are allowed for carrying groceries and suitcases. All streets are little narrow boardwalks that wind their way uphill and down to the beach houses. The vegetation is lusher than most beachside locales, with mature trees and bamboo shields, carefully manicured landscapes, and an overall feeling of remoteness and privacy, each house tucked back from the boardwalk and nestled into its unique, carefully sculpted context. On one walk into town, Barrett asks why the boardwalks are painted with a white stripe at the edges—like highway stripes. My brother John, celebrating his twentieth year of sobriety, laughs casually and says that in his first years of

AA in the city, everyone used to talk about falling off the boardwalk at Fire Island as an example of their debauchery. He heard the story repeatedly from different sources and didn't understand it, long before he ever paid his first visit to the island.

Tame dwarf deer are everywhere. They allow us to walk right up to them and pet them, although Mark cautions against getting too close, given their tick infestations. I am struck when we turn to my brother's cottage, first by Mark's elaborate landscaping that rivals any of their neighbors, and then by our parents' racks of deer and antelope that adorn the cottage walls, horned stuff I didn't want when we divided up the estate. There are also lamps, chairs, and tables composed of various parts donated by larger cousins of the friendly animals that roam the island.

John wants to show us the impressive houses on the bay side. We walk by the hordes at Low Tea enjoying the pulsing ya-ya disco beat accompanying a Dido song. Every day on Fire Island, Low Tea (7:00–8:00 P.M.) is followed by High Tea (8:00–10:00 P.M.), then by Sip and Twirl (10:00 P.M.-12:00 A.M.), and then, from midnight onward, a final unnamed party at the pavilion for those truly in want. We hear rumors of the meat market, at the far edge of the community, where any man—and I'd guess he would *have* to be male—can find anonymous sex at any time. In the midst of all this jubilation is a quiet community of gay couples in a peaceful beachside setting. My brother and his partner are two who don't participate in the high life, although Mark enjoys visits to Low Tea. I get a little crispy sunbathing on the beach and finish a novel. I return to my brother's house to help him with his wedding vows, but Barrett and he are in the midst of a Judy Garland DVD festival and don't want to be disturbed. I let my mind stray to the horses. I want next weekend to hurry up and get here, when Redmond will make his comeback at Surefire Horse Trials, "Somewhere, Over the Bank Jump . . ."

We have a late rehearsal dinner with my brother and Mark and a dozen of their closest friends at the Botel, a small hotel shaped like a boat. This is followed by entertainment from a drag queen who sings a Madonna tribute, then Handel and Puccini. Caitlin comes in off the ferry midway through dinner, and we all sit mesmerized by She-Quita's long blond hair and dark skin, her 18-ounce cleavage and long, sleek body and even sleeker voice—

its impressive range from baritone to operatic soprano. I wonder if Caitlin thinks I'm disgusted. My conservatism would give her something to turn away from. Why is conflict so essential? If I could solve this riddle with my daughter, maybe I'd be happier in my yo-yoing relationships with everyone. Confucius says, "The answer is as simple as a person's innate sex."

July 10

My brother and Mark exchange vows at their house under a gazebo. It has an altar-style table placed at one end, which is adorned with vases of birds of paradise and pewter candlesticks from our parents' house, suggestive of our original home and shared past. The "minister" recently bought his ordainment online so that he could perform the ceremony. I question the need for his presence at all. His role is so small, and there's nothing in the eyes of either God or the state that needs his blessing in our country, which still does not acknowledge gay marriages. Mark has masterminded the ceremony, and, in tribute to his foster Jewish upbringing, brings out the linen-wrapped wineglass, on which they both heartily stomp before a cardboard box is opened to release hundreds of monarch butterflies, half of which never make it alive into the scorching atmosphere above them but lie stunned on the deck, some clinging in a last-ditch effort to our pant legs and shirts. There's not a dry eye in the house, including my own, though I usually hate weddings. But I am moved by my brother's celebration of his love for Mark and the ease with which he makes his commitment—so far from his days growing up in our closed-minded house, where his homosexuality was never acknowledged or discussed. My brother is one of the butterflies that made it into the air, while I am clinging to a pant leg, still bogged down by grief and the complexities of being the executor of my parents' estate, both of which have kept me from resolving my feelings.

Barrett and I lived in sin for eight years. I had vowed not to take vows again. After our exes remarried, it was easier to think about getting remarried ourselves. We decided on the moment's spur and didn't even tell John or Caitlin. I mail-ordered a simple skirt outfit from J.Crew, met Barrett one March afternoon at the Towson town hall while the kids were in school, and the deed was done. I don't think Caitlin ever forgave us for our secrecy, and her resentment was probably deserved. Now I wonder why on earth I wouldn't have wanted to share our ceremony with my children and with my parents while they were still alive. I especially wonder why on a festive day like today, at my brother's wedding day.

The reception is at the Pines' fitness center. We have to catch the last ferry to the mainland so we can drive back to Baltimore in time for day two of the John Williams clinic, and so, sadly, we must be prudent with our time and with what we eat and drink. Another drag queen DJ keeps us well pumped with tunes. When one of the floats in the swimming pool catches fire, an ex-porn star, now famous for her local New York TV show interviewing strippers, parts her beach wrap, flashes her somewhat-slacker-than-*Debbie Does Dallas*-but-no-less-riveting body, and jumps into the shallow end to rescue the float. I'm sure the party will become even wilder after our 10:00 P.M. departure on the ferry and our long trip down the New Jersey turnpike to an agonizing 3:30 A.M. arrival home.

July 11

Bleary-eyed, I check on all the horses and get a couple of rides in before my clinic times in the afternoon on Surf and Calvin. Katie tells us that there were boogeymen in the paddocks Saturday night causing the horses to run. Calvin threw a shoe and was sore, although after soaking the foot and getting the shoe put back on, he came sound. But sure enough, I feel something ticky when I trot him in warm-up. He jumps well, but is hesitant to pick up his left lead canter. After the clinic, John Williams confirms my suspicion—"He looks a bit katywhoompus behind," he says. And with this comment, Calvin is no longer the soundest horse I own.

Surf is bold and rideable in the cross-country school, although John feels he's too big and not supple enough to make an Advanced horse. What I've got going in my horses is more than the potential levels of the horses. "At some point, we have to think about the soul of the farm," Barrett says, when I tell him John's assessment of Surf Guitar. John is a careful, considered speaker and teacher, not one to pass around the compliments. He feels Calvin is too lumbering and Surf too stiff. Yet I love them both, despite their flaws. Body type is only a fraction of what creates success, at least in my own style of eventing. The rest has something to do with faith.

And try. Even so, I feel weighed down by John's critique of Calvin and Surf, and by Calvin's new lameness. I cannot fly above the gazebo and be any symbol of freedom for anyone.

July 12

I postpone a lameness assessment of Calvin until after my lessons with John. Redmond handles John's gymnastic as if it were made for him. It's a line of several jumps set at 15 feet apart, a tight distance that requires the horse to take one short stride between jumping efforts—a real challenge unless you're a jack rabbit. Which, of course, Redmond is. Eighteen-hand Surf, on the other hand, has more difficulty with the exercise and bounces through it a couple of times until even his long body is able to figure it out. John has also set up a turning exercise geared toward schooling lead changes over jumps.

Both of my horses handle the exercise well—even Surf, who manages to get the turns done and not lose his impulsion. John emphasizes the need for dressage over fences—and for riding my horses every stride, as I would in the dressage ring, asking for suppleness and softness right up to the base of the fences. Both Jimmy and Grace, on the other hand, stress the importance of getting my homework done early, then leaving the horse alone three strides out and softening my hands forward. All three roads lead to Rome, and yet I don't trust that I'm sensitive enough as a rider to be successful with the more active ride. Remember show jumping at Morven Park on Surf Guitar? To get John's gymnastic done requires more involvement. He explains that this is the way to get Surf to coil his spring and compress his long body before the fences, something that he must learn to do before I attempt to move him up again to Intermediate. I can't wait to talk to Grace about this strategy.

After my lessons and John's departure, we jog Calvin and then put him on a lunge line. We scratch our heads as he trots up and down the driveway. I spot something in the front end. Barrett believes it's in the hind. We put him on a lunge line in the indoor, and there it is: an obvious hip hike, worse going to the left. Vet can't make it out until tomorrow, and I spend the rest of the evening fretting over the state of the soundest horse in my barn and wondering what boogeymen were scaring Calvin. It makes me never want to leave the farm again.

July 13

Vet diagnoses a bad nail in Calvin's left hind. She pulls the shoe, and he's 50 percent better. I ask for x-rays. Vet flexes the leg and torques the ankle. "This is a sound horse," she says. "A couple of days in a stall, and he'll be ready for a shoe and work. There's no need for x-rays." I take a deep breath and turn her attention to Surf Guitar's knee. "That's a whopper hematoma," she says, and seems more concerned about Surf than Calvin, suggesting a DMSO cortisone stack wrap along with Naquasone for a week. She warns that if the swelling doesn't come down, she may have to draw out the fluid with a needle or lance it. She adds that the lancing would mean about a month of downtime. I'm not thrilled with either option, and I cross my fingers that the more conservative method of wrapping and administering steroids will do the trick.

I've stood by Vet for eleven years, despite lots of ups and downs. I've come full circle since Houston's death. Her negativity and hyperconservatism are just my ticket in the long run. Though she's not wild about a couple of my horses and would have a lame horse stay in a month when most vets would call for a week, I'd rather take the slow route than hope for the best and end up with a dead horse on my hands. I trust her careful judgment, and that means more than her not having the latest gadgets. Stifle ultrasound, digital x-ray machines, video endoscopy, shock wave devices . . . so much of that equipment is a kind of veterinary conformation. Good conformation is good, but hang out in the winner's circle some afternoon and you'll see all kinds of crazy legs. Good conformation might help you hold up, but something intangible—quintessence—helps you win the race, and Vet has barrels of that quality.

July 14

The great thing about sex in the morning is that I've had the whole night to sleep away the knots and kinks and aches. The problem with Barrett is that he's always out of bed at 4:30 A.M. like a rocket, trotting downstairs, buzzing the coffee mill. I have to be quick to get his attention at this hour, and I'm not that fast. He has energy and happiness to boot. Even while he's getting dressed in the laundry room, I can hear him humming the theme song to *Gilligan's Island*—he doesn't even realize he's doing it. "Your loss," I say to his shadow as he shuts the front door and jogs up the driveway to the barns. What man would turn away from a bed full of retrievers? I get up and don't hum anything and proofread yet again the galleys of *Dark Track*, soon coming out from WordTech Press. The publisher has lost the last corrected set I returned to him, and I stupidly did not make an extra copy, so I have to read through the manuscript one more time, looking for the errors I already found once before. I'm annoyed and bored when I notice the half-dead Japanese maple in the backyard. Barrett comes back to the house after seven o'clock for a second cup of coffee. He tells me he'd like to go to the track this morning. I fetch him a pair of clippers.

"Why don't you prune that tree before you go?" I say. "Shouldn't take more than an hour." My need to pass on my bad mood to my husband, like a cold, is wrong. But I do it anyway.

"No problem," he says, trying to keep ahold of his optimism. He carries the clippers like a dead animal whose germs he doesn't want to get on him. The truth is, I hate it when Barrett goes to the track, which leaves the responsibility of the farm all to me.

How many times have I read these poems? Writing and rewriting, at readings, and now through the publication process? Maybe a thousand? Some of the poems are almost ten years old. Others are younger, and they represent my life here at An Otherwise Perfect Farm, my ups and downs with horses and how the four-footeds and farm life relate to my interior life. But I am deathly sick of the poems as I plow through them a final time and hope that I won't have to read them again in the near century. Barrett has traded the shears for a machete. He looks like Paul Bunyan. Whack. Whack. Whack. Must be something really big going on at Pimlico today.

Chandler begins her dressage lesson by telling me a story from work, which she prefaces by admitting that she's sold her soul. She is a drug rep for a manufacturer of pharmaceuticals for small animals and up until recently has been consistently the top rep in her region. But her sales have slipped lately. I hope that it's not because she's been ducking out of work early to make her riding lessons with me. She tells me how she doubled a sale when a vet spied her old Passier dressage saddle in the backseat of her van. "I'll double the order of Revolution if you throw in the saddle," the vet offers. My student hated the saddle and was about to put it on consignment anyway, so . . . what the hell.

"You're on," she says. "So I sold the Passier for $10,000." She adds, "You've got to promise you won't tell a soul."

"My lips are sealed," I say.

July 15

I'm at my desk upon waking, armed with Cran-Grape juice and a foggy head, thinking about Redmond's comeback this weekend at Surefire Horse Trials. I look out my office's glass French doors to see something I've never seen in these parts before—a pair of pelicans skimming the row of Leyland cypresses just beyond my window. I first think blue heron, which are much larger and usually solitary, without the telltale pouch under their beaks as these two have. Maybe the birds are hungry. We've got tins of smoked mussels. Anchovies. Tuna. When the coffee kicks in, I'll look for the can opener.

Redmond gives me a solid tune-up over stadium fences, and Calvin is sound under tack in the indoor. But the best news of all is that Pruitt marches up and down hills with Surf Guitar without blinking. He thinks about being bad only once, when I ask him to negotiate a steep, rocky tunnel of a slope, but when I wiggle the right rein to remind him that he's wearing the powerful Segunda bit on loan from Kim, he straightens up instantly and heads down the slope like an old school horse. I give my four-year-old his first gold star for his efforts. Selery flies over to the fence line and peeks out between the second and third fence boards just below his eye level, as if to say, "Hi there, my name's Selery, what's yours?" Maybe we should have named him Curious George instead. What a doll.

Before I know it, the day's complete. We pick up our books—mine about a cold-blooded killer and Barrett's about mitochondrial DNA. Barrett turns to me as we get to the fascinating parts: "So, what's with the fish in the backyard?"

Purcellville, Virginia

Saturday afternoon I walk the cross-country course at Surefire Horse Trials. When I get out of the car, I'm smacked by an intense cliff of heat. It must be 95 degrees in the shade. It's a haul to the start box, and on my way there, I run into a neighbor who's just finished Beginner Novice stadium jumping on her young mare and is heading over to cross country. My neighbor looks green, and when I ask how things are going, she says that she had dry heaves after stadium and admits that she doesn't do too well in the heat. As I'm walking the Preliminary course, she gallops by, and then a little farther into the course, I see her again. This time the horse is walking, and my neighbor is leaning over the side of her saddle and vomiting. I ask if she needs help. An official steps out of an air-conditioned car and warns me not to interfere: I can only offer help if the competitor asks for it, by the rules of competition. Someone who's tossing chunks horseback probably shouldn't continue, even on a cool day. Nonetheless I back off, and about thirty seconds later, the rider perks up and turns around, asks if she may please continue, and gallops off.

Sunday dawns at about 75 degrees, with a forecast of being hotter than Saturday. I hope it won't stop either Redmond or me. I'm nervous about the heat and about Redmond's legs, but my overgrown pony doesn't seem to have a problem with either. His dressage is fairly good, though it is never his forte. Not so much because of any fault in his training—he knows and does all the movements well and is generally obedient in the ring—but because he moves basically like a penguin—short strided and choppy. It's hard for him to be competitive in the dressage ring when set against so many of the fancy movers you see nowadays at the upper levels of eventing. Still and all, I'm happy with the test, except for a spook at the canter, which tightens up his back and stride.

The jumping phases are altogether different. As soon as Redmond realizes he's jumping, he bucks and tosses his head—and charges his fences. I count one gorilla, two gorillas, three on our way to the fences and try to keep my body as relaxed as possible. He takes the slightest move with either my mind or my body as license to break his rhythm and jump faster than a speeding bullet. We have one disappointing rail when I don't think ahead and badly negotiate a tight left turn to a skinny. He ticks it ever so slightly with a hind leg, and it comes down. Redmond doesn't usually hit too many rails. Chalk this one up to heightened enthusiasm his first time back and to my being a little slow on the draw.

Redmond's exuberance carries over to cross country, which isn't necessarily all bad. He's happy to be doing his job again. At the Preliminary level, I find that the jumps aren't big enough to hold him off, as he's used to jumping Intermediate and Advanced fences. His cockiness continues around the cross-country course, until he gets up too close to one larger oxer and clips it. Ouch. The stride isn't quite there, even for clever Redmond. After he gets too close for his comfort, he backs off ever so slightly around the rest of the course and starts to jump with his head and not so completely with his huge heart. I'm a little unnerved by his speed and exaggerated gusto over which I have little control, but it's not a bad first go. It will take a time or two for me to get back into Redmond's superman style, especially after becoming more accustomed to the long strides and quieter natures of Calvin and Surf Guitar.

Rainey Andrews's rig is parked beside mine. She is hugely eight-and-a-half months pregnant with her first. After our run, I catch her sprawled on a lawn chair underneath her gooseneck, fanning herself with a fly mask.

"What are you doing out in this heat?" I ask her. She shrugs, like it was a dumb question.

"So, what are your plans for Redmond? Are you thinking of Fair Hill?"

She is referring to the Fair Hill International Three-Day Event, which takes place each October in Fair Hill, Maryland. It is the pinnacle event for Advanced riders and horses in my sport, who come from several different countries to try their best to conquer Derek di Grazia's arduous course. It is a goal I have never dreamed of attaining until Redmond came along to show me it just might be possible.

No one besides Barrett has mentioned those words to me. I cast my eyes down at the ice boots I'm struggling to fill.

"Oh, we'll see," I say. "Everything would have to go pretty perfectly for that to happen."

I consider my chances of that, especially with my luck—although I have definitely been thinking of the Three Star for Redmond, and I'm sure she can tell.

"One step at a time," I tell her.

Though that's all we say about it, she knows me and my ambition well enough to know that the race is on.

July 18

I hurry through a couple of rides so that Barrett and I can leave the farm by 7:30 A.M. and head down to Pimlico, where we are to pick up our grass specialist Winged Sumac and, more importantly, say hi to John. I've yet to see him working his summer job as hot walker, and since he's only got a couple of weeks left, I'd better get my peeks in now while I can. "I hope I don't see any rats."

"Don't worry, they got rid of them all this morning for you," my husband reassures.

John is sitting in the hot-walker chair, waiting for another hot one when we pull up in the rig. "What, sitting down on the job?" I tease. He pops up to greet us. Then a horse comes in from the track, and he takes over.

"Come on, sweetheart," he says, as he puts the chain shank over the filly's nose like he's been doing this all his life. "Watch out for that one," he says over his shoulder as he walks away while motioning with his head at stall number three. "That's the colt. He'll eat you if you don't watch out."

Beyond giving me a friendly warning, John wants to point out his favorite horse in the barn. The colt has a tiny, expressive head that is in constant motion, now bobbing up and down, as if to get my attention. I go over to give him a pat, and sure enough, he tries to take a chunk out of my arm. At the track, you're always asked to move over to the side of the shed row where the horses' stalls are when a horse comes through, which they do about every five seconds. For the innocent, it's a dangerous place to be—there are a lot of bored teeth on that side of the barn. You have to look out for your back—and fingers, and arms, and shoulders.

Sylvia Plath is next out of the stall. I'm told she's gotten pretty keen since she's been at Pimlico. She's as beautiful as ever, and if money were won based on looks, she'd win it all, hands down. The news is she's fast, too. She blew her field away on Saturday during her first work, and the barn is abuzz about it. We head out to the track to watch this one gallop. She runs away with the exercise jock, Mark O'Dwyer, and comes back with rubs on both of her shoulders from Mark's boots because she pulled so hard. "It's booties for Mark next time out on Sylvia," her groom, Tony, says. Tony and I talk about the blocks that some of the racehorses have in their hind shoes for better grab on the track, and I show Tony my array of studs, with which he is duly impressed, particularly because they can be screwed in and out.

"I've never seen anything like that before," he says. "You've got to show them to J. W."

"Watch this," I say as an aside to Barrett. "Next time we visit the track, all J. W.'s horses will be drilled and tapped for studs."

The afternoon takes a downward plunge when, after a midday break to run out for my annual mammogram, I spend time fretting over Surf's knee, which has swollen again since he's been off medication. It's huge, and though he's sound on it, there's no way I can take him out in public looking like this, nor can I imagine that he would have full range of motion with its size, particularly over the bigger fences. We decide to have Vet draw out the fluid.

Calvin gets his shoe back on, and I saddle him up for a hack about the countryside. As soon as I trot up the back hill, I feel his lameness, and so I return to the indoor, where I trot him again on good footing. Maybe I'm imagining it. Maybe he'll work out of it. Maybe I'll stop making excuses. Barrett walks into the indoor midway through my vain examination and draws a finger across his neck. It's another vet call. This time I want x-rays of every molecule of Calvin's left hind leg. I don't care that there's only a one in a million chance that anything major is wrong. I don't care that the pictures will be expensive at a time when we are watching our pocketbook. I feel the ghost of Houston at the end of his last shank, advising me to take the x-rays to make sure there's nothing broken or about to be.

I fret the rest of the day. I pull out my fall event calendar, in which I've marked upcoming events for each horse. I throw it down on my office floor and go pour myself a glass of Anapamu, in a quantity to rival what's in Surf's knee. At least I didn't see any rats today. That's the most I can say about this one.

July 19

Vet returns for Calvin just as Suave Rhapsody is pulling into the driveway with Jeremy Gillam at the wheel. I wave to Jeremy and motion where he should park his rig as we're heading into the indoor with lunge line and Calvin in hand. Vet is perplexed that Calvin isn't any sounder after several days of stall rest with his "toe bruise," although she guesses it's because the shoe went back on too soon. She flexes the hind leg, and the horse is positive to a lower leg flexion. She then blocks the foot so that he won't have any feeling in the area she numbs to better pinpoint the problem. He responds, not to a lower block, but to the second, higher block that encompasses the front of the foot as well as a portion of the pastern and fetlock, and he comes sound. She is still sure it's a toe bruise but nonetheless asks if I want pictures, and I do. She agrees with me now. Out comes the x-ray machine and a long day of waiting until they're developed.

I give a midday poetry reading for the Harford County Poetry and Literary Society, where I read to a small audience from an easy chair at Rockville Manor in Bel Air, Maryland, somebody's private house now converted to a community arts center. This group of avid retirees gets together weekly to share their poems and listen to guest poets read from theirs.

Back home I meet with Jeremy to go over Jerry, whom he suspects may be working on a tendon. We stand with a blank piece of paper and a flashlight to better see the outline of the tendon in its shadow thrown on paper. I strain to see anything but absolute straightness of the tendon in question. Jeremy admits that he's sensitive right now, as he just had one of his racing mares break down with a bow last week at Colonial Downs. He wants me to ride Jerry and assess the tendon over the next few weeks, and if there's nothing there, then he'll be glad to put him back in steeplechase training. "He will win," he says, leveling his eyes at me. My jump builder, Dave Wisner, stops by for a meeting about plans for new jumps on our cross-country schooling course and revisions to a couple of others. There's just enough time to fill my glass with ice before Vet calls.

I answer the phone while pouring in the dregs of an almost-spent bottle of vodka.

"Should I be standing or sitting?" There's an equivocal pause on the other end.

"Well, hmm, I guess you can be sitting," she says. My heart sinks. A bone abnormality of the pastern has shown up on the x-rays, she explains, probably the result of a traumatic injury within the last month. "Did he have a puncture wound? Or hit a jump hard?" she asks. I draw a blank, take a huge gulp of my weak vodka tonic. She explains the problem as osteomyelitis or bone infection on the long bone of the pastern, which is not in the joint, she says brightly, and most likely treatable. She wants to come back for more x-rays, however, to make sure there's no fracture.

I spend the rest of the evening feeling sorry for myself. "Do we have any tequila?" I ask Barrett.

"Do you think you're the only one in the world with bad luck?" he says. "Everyone in your sport has these problems. There's not an event horse or any other kind of horse who makes its living as an athlete who doesn't have issues. And a lot of them."

"Tell that to Houston," I say bitterly. When I think of the probabilities of two pastern fractures in my barn within six months of each other, which would brighten the pockets of most other gamblers, I shudder. "And remember," I say, "I've never seen the winner's circle."

I follow Barrett into the living room. He pulls three encyclopedias off the shelf. At first I think he's going to produce the scientific explanation for why I'm a pathetic moron. But there, hidden behind the M volume, cool and yellowy and shimmering, a bottle of Aztec gasoline. "Fifty miles to the gallon," Barrett says. He holds onto the first gulp so we can swallow together.

Rhapsody

Scotch pulls from her mother,
stamps the stall floor
when the mare turns away toward her timothy.

This one's the best in the barn—
short back, long runner's legs, good angle to the shoulder.
"Who does that?" I ask my husband,

as we turn out mama and baby,
Scotch trotting circles around her feather duster of a tail.
Just a week old, she could run for days if she had to.

It's enough to tempt faith in lesser prophets:
someone's got to be responsible for perfection.
We pause at the gate,

our arms flung over the oak board fencing,
watch how near Rhapsody's flank
the newborn stands, gallops in the sheen

and shadow at her mother's side
so even the wolves who see all can't see.
She's safe in her world

as long as she stays close, which will last
a few months if she's lucky,
or only forty-seven years if you're me.

In memory of my mother

Redmond

Selery Salt

CHAPTER ELEVEN

The Nature of Longing

※ July 20

Vet lugs out her x-ray machine and gets down to business with Calvin. She pokes and prods his pastern, sure she's going to find the scabby remnants of a puncture wound. The outside of his leg is clean. She doesn't understand why there's no history of trauma and asks again if I had hit a jump during one of my competitions. I say that I was up all night replaying all of Calvin's jumps in the last six weeks and couldn't come up with a single blow. Why would radiographic changes show an inflamed bone when there's no external injury? She returns to the possibility of a fracture, which is why she's here for more x-rays. "Maybe he's got a bone infection. Or maybe there's a comminuted fracture like Houston's," she says to me, just to be reassuring. His temperature's normal, he's clearly not sick, but she draws blood anyway. "Maybe it's bone cancer."

"Bone cancer!!" My voice goes up about 10 decibels.

"Relax," she says, "I've never seen it in horses."

The phone rings at dinnertime again. It's Vet, this time with good news. There's no sign of a fracture, no sign of the problem infiltrating the joint, and no sign of the inflammation wrapping around the pastern bone. She concludes that Calvin must have simply hit himself. She prescribes two weeks in a stall, mild riding in the indoor, and a course of bute.

We go up to the barn after dinner to turn out the horses and check on Calvin. Though he looks unhappy to have been left in the barn by himself, he still pricks his ears as I walk down the barn aisle to check his water and leans into my rubbing of his forehead. He may even be ready for Fair Hill Horse Trials in August.

July 21

Redmond is a beast in a jumping lesson with Grace She has us jumping 3-foot fences, and Redmond takes their puny size as license to blow them off and charge them. Grace gets annoyed with my speeding bullet when he runs up to a small vertical, starts to leave the ground, but then changes his mind at the last millisecond and puts in an extra pat before jumping. I feel like a human yo-yo. Henceforth we circle and pull up before and after jumping, until my good pony's evil twin has a semblance of a half halt again. At least with the Redmond I have today, and the Julia he has today, I have to keep ahold of his mouth in order to check his enthusiasm. Unlike my other horses, with whom I've been working on a much softer ride, if you give Redmond his head he'll run off with you. Grace wants me to slow the canter down, to keep the connection to the base of each fence, and in general, to think about dressage over fences.

I have a nagging suspicion that Grace is not fond of Redmond. She admits she cares less for the eager beavers who like to drag their riders around a course and prefers the shyer, push-along types like Surf. Because Redmond is not her cup of soup, I worry that her coaching won't instill the confidence I'll need to ride the bigger fences and see me through the Three Star. Moreover, Grace won't be at the second Intermediate Surefire Horse Trials this weekend.

I pick up the phone to call my other coach . . . would she mind if I joined in her Intermediate course walk this weekend?

"Not at all," she replies.

My brain is a lake, and there, swimming rhythmic laps near the shore, is Coach, commenting on Redmond's unique style of jumping. "The faster he goes, the better he jumps," she calls out to me pacing the shore. Farther out in the cooler, deeper water she glides, flips over onto her back. "Redmond is a freak of nature that way," she cries. I want to swim out to her, ask her what she means by that. But I've forgotten my suit.

July 23

The first crickets of the season, chirping right outside my back door, harbingers of the end of summer, as well as my forthcoming birthday in August. Six legs, wings, antennae. I mark half a century with their song. What do they mark with mine?

Purcellville, Virginia ·

I screw my courage to the sticking point and let Redmond run his first Intermediate Horse Trials since his bowed tendon. His dressage is good. He's not as in front of my leg as I'd like, but I work hard to cover up that fact while trying to look like I'm not doing anything—i.e., the art of dressage and putting on a good show.

We show jump in cross-country attire—body vest, stopwatch, armband, lots of color—then go right to big terrain after warming up over pickup sticks. This is a recent tactic often used now at horse trials to make scheduling easier and more efficient. Though show jumping is where I get the most nervous, there are no worries today. Redmond jumps clean. There's a hold on the cross-country course because of a fall, so there's more time for both of us to fret. This is a new Intermediate course, and I question my selection for Redmond's first go at this level since his injury. You never quite know what you're getting with a new course. So far, there have been a number of problems—at the water, at the corner combination, and at the sunken road in particular.

Coach comes back on her fourth Intermediate ride. "Take the option at 10 and 11," she warns me. "Hold for four strides to the hay bales after the corner, and keep your eyes on the last element of the sunken road. The horses don't read it well."

Redmond jumps around like he designed the course. I take Coach's warnings to heart, though, and tack seconds onto my already slowish time at the option, get four strides at the corner, and ride determinedly forward with my eyes burning a hole in the sunken road when I feel Redmond's shoulders start to wiggle, signaling a potential run-out. I come off the course beaming and run into Kim Meier on my way back to the trailer. "I saw you at the water," she says, "Redmond looked just like his old cheeky self." And Kim doesn't pass out compliments much.

Barrett divulges my dressage score back at the trailer, as we're stripping off tack and throwing ice water on Redmond. He's been dying to tell me the news, though he knows better than to reveal my scores before I've finished. Barrett's a scoreboard hound, handicapping the circles and rails and combinations of my sport. That's okay, someone's gotta look if I won't, in the same way I refuse to get on scales. "You got a 32 and are fourth after dressage," he tells me. "You're laying third after show jumping, five lengths off the pace."

"Well, I probably moved way back down again after all of my time on cross country," I say.

I'd like to think my time faults were a function of caution, of my being careful and protective of Redmond's tendon. Although that may have been a factor, in reality our time penalties were probably more a function of my fear and rustiness in not having run Redmond at this level for a year. As it turns out, everyone else had a lot of time, too, and several had stops.

We pin our white fourth-place ribbon to the sun visor in the truck for all to see on Route 70, as well as for Katie and Chandler, who are sitting on Chandler's tailgate having a beer when we pull into the farm driveway. Barrett waves my fourth place at them, yelling from the truck, "Pay the lady! Pay the lady!" What a guy.

We'd put ice boots on Redmond at the event, and now we soak his front legs in Baden's knee tub. The tub has become a ritual for Redmond, who adores his ice bath. It's kind of like standing in a giant margarita with its generous ingredients of ice, water, salt, and Vetrolin Liniment—the one remaining question in my pony's eyes: *Where's the lime?* We turn him out for a while, bring him back in, pack his feet, mud his front knees down like he's a racehorse, dry wrap him behind, and put him to bed for the night. We toast to Redmond's return over Anapamu and crab cakes before we crash for the night.

July 25

Used to be, I'd try my best to have an inside day after an event to get caught up on office, house, and writing work. But my barn days have become too demanding, with more horses to ride and lessons to teach. If I'm in the barn by 7:00 or 8:00 A.M., I'm not through till 4:00 or 5:00. This leaves little time for my interior life, and today I get cranky at my patient husband as 5:00 P.M. turns into 6:00 before I get all of my barn work done. His days are much longer than mine, and he rarely complains. I contemplate cutting back—maybe back-burner Huey or Surf, let Surf's knee heal, let Huey retire for what would be his fourth time. The heat makes me want to quit the day before it's done—there's a 105-degree index out there, with promise of a hotter day tomorrow. The house AC unit chooses today to go on the fritz, so after pasta and night check, Barrett and the dogs and I head over to the pool barn to sleep.

It's blessedly cool over here. The second floor is at a third floor level, so that looking out those higher-up windows feels like peering from a widow's walk. I scan the dark horizon of the farm, and its waters are sleepy-still. I watch the lights of cars listing their way along old Route 88. The dogs and Barrett settle in more quickly than I do to this new sleep place, while I toss and turn, until Pie, the orange tabby who matches the interior pine walls of the pool barn and who lives over here with my mother's nineteen-year-old Ragdoll cat, Toynbee, jumps up on the bed, glad to have company for the night. She nestles beside Barrett and me, and all six of us fall asleep.

July 26

My days are getting even longer. A heat advisory is in effect, and Lord knows how far the mercury climbs. We bring in the mares and foals to get a break, and they seem gratefully cool and sleepy in their stalls. This gives me a chance to play with Ditto and Selery: Curious George and the Princess. Ditto is refined and elegant, just like her mother. She looks more like a little horse than a foal, perfectly proportioned, not gawky and awkward like most foals her age. Selery, on the other hand, is all legs and gangle, and still has his shaggy foal coat, which has bleached out almost to a buckskin, though we're pretty sure he'll end up a light bay. Selery is all over me when I go into his stall, but Ditto is more reserved and self-possessed, just like her mother.

By five o'clock, after a long day in the insufferable heat—lessons, rides, lunges, barn work—I'm wilting. I make a valiant effort to pull Huey out of his stall—my last ride—and hook him up in the cross ties. I look at him, he looks at me, and that seals it—back in the stall he goes, while I go in search of newly-fixed air-conditioning. I plop down on the couch, and that's pretty much where I stay until early bedtime. In addition to actual interior space, I'm craving more time for my interior life, but the demands of the horses and farm have been too great. I am feeling a little unbalanced, as if some decision needs to be made.

July 27

Calvin comes up lame during the weekly jog. We attribute this to the increase in his work. Vet had wanted me to get on him in the indoor the last few days, which I have done, and apparently his bone bruise has not held up to this intensified exercise. When the stack wrap comes off Surf before his jog, I notice an increase in the swelling that has now migrated below his knee. He is sound, however, so all is not lost, but I'm worried that the leg is trying to reinfect. It is 90 degrees by 9:00 A.M., and Barrett decides to bring in the mares and foals.

As soon as Ballerina gets in her stall, she starts to fuss—up and down and up and down. When she begins to paw and break out in a sweat, Barrett brings out the Banamine. But the drug does little to relieve her discomfort, and so he calls in the vet to oil her. Vet is away, and her associate assures us that Ballerina's heart rate and temperature are normal. Her bowel distention is only mild. Once oiled, we should monitor her progress, walk her, and hope for the best from this colic incident.

Ballerina spends the rest of the morning and early afternoon lying down in her stall and groaning from the pains in her stomach. Little Selery keeps nudging her, clearly hungry. When she won't get up, he stands over her and nurses while she's splayed out, and despite how miserable she feels, she offers the nourishment to her son.

The afternoon does not go well for Ballerina, and she continues to crash. When she's up, she's pawing and sweating; when she's down, she's thrashing and groaning. We repeatedly take her and Selery out to the paddock to walk and get her stomach to settle, but every few steps she throws herself down and won't get up despite Gregory and Barrett's and my proddings and punchings. Every hour or so we make an attempt at walking her, with little success. I call Vet's Associate midafternoon to report Ballerina's status and my concern that her condition is worsening. "Is she a surgical candidate?" she asks me. I don't quite know how to answer.

"I guess Barrett and I should talk about that," I say.

"Yes, now would be a good time to do that," she says, meaning that if we decide she's not worth the risk and expense of surgery, then we will opt to put her down if her situation does not improve. I call Barrett. Ballerina is his, and so the decision is up to him.

"No," he says, "We're not putting her on the trailer."

After teaching, I go back to the barn. Associate's car is still there, as are Katie's and Gregory's, though they should be long gone. I sense what's going down. I find all four of them in Ballerina's stall, pushing and pulling and slapping and kicking her to try and get her up, so she can walk outside one last time and see the blue sky and green grass before she dies—and so the vet can put her down in a place from which she can more easily be carted away. Her tongue is distended and her eyes glazed and the mare already has the look of death about her. But she won't get up. It takes us twenty minutes of coaxing, with Selery looking bewildered from the corner of the stall, before we're able to pull and prod his mother to standing, and lead her out under the apple tree just outside the mare barn. Within a minute, Associate has the pink barbiturate in her vein, and she's fallen over on her side like a bombed skyscraper. We all crouch around her and wait. There's nothing left to do but witness her final breaths and heartbeats. I pat her face and scratch her ears, and when her eye starts to soften and go limp, I try to close her lid, and when it won't stay shut, I hold it closed as softly as I can, as if I'm protecting her from one final indignity. We won't leave her until there's nothing left, but it's hard to tell, even with the vet's stethoscope, even after her sides stop heaving and eyelashes fluttering. Her muzzle keeps twitching, and her legs do, too, until minutes that are hours go by, and there's one final exhalation that lets us know she has escaped the body lying before us. Nothing is ever easy when you weigh 1,200 pounds.

Confused, two-month-old Selery whinnies from his newly imposed solitary confinement. Barrett moves Calvin, who is back on twenty-four-hour stall rest, next to the lonely foal. Selery calms some in the presence of Uncle Calvin, who seems pleased to be given something so important to do to break up his monotony. They touch noses through the stall bars, and then Calvin nestles up against the bars and finally goes to sleep as close as can be to the fretting colt. Why didn't I put myself in a stall next to Calvin when my father died? The foal will learn how to cope, how to drink the milk supplement from a bucket, and later to eat the milk pellets we will mix into his sweet feed. He will quickly learn how to live without his mother because he has no choice in the matter, because his own will to keep living and growing is that strong. I call Dave Wisner to ask if he will do me a favor: there is a horse to bury.

New York City

I plan to take the train to visit Caitlin, although I'm worried about leaving the farm so soon after Ballerina's death. Barrett comes into the indoor to say goodbye while I'm catching a ride on Redmond before I head for Baltimore's Penn Station. He has to take two of the lay-up racehorses back to Pimlico. Barrett leads Hot Kisses while Gregory leads Hillflower Grace out of the barn to the trailer. Redmond, cantering around the indoor, throws up some footing on the metal sides of the arena side doors. Hillflower Grace spooks, lunges, throwing Gregory to the tar-and-chip driveway, and falls down, degloving one knee to the edge of the joint capsule. It is a critical injury requiring emergency vet attention. The horse will need immediate surgery.

After making plans for her transport, Barrett comes into the house to say goodbye to me while I'm zipping my suitcase shut. "I'm a little low on confidence right now," he admits. I try to convince him that confidence has nothing to do with it, that both Ballerina's death and Hillflower Grace's unfortunate accident are freak occurrences. It's bad luck, nothing more.

"But if you or I had been leading her, it wouldn't have happened," he says. Maybe, maybe not. Secretly I question Barrett's decision to let Gregory handle the racehorses. Even the quiet ones. I won't say that to him now.

I arrive at New York Penn Station and stand in a long queue for a cab. When I finally earn one by waiting, I spend a good forty-five minutes battling the short twenty blocks through noon-hour traffic to my daughter's sublet on the East Side.

Caitlin's idea of showing me a good time is to comb the hot streets in search of food. I put on my walking shoes and we trek for miles, taking small breaks from pavement trotting to endure the Hades of the subway, which is about as pleasant as being locked in a stinky sauna. The restaurants are on a par with the subterranean tram: hot, cramped, dark, and noisy. I can't get the last few days out of my mind. But I'll bite my tongue a thousand times for the sake of my daughter, who wants to eat and eat as if she hasn't eaten since the last time I visited her—which is probably close to the truth. She also wants to show me her extensive knowledge of the city and new sophisticated ways after having lived on her own for the first time. Though she's only nineteen, she orders a mojito at dinner. "I'm the D.B.," she says, "the director's bitch."

This is the short version of her internship as a production assistant on the *Fast Track* movie set. The longer version is she gets to rub elbows with the rich and famous, especially with the star, Zach Braff—who has been one of Caitlin's idols ever since the movie *Garden State*—by running to buy him coffee when he wants it, either iced or hot.

I keep thinking about Ballerina. I call Barrett when I can get a minute—between all the hot walking on horseless cement and the lukewarm delight over the volumes of food Caitlin wants us to sample—to check up on Hillflower Grace. Maybe she can be salvaged as a broodmare. Although surgery is expensive, the owners have made more than $35,000 on her racing efforts in the past three months alone. The decision will be a difficult one. Racing can be ruthless, horses no more than commodities—and that's why it will never be a sport for me. I cringe to hear this—a three-year-old, who spooks and slips on our driveway, and now her life is on the precipice. Such a waste. Barrett sounds level, his confidence bolstered. Either that or he's putting up a good front for me. Several of the boarders have been passing the hat so we can find a way to keep the mare if the owners don't want her. Chandler can't get over how Barrett has lost one chestnut mare and now there's a prospect of this other one the next day. "I'll do her stall," she says.

"I'll buy supplements for her," Audrey says.

"I can hand graze her," Alex says.

July 29

Caitlin's sublet in Tudor City which overlooks the East River spurs on my claustrophobia. Its air-conditioning is as cranky as I am and only half works in one of the apartment's two tiny rooms. I yearn for the quiet of the farm as sirens squeal sixteen stories below. I find some new threads for myself at Anthropologie and get all dolled up for our second night on the town at Sushi Samba, a Japanese/Brazilian fusion place with a loud disco beat. Caitlin wants to go to a Russian bar after dinner where they serve exotic martinis and caviar. Though I've had my two-glasses-of-Chardonnay-for-the-day quota, I say yes, and we take yet another herky-jerky cab ride to SoHo and head down some basement steps into the intestines of another dark space. We order pear martinis. I don't hesitate to blink at her request. She loves putting on her sophisticated demeanor when she talks to the waiters, as if she's been ordering martinis since the day she stopped wearing diapers, although in her 5-foot-2-inch cutesy frame, she doesn't look a day over sixteen. Down our sleepy, already-buzzed gullets go the pear martinis, which assures that my headache will increase and expand well into tomorrow. I love my daughter, but our individual loves and perspectives have split, and I can't help counting the hours till I can escape this hot, noisy sea and return to the quiet of my bucolic existence at An Otherwise Perfect Farm. My mind wanders back to Ballerina and Selery, and to Hillflower Grace, whose fate is still in the balance. I ache to be with my overworked husband to help him through his current streak of otherwise perfect luck.

July 30

Over coffee and smoothies and scones at a neighborhood deli, Caitlin asks how her pony Sunny is doing. "He's okay," I say, "but he's still quite off." Caitlin has grown accustomed to our care of Sunny in her absence, as well as reports of his intermittent lameness.

"So what's wrong with him?" she asks.

"He's got old pony disease," I say. "Everyone has been asking what the new barn kittens' names are," I change the subject, "and I say I don't know because I haven't talked to Caitlin." I describe the kittens and their traits as I've come to know them in the short week since we've had them. Caitlin offers up Gabby for the purrer and Turtle for the gray tortie. "So Gabby and Turtle it is," I say. "They're good names," though I'm thinking not. I want to make her feel that she is still needed to name things. I drag out our last conversation. "Promise me you'll come visit soon," I say.

This will be the fate of my relationship with my grown children from now on——my never-ending requests for them to return to me. My mother did the same, and over the years, my excitement about returning to my childhood home in Warren, Pennsylvania, and to my parents waiting for me there turned into a middle-aged sense of dread and obligation. At least for now, Caitlin still looks forward to my visits and to spending time with me. She admits she doesn't want me to go. The streets are the quietest they've been since my arrival. I get teary as she locks up her sublet and we head out to find a cab. I hug her hard and climb in for yet another chrome-yellow roller-coaster ride to the train station.

The Nature of Longing

My lab, lame these past months,
has grown accustomed to running through it,

small chip floating in its bony sea
to some calcified recess

where it settles for a while,
returning her to the realm

of manageable pain.
She gallops across the farm,

chases Mr. and Mrs. Rabbit under the garden fence,
bounds up the driveway into the bruised dusk,

smiling with her whole body
when she pinballs back to greet me.

She cocks her head as if struck
by a new idea—the absence of pain,

defined by the memory of its opposite.
This morning, from my loft window,

the fog drapes itself over my ability to see
any farther than the backyard

hemlock or the barracks barn.
My back seizes up

as I pry myself to standing.
Everything goes lame,
and everything goes missing.

And absence can be
a beautiful thing.

This poem first appeared in *The Louisville Review*.

Seventh Heaven

Redmond

CHAPTER TWELVE

The First Time

⁂ **July 31**

Reveille on the farm—horses to groom and ride, lessons to teach. Surf's leg is better, Calvin's hind ankle a little better, too. Redmond's fine. Huey gets the gold star for his jumping efforts in a grid. Jerry's bored on his day off, spends the afternoon rubbing his tail on his stall guard. Selery is still in a stall. We try to buddy him up with my very first event horse, but It's My Show does too much squealing through the stall bars. We're back to ground zero with the orphan colt—we must find a pasture buddy for him soon. I'm leery of confusing Calvin with dual roles as babysitter and event prospect for fear that would be too much for his fragile, somewhat unreliable mind. I pull Pruitt out of his stall for my last ride of the day and see that in my absence he's popped another splint on his other front leg. It is hot and tender to the touch—and I hope it's not fractured this time. It will mean time off, possibly as much as a month. And just as I was making such good progress with the unruly adolescent.

August 1

I forget to walk upstairs backward. It might have been prudent to remember, as this is my birthday month, and I need all the luck I can get. How many wishes do we get in one lifetime? May John have a great time in Europe. May Calvin come sound. May Surf become a better jumper. May

Pruitt's new splint disappear. May Ballerina return from the dead. May I win the lottery to help maintain this farm. May I turn forty rather than the big 5-0. May I sail through the Three Star with flying colors. The genie in my lamp will be working overtime.

We turn out Selery and Show together. Selery's nursing instinct is still strong, and he tries to nurse from Show. Back in they come. "How about we graze Show just outside the paddock and let Selery run around inside?" I say. This method works pretty well. Then Barrett gives Show some Aceproma-zine tranquilizer and tries turning him out again with the foal. Selery still wants to nurse. Show turns his butt and lifts his leg, but only as warning. I am once again impressed by Show's tolerance. He was a mediocre racehorse, finishing third some twenty-seven times, and never made it in the eventing world because of his penchant for stopping in front of fences. The only time I could get him to jump reliably was to jump out of the dressage ring. Late in life he discovered his forte as teaser (lots of foreplay but no Shangri-las, just like his races), and now, apparently, as babysitter, though you wouldn't assume that the two would go together. Maybe after having teased the mares last year, he thinks he may be the dad. Selery seems happy enough, nibbles a few blades of grass in between nudging Show's penis. They both get a peaceful hour of sunlight and fresh air before Barrett brings them in again. The adjustment for Selery is going to take a while.

I was forty-seven when I lost my mother; Selery was two months when he lost his. I'm sure he feels an absence and a frustration that his suckling reflex is not being satisfied. He still seems ill at ease in his stall, backing up to the wall repeatedly, not knowing whether to eat the grain and drink the milk supplement, which don't taste as good as mother's milk, or pace the stall and stick his nose through the stall bars to try and make friends with the new guy next door who is at least the same color as his mother. Rarely do I catch him lying down and sleeping. The foal looks ribby; he has lost a few pounds since his mother's death. Barrett makes an appointment with a foal nutritionist, a specialty I never knew existed until today.

Both Pruitt and Jerry have the day off. I decide to let Redmond chill as well. That leaves just three rides for me—two hacks on Surf and Huey and a light flat session on Calvin, whose soundness I'll try to get a handle on. I obsessively watch his hind end in the indoor arena mirrors. The hips are pushing evenly, and the hip hike indicative of hind-end soreness is gone. This is the highlight of my day: Calvin is sound.

I call Dave Wisner to ask if he's found a horse. He thinks so, is excited about one that hasn't vetted yet. Dave is hunt master of Mount Carmel Hounds. He is looking for another hunt horse to replace his best friend who died last winter in a paddock accident. "If it doesn't work out, get back to me," I say.

"Oh?" he asks.

"Would you ever be interested in leasing Surf Guitar?" I say.

August 2

A crazy day in the heat with rides and lessons and jump patterns to set up. Dessert is a meeting with Dave Wisner, who is building a slide jump in our front field. I try to use the farm's undulating terrain to best advantage when it comes to our cross-country schooling course. This one's my idea: small 2-foot to 2-foot-9 logs that Dave has anchored at the top of the front-field hill that we will jump before running down the steep grade on the other side. It's a solid question I've not seen much on schooling courses, although I have had to jump slides in competition.

"Do you have a minute more?" he asks, after we finish our planning session. "Were you serious about the offer of Surf Guitar?" Although yes, I was, my heart sinks: it is hard for me to give up on a horse, although I know that taking a break from Surf would be the right thing for both of us. It wouldn't be fair to ask Surf to jump the Intermediate fences. My back is still aching from having wrenched it a couple of weeks ago when Surf found a deep spot to a big stadium fence, made a muddle of it, and I nearly came off. With the Fair Hill Three Star on the horizon, I need to play my cards like a boxcar bandit. Riding a horse who toys with my self-confidence at the upper levels is not the way to go. "How big is he?" Dave asks. At 6 feet, 4 inches, Dave likes a huge horse, but when we go into the barn and stand next to Surf Guitar, it's Dave's eyes that get huge.

"I have every confidence that this horse would be big enough for you," I boast.

Surf stands at 17.3 hands, far bigger than most, bigger than any other full Thoroughbred I've had the pleasure to know. I tell Dave the short version of the long story of Surf Guitar. It's late, past cocktail hour, and I've had a long day. Dave is a good friend, and I know he would take good care of Surfie for a while. Even so, I can't help but question the steely wheels I've put in motion.

I confess to Barrett what I've done, and surprisingly, he's in support of Surf learning a new job to help his old one. I call Vet, who's back from Nantucket. I hear her new baby fussing in the background. "Oh, poor Ballerina," she says. I can feel how sorry she is about our loss of the mare she helped take care of for six years and about little Selery's fate. I may not always agree with Vet, but I know she cares about the horses in her charge. I report that Calvin is still oscillating between sound and lame, and she suggests we have a meeting about him in the morning. "This is the first horse you've lost to colic at the farm, isn't it?" She returns to the subject of Ballerina. I think of all the colic incidents we were able to resolve over the years. This one, however, was shocking in its speed, intensity, and outcome.

Barrett and I head up to the barn for night check. The dogs run off as is their custom, just under enough fence boards and far enough away to say they did, looking back over their shoulders for us every few strides. I slip into Selery's stall to see what he's up to, and when I find him lying down, I lie next to him and scratch his neck and muzzle for a while, while he feigns sleep. I have a confident new thought that this foal and I will be fast friends for a long time. I felt this way about Surf Guitar when he first came to the farm as a yearling. I knew with the same kind of knowledge I now have in Selery's stall that one day we would get him back. We had to work to make it happen, and we had to be patient. We waited for four years while he made a lot of money for people who never understood that the real money to be made is in slipping into a stall at night check and lying down beside an orphan colt when he'll let you.

August 3

The riding director of Garrison Forest School often comes to our farm with a group of students to cross-country school. On one of those visits, the director encouraged Barrett to sign me up for a show jumping clinic at Garrison.

It's hard when a clinic instructor has never seen you ride, knows nothing about you, and knows only a little more about your sport. There are three horse-and-rider pairs in the 3-foot-6-inch lesson, and I'm the sole eventer. The other two rode yesterday in day 1 of the clinic. I feel like a guest who's arrived late for the party.

The clinician asks for some background information on me and Surf, then scrutinizes our riding as we warm up. I warm up with dressage work—stretching, all three gaits, a little shoulder in, leg yield, turn on the haunches. He says I'm too restrictive and have two positions: two point and sitting in the saddle. I need to develop one that's in between.

I explain my difficulties with Surf. He tells me before he even sees the horse jump that he rushes to his fences because I'm too tight. He wants me to build more canter, then decrease the stride before and after the fence. "Start with more, and end with less," he says. This advice is nothing that I've heard before. The clinician thinks that I promote a crooked horse because I'm crooked myself. He's right about that. He wants me to look down at my horse's outside ear. I try it, but it makes me dizzy. He tells me that I'm riding to see my spot and not riding the rhythm of the canter. "That was shockingly awful," he yells as I land after a line of fences. He says that what we eventers ask our horses to do is unreasonable—jumping into water, across ditches. He's delighted when people bring a horse to him and complain how the horse doesn't bend. "Finally, I have a straight horse," he says. "I love it when horses don't have any dressage training. It makes my life so much easier." He's looking right at me when he says this.

"There's straight and rigid and there's straight and flexible. Where I come from we teach horses to be straight by teaching them to bend," I blurt.

Despite the ordeal, Surf tries his heart out. I'm proud of him, but I allow myself to feel unnecessarily bad on our way home. I make a mental note: no more clinics with new people until I've audited one with them.

I hearken back to Jimmy's clinic exercises, simplified and geared for success, a critical ingredient in an educational setting, particularly when the clinician is dealing with horse-and-rider teams he's never worked with before. Now that I'm teaching, I tend to view all riding lessons a little differently, more from the teacher's than the student's perspective, which is giving me new ideas for my own riding, as well. Finding the right exercise for the horse-and-rider team is half the battle——then a quarter is progression of the exercise, and maybe another quarter is constructive criticism embellished with lots of encouragement.

I had some horrendous teachers at the Iowa Writer's Workshop who were fabulous poets. In fact, there are similarities between riding and writing teachers. There's no money to be made in either eventing or poetry, and the only ways to make a living in eventing are to teach and to buy and sell horses, and the only way to make money as a poet is to teach, as well. But it doesn't make you a good teacher just because your passion requires you to teach in order to eat, nor does it make you want to become engaged in the art of teaching. What do they say?——something like good teachers are born, not made. My father, who had earned his Ph.D. from Princeton and used to teach there, was an example of a horrible teacher. As I was struggling to learn the sport of tennis that would never come to me, I took a few lessons from my father, who was also a nationally ranked tennis player. I remember him screaming at me to "Hit the ball! Just hit the ball!" Occasionally, he'd expand his repertoire to "Look at it, and hit it!" But he didn't know how to break down the parts of tennis in a simple, well-articulated fashion, with a systematic program in his head, a series of exercises that would lead me to success. I got frustrated early and gave it up.

August 4

Vet's Associate returns to the farm to take more pictures of Calvin's hind leg. We get the bad news several hours later, after a long day of heat and rides and lessons——a hairline fracture at the front of the left hind pastern about the length of my pinkie fingernail. This is similar to Houston's comminuted fracture in his front leg. The difference is that Vet has caught the problem in Calvin, we hope in time for it to be corrected and healed. I had feared the worst when Calvin wasn't getting better and when any form of exercise made his lameness worse. The chances of having two horses within five months of each other display a hairline fracture in a pastern joint are one in who knows how many million. I scan our management, turnout, nutrition, shoeing, training. I can't come up with anything that would help explain the commonality of the injuries. Neither can Vet nor Barrett. Vet attributes it to chance and my unusually bad luck.

I knew I should have walked up those old month's stairs backward when I had the chance.

What it will mean for Calvin is four months in a stall with a Robert Jones bandage. New x-rays reveal that Pruitt's new splint is fractured, too. This is less of a problem because the splint bone is a non—weight-bearing bone, but it will still mean six weeks in a stall and yet another enormous bump for the rest of Pruitt's life on the inside of his other cannon bone. I feel like crawling under a rock. Barrett's and my evening is fraught with heated discussions. When I start to feel sorry for myself, Barrett steps in. "I'll tell you what bad luck is," he holds up his compromised paw. "You've never been badly hurt by a horse. That's good luck. You have enough money to help supplement the farm. That's good luck. You got Redmond through two Two Stars, Huey through a One Star, and Surf through a One Star with a bruised foot. That's good luck." He goes on: "You've got two wonderful children."

I think of John, Eurailing with his buddies from Amsterdam to Milan. Another swig of wine. Caitlin calls in a whisper. She's still on set and can't talk, yet she's dying to be calling me from a movie set. I take a deep breath. At the back of my mind, I hear Rainey Andrews, whose luck with horse injuries about matches mine, shrugging her shoulders over some recent bad news and saying, "That's horses for you!" And so it is. It is what it is. How does the song go? "Thaaaat's life."

August 5

I travel to southeastern Pennsylvania with Redmond, who jumps around Coach's ring like a maniac. He starts out a little slow and wary, as if he were waiting for me to put the breaks on and try to contain his energy. But once he realizes that my leash is looser, he takes over, pricks his ears, and attacks the fences.

I've brought him here without telling Grace I've been leery of her tendency to change Redmond's overly enthusiastic style of jumping. It would be one thing if he brought the rails down, but he jumps well out of his speed and aggressive manner of going. But maybe Grace is right— maybe his zeal will get him in trouble at the bigger fences. Something tells me that if I interfere with him too much, that will cause a problem, too.

Coach jacks the fences up, and my eyes get big, not having jumped 4-foot jumps with Redmond since his return. I need to do just that, to get my own eye back up to this height before I go into my first Advanced show jumping course in a couple of weeks at Millbrook Horse Trials.

I tell Coach that I would like to try to get Redmond to Fair Hill. "If he's sound, I wouldn't wait," she says. Who knows what will happen to the horse next spring? I'll have to muster the gumption somehow, and part of that process is to have enough faith in the way Redmond goes and not fiddle too much with his jumping style.

I have a long talk with Coach about my horses and all of their current troubles. She takes me around her barn and reintroduces me to her horses. There's one who's been recently diagnosed with ulcers. Another with Lyme disease. There's her best mover and jumper, who is coming back from colic surgery. Her Advanced horse, who has torn his check ligament. I read between the lines: in a barn full of competition horses, they all have their problems at one time or another. She's heard through the grapevine about my recent difficulties, including Ballerina's death.

"Who in the world did you hear that from?" I ask.

"Julia, you need to get yourself some new neighbors." In other words, someone is talking.

I don't know what I will say to Grace, if I say anything at all. I believe in being up front, but I've found it hard to be mobile between instructors in this sport. It's not at all like taking different classes from different professors at college, which is the way I wish things were in eventing. Grace doesn't seem to appreciate Redmond in the way I need my coach to appreciate him if I am going to cultivate enough guts to get us through Fair Hill. I need Redmond's instructor to have as much faith in him as I do. Coach has faith in the horse and Grace has faith in the rider, and right now I need both kinds of religion. East must meet West. Hail Mary, Mother of Buddha.

Downington, Pennsylvania

Pleasant Hollow Horse Farm Horse Trials. Surf Guitar is second after the dressage test of his life with a 34.5. He flies around the Preliminary cross country, pulling both a front and hind shoe in the process and ending miserably sore. We have to scratch him from the competition and not finish show jumping. I am surprisingly not unhappy about this. Last night he pulled the wrap off his knee all by himself, and when we found the huge mummy unwound in the morning, his timber knee was about twice its normal not-so-normal size. Something needs to change. I decide that we need to lance the knee and give Surf Guitar time off. Pleasant Hollow will be his swan song for a while. Still, his good effort today makes me want to continue on with him, when the continuing is right, and not give him up to Dave as a foxhunter.

Huey's dressage is not so good. I can never seem to mend the tension that shoots through our bodies every time we trot down center line. As soon as there's tension, there's a shortening of his already short step and a stiffening in my already big brittle hands. He pulls his way around cross country and jumps clean. He's too strong, and I have to work harder to get him organized and balanced before the jumps, so we end with a smidgeon of time over the optimum. Then he produces a flawless show jump round and finishes fourth. This, along with Surf's dressage, are the highlights of my day.

Having left at 3:30 A.M. so I could walk the cross-country course before dressage, we pull back into the farm driveway around 7:00 P.M., just in time for cocktails and dinner, which Barrett mercifully provides from India Palace. I practically fall out of the truck, my back is so sore. An appointment with the physical therapist is in order. My bad back is my perpetual timber knee, though there's no easy lancing in store for me.

August 8

I wake and can hardly move. My back shouts pain with each rollover in bed. We used to joke about having to turn off the alarm clock with our elbows, but we can't joke about it anymore. I tumble from my Tempur-Pedic mattress onto the floor toward the stretches and exercises I rely on to help me limber up enough so that I can get on my first horse. I down four Advil and—what the hell—a couple of muscle relaxants for good measure, making a mental note that I should call the physical therapist for a dose of electricity, moist heat, massage.

Barrett gets not-so-good news from his orthopedic surgeon after an ultrasound of his bad hand. The vibration of the farm machinery has caused the plate in his wrist and arm to rub against the ligaments, creating pain as well as further damage. He is advised to lay off the equipment for a long while—an unrealistic option when you're a farmer. We spend part of our afternoon in a business meeting, discussing choices—whether to hire someone to do the grounds work, the mowing and lifting, the fence repairs, and the countless other facets of farm maintenance requiring tools that vibrate, spending money we don't have right now. Whether to keep Katie or let her go. Whether to put the event horses on the back burner, to which I give only the most fleeting of considerations. How to rearrange the farm and our schedules to accommodate the changes in our bodies. Or whether to sell. We always come back to this topic of selling when things aren't going well, and we always throw the option out. But we end this discussion without any answers. We'll return to the painful subject tomorrow, and the next day, and the next.

I find myself down to three horses with Surf, Calvin and Pruitt on vacation. Lameness in horses, like a lot of things—including the writing of poems, in my case—tends to come in threes. I'm grateful that I have as many other sound and willing event ponies to fall back on in a time of drought. Good ol' Huey rises to the fore, once again. And of course, Redmond.

August 9

I can't get old fast enough. Twenty days early, I'm taken out for dinner by mutual geezers to celebrate my fiftieth. I share the birthday with my friend, David Fenza—same month, day, year, and state. Barrett offers the first toast: "To November 29th, 1954, when all of your parents were having sex!"

Fenza and I were in graduate school together, along with my ex-husband. That was half our lives ago. Michael Collier and his wife, Katherine, have organized the party with E. J. White, who once waited tables with David at various chichi restaurants in Baltimore and has become one of my most enduring pals. Jean-Claude is with us tonight, too. Jean-Claude waited tables with David and E.J., then moved up the ranks to own his own restaurant in Baltimore's choice Inner Harbor, where we literary desperados would meet for a drink or two or three in the early days of our life in Baltimore in the eighties. Michael and I started out as career peers twenty-five years ago, struggling to get our first books published. We both eventually did, he with a much more prestigious press than mine. That, along with being offered a position at a university, instantly skyrocketed him to a different plane of success. I tell him about my nonfiction project and ask whatever became of the one he was working on about his dives in a deep-sea ocean pod down to the absolute bottom of everything. He shrugs his shoulders and tells me that nothing ever came of it, but I press him. This is where we can connect, and I am eager to hear more about another poet's experience writing all the way across the page. "The great thing about prose," Michael says, with his signature warmth, "is that you can always write it." The chronological nature of my piece gives me something to write about every day, and so I shake my head as if I agree with what he's said. But I don't, really—I probably could get as blocked writing prose as poetry. No one at the table wants to talk much about writing. Put a group of eventers together, and horses and eventing are all you'll ever hear talked about for the night.

For our fortieth, Fenza gave me a bottle of Nuits St. George Burgundy with a note attached: "For drinking on our 50th birthdays!" No one can believe that I've kept the wine for ten years to be consumed this night. I'm afraid it might have turned after all of my hoopla about the gift. The nine of us only get a dollop each of the precious liquid and toast to our fiftieth, and then to our sixtieth, and sip what is a full-bodied mature wine, with notes of currant and pear—even if it is slightly over the hill. It is as complex as I hope to be at sixty—wiser for the years and yet with hints of my youth that can be tasted if I'm still the sort of person whose life is based upon my imagination.

These friends were mine and my ex-husband's during graduate school, when we were as frivolous and young and as ready to consume as any Chardonnay, before marriage and after, and through the early years of parenthood. Our cravings changed, and my husband's and my paths diverged, much to the sadness of these same friends. Though I have tried and tried, I cannot shake off that old identity as Jack's wife when I am sitting at a dinner table, sipping something I have managed to horde for so many years.

August 10

My concentration is broken by the cardinal flying into my loft window in search of her mate. She has come around the house, in Caitlin's absence, to bother with my window instead of my daughter's, and the rat-a-tapping and flutter of frustrated wings against the glass, along with our house cat Bitten's incessant growling for attention without Caitlin to give it to her, makes poignant what is missing. I have nothing on these windows to pull down or close to deter the bird from hurting herself against my window. As for the cat, I toss her outside, knowing that with the next open door, she'll dash right back in again, afraid of the loud, big prehistoric birds screeching their sweet songs.

I am trying to settle Jerry after his steeplechase career. I trot fences and halt to calm him and reintroduce him to the half halt. I head him to the third element in a line of fences. He swerves and ducks out of the oxer at the last minute, and I tumble down. I jump up, trying my best to seem unfazed. "Did you wrench your back?" Barrett shouts from across the ring. I ought to know better: if disaster is going to strike, it always does when Barrett is helping me jump school. His presence gives me just enough confidence to go too far.

"It's already wrenched," I say, bending over to unlock my scaffolding. I could tell as I was going down that I wouldn't be seriously hurt, reminding myself of one of the great laws of gravity that gives you foreknowledge in transit. I jump up, tell Jerry how naughty he is, find the stirrup and my balance and strength to get on the bastard from the ground. I ask Barrett to deconstruct the jump so it's not so scary to the big, brave steeplechase horse and proceed with the school. All the gold stars today turn out to be made of copper.

August 11

I jump Huey and Redmond. They are clearly both ready for Fair Hill Intermediate Horse Trials this weekend. The day is relentless with heat and lessons. My student, Dan, in particular is a challenge. We have followed each other around from instructor to instructor, starting back ten years ago when we first met when working with Kim Meier and

Marty Morani. We've been riding peers for years, and now he's come to me for help with his new horse, with whom he's been having difficulties in competition. Dan, like me, is plagued by strong hands and weak legs. I consider asking him to ride upside down. If he could put those hands in the stirrups and take the reins with his toes, he'd be ready for Burghley. When his horse begins to stop in front of fences because he is pulling on his mouth, I suggest he reverse his aids. But Dan is also plagued, as are most of us, with not always being able to translate what he can mentally process into a physical reaction. Dan also talks at the speed of light and is sometimes difficult to understand, so about half of what he says goes over my head. He is also a good friend—will fix my computer or chop down a dead tree at the drop of a hat. And so our relationship is multifaceted *while* being conducted in a foreign language. He tells me he can't ride this horse with low, soft hands because his other coach has told him to raise his hands and ride the horse up into the bridle. "Won't you at least give my way a try? If it doesn't work, then you don't have to come back," I advise.

He makes another go of it and ends the lesson on a good note. Little does he know that my insides are roiling with uncertainty about whether I've directed him wisely. I've only been teaching for a few months, and I'm the first to admit that I don't have all the answers.

Fair Hill, Maryland

Horses fare better than humans in blazing heat. For the most part, the horses are fitter than their riders, and it's the level of fitness that determines how well an athlete can cope with the heat. Horses also eat and drink properly, unconcerned with how they might look in a bikini. Plus, they descend from creatures bred in the desert. In the case of Surf Guitar, that would be a camel.

I put the double bridle on Huey to help with the increased difficulty of the Intermediate dressage moves. He is relaxed in warm-up but tenses, as usual, as we trot down center line. Still, he's quite rideable and keeps his cool throughout the test. The judge crucifies us with a 50 for being behind the vertical—when a horse tucks his nose toward his chest so that his head is no longer perpendicular to the ground, signifying that the horse has come off the rider's aids. I don't feel the problem from his back, so I don't correct it. Barrett's take is that any time you score your age or better, you deserve a prize.

Redmond's dressage ring is running late. We have to kick rocks in a shadeless hundred degrees until it is our time to go, while Katie gets Huey ready for stadium and cross country back at the trailer. Which means no water for Julia. By the time we trot down center line, I am seeing Little Dippers, Andromedas, Cassiopeias. I am desperate to get the test over with. Redmond is sluggish to my leg—no small surprise in this cauldron—but still manages to pull off a 38.

I drink three bottles of water before heading down to stadium and cross country. Huey jumps well and ends with only one rail, then flies around cross country slick as you please. When you're a Jet, you're a Jet all the way. When we pull up at the finish, it feels like we've crossed into Hades. Huey's sides are still heaving when we arrive at the trailer. I have to pass him off to Katie long before he has caught his breath.

I down some more water before heading back out. Redmond attacks the stadium course, is clean and fast. As we're walking over to the cross-country start box, the stadium clocker calls out to me, "Fastest time of the day!"

"A little nuts," I say. "Good, but nuts."

Redmond keeps his horns down around the cross-country course. I wrestle with him to get him back before a jump or combination, but when I settle into the saddle before a fence, he takes advantage of my signal, increasing his speed and rhythm, but still managing to jump well. He thinks he knows it all, and I think I don't know anything. I'm beginning to realize we're both right.

When we get back to the trailer, Katie is still cooling Huey out—he's in the ice boots now. I pass Redmond over, who's panting and heaving. It takes a solid hour to get his breathing to return to normal. That means a lot of ice and water and walking. Then ice boots and electrolyte paste, Bigel Oil and alcohol wash for both, leg wraps and long grazes in what little shade we can find.

Once the horses are as cool as we can get them in this heat and snoozing by the side of the trailer, I search out Grace's rig to find her sitting on a bucket, enjoying a Gatorade after a Training cross-country run on a student's mare. "Well?" she asks me. "How did it go?" She wonders when I'm going to make a decision between the Radnor Two Star and Fair Hill Three Star.

"I don't think I want to do Radnor again," I admit. "It's the long version, and the footing on Radnor's roads and tracks sucks." Fair Hill will offer a short format without roads and tracks and steeplechase. "I almost think Fair Hill would be easier on Redmond's legs," I say, but dreading the increase of guts that his rider will need to negotiate the monster fences at the Three Star.

The season must go perfectly for the Three Star to happen, and perfection is not normally in my small lexicon of equine experience. If there's a hiccup in the next month, we'll be packing our bags a week early for Radnor. I neglect to tell Grace how I've hooked back up with Coach. I do tell Coach, however, and admit to her that I'm not sure what to say to Grace. "Maybe not saying anything is okay," she suggests. "Sometimes things just have a way of sorting themselves out." I'm hoping that all the pieces of this fall-season puzzle will fall into place, but something tells me a lot of head scratching is in store for me.

It's late afternoon before I find out that Redmond was fifth this weekend. We head out of the show grounds toward home. It's early evening before it dawns on me how well we have fared in the awful heat, and very late after the horses are munching hay in their stalls before I settle into the realization that we just might be Millbrook-bound next weekend. Our first Advanced run in a year.

August 14

I run my hands up and down Redmond's legs about a million times before Gregory jogs him up our driveway, sound as a dollar. Big sigh of relief as I tack up Jerry—my only ride of the day. I head out with him and the dogs on a long early-morning hack to "beat the heat," as my father used to encourage us to do, whether it was starting a road trip or mowing the lawn. Today it is already 90 degrees at eight in the morning, and it will be hard to outrun. We aim straightaway for Baden's Stream. It takes a little coaxing on my part to get the ex-racehorse to walk down the steep, rocky grade to the pool of water that he gingerly enters as the dogs dive headfirst. When Jerry realizes there are no monsters on the streambed, his courage deepens with the water that rises to his belly. For the first few moments, his whole body is quivering with anticipation, before he settles into enjoyment of the cool bath. The dogs are paddling circles around us, in no hurry to get out. We stay a while longer, in no hurry ourselves to leave the calmest, coolest highlight of our day; the world stops, and we stop with it for a while. I plan the day ahead: I am taking off from farm-work to be on hand for Caitlin, home from New York for a few days. I would like to coax her here, as this used to be her favorite spot to hack Sunny. But New York has taken such a hold on her heart that she barely comes to visit the horses in the barn when she's home, let alone ride them. Neither John nor Caitlin ever got the bug, as my father also used to say. They chose to leave the farm and go out into the world to discover their own passions, completely separate from my own. It is probably healthier that way. After all, it's not like I followed my father into the oil business. Jerry takes a few steps in the stream to indicate that he's ready to move on. We negotiate our way up the rocky surface, then back down into another watery crossing, which this time he plunges into, until we are on the other side of the stream, heading for home.

August 15

Redmond enjoys the same trail ride and soak in the stream. He's feeling sounder than sound, ears pricked, ready for whatever's next. I get my rides done early so I can spend the afternoon with Caitlin. With three on the vet list right now—Surf, Calvin, and Pruitt—my riding time is considerably compressed. Surf's leg has exploded from the iodine blister that Vet packed in his knee when she drained it last week. On returning to the farm, I check in with Barrett to see if I can help out with the afternoon shift. "I hope she knew what she was doing," I say, walking by Surf's stall and wincing, on my way back to the house. I throw together a dinner of sun-dried tomato pasta, corn on the cob, cucumber salad, and garlic bread. It will be our little secret that Barrett inadvertently grated a nerveless part of his hand into the parmesan. Dinner is served just in time for John to appear, back from his two-week backpacking junket in Europe, with news of Milan's Duomo, the Van Gogh Museum in Amsterdam, the ups and downs of life in hostels, highlights of Rome, Paris, Florence, the statue of David, the Uffizi, Notre Dame, the Coliseum. We laugh until our sides split—we're delighted to be all together again. But Barrett is exhausted and needs rest early—with his bum hand, his days are unbearably long. Life has been made even harder by the challenge of getting the farm mowed, the cross-country jumps weed-eaten, and the barns scrubbed, decobwebbed, and tidied for all the visitors to the Jimmy Wofford clinic happening here over the next couple of days.

August 16

Jerry the Racehorse shines as Jerry the 2-foot-6-inch event prospect on day one of the Jimmy Wofford clinic. It's nice to hear Jimmy's little pearls of wisdom again. Today he focuses on what makes a bad jump bad. It doesn't have to do with where the horse takes off, or even how he jumps the jump, but whether the horse and rider are in sync—if the rider gets left and yanks on the horse's mouth, then that's a bad jump, says Jimmy. Or if the rider leans forward too early, causing the horse to lose his balance and chip in a stride, then that's a bad jump. Makes perfect sense to me. So why worry so much about where the horse is taking off? Just try to be prepared. I love Jimmy's method because it doesn't require a lot of talent on the rider's part. You don't even need a good eye. You can have your boots on the wrong feet, your undies on backward. Well-trained horses are clever enough to post bail for their felonious riders.

Jerry is on the muscle, but he's not rude, jumps well, and is listening to me. "He's crazy but he's not stupid," Jimmy says. As an aside, I tell Jimmy the history of Jerry, and how Barrett and I are wondering whether to send him back to the races.

"What do you think?" I ask Jimmy, as if his blessing would be ammunition for my Saturday night special.

"Our sport is changing," Jimmy says with a sigh. "You can't trust your old instincts anymore. One day, this would have been *the* horse—actually, he's my kind of horse: he's a game Thoroughbred who can jump the moon—but you'll spend year after year saying, if only I could get him to relax in dressage. You need an R. J. Renegade to be successful in our sport, nowadays; you need a Twinkletoes."

"I just want to get through a Three Star before I'm done," I say.

"You need a Zydeco, then," he counters, referring to Gretchen Butts's relative of Redmond who took the talented adult amateur all the way.

"But I've got Redmond!" I say. "Redmond's back!"

"Redmond's back?" Jimmy says, and I see him reminding himself of Redmond's jump. I intuit his silent calculations of the horse and his potential as a Three-Star horse. He's probably wondering if he has the scope. Or if I can keep the horse sound enough to do it. After all, in the six years I've owned Redmond, he's spent two of them on the shelf because of various injuries.

An amateur with my goals doesn't need the movement so much, but she needs the jump. And the mind. And the soundness. And all the luck in the world. As Kim said the day I bought Redmond, "No one ever died doing dressage."

August 17

Day two of the Jimmy Wofford clinic—cross country with Jerry in the 2-foot-6-inch division. We do ramps, we do steps, we do skinnies and ditches and water, and Jerry handles it all. He only has one skid off when three skinnies are presented to him in a row, with flags on the last element—he's never seen flags on a jump before. As soon as he realizes he's supposed to go through and not around them, he handles the question with ease. He bucks and farts on landing, because he's having a good time, not because he's naughty. It becomes clear how Diana Gillam fell off in his last hurdles race. Jerry is a bit of a player.

We sit down to crabs and Caesar potato salad, corn on the cob and fresh tomatoes from our garden, and as we're pounding and picking away, we muse that this is the fourth time we've had crabs this year—a family record. This will also be the last time we sit down together for a while, as Caitlin returns to New York tomorrow, and Barrett and I head off with Redmond to upstate New York and the Millbrook Horse Trials. John's friend, Andy, with whom he backpacked through Europe, stops by after we are stuffed and the newspaper tablecloth, with its heaps of shells and pickings, has been crumpled and tossed. He shows us digital pictures of their trip on his laptop. We see goofy close-ups of John and his gang, we see the Senegalese friends they made and pictures of the wrapped joints they legally bought and smoked. "They even came with bar codes," Andy pipes up. We see the Panama Reds in their official package followed by a shot of John stoned and lost in a haze of marijuana smoke in a neon pink hostel room. My son.

Then it's good night, sleep tight, good luck getting your visa at the Indian embassy in D.C. tomorrow, John. Good luck finding a ride to the train station, Caitlin. Your mother is off to chase her Sirens, somewhere in the depths of her own Indian ocean, which this weekend happens to be over some 4-foot oxer smack-dab in the middle of the lower Catskills.

August 18

I head up to the barn to finish loading all our gear. Little Selery and It's My Show are at the gate, standing head to tail, scratching each other's backs. It's a match made in heaven, and I thank my lucky Little Dipper for Show, even though he was a mediocre racehorse and a poor man's event pony. I can't say I blame him, with oatmeal for a knee. So many bone chips showed up on x-rays that Vet couldn't count them all. But he's an extraordinary teaser and an even better babysitter—just ask Selery, and he'll tell you. Selery sees me coming, stops his scratching, and walks over to the fence line to ask what's up. Hurry up, it's time—but I can't help myself. I take a few moments to do my own scratchings. I see more of his light bay, grown-up coat coming in and his baby fuzz falling out. He's the best time waster in the world.

We stop in at Coach's on our way to Millbrook for a jump school. Barrett is against the detour—too much like working on Friday to practice for Saturday's race. Coach puts the fences up pronto to Advanced height, which feels almost twice the size in her tiny sand ring where Redmond has to go skidding and scrambling around the tight turns to keep his momentum going. One vertical she jacks up to more than 4 feet. We get a good stride to it, but he stops, anyway—his first since the jump school right before his bowed tendon was diagnosed. I'm shocked, and Coach is a little surprised, too. "I thought you had it," she says, but then adds that I probably didn't have quite enough canter going. Redmond can't be beat, as long as he's going full tilt.

I'm not riding well today—I don't feel in sync with him and find myself either folding with my upper body too much or not enough. I feel claustrophobic in Coach's ring. Feeling out of whack with myself, I happen to look up at the 300-year-old dead tree at the side of the ring with a family of vultures glaring down at us. "That's where they hang out when they're not eating something dead," she explains. "Cheery, aren't they?"

I kick myself and start riding my horse, and the school ends well enough—except I can't get the stop out of my mind. "Do the jumps look big to you?" Coach asks. They resemble Mount Olympus.

"No, not really," I say, thinking this is the part where Coach will recommend I drop back down to Intermediate this weekend.

"You'll be fine, Julia," she says. I hope she knows what she's talking about.

Millbrook, New York

Millbrook Horse Trials is a big deal, plus it takes seven hours to get here. It is a Gold Cup Event and attracts distinguished company to the upper-level divisions. Both Advanced divisions are filled. I don't ride dressage till midday on Friday, which gives me time to ride Redmond early in the morning and then put him away for a lie down before the test. This strategy serves us pretty well. His dressage test is consistent and obedient. His only display of naughtiness occurs during his first flying change. The test scores so-so, but respectably, relative to the other scores in the division, with a 42.

I walk the Advanced cross-country course four times before riding it in hopes that the track will become second nature to me and the jumps will shrink by the final course walk. It's the same track as last year, but when you haven't jumped around an Advanced course in a year, the jumps have a way of growing. Four-foot-high solid fences with 9-foot spreads are big by anyone's standards. Size does matter.

I'm nauseated with nerves. Shouldn't I be at home in my rocking chair? Coach warms me up, and I hold it together for the excruciating minutes until I'm out of the start box. I gallop out toward fence 1 and 2. I try to establish a rhythm despite Redmond's pulling. Fence 3 is a huge oxer, whose back rail Redmond won't see until he leaves the ground. Redmond comes flying at it; he twists and still knocks it with his hind legs. I get jarred, but manage to stay on. Deep breath. Should I keep going? Fence 4 is a big drop oxer with a decorative arch over it, and he jumps that well. Fence 5 A and B is an open corner with a mammoth ditch under it and a turning three-stride narrow hutch after. Redmond comes running at the corner, balloons over it, and I barely get the turn to the skinny. Another deep breath. We've survived this far, keep going. Redmond starts to run and jump in more of a rhythm and is clever at the rest of the combinations. The water involves a drop in, three strides to a double bounce up a bank and over a log and back into water, and four strides to a skinny out. He's got it, and off he goes to attack the rest of the course, over the corner to the double-bounce bank complex, jumping a blind landing ramp with an arch over it and rolling down the massive slide on the other side as if we're tobogganing toward course's end. Just two more fences, then the finish flag. It feels as though we're flying, but we have a lot of time faults. I'm a slow boat when I'm unsure of myself, and Redmond's little pony legs feel like they're going a million miles an hour but don't cover much ground. We finish with 26 time penalties toward the bottom of the pack. Clean, but slow. Even so, I couldn't have asked for more from Redmond's first Advanced run since his bow.

We walk Redmond, and walk him some more. We spend the rest of the day with water, ice, and walking. We poultice Redmond's legs, and feed him, then graze him and put him to bed, all in time for the competitor's fiesta, where we drink and eat tacos and dance to a DJ's favorite platters, and let loose with the other competitors who had a good day. If Bonnie Mosser can swing from the tall rafters of the competitors' party tent, then so can I. They show a video of all the rides through the water and up the bank: there goes my Bucephalus bouncing his way through those mammoth combinations. We all have a good time admiring ourselves and dancing and drinking for the rest of the evening.

We wake to hangovers and more walking and grazing and a long day of waiting until the Advanced Divisions show jump late Sunday afternoon. I run into Peter Green on one of my grazes, and we take to chatting about the Advanced course. I admit to him how nervous I am. "What are you afraid of?" he asks. I pause. "Is it fear of failure or fear of getting hurt, or what?" he goes on, "because if you can identify what it is you're afraid of, then you're that much closer to understanding the fear and overcoming it."

"I guess I'd have to say fear of failure," I admit.

"There you go," he says. "Now you're that much further ahead." I'm not a hundred percent sure I've responded accurately. In reality, I think I'm afraid of a lot of things all at once, and the psychology of isolating my fear isn't all that simple. I'll have to come back to this concept, over time.

The show jump courses are huge and windy and technical. Coach heads out of the show grounds long before I jump, as she only has her Intermediate horses with her and needs to get home. I tag along on Bonnie Mosser's course walk. I wait for my turn. And wait. We have a good warm-up. Redmond is game and sound and jumps the practice fences well. I take Bonnie's advice to turn inside a fence on my way to fence 2, but my brain doesn't calculate the torque of the turn until I'm halfway around it. We never get quite straight to the next fence, and Redmond knocks that rail. Bonnie's advice was based on trying to save time on the course; she didn't realize how unnecessary that is with Redmond's unique whiz-bang show jump style. Redmond jumps the rest of the course well, putting to rest my fears that Thursday's stop in Coach's ring was a premonition. We may not have finished in the top five, but we certainly held our own this weekend in distinguished company.

We throw all our stuff on the trailer, wrap Redmond's legs, load him up and head out of the show grounds for the long trip home. Barrett proposes we take a short cut, veering more or less toward Canada to avoid I-95 at all cost. When I doze he gets the rig up to 90, so that I'll think it is really shorter. The truth is that he doesn't want this weekend to end. Hours later, we are still miles away from our tiny little planet of Upperco.

August 22

The days have cooled and have that end-of-summer ripeness I associate with back to school and my birthday. The crickets are well into their churning, too, always a sign that some end is forthcoming.

I arrive home to a box filled with copies of *Dark Track*. I hunker down at the house in the early A.M. to see off John, who is helping Mollie move back to my old stomping grounds at Cornell, with which John is falling in love because Mollie is there.

Redmond is glad to be home and will enjoy a couple of days of loafing in the paddock. Vet shows up to check on Surf's knee, which she had to relance and put in a drain while we were away. It has blown up again and may require surgery. Vet is trying to destroy the secretory lining that is holding the fluid and enabling it to reform, but the lining is proving harder to kill than she expected. The nasty process is nowhere near a resolution.

I have a lot of catching up to do, but Huey and Jerry come first. Huey has apparently forgotten his manners during his week of vacation. He breaks out of the cross ties and cuts his head on the cross-tie snap, then spooks and shies at every twig on the trail. I almost have to laugh at his jerky display of adolescence. It's nice to know such an old man would still want to burp the alphabet to crack up his classmates.

Jerry and I head over to Grace's in hopes of catching her for a powwow about Redmond's weekend and his conditioning schedule before Fair Hill. We chat for a good half hour outside her barn, while Jerry the Racehorse stands politely. We go back home a different way, where I get vaguely lost. I think about my early years of riding, when hacks were everything. I take a moment to look out over the rolling vista of my Maryland. Maybe I'd be happier if hacking were my only goal and not the high-powered events with the electric pressure of competing and succeeding. One day, I'll return to the quieter ride, the simpler life. But not quite yet.

August 23

I wake again to a cricket orgy and a feeling of general decline, every flower and tree and bush just a little past its prime. Only six more days of being in my forties. I do a little flatwork and office work, then spend some time sending out comp copies of *Dark Track* to poetry distributors and tack shops, in hopes that I'll be able to widen my audience beyond relatives and school chums.

August 24

Katie and I head out on the trail with Redmond and Huey. With Huey's nervous help, Katie opens the hand gate at the top of the O'Donovans' hill, and we press into the Degarmo's cow pasture. Huey has a Nervous-Nelly fit when he smells the cows, jigs his way down the hill, through a second hand gate, into the Dorseys' woods, and away from the bovine monsters. The ground is littered with old leaves that soften the footing on these trails that go on for miles, crossing over themselves. The overhanging trees will keep us cool. I start my stopwatch, and we begin to trot, letting the maze of trails take us where it will, constantly trotting. The Beginner Novice logs we find here and there are barely blips on Huey's and Redmond's radar. Around and around, under the trees, we listen to the metronome of our trotting horses, getting fitter as they go, pressing on toward Fair Hill—one-two, one-two, one-two—until my watch beeps twenty minutes and we pull the horses to a walk. The dogs are still following, though their tongues are starting to drag. They're glad time's up as we head back through the alpaca farm, stopping for a brief doggy swim in Dorseys' pond. The horses stand patiently watching Daisy and Simon do their Esther Williams routine—side by side, slo-mo across the parting water, with strokes we'd swear were synchronized. We head up the farm drive toward home, stopping to admire the miniature paint, who tears around his paddock as we walk by. "I want one of those," I say to Katie. Summer is almost over. Aladdin will be leaving the farm tomorrow and heading back to Goucher College. Goodbye, bitsy paint and Aladdin and son John, so soon off to seek his spiritual fortune at the head of the Ganges River. Goodbye, Caitlin, attempting to take another stab at Sarah Lawrence. And yet another decade of my life, so long.

The First Time

The first time I saw a horse race—
all steam & speed & spinning arcs
of delicate arms & muscles & bones,
a score of front legs digging into turf & tucking up
the exact moment hind legs thrust under bellies
& pushed off, three beats barely one times twelve
blurred shapes all willed by the heart to get there first—
I knew I would never leave this animal.

The race, the before & the hush
in the quiet after,
relaxed backs & rumps turned
to us, their various pastels
melding with the sky.

How does the horse know
to stick his nose out front to touch the wire
& win by a shadowy inch?
What makes us court perfection?—
the peculiar thing that makes us love & last.

This poem first appeared in my chapbook, *Scared Money Never Wins* (Finishing Line Press, 2004), and again in *Dark Track* (WordTech Editions, 2005).

✦✦✦✦✦ *Fall*

Into the barrel we go, over some Niagara.
—Ted Hughes, *Birthday Letters*

Huey

CHAPTER THIRTEEN

Rain is Rain

///

※ **August 25**

Cooper comes to shock wave Pruitt's splint and to give Redmond a once-over. "Looks solid to me," he says, as he runs his hands up and down Redmond's legs and over his back, which doesn't flinch at the vet's decisive foreplay. "You've just made my day!" I say brightly.

"This horse has made mine," he says.

Cooper recommends that we inject Redmond's hocks closer to the Three Star. We decide to wait until after his run at Plantation Field Horse Trials, mid-September.

We no sooner get Cooper out the door than Vet arrives to administer farm fall vaccinations. Vet knows that Cooper injected ACell into Redmond's bowed tendon and that he has been following the progress of the tendon's healing, but what she doesn't know is that we've decided to let Cooper follow Redmond's progress to Fair Hill, as well. It's a little like my game of playing multiple instructors. Coach knows Grace is my primary instructor, but Grace doesn't know that I've gone back to Coach for the occasional lesson on Redmond. I'm usually honest with people when it comes to lessons and medicine and have historically been the first to let a vet or instructor know when another was involved. But it's gotten me into trouble, too, when I've provided too much information and explanation, and I've ended up maddening or hurting. So this time I've decided to let sleeping dogs lie and be discreetly secretive—and let the situation work itself out. But I am sweating it this morning until Cooper gets safely out the driveway before Vet pulls in. "What should I do about these secrets?" I ask Barrett.

"Why not call your boyfriend and ask *him?*" my husband says, with an evasive wink.

He enjoys my squirm, pointing his six-gun at my boots and telling me to dance or lose my toes. Nobody but Barrett would schedule routine vaccinations on a tendon day.

August 26

We continue the Battle of the Bulge: Surf's knee. Vet has now lanced the knee twice, put drains in it, instructed us to cold-water hose it and squeeze out the fluid several times a day, yet the knee continues to be three times the size of a normal knee. Katie takes satisfaction in squeezing out the chunks of destroyed secretory lining and fluid. If it's been allowed to build up for several hours, the first good squeeze produces a jet spray of fluid across the shed row. Katie has the stomach of a moose, or a surgeon. "Hey, look at this," she says to Gregory, or the farrier, or to any other innocent passerby, and pop, there goes the knee again. Vet assures me that we will get to the bottom of the problem, though it may take several lancings, and that we should put off surgery until all else fails. I try to be patient, having long ago given up hope of a fall eventing season for Surf Guitar. I'm afraid we may have run over this good dog one too many times.

We play musical stalls in the barn, giving Redmond back his old one and giving Jerry a window view, but it necessitates moving Surf, at least temporarily, to the windowless corner stall, which makes him exceedingly grumpy. He pins his ears and lunges at all passersby. Selery gets the stall adjacent to the wash stall, so he's now closer to the action. Anyone entering the barn notices him and makes a fuss over the poor little orphan Andy. He plays his role to the hilt, loving the sweet smack of attention.

Barrett calls me from the barn. "When are you going to tell me that you want to keep Suave Rhapsody for yourself?"

"Well, yes," I say, "we need to talk about that."

Barrett was pushing to get Pruitt back in work sooner rather than later. Maybe with another horse to ride, I'd let Jerry return to his steeplechase career. I had sent Jerry away after Houston's death because I was feeling overwhelmed and somehow responsible for everything that was going wrong with my horses—and I needed to pare down in order to get myself back on track. It seemed like a good idea at the time, but I knew as soon as Jerry came home for a break that he wouldn't see a starter's flag again. Though he won a lot of money for us on the flat, he'd come home before he'd proven himself as a steeplechase horse, making the decision easier. And, truth be told, he's got one of the best minds and one of the cutest jumps on the farm.

A call comes in from Caitlin. "I'm in the hospital with my second A.D.!" she says, breathlessly. I'm thrown into a panic, searching my memory bank. When did she ever have her first A.D.? Have I overlooked some new venereal disease running rampant among college girls, or bakers, or movie set interns? "Yeah, she fell in a hole." My daughter is referring to a person, not an illness. "She stepped off a curb in Times Square and there was this big hole in the street she fell right into." The Hollywood hierarchical lingo comes back to me: assistant director, first assistant director, second assistant director, production assistant, then intern. "I told her that in all my years of riding, I'd never seen a worse fall." Caitlin loves to play the farm girl to all of her savvy city-slicker friends. Her background is certainly exotic to those whose idea of vegetation is a salad bar. "We're waiting for x-rays. They think she may have broken her wrists. I'm helping her," she adds. Ah yes, and the other well-played role: Florence Nightingale.

August 27

My ex-husband and his wife unexpectedly swing by the farm on the last leg of a summer's cross-country road trip. John arrives home road weary from Ithaca about two seconds before our surprise company pulls up. I invite them to stay with us, then spend part of the afternoon engaging in awkward chit-chat. My ex pets Simon, then asks where the bathroom is so that he might wash his hands. Good thing I can't see his reaction when he finds horsehair on the hand towels. Needless to say, he doesn't inquire about the horses, nor ask to visit the barns. They spend the late afternoon playing pool with John and then head out for a dinner of crabs. I know that John feels guilty for not having visited his father and stepmother earlier in the summer, and I want to help make this visit as easy as possible. That has always been my goal with my firstborn—to make things easy—and it is not always for the best. For some reason, I've let Caitlin struggle more than John, and she is stronger for it.

Jack and his wife will return later, after we're asleep, to crash in Caitlin's room. The history of my younger life married to my first husband, before the farm and Barrett and my life with horses and older children, visits me in my dreams. I'm grateful to wake to Barrett beside me, sawing away. Thankful that he was good enough to let this one slide.

August 28

It pours in the morning. I modify my riding schedule to include only flatwork in the indoor on Redmond and Huey. I can't complain—the ground has gotten hard, and we need the rain to soften up the footing if I'm going to trot Redmond into the three-day.

Chandler has a tough dressage lesson. She is on the verge of getting her horse on the bit but doesn't quite have the feel for riding a horse from back to front yet, nor for the kind of elastic connection needed to make it happen. She gets frustrated when Smarty throws his head up in the air. I tell her that she needs to soften within the connection and give him something in the reins to move into. She makes progress on one side and then loses it when she changes direction and has to start again. I tell her that it took me years of lessons to learn how to ride a horse into the bridle, but she wants it now. I try to make it possible for her, but I'm not good enough to teach her patience.

Hurricane Katrina makes her way landward and heads for New Orleans. She's a class 5 hurricane, a fact which rivets us to the weather channel while I make a feast for John and Barrett: prime rib and Yorkshire pudding, roasted potatoes and Caesar salad. I pooh-pooh the hurricane. I say it will never reach New Orleans. It will be downgraded shortly.

Everyone is making a big fuss over potential natural disasters after the tsunami. I get booed off the couch by John and Barrett, who are sure that the hurricane will not only reach New Orleans but will remain a class 5 after she hits land and then makes her way up the East Coast and all the way to the farm, where she will wreak havoc and change our lives forever.

Secretly, I crave the worst when it comes to weather—snowstorms, rainstorms, tornadoes, hurricanes. I can't explain this desire for the extreme, except that bad weather has a way of creating a kind of time warp where life as you know it stops and everything becomes a matter of survival. Like war, I would imagine, or illness. For people who are always marching forward with a million things on their plates, bad weather is a kind of reprieve from the ordinary: you get snowed in, and you have to stop what you're doing and dig your way out.

I've never been in a hurricane, although I have had a tornado come across my backyard at my old house in Maryland, and that was like nothing I'd experienced before. We hunkered down in the basement until it passed, and then spent days cleaning up our yard, cutting up the fallen trees, repairing the picket fence, cleaning all the debris out of the yard. We got it a lot easier than our neighbor, though, who had his roof ripped off.

I've never understood how anyone can call Maryland's a temperate climate—I've seen some of the most extreme weather ever in the twenty-five years I've lived here—and I grew up just south of snowy Buffalo. The weather patterns are changing, they tell us, as our expectations of weather change with them. I turn off the TV for my last slumber as forty-nine, just as Katrina is trying to make up her mind which city to visit first.

August 29

Katrina pummels the Mississippi/Louisiana state line. So much for my weather predictions. Early morning we are glued to CNN. I finally excuse myself to get my rides done, the last being a hack on Huey. We head to Baden's Stream with the doggies, who plunge in, with Huey right behind them. Huey and I watch them draw circles around us. Huey enjoys the water as much as the dogs. When I ask him to walk on, he's dead to my leg and wants to stay put. I can relate—I would love to spend the afternoon here—one of my favorite places in the world, with no one else around and the lush trees canopying and hiding us, and the deep water seeping into our ankles and knees, its coldness so delicious when we bend our heads to it and drink. But people are being pummeled by bad weather, even as children are expecting their mothers to come home.

After another news check, John and I head out for an afternoon together of lunching and working out at a local gym, then to the grocery store so he can buy ingredients to make me one of my five favorite foods in the world—cheesecake. He insists on buying three packs of candles so he'll have enough for fifty years, after I put the kibosh on the oversized candles, an enormous 5 and 0. He listens to some Senegalese rapper as he cooks, while I get work done in my office. If my son doesn't make it as a musician, there might be hope for him at Caitlin's famous bakery. There's not enough room for fifty little candles, so the cake ends up with only a handful, which I am able, with my half-century-old lung power, to blow out in one breath. I'm selfish this year. Everyone knows what I wish for.

August 30

Kim Meier comes to the farm with Test Run, to gallop our hills and point him at some of our cross-country fences in preparation for Loudoun Horse Trials. She is also returning one of our neighbor's horses whom Kim's had in training. The neighbor shows up with her daughter, plus two other horses and their Bichon Frise. As I'm getting on Jerry to get Kim's help with him over fences, another neighbor shows up to chat and watch the rodeo.

Kim asks me to trot the skinny fence. It seems unfair to ask Jerry the Racehorse to jump a skinny right off the bat. Sure enough, he runs out on the first attempt. We come again, and he jumps it fine. Kim wants me to do something different with my hands, shortening the reins until they're way up the neck and in front of the martingale and pressing into the crest with my knuckles while putting a ton of leg on the horse to make him come into the bridle. This strategy should encourage him to keep a regular rhythm to the jumps and not rush, as Jerry is prone to do, Kim explains. But the new position takes a bit of getting used to and is confusing to Jerry. He crashes through the grid of two jumps that Kim has set up. Next time through, the Belgian dog dashes into the ring, heads straight for the grid, and stands there as we come through. Jerry has to jump the dog, too. I bark at my neighbor that the dog has to stay out of the ring. I'm annoyed to have an audience I never asked for in my own backyard.

We move to the green-carpeted rolltop. Kim has me jump on a circle at the canter, which is difficult for my green bean, Jerry, but he handles the exercise well. He treats it like a steeplechase fence without the brush. On about the tenth circle, in midair over the jump, I feel something go. I think the horse is going down with me. I hit the ground hard. The horse careens off with the saddle down around his side before slipping in front of his chest. "The girth snapped!" Kim screams. I shake my head. There are stars in the dirt. "Are you okay?"

"I don't know," I say. "I guess so." Jerry can't rid himself of the skewed saddle despite his bucking. He gallops down the hill toward the barn, the saddle flapping wildly in front of him. I'm bruised and dirty, and a little bloody from some ring rash on an arm. I head back to the barn to collect my horse. Katie has already caught him when I get back down the hill. His front legs are cut up, and he's blowing hard and obviously rattled, but basically okay.

I study the culprit—sure enough, both elastics have snapped off the buckles—one of my favorite girths, which I have recently competed Redmond with. I shudder to think of the outcome had I been jumping a 4-foot-3-inch oxer in competition with Redmond instead of a 2-foot rolltop when the girth snapped. "I've seen two people end up in shock trauma because of a loose girth," Katie says. How it ended so minimally for Jerry and me, I'm not sure. Because the girth came completely off, centrifugal force threw me clear of the horse—always a safer fall. I'm sore, particularly on my right side, which took the brunt of the fall. I'm sure to get sorer over the next couple of days.

I clean out Jerry's cuts, throw out the girth, instruct Katie to check all the others, ease my worried horse, tack him back up with our newest Professional's Choice girth, say no thanks, no more today to Kim, and head out for a quiet walk hack to restore Jerry's confidence in having a rider on his back whose elastics snapped off years ago.

August 31

New Orleans disappears before our eyes. The Gulf Coast has been devastated while I've been composing poetry about how much fun bad weather can be. Shame on me. The floods have an Armageddon-like feel. Memories of 9/11 return, as we sit mesmerized by the news on TV watching stranded families being airlifted off their roofs.

I show jump Huey in preparation for his horse trial this weekend and bump up the fences, even though I don't like jumping big when I'm on my own. He's full of vinegar and wants to take over, but I manage to channel his energy, and the school ends well.

Jerry is frazzled from his bad experience yesterday and is on edge when I first get on him. I want to give him a positive experience over a few small fences, but he seems rushy and frightened. Because of his setback, he may not be ready for his debut in two weeks.

Barrett and I are invited to dinner at a neighbor's house, along with a few other fellow eventers. Everyone is focused on his or her own horse tonight, and no one, myself included, wants to talk about much else. Over cocktails, one neighbor asks what happened to the new horses I bought last fall. This is the last story on the planet I want to tell, especially because everyone present already knows what happened to Houston and Calvin, and it feels as though I'm being put to some narrative test by having to tell it all over again, like Scheherazade on acid. Midway through dinner, the same neighbor turns away from her own stories to ask, "Are you doing a three-day this fall, Julia?" I answer, as quietly as I can, "Fair Hill." But she's already moved on to ask everyone else at the table the same question. Ten minutes later, she asks me again, "Are you planning a three-day this fall?" I repeat the two words that have been haunting my days and nights a little louder this time, as if I either really mean it or am speaking to the deaf. Once again, she doesn't respond, either doesn't believe me or is engrossed in her own plans.

John has spent the evening watching *Apocolypse Now Redux*, having recently finished Conrad's *Heart of Darkness*. The movie was three hours and twenty minutes long, and he's just turned the DVD player off as we walk back in the door. I find his choice of movies ironic and poignant, considering what's going on in New Orleans. "Why not just watch CNN?" I say as an aside to Barrett as we head up for bed.

John leaves for India in five days. I've just turned fifty. A waning summer finds three of my horses broken. And yet, no squadron of choppers is flying over the farm that is perched safely on top of a hill. At least no levees are breaking.

September 1

I trailer Redmond to a farm in Forest Hills, an hour's trip north and east of our farm, where Coach now comes to teach. There's a big sand ring, which I have been warned might be too deep. I feel Redmond bog down and labor in the footing. It should be all right for one day, but I probably don't want to make a habit of coming here for lessons, especially for a horse coming back from a bowed tendon. I am reminded of the old maxim I learned long ago from Barrett: a good cushion with a firm base for soft-tissue injuries.

Redmond is lit and plays over the jumps Coach jacks up to Advanced height. I am using a new twisted snaffle bit, with hopes that he will respect it more than the softer bit I'd been using, and I'll have brakes for a change the next time I run him cross country at Plantation Field. There's little to complain about or fix today, except Redmond's tendency to cut corners. I correct this problem by exerting a little influence on my outside rein and leg when landing off a jump and then around corners to help keep him out on his turns. I just have to remember to do it, which is where Coach comes in like an alarm clock. "You two look solid today," she says at the end of the school. That's the second time I've heard that word in a week in reference to Redmond.

I untack him, cool him out, load him up, return to the ring to pay Coach. "So he bit his tongue," she says.

At first I wonder if she means figuratively or literally. I cut my own internal corners and cover up my having not noticed. "Maybe a little," I say. What red gushing had she seen that I hadn't?

"I wouldn't let that not let you use the new bit," she advises nonchalantly, and then adds, "How's that for a double negative?"

"OK, sure, thanks a lot, that was terrific." I race back to my rig, climb in the trailer, go over every inch of Redmond's mouth, which is still smiling from his beautiful effort, but absolutely blood free. Then I turn to the bridle and bit, which is crusted over with residue of the pink peppermints I plied him with before the lesson. I guess I'll keep the bit, after all, but will go back to apples and carrots.

I head home, pack Redmond in ice, feed him, turn him out, and settle down to a quiet evening with Barrett and John of vegetable pad Thai and *Sideways*, a movie about a wine snob, who is really just a drunk, and his soon-to-be-wed *compadre*, who taste their way through the California wine country and get into lots of misadventure along the way—too much wine and women, but not enough song. It should be sad, but it is hilarious, and we laugh our heads off, as we sip our own tumblers of Chardonnay.

Leesburg, Virginia

I'm by myself with Huey this weekend, toodling back and forth on Saturday and Sunday to Loudoun Hunt Pony Club Horse Trials. It's a two-hour haul, my magic limit. Two hours or less, and I commute; otherwise, I stable. Except now that the gas prices have skyrocketed, I may be more into staying. With diesel at $3.69/gallon, it takes more than a hundred dollars to fill up the truck. The lines are growing at the gas stations, too, reminding me of the seventies.

Huey tries hard in dressage, despite his repeated heart attacks over a blob of stone dust with which they've filled a hole in his ring. He shies at the patch every time we cruise by it and then almost falls to his knees after a major stumble near the judge. Suffice it to say that the footing is irregular and as hard as a rock. We have the same judge who nailed us three weeks ago at the Fair Hill Horse Trials. She nails him again with a 46.5 and slams the scaredy-cat for having his poll too low and being overflexed.

I change my tack as fast as I can for stadium. Which isn't all that fast. Without any help, everything takes twice as long. I neglect to review the course in my head.

I get a little rattled warming up, as the stadium stewards are trying to rush us into the ring. Midway through the course, as we negotiate the first combination, Huey catches the rail of the in, which instantly makes my mind switch to a backward, evaluative mode. When we come down off the second part of the jump, I can't find the next one and turn wide to stall for time. I spot jump 7 out of the corner of my eye, which only comes into Huey's field of vision in the last stride. He jumps it cleanly nonetheless, and we're on our way to finish the course without another rail down. Quick thinking, Huey.

I walk the cross-country course—once with Kim Meier, who's in my division, and twice by myself. Grace's husband gives me a hard time when I admit how many times I've walked the course, but I laugh it off. Everyone knows about my tendency to go off course, and now that I'm fifty, the friendly jabbing doesn't even bother me as much. Depending on my mood and how much I want to put my tongue in my cheek, I either call it the senior moment or the Einstein syndrome. I figure I'll have walked a good 10 miles today when all is joked about and ridden.

Back home, it's blessed turnout for Huey, and sushi and family for me. John is staying close to home lately and seeking out my company. It is an almost palpable feeling, and I am taking full advantage of it, filling up his tank with mothering that will send him halfway around the world and back and last him a full three months till his return in December. Barrett is more worried than I am. "What's he gonna do about showers in India? He'll have to pay somebody to throw buckets of water over his head. For Chrissake, the boy takes forty-minute showers! That's a lot of buckets."

I see 3:30 A.M. on Sunday, leave by 4:45, and arrive at Loudoun by 6:30, which gives me plenty of time to get ready for my 8:16 ride. I love starting out for an event in the dark and watching the sky take shape and color as I get closer to my goal. It's barely light when I pull in, and I'm one of the first rigs. I dress slowly and tack Huey up slowly, paying special attention to the way the galloping boots are Velcroed, how the saddle is set just so on his back; combing through his tail one more time; cinching the girth by inches as well as the figure-8 noseband. And the Saddle Tite—lots of that, applied at least twice, to the calves of my boots, as well as to the saddle. I'm a little more obsessive not only because I'm alone, but because I have the luxury of extra time.

Huey cruises around cross country eager yet relaxed. Despite the hard ground, I'm able to let him go, and he comes back to me before the fences. We tick them off, and before I know it, we're crossing through the finish flags. He's still pumped when I dismount and lead him back to the trailer. He cools out in a jiffy, then gets lots of treats and mom love for the rest of the morning. Not bad for almost eighteen. When we were racing him, it was so heartrending to watch his style. He was a true rabbit who loved putting 10 or 15 lengths between himself and the field. Of course, the field always caught him, except three or four times. I wonder if every cross-country run doesn't leave him feeling like he's won by 2 miles or more, since it takes so long for the next horse to finish.

The highlight of my day is when Jimmy Wofford pulls up by my rig and calls out the window, "Good, Julia. You had fun out there today."

"Yes I did," I say. Twenty feet is the closest I have ever gotten to a compliment from Jimmy. I'll take it.

Because we were positioned low on the ladder after dressage, I pack up and head out without waiting for times and scores to be posted. So I'm even happier when I call Kim to ask if she won our division, since she was tied for second going into cross country. "No, but I was third!" she says, and then adds, "Hey, you only had a few time faults, eleven, I think."

"That's not exactly a few," I say sourly. She explains that no one at Intermediate made time, and the fewest time penalties in our division were eight, followed by her ten and one other, and then my eleven.

"I'm sorry, I didn't notice where you finished up."

Linda Reynolds calls me a little later. "You finished eighth," she informs me, "right after our seventh. There was only 0.3 separating our scores."

I'm happy for her husband, Walter—he finally got the clean round in stadium he'd been working toward. He deserves that ribbon.

I turn my attention to ending my day with a mouthful or two. Barrett makes a new chicken recipe with thyme and sage, and I make a gingerbread cake. We eat heartily, and John asks to come with us for night check. So we slip up to the barn in the early dark, pat the ones that come up to us from nearby paddocks, check the water and hay of the ones left in their stalls. Then I listen to John play some jazz. I can feel him want my presence, and so I sit and let his music fill me up, even though my body is aching and I am exhausted from my long weekend. I sit and sit, until he finally stops and silence tells us that it is time for bed.

September 5

John's backpack and guitar are lined up at the door. He's got three months' worth of gear stuffed in the pack, including his sleeping bag, which has been smooshed down to the size of a football by his sleeping bag compressor. "That amount of space would pack about a weekend's worth for me," I say. I'm a famous Cleopatra, always taking with me on a trip about ten times more than I need or will wear along my Nile. But then, I'm usually traveling in my 200-square-foot rig, where there's room to burn. My horses, with their hundreds of pounds of gear, are impressive Cleopatras themselves. John is excited, and nervous, too. I can tell this by the fervor in his preparation for the trip, his need to be close to me, as well as by his frequent phone calls to Mollie, already buried deep in her semester at Cornell.

I'm torn between being there for John on his last day at home and getting my work done. Huey comes in from turnout like a stakes horse and is apparently no worse for wear. He tacks another onto his daunting eventing record of around fifty horse trials at the Preliminary level and above. That's a lot of miles and jumps. Add more than fifty race starts to that career, and you have yourself a horse.

I take Redmond out for his conditioning hack. We're up to thirty-five minutes of trot, with three canter sets interspersed. The ground has gotten rock hard, and it's a worry, having to trot and canter for miles. I pick the softest spots, but my choices are limited. The aftershock of Katrina passed us by. On my return to the barn, I ask Barrett about the possibility of taking Redmond down to Pimlico on Friday to condition him on the track's perfect footing, and he agrees to it. That promises to be its usual hoot—fatty Redmond in the midst of all that sleek tucked-up tightness, showing them all how many times he can trot around the track.

I honor John's request for filet mignon, as he needs to get his fill of the cow he won't be eating in India. Barrett adds chocolate-sauce fixings and a good burgundy to the shopping list, and we have ourselves a lovely last supper. John wants to help again with night check and specifically to say goodbye to Selery, so we head out to Show's and Selery's paddock, where the cutie is delighted to have this late-night attention. He's all over us at the fence line, while Show stands as close to Selery as possible, a little irritated that we've interrupted Selery's bedtime story...how the zebra got its stripes, how the camel got its hump. John wants to let this life seep in, every ounce of it, pack all the memories into the sleeping-bag compressor, then rotate and pull the tabs one by one until the farm is all in there, now the size of a black walnut that he will be able to put in his pocket and take with him, and slip his hand in from time to time to feel the round hard density of the life he has left back in Maryland as he's trekking through the Himalayas or meeting his Indian host family for the first time.

The crickets are churning, the days are cooling, John leaves for India tomorrow, and we slip into fall.

Drought

Spent grass crunches when I walk on it.
Paddock weeds straggle upward,
spider-yellow, dust
coating every leaf and twig, the ground,
as hard as tarmac. Clouds well up
but then subside, that awful blue appears
between them.

I turn to the sapling apple trees
that made the most of April,
hoarding moisture at their cores.
Branches almost kiss the ground
with their bright freight, are made to bear
too much. Another twenty years
and I'd think nothing of it—
the heavy sighs and heavy arms of
what outlives and what out-hoards.

Finish Line

CHAPTER FOURTEEN

Contours

✕ September 6

It's like another day of school as I try to get John out the door for the airport, sweating the minutes. I repeatedly call up the stairs—my own way of expressing anxiety over his leaving—until I finally get in the truck and start the engine. Barrett has changed from his work clothes into something nicer for the occasion, and I compliment him as he gets in the truck to wait it out, too. John finally makes it out the door with his back-crippling pack and one of his beloved guitars. We head out, a half hour late, 6:30 A.M. or thereabouts, just in time for the worst of rush-hour traffic on the Baltimore highways.

Even so, we make it to BWI in plenty of time for check-in and to locate an ATM so I can ply John with a little extra cash. We order coffee and muffins at the Euro Cafe, where we talk about time zones and the international date line, and what he's to do and where he's going to meet his group upon arrival in L.A. John whips out the map of India, points to Delhi, then to Benares, where he will spend most of his time, a city about four hundred miles (or a thumb's length) away from Delhi along the upper Ganges River. The first leg of his trip will be a three-week trek through the Himalayas. Now it's hugs and teary goodbyes in front of security, and he walks away in his REI quick-dry hiking shorts, his hiking boots, new ball cap, and daypack, clutching his boarding pass. He turns back to us and smiles and waves. "He looks like such a little boy," I say.

"Such a good kid," Barrett replies.

Huey jogs sound and has apparently come out of the event well. I take him on a long hack with Katie and Alex. The ground is still like cement—no rain in sight yet. In a dressage lesson with Grace, we fire Redmond up, getting him as forward as possible while trying to contain the new energy created in the front end. Our plan is to increase his engagement, which the judges usually complain is lacking. It feels like squeezing an orange with the rind on; I know there's more juice inside, but it's too hard to coax it out through the skin. Redmond, despite his lack of inherent movement, tries his heart out as I press and press him.

September 7

Two weeks ago, Barrett wrote on the whiteboard of the mare barn: "Fifty days till the first vet inspection at Fair Hill," and every day he has remembered to subtract a day. The first vet inspection is cause for great anxiety at every three-day event, when the horse-and-rider pair must jog in front of a ground jury composed of dressage judges and veterinarians who will decide whether the horse is sound enough to begin the competition. We're thirty-five days out, as of today. Each day as I walk by, I burn a hole in the number. Each day closer is another thousand steps up the wall of this Everest.

I follow Walter Reynolds and his rig a short fifteen-minute trailer ride to Bruce Fenwick's farm, to use my neighbor's hills for trot work with Redmond and Stoney, Walter's horse. The horses perk up at having company, as well as at the change of scenery. The hills on Bruce's farm have held some moisture in. His mature turf has deeper roots and is therefore preferable to the harder, inconsistent footing at home. We are in desperate need of rain.

As I'm untacking, I see Bruce instructing one of his employees on the repair of a manure spreader. I thank him for the use of his hills. "Any time, Julia," he says. "After all you've done for us, you don't even have to call, just come on over." I am struck by this. I haven't done anything much for Bruce except host a few clinics that he has taken advantage of.

When homebred Cherie contracted strangles at the track, Bruce offered our race filly three months' use of an isolation pasture at his farm. I didn't know Bruce all that well at the time, and to this day I am grateful for his generosity and good will toward my sick horse. Since we don't have an isolation field, my only other alternative would have been to bring the filly home and put thirty-five horses in quarantine. It worked out for Cherie. She got better in Bruce's lush, lonely field, came home, bombed out as an event horse, and is living happily ever after having sex with stallions, which always was her goal in life anyway. Some mares are mares, through and through. And some people are just born generous.

Huey has gotten into Seneca Valley Horse Trials this weekend, and—best of all, I get an email from "Subcontinentaljohnny" who has made it as far as L.A., likes his group, and is looking forward to a twelve-hour plane trip to Tokyo, then on to Bangkok and Delhi. Up, up the mountain he climbs.

September 8

I set up a difficult pattern in the jump ring. As usual, I replicate the course from the previous week's event and add a gymnastic where the triple would otherwise be. Redmond is all fired up—he is in attack mode in a jumping lesson with Grace. She laughs and shakes her head, as if she's out of ideas on how to change him, so she might as well join him. It feels like I'm being fired from a slingshot—my job is to learn how to sit still on the stone just launched from the rubber band. Grace might not like the lightning quickness of Redmond's style, but she can't complain about the way he jumps.

As we attempt to negotiate a difficult line from a corner to a narrow oxer, I feel Redmond start to turn left too soon as he leaves the ground over the skinny. I catch the left standard with my leg, and the jump goes flying, as do I. I land flat on my back, hitting my head hard. As I lie there, my first dizzying thought is, *hope it's not another concussion*, and my second—*oh shit, my back*. I sit up, count to ten, assess the damage, get up, get my horse, get back on, and reschool the line, this time with circles thrown in. Redmond isn't rattled, the school ends well, and I pretend that I'm unfazed by the event. I get on Huey and jump school him next. After that, I take a student and her horse and Jerry the Racehorse over to Weave a Dream Farm in Hampstead for a cross-country school. Chin up, no problem, keep riding—without a second to evaluate what just happened.

My back is a fragile creature, and it occurs to me as pains start shooting down my legs that I better call the pain doctor for another back injection before Fair Hill. Redmond is getting his hocks done, so why shouldn't I get some juice for myself? I try my best not to walk stiffly, but it's obvious to all that I'm hurting. "I can't believe you can ride that," says Katie. "I mean, he's amazing, but how do you find your center?"

"Mane," I say. "I grab a lot of it."

I down as much Advil as I dare, add a little wine to the recipe for the familiar pain. I go out to dinner with an old friend who's known me longer than I've owned the farm. She doesn't understand my passion for horses. A recent divorcée, she wants to talk about the current dating scene for forty-five-year-olds. Which is just as well, because I don't want to talk about my fall. I know how she'll respond. Something about the danger and my advancing years. So I keep quiet, down more wine and Advil, and while thinking how I'd rather be riding than dating, listen to my still-beautiful friend talk about a new beau. I can barely move while she's still avidly arching her back. I head home for a painful night of sleep. I can't get comfortable even on my magic-carpet mattress, but roll from side to side all night complaining to no one how sore I am. Barrett and Simon snore in stereo, a duet for tuba and clarinet.

September 9

Barrett and I meet up with Kim Meier at Pimlico. She brings along a filly whom she just broke for clients of J. W. Delozier, and we've made plans to trot and gallop Test Run and Redmond together on the track.

The last time Redmond galloped at Pimlico was on the morning of 9/11, as I was getting him ready for Radnor. I remember the apocalypse feel on the track as one, then two World Trade Center towers collapsed. Before I could finish my trot sets and slow canters, word spread like a sick game of telephone from galloper to galloper that the Pentagon had also been hit. We hovered around the tiny snowy TV in Baden Hughes's spartan tack room watching the world as we knew it collapse before our eyes.

Though the world is far from quiet now, particularly in the aftermath of the New Orleans tragedy, the track at Pimlico is blessedly still this morning and the air autumn cool. It is an oasis set smack-dab in the middle of bustling Baltimore City. Kim has never galloped on a track before, so for once I know something more than she does. It's been so long, my memory strains to recall where and at what speeds we need to be on the track—the slower, the farther to the outside, the faster, the closer to the rail. I remember that much. The last racehorse I galloped was a two-year-old filly who's now eight. The last horse I worked a black-type half mile is now fourteen. That was 4000 bottles of wine ago. Today, the footing feels fabulous, and it's easy to follow the rules. Kim and I chat our way through a half hour of trot, with two four-minute canters interspersed. I feel so far away from the real world, yet ironically, I'm right in the middle of it.

I introduce Kim to J.W. I suspect my matchmaking efforts will be futile, as Kim has at least fifteen years on J.W. "I have two other single men to introduce you to, and then you can take your pick," I say to Kim, with a wink.

"Who's the first one?" she asks, watching J.W. chase his four-year-old son around the barn.

"Just because they've got kids doesn't mean they're not available," I explain. "Though I don't think he's young enough for you."

"Well, just how old is he?" she asks, vaguely interested now. I've probably stuck my foot in my mouth, but at least I've got good intentions.

We say our goodbyes to Kim and hustle out of Pimlico, to give the potential lovebirds a fighting chance, and head back to the farm to flat Huey in preparation for Seneca Valley Horse Trials on Saturday. I leave the farm again in the afternoon for Bittersweet Field and an Intermediate course walk with Coach.

I tell Coach about my fall from Redmond. No reaction. Midway around the course, I tell her about taking Redmond to Pimlico. She gets steely on me. "Be careful of that footing," she says. "I once did that, three sets of five on a racetrack, and broke the horse down."

"You mean, because the footing's so deep?" She nods yes. I had just been thinking how good the footing was at Pimlico, and shallower than I'd remembered. Coach's warning alarms me. Some days, you just can't seem to do anything right.

Poolesville, Maryland

I'm struck by how much of anyone's year is marked by anniversaries. Until now, other than the obvious birthdays and holidays, I've recognized such annuals silently—my parents' deaths, my first wedding anniversary, my ex's and my parents' birthdays: my father would have been eighty-six yesterday. I pause to think of him shuffling around Radnor, months before his sudden death in 2004, relieved when I didn't make it out of the ten-minute box because he doubted my ability to handle that steep course, even though I'd already run around it two years previously in his absence. I think of my brothers and me going to Warren to help him celebrate his eighty-fourth, just two months after my mother's death and five months before his own, though none of us would have guessed what was in store for him, his death was that unexpected.

I arrive at Seneca Valley's show grounds to find Barrett already there with the rig and Huey all braided and ready to rock 'n' roll. This is the first time I've decided to come ahead—both the long drives and the back have been wearing on me. But after a bad burger at Red Robin's and a fitful night tossing and turning on a doughy mattress in Gaithersburg, I vow not to do it this way again.

Huey keeps his composure for dressage. Even Barrett likes the results, and he's not much into dressage. Huey scores below 40—by a whisper at 39.50—but it's still under 40, my upper-level goal on my noncompetitive movers, Huey and Redmond.

The footing in show jumping is like concrete, and I can't get Huey forward in warm-up. "Don't worry," says Coach, "he'll open up once he's in there." Coach is Number 1, there is no Number 2, and I'm Number 3 in Open Intermediate Division A. Coach enters the ring on her first of four. "Watch how it should be ridden," I say to Barrett.

"She's dropping a Three Star horse down to Intermediate," Barrett says. "If she doesn't win by ten, she ought to drive it straight to New Bolton."

"Sssh!" I say. Coach *does* put in a perfect round, and I don't care who she's sitting on, I just want to learn how to ride the course by watching. Then it's my turn. Just as Coach predicted, Huey goes forward once he's in the ring and puts in a good round, knocking only one rail, the second element of the triple, at the very end of the course. Barrett seems a tad disappointed—he's the competitive one. "Thought you had it," he says.

I throw Huey's boots on and hurry down to the cross-country start— but Coach isn't there. I suspect she's still in show jumping with her other mounts and will go cross country out of order. I sure don't want to be the first out on course, and I say something along these lines out loud. Karen O'Connor, who is the only other rider in warm-up, pipes up, "I don't care, I'll go first." Whew! Saved by an Olympian. She heads out of the box on Theodore O'Connor, a literal pony, not even 15 hands, who obviously has no chance of ever going Advanced or to Rolex or the Pan Am Games. I guess as we get older we temper our dreams.*

A couple of minutes later, just as I'm about to go into the box for my countdown, I hear the announcer say, "Fall of horse and rider at fence 4!" They're up and okay, but fall of both means mandatory retirement.

Hell's bells, as my father would say. Now it's up to Huey and me not only to set—but also right—the tone for the others that follow. Huey sails around the course and crosses the finish line with lots of energy to spare, so much so that I have a tough time pulling him up. "I don't know," says Barrett, "that Two Star is looking better and better." He's referring to the modified Two Star that will take place at the Virginia Horse Center at the beginning of November.

"I'm not sure I want to go there," I say to him. "I don't know if I can take another disappointment."

"I don't know about you," he says, "but I'm getting pretty good at handling disappointments. We ought to consider ourselves experts."

Barrett heads home in the zip-around car, and I hang around getting Huey cooled out, wrapped, and settled. I check the scoreboard and wait for the thirty-minute protest period so I can pick up my fifth-place ribbon. Happy birthday, Dad.

* Karen and Theodore O'Connor captured the Individual Gold Medal and helped the United States win the Team Gold at the 2007 Pan American Games in Rio de Janeiro.

Namaste! John writes. *L.A. to Osaka was about 11–12 hours, followed by a couple hours in the airport and then a 4–5-hour hop to Bangkok. We stayed overnight there and got a little wandering in the next day before flying to Delhi (another 4–5 hours). Needless to say, the jet lag won't wear off for about a week. It's very, very hard to describe this place . . . so many new sights, smells, sounds, spice, heat, PEOPLE, beggars, cows, dogs, haggling, auto-rickshaws, bicycles, dirt, horns, proximity . . . Well, it's about 16:33 in India, which would make it about 5:33 back home. Good morning!"*

September 11

I don't make it up to the barn till 8:30 A.M., but as usual, Barrett has a couple of hours' head start on me. Huey is relaxing with his head out the back window—one of his favorite stances, surveying the goings-on of the back pastures, particularly the mares and the foals, whom he adores. When I come into the barn, he turns slowly around and sticks his head over the chest bar to greet me. "He's been at his back window all morning," Barrett says. "Wouldn't even turn around for a flake of alfalfa. Crustacean loves the mommy," he adds. Huey noses my armpit, then focuses on me as I tack up Redmond for a conditioning hack. He always gets jealous when I have another horse in the wash stall, which is right next to his stall—tosses his head up and down, pins his ears and nips the air in Redmond's direction. Redmond couldn't care less—he knows who is on his way to Fair Hill.

Huey has apparently come out of the event well—there's only a slight warmth in his left fore, but he is sound and not all that stiff. "He's telling you something, Julia," Barrett says. But I won't go there today. I'll think about that à la Scarlett O'Hara: I don't have room in my head for yet another challenge. I need to focus on Redmond.

I trot and canter Redmond for thirty-five minutes, then we go on a long walk over to Baden's Stream. The dogs—annoyed by the ride so far because it hasn't gone anywhere but stayed repetitiously in the fields best for trotting and galloping—start wagging their tails and trotting off happily the moment we head in a straight line. Redmond plunks into the stream up to his hocks and stays there. Daisy, who's usually an in-and-outer, can't seem to get enough. All of her grace is destined for water as she swims figures endlessly around us. This is the one place where time doesn't matter, and suddenly I have all of it I could ever need because none is needed here. The significance of today's date hits me, as well as everything that has happened in the last four troubled years. I am nonetheless deeply grateful for having lived them.

September 12

My brother's atrial fibrillation has returned. His doctor recommends a procedure called an ablation, which involves a catheterization and zapping of a nerve by the heart that is causing the muscle to beat irregularly. I phone a cardiologist friend who used to keep a horse at the farm to get her take on my brother's condition and to see if she would recommend a second opinion before he undergoes the procedure. We begin the process of getting an appointment with one of her compadres at Hopkins. Barrett is off returning a racehorse layup to the track, leaving me blessedly alone on the farm. Just as I'm finally getting on Redmond, the owner of one of the yearling fillies shows up. I bark that I can't talk right now, but my guilt over being rude ruins my focus, and I end up having a mediocre ride. Next on my plate is a visit from my computer man, who spends hours trying to get to the bottom of my endless computer problem, which he fails to do. As I'm on the phone ordering a brand-new computer, which takes another eon out of my day, the heating man shows up to replace our flue so our house doesn't burn down, which it has been threatening to do the last few days, with smoke billowing out of the boiler chimney. My day fits to a tee the book I'm reading by Terry McMillan, *The Interruption of Everything*. For the heroine, it's an unexpected late pregnancy. For me, it's everything that can possibly get in the way of my riding.

September 13

I take Redmond to meet up with Walter Reynolds and Grace at dressage judge Cathy Tucker-Slaterbeck's farm to practice the dressage test I'll be riding this weekend and to get her comments and critiques. She and her husband just built a farm outside of Glyndon, Maryland. The house is built on a hill with an expansive view. The new eight-stall barn has been built exactly the way they want it. "Even better than the last one," she says.

I turn to Barrett. "This is what I want," I say.

"You could have had it," he says, "minus twenty-seven stalls, minus the indoor, minus the fencing." I tuck this farm away in my memory bank— it's what I hope to have someday—everything on a much smaller scale.

We ride through the test, get our critiques from Cathy and Grace, and then ride through it again. Redmond gives me a little trouble with the flying changes in the first test. Cathy's overall comment is that he is stiff in his back and a little short strided. She is sensitive to the limitations of his gaits and makes suggestions not only on how to improve his movement and overall look in the test, but also on how to "fake it"—a shoulder fore to correct the lateral nature of Redmond's walk, for instance. Though shortcuts may not be classical, they're effective and can be deceiving to a judge's discerning eye.

I switch Redmond to the double bridle for the second test, and he's softer and improved, particularly in his flying changes. We have fun bantering with Cathy, too. All these years of being judged by her at events and being a little intimidated by her presence, and come to find out she wants to help us eventing dressage riders improve and wants to give us good scores when we earn them.

After a busy day back at the farm with lessons and rides, I nestle into my office to find another e-mail from John awaiting me from Manali, India, on his way to Leh, base of operations for his week of trekking in the Himalayas. He sounds tired and overwhelmed, having last slept on an overnight bus his group took to get there. I try to imagine how long it would take to get over jet lag with a ten-and-a-half-hour-plus-one-day time difference. I try to imagine the town, and the bus, and the alien scenery. I imagine him sitting at the sole computer in the Internet café in Manali, where the connection is so slow that a computer crash is possible at any moment. I don't go anywhere except to Hampstead and an event here and there, and yet I feel like I'm always traveling to faraway places. Everyday, when I get on Redmond, I'm someplace new.

September 14

I trot Redmond for a half hour before Grace shows up to help me school the bounce into water. She doesn't ask why I don't want to jump more, and I don't tell her that I'm also taking him to Coach's tomorrow for a jump school.

Grace uses plastic cavaletti boxes and standards and poles at the water jump to mimic the bounce into water that I will face at Plantation. This is the jump we ate at my first Advanced horse trial in April 2004. We had flown around the course with Redmond's exuberant wings like it was just another Intermediate course, until we got to the penultimate jump—the water, which required us to bounce in. Redmond misread it as a one stride, caught a leg on the in, and I went flying head over teakettle into the water. It was 40 degrees and raining that day. I kept hold of the reins, got up, got back on, jumped the last jump, and went through the finish line, relieved not to have to jump the bounce again. After all, we had already negotiated the obstacle in a manner of speaking and didn't have to do a do-over to keep going. I was drenched from stem to stern, running on adrenaline, and tickled just to have finished my first Advanced run, despite the fall. A half hour later, the shakes set in as I peeled off my layers, including my underwear, which was also soaked. That's the one article of clothing I didn't have spares of, so I went commando for the rest of the day. Since then, I always pack a second of *everything*.

We zip around the corner and head for the water, but Redmond miscalculates the in, as there's no ground line and the water behind the jump is shimmering underneath the cavaletti. He catches the pole with a toe, and we both bobble into the water but manage to stay upright and not get too wet. Second time through, same thing. Grace puts a ground line down, and that does the trick. She shortens the distance, and we come through again for good measure. I don't admit to her that my heart started racing when we bobbled the first time. One nice thing about Grace is that she knows these things about me without having to hear my confessions. I cover up so much these days: whom I'm working with, my fear of making mistakes and of running Advanced, my soft addiction to Chardonnay, my deep-down relief that both kids are out of the house—after twenty-one years, my days are finally all mine—and sometimes, even jumping a jump in my own backyard makes me afraid. I uncover the uncoverable in these pages, because it's the jump in front of me here, and I have to get to the other side.

September 15

The land is beginning to look worn, partly from lack of rain, and partly because summer is becoming *passé composé*, as Barrett would say—his way of bringing an international flair to the eternally mundane. The cornstalks have browned and withered, the soybean fields have that golden, ready-to-harvest appeal, the occasional dead leaf flutters to the ground, and everything feels dusty and overripe. Rain has been promised for days, and now that Hurricane Ophelia is pelting North Carolina, we may finally get what we've been pleading for. Yesterday, I heard rumors of pockets of rain all around the Baltimore area, but the farm stayed bone dry.

I drive through rain showers on my way to Coach's for a jump school with Redmond, hoping that the rain is finding the farm as well. The 4-foot-3-inch jumps look twice their size in this small ring, where the turns come up wicked quick. Claustrophobia doesn't get in my way like last time. The lesson is short, sweet, and effective.

When the subject of my new student, Dan, comes up, I get quiet. Dan was a student of Coach's, but now he has come to me for help and hasn't said anything to Coach about the change. I insert a toe in my mouth when I tell Coach that I'm doing a little teaching. I'm pretty sure she's figured out what Dan is doing. So many little lies and deceptions. I've withheld saying anything to Grace about working with Coach. I've withheld from Coach news about teaching Dan. I've not said anything to Vet about getting Cooper's help with Redmond. I lie to myself that I'm saving feelings by my silence. Deep down, I know this strategy will eventually backfire. White lies too often turn into black ones; sleeping dogs can turn ravenous. But then again, I've had people turn against me for my honesty.

The bottom line is: I'll do most anything to get to the top of my Everest.

The sky is as closemouthed as I've been. On my return home, I see that not one drop of its honesty has escaped over the farm.

Unionville, Pennsylvania

Plantation Field Horse Trials. Redmond puts in a steady and obedient dressage test, which scores so-so but still in the pack, 40.9, eighth out of twenty—not bad. Barrett calls these bottom of the first third placings stalking scores.

Lucky ducks—they've had a lot of rain in Unionville, so the footing in show jumping, which at its driest is mediocre at Plantation, is deep and mucky. Unlucky horses—rails fly all day long. In warm-up, Redmond knocks one hard. After that, he makes a huge effort to jump out of the muck and not touch a rail, and puts in a clean fast round. Steuart Pittman comes up to me afterward. "He's one sharp motherfucker," Steuart says.

"Thanks," I say.

Katie takes Redmond home early while I stick around to walk the cross-country course with Coach, before heading home for my pre–cross-country dinner of steak and potatoes. Sylvia Plath has won her first race, and Barrett is abuzz with the news from his day at Laurel racetrack. It doesn't happen often that we both have such good days. This one lasts into the night when Barrett gives me a one-handed back rub as soon as I'm horizontal. "Here?" he says.

"Lower."

"Here?"

"Lower."

Sunday morning John calls from India. It takes a few seconds for him to respond to what I'm saying, confirming that it does take awhile for sound to travel all the way around the world. He's sick with Montezuma's revenge and is taking antibiotics. He loves the group and the group leaders, loves the countryside of India. He tells me of the town of Ladahk, which took them an eighteen-hour cliff-hanging bus ride to get to, and which will be their home base as they day-trek for a couple of weeks. He describes the jagged mountains and the juxtaposed deserts, as well as the second-highest pass in the world, at 17,500 feet, that they traversed. He is happy, and yet I can tell he is also a bit homesick—not a bad combination. It only cost him 70 rupees, or $1.75, for this call. I imagine we'll be hearing from him again.

Because I don't ride cross country till two, we have a leisurely departure at nine, and time for yet another course walk when I get to Plantation. One jump at a time, I tell myself.

The Plantation course is a big open battlefield with a panoramic view of many of the fences from warm-up. Of the first twelve horses that leave the start box in the Advanced Divisions, nine of them either fall or stop or are eliminated at the water jump. The jump is my nemesis bounce into water, followed by a bank up to a skinny. After jumping a huge elephant-trap oxer aimed right at the horses in warm-up, the horses have to turn away from their buddies and canter forward to a difficult bounce into water, going counter to where instinct is pulling them. Horse after horse either lugs through the turn and the rider can't get him straight, or the rider, in an effort to compensate for the horse not turning well, rams the bounce, causing the horse to jump poorly or not jump at all. "Let's see what Kim does," Coach says, pacing back and forth on her first ride in the warm-up area.

Kim Meier and Test Run come through. "Merle" catches a leg at the in, and Kim flips over his head and lands in the water. She stumbles to her feet, bends over for a few moments to catch her breath, hauls herself back into the saddle, and courageously continues on. I almost call it quits.

A group of riders, including Sally Cousins, Bonnie Mosser, and Jane Sleeper, are in a huddle now, trying to form a plan to refuse to go out until the technical delegate—the head honcho of the event—decides to take the bounce off the course. Nothing happens, except more thrills and spills. One rider runs through a gap into the water and comes to the bounce off the left and gets it done, and then another comes straight through easily, so I'm reassured that it is statistically possible to jump the jump. I ask Coach if she's going to run, and she nods yes, but there is concern, even in this veteran's eyes, when she says it. I contemplate the long way around the water. "I don't know what I should do," I say to no one in particular. I am as terrified as I've ever been, at a horse trial or elsewhere.

Bonnie Mosser turns to me and smiles, "Just ride to the water, Julia. He's a really good horse."

We pick up a rhythm out of the box. Redmond jumps the first three fences well—kiss, kiss, kiss. We start cruising, I relax, settle into the racy foreplay of the narrow at the top of the hill and the elephant trap at the bottom. I turn to the water, and he turns, we bounce the in and run right through it, to the bank and skinny and out. I hear clapping in the background, and we keep going, jumping one jump at a time, through the cliff and the ruins, the coffin with its offset ditch, the trakenner to the two-stride bounce bushes, the huge turning oxers and double corners on a hillside, until we get to the last and the finish flags. I glance down at my watch—wow, maybe only five ticks slow.

Redmond is blowing. And blowing. It takes us a long time to cool him out before we can ice and poultice him. I am blowing too and happier than I've been in a long time. Barrett goes away and then comes back waving a third place, yellow ribbon, with news that only eight out of twenty Advanced horses even made it through the finish flags.

John

As a child I'd ask to see
your grandfather's bear claw,
would he please turn it over
so I could trace Alaska on his palm?

He'd rotate the much larger
version of my own
to show the contour of his flaw,
a red, angry birthmark I was miffed

not to have myself.
I would reach to touch that state,
but he would close the fist,
put a glove back on. *Too cold.*

Mornings, when I go into your room
Give me a foot, I say,
which emerges like a turtle's head
from under the warm shell of sheets.

I pull each long, slender toe, both of us hoping
for that satisfying snap. *Give me the other*, I say,
noting the dime-sized freckle
stamped in one drowsy curve, grateful
for your uninhibited scars, your bones.

Hacking

Oops!

CHAPTER FIFTEEN

Rain after Ninety Days of None

※ **September 19**

Cooper is pleased with Redmond's condition and the state of his legs. The horse stands like a pro for his cocktail and his hock injections, and then we guide him drunk and swaying back to his stall for a day of R and R. I bring Huey out. I narrate his more than sixty race starts and more than sixty horse trials, his advancing age, his first year at the Intermediate level this past year, and my hope to take him to the Virginia Two-Star event. We flex and jog him, and Cooper detects a fair amount of arthritis in his ankles and hocks—no big surprise—and yet he feels that it's worth a try. So he injects his ankles as well as his hocks and recommends that we follow up the injections with a series of shock-wave therapies in an effort to make him as comfortable and as sound as possible. Huey stumbles back into his stall. I've got two drunken sailors on my hands, and it's not even twelve o'clock.

After Cooper has packed up and left, Barrett announces that Vet should be here in fifteen. "For what?" I say, a little panicked. "Glad I didn't know she was coming so close on Cooper's tail."

"For Selery," Barrett says. Little Selery's cold has morphed into pneumonia. When Vet shows up not more than ten minutes after Cooper drives down the driveway, she mentions rotococcus as a possibility and takes blood to measure his white count. Though he doesn't have a fever, the foal is listless, keeps lying down in his stall, and is having difficulty breathing.

"I am really worried about him," Vet says. She changes the antibiotic to erythromycin. We set up fans outside the colt's stall to keep him as cool as possible.

"We should rub on him a lot," says Barrett, "get the blood flowing." This bad news is pretty much a 5-gallon piss on my parade.

"That's how you spell it?" Vet says, eyeing the orphan foal's medication dosages on the barn whiteboard. I explain the genesis of Selery Salt's name, hoping that we will be able to use it and keep it and race it and event it for years to come and that it won't just be another one we file away in our cabinet of lost names and lost foals.

September 20

I pack Jerry up for a cross-country school at Fair Hill. Coach has a crew of Beginner Novice horses and Beginner Novice riders. A couple can't get their horses down an 18-inch drop. The drop is so tiny that the horses could have been led down it, as if across a stream, but . . . Close your eyes and even a curbside can feel like a cliff. After ten minutes of contrary shenanigans—kicking and rearing and wheeling—out comes the broom. Coach tries to sweep the horses down the drop. When that doesn't work, she throws it at them. Jerry is patient, and when he finally gets a chance, jumps all the Beginner Novice fences, with only a minor blip—a log later in the course that he ducks out of with the speed of lightning. I have to catch myself not to fall off. "Good save," Coach says. I feel my back go *tweak*, then *rip*. We circle back and jump the jump and go on.

After the jump school, I run into my eventing pals, Pam Wiedemann and Courtney Cooper, who make a fuss about my ride at Plantation. "Nobody gets around, and Julia Wendell only has two time faults," Courtney says. "Good for you!"

"How much money did you win?" Coach asks.

"Money?"

"Yeah, money. Mine got $150 for fourth place."

"I didn't get any money," I say.

"Well, you won it," she says.

I call up the Plantation secretary to inquire about my winnings and get Denis Glaccum, course designer and organizer of the event. "Julia!" he says to me. "You sure rode the hell out of that course. Good for you. It was like a course in the Psychology of Riding 101," he adds. "The first few riders had a problem, and it psyched everyone else out." I replay the huddle of terrified riders in cross-country warm-up. How I was one of them. I wonder how it is that I didn't succumb to this negative pressure when I so easily could have. I forget about asking Denis for the prize money. Apparently, you get $150 for fourth and $350 for second, but all you get for third is rapturous flattery.

Once home, I return a phone call to Caitlin over a fishbowl of Chardonnay and bags of popcorn. She is having trouble with life at Sarah Lawrence and is thinking about transferring. She is missing out on the traditional college experience. She wants to go to a school that offers football and sororities. I could easily see Caitlin in that other environment, but I also feel that it's not a matter of environment at all. She's got to learn this for herself, though. I bite my tongue so I won't meddle in a situation that needs me to be supportive but not interfering. Instead, I tell her the latest on the new barn cats, how Barrett has given them the names This, That, and Th'Other. "Which one's Th'Other?" she asks. "No, let me guess, the black one, right?" she says, trying to remember the two gray sisters and the black other one recently deposited on our tack room doorstep by a desperate neighbor, along with cat box, litter, bowls, food, and six months' supply of Revolution.

At night check, we find a perky Selery with a clean, unsnotty nose for the first time in days. We've hung a stall guard on his stall, a fan is blowing soft, cool air on him, and he greets us with his forelock and mane wisping about him. Maybe the circulating air makes him think he is running. He gulps down the syringed pink medicine Barrett inserts in his mouth as if it were candy—what a good boy. Some are just born happy and friendly, no matter their circumstances.

September 21

I flat Huey and Redmond, and both are glad to be back to regular work. I have lessons scheduled for later in the day, so Katie and I have to use the late morning to set up a new jump pattern. I've been having fun with this weekly task of recreating the courses I've jumped at the shows the previous weekend, adding in a gymnastic that helps to tune up the horses as well as put them back together. I set a basic grid for my students.

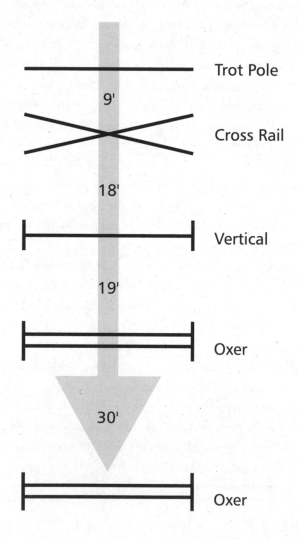

It's an old tried-and-true gymnastic of Jimmy Wofford's, which will be beneficial for my students who need to work on their position and for their horses that need to work on negotiating several fences in a row set close together. The horses will trot in to a crossrail, take one stride, jump the vertical, take another stride, jump the first oxer, take two strides, jump the second oxer, and canter away.

For Redmond I set this:

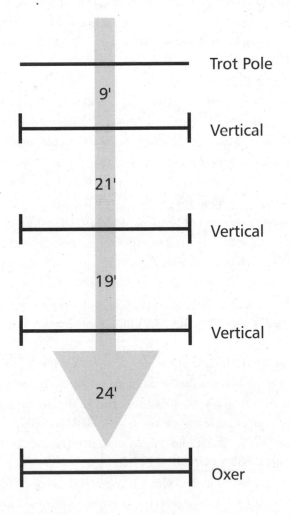

Trot Pole

9'

Vertical

21'

Vertical

19'

Vertical

24'

Oxer

Redmond will start the exercise with a compressed canter stride but will stretch out by the.end of the gymnastic. We want to remind him how to lengthen his stride and reach through a combination.

In the evening we watch Hurricane Rita rip toward Galveston, Texas. The new hurricane still has days to change course and lessen—we know about when it will hit, but we don't yet know the outcome. We sit glued to our lives, stocking up on cases of wine, popcorn, toilet paper, condoms made from sheep guts. Add boxes of fitness and schooling and bravery, and we are prepared to tackle anything.

September 22

I'm surprised to find an e-mail waiting for me—not from India—but from Mollie. The e-mail's header is "Advice." I take a deep breath. For some odd reason, I know what's in it before I read it, even though it's perplexing she's writing to me. She is asking for my love advice. She's lonely, she loves John, always will—but, well, she feels very disconnected from him, halfway around the world . . . what should she do? I write a reply asking her to please not break up with him when he's 14,000 miles away. I don't send it. Instead I call Caitlin for *her* advice. She's happier after getting a role in a musical at school, as well as a job offer as a production assistant for a TV pilot that's being filmed in New York. Caitlin loves to give advice, and she's good at it. She agrees with my vow of silence, even though silence is not the modus operandi for either one of us.

I school dressage with Grace Our goal is to finesse the Advanced D test that I'm to ride at Morven Park in a couple of weeks. Test D is far harder than C, which is the only Advanced test I've ridden to date. It includes four flying changes, counter canter four-loop serpentines, full passes from quarter line to quarter line, three efforts at medium and extended trots—egads!—bad news for short-strided Redmond. I enjoy the challenge of figuring it out with Grace's help and then squeezing the most out of my four-legged sponge, who tries his heart out. I have my work cut out for me over the next couple of weeks.

Selery is perkier still—he likes his erythromycin smoothie—and we have hope he's through the worst of his illness. In the evening, we watch the state of Texas evacuate while I make a prediction that the storm will miss Galveston and won't reach Katrina's magnitude. I'd rather have my optimistic outlook than that of Vet, who always prepares for *Paradise Lost*— maybe so she'll be pleasantly surprised when Paradise is regained. My fingers are still crossed for Selery.

September 23

Storm clouds come and go, they lure and beckon and entice, and then pass over. We've been watering the garden flowers every day. I can't remember the last time it rained. Rita barrels her way toward Texas. The whole state takes cover. When Katrina did her damage, we didn't get so much as a drop. Even for a hurricane, it's a long way from Louisiana to Maryland.

I jump school Redmond with Grace He is motherfucking keen, as Steuart Pittman says. Grace puts us through the exercises and doesn't say much. Which is fine by me. Because I don't want to change anything. And Grace seems to have surrendered to the red rocket.

Vet comes to check on Selery, whose lung sounds are improving. The whole barn takes a deep breath. Then another little one comes to visit: Jennifer Tanio and her newly adopted baby. Huey loves kids. When I hold the baby, Huey tosses his head up and down over his stall guard, wanting to hold the baby too. I bring Michael over to meet him. Huey puts his velvety nose gently on the arm of the baby, who stabs him with a quick, fearful pat. Every time I walk away from his stall with my prize, Huey tosses his head.

I make a touch-base call to David Fenza. He asks after the kids and Barrett, and Barrett's bad hand. I tell him about my tumble from Jerry and admit that my back has been killing me lately. "When you take a fall like that," he says, "don't you ever wonder that it may be time to quit?"

"Not for a minute," I say. "Why would I quit the thing that makes me want to jump out of bed every morning?" As soon as I say it, I realize that I'm one of the lucky ones. And from David's silence, I guess that he's not.

I come back up to the barn to find Calvin out of his sick stall and strolling around the barn, rummaging through the buckets of supplements that hang on all the horses' stall doors. Calvin still has his Robert Jones bandage on for his cracked pastern and has not been out of his stall in weeks, so he's taking full advantage of his newfound freedom. I catch the blasé escapee, put him back in his house, close the stall door after noticing how he broke through the stall guard hanging in his doorway, and then check the feed room to see if he got into grain while he was out. But the feed room and all the bags of grain look untouched. I ask Katie if horses can colic from too much Farrier's Formula, Cosequin, and Platinum Plus.

I finish my barn work around six, in time for a quick bite before Barrett and I pick up Caitlin at the train station. I wish all it took was to lead her over to Huey's stall. She is bubbly and bossy when we greet her. I have done everything wrong in her absence: my hair is an awful color, the new shades in the upstairs hallway are tacky, and I look downright anorexic. I take a deep breath, knowing that brassiness and faultfinding are her ways of giving me a quick pat and showing how glad she is to see me.

September 24

I've been asked to read from *Dark Track* at the Baltimore Book Festival. It's a street festival, it's about books, and it's in Baltimore, an odd combination that makes it raucous and literary and blue and white collar all at once. The venue for my reading is one of the many tents lining the block of Charles Street. When Barrett and I arrive, they're still setting up the literary tent, attempting to put up a large sign at the entrance that is a Scrabble board spelling out THE MARYLAND POETRY AND LITERARY SOCIETY and BALTIMORE BOOK FESTIVAL and CREATIVE CAFÉ—but all the letters keep falling off, and the workers are scrambling to glue them by the start of my reading, the first of the day. One person wanders in— enough for an audience, along with the construction workers who will hear the poems and be a part of my audience whether they like it or not— then a few more straggle in.

Dark Track

One board for the preemie foal we encouraged to stand
before his legs were ready,

one for the gelding who ran out on our busy road
in an ice storm. Another slat gets the name
"Charred Angel," for the wobbler we had to put down.
We paint the 4-inch letters high on the round pen walls.

And now we have to add the letters
spelling "Diamond Mesa," the 3-year-old
who broke her leg in the home stretch,
pushing for a win.
And though it is not a dark Tuesday
of no races when we get the news,
our darkness goes on a long way.

We trained her through a fear of crowding
by galloping her straight into a band of brood mares,
we practiced tapping her croup
from the saddle, so she wouldn't spook at our touch.
After she got over pneumonia, we ran her,
after she healed a pulled muscle in her shoulder,
we ran her again. Because we needed her
to earn our keep. Human beings

are the strangest of all, they need so much
light & air & proof to keep moving, every poem,
a name on a fence board.
Today we'll paint her high up & close to the others,
& for a while, the heaven of a filly's
sleek bones & speed translating fear
will make anything possible,
her dark track illegibly within us.

The poem "Dark Track" first appeared in *Southern Indiana Review* and then in the collection of poems *Dark Track* (WordTech Editions, 2005).

The poems in the book are mostly about horses, or at least use horses as conduits for human issues. So an audience like this that knows nothing about horses is a good test for whether the poems go beyond their subject matter. My audience of about ten nods heads as I read. Sometimes they even sigh and say *hmmm!* at the ends of poems, all of which are good indicators that they're enjoying them. I take wicked delight in reading a poem about Caitlin in her absence, and preface it by saying that my daughter is in town but has declined my invitation to join me today because my readings make her feel "uncomfortable"—so I'm taking advantage of her absence by reading one that would really make her squirm.

The Museum of Modern Art at 6:00 am

It's a Degas in the shower,
my daughter bending from the waist,
one leg propped on the tile,
her skin dolphin-slick
with shaving cream & shampoo,
breasts & sex obscured
by rippled glass.

She's got tendonitis now, can't dance
when dancing is the passion.
I bring her *Wuthering Heights*, chewing gum,
new reins for her pony's bridle,
confide a few of my own blues.
Because I'm no dancer & cannot comprehend
the meaning of sore ankles,
she asks me to knock
before entering her room,
greets me by turning away.

Without knowing, she gives me a gift
as she does her ankle exercises
to Joni Mitchell before dinner
& Cass Elliott after,
tremolos that infiltrate our house,
as do the dancers in their hushed pinks
stretching & bending at the barre
from the poster on her wall,
each wincing moment a foreboding
of what they want most yet won't be able to have.

"The Museum of Modern Art at 6:00 am" first appeared in *Bayou* and then in the collection of poems *Dark Track* (WordTech Editions, 2005).

I sell a few books afterward, place more at the MARYLAND POETRY AND LITERARY SOCIETY booth, and wander around the festival with Barrett, talking to a couple of old literary pals I've known since I moved to the area in 1982. We head home so we can get our barn work done and I can ride Huey, who is now following Redmond's rigorous schedule, which includes conditioning trots and canter bursts three times a week. I've made the plunge to attempt to get him through the Virginia Two Star. Old fools die hard.

September 25

Calvin's legs are stocked up. He may have gotten into something during his Great Escape. Worried about founder, we call in Vet. I don't look forward to seeing her, as she's always cranky when she's called on the weekend. I hunker down at the house when she shows up. I wait for the call. "I think it must have been the apples," she says, referring to the overburdened apple trees right outside the mare barn. "He probably gorged himself." She prescribes bute and Banamine, and assures us that we caught the problem early. What she says to Barrett is, "This creature is suffering from carbohydrate overload."

The clouds well up and then subside. I write a rain dance—maybe that will help. The land is in desperate need of sustenance.

Nope. Not a drop. I flat Huey and Jerry, say my goodbyes to Caitlin, check in on Calvin, then start cooking. Old friends are coming for dinner tonight. I'm not much of a socialite, but I do like to cook. I start putting together a dinner of—once again—Maryland crabs, Caesar potato salad, tomatoes with mozzarella, and a gingerbread cake to top things off. I get the ordeal organized, then head back up to the barn to hop on Redmond. "I can't think about anything except Fair Hill," I admit to Barrett. "Everything else seems like an interruption."

"As it should be," he says. I feel selfish, but I also know that my focus has to be that clear and intense if I am going to get through the Three Star. Time to clear the table, as good as this dinner promises to be.

September 26

My day starts with a phone call from India. I detect a quaver in John's voice. We talk some about the trip, his trek in the Himalayas, his upcoming train ride to Delhi. There's a pause from across the world. "I hear you got an e-mail from Mollie," he says. My heart sinks.

"You've got to put it out of your mind, John, because there's nothing you can do about it. You're there and she's here, and you've got to live your life and soak it all in. And report back to us." That's it, he's a reporter, he's on a mission. His job is to bring us news from India, which is more important right now than his other job as boyfriend. Before I know it, I've given the advice I didn't want to give. The phone cuts off. He calls back. This time he sounds like he's underwater, and my own voice echoes back to me. The last thing I want is to hear me repeat myself. "Just squeeze the experience dry," I tell him, and it echoes, sounding ridiculous the second time. The phone goes dead, I suspect because he's run out of rupees. It doesn't ring again.

I take a dressage lesson from Grace to work again on the movements of the Advanced Test D that I'll have to ride this weekend. It's the most difficult dressage challenge I've encountered. Redmond gets fussy in the double bridle, and I'm not sure if it's the severity of the bridle or what I'm asking of him.

All day, storm clouds brew and the wind picks up. Blessed rain is in the forecast, but the sky takes all day to make up its mind. I finish my rides, get some office work done, teach a couple of lessons. The heavens open during my second lesson at the end of the day with a new boarder. Who cares if we get cold and wet? Rain is rain.

September 27

Barrett gets up at 4:00 A.M. to let the dogs out and start his day. Ten minutes later, I can expect Simon's running leap onto the bed to join me for some snuggle time after his early-morning pee and prowl. It gets harder for me to rise at my usual 5:30 with the air cooling, fall brisking on, and morning light holding off until almost 6:30. I'd rather burrow under the covers with the brown dog.

I find out that I ride dressage on Redmond at Morven as early as Thursday, which puts my week's schedule into a tailspin. I do some rearranging of Redmond's conditioning workouts before heading up to Coach's for a jump school. I am beginning to feel the pressure of impending Fair Hill. I over-analyze Redmond's every step and twitch and bump, needing everything to go perfectly between now and then. Jump schools are no longer enjoyable, but a hurdle to get over before Fair Hill. My mind is playing fretting games with me, and I'm not sure what to do about it, except to grab mane and hang on. I talk to Coach about my pre–three-day jitters. She shrugs it off while admitting that she can relate to it, but without giving any advice to speak of for dealing with it.

Her ring is as spectacular as ever. The tight turns make me ride defensively and backward on my speedball. To give Redmond his usual forward ride over fences and make the turns on the other side, I get slingshot to the outside of my horse. I feel like I'm on an amusement park Tilt-A-Whirl, catapulted from one stirrup to the other as I struggle to stay centered around the turns—and not throw up. Coach quickly maxes out the fences. I prefer to take my time building up to sizey fences rather than attempting to read a compressed CliffsNotes version of *War and Peace* in an hour. "Good job," Coach says at the end of the school.

"Well, he did better than I did," I say. "I guess I'd rather have that than the other way around." I'm relieved I didn't fall off. Or lose my cookies.

On the way home, I review what I learned today about riding

Redmond from Coach, then start to feel a little down. As Fair Hill gets closer, I am enjoying my rides less and just trying to get through them without a mishap. And checking off the days. I make myself a whopping vodka tonic on my return, hoping I won't regret it in the morning. Half-assed resolves to quit drinking come easily in the early hours when I feel like the stall I'm mucking out. I dump whatever happened last night off the ramp onto a huge pile of everything that happened last month. But by 4:00 I'm looking forward to 6:00, when all my promises disappear. "Don't wish your life away," my mother would tell me that her father used to say, and today, that cliché has resonance. I make another resolution as I'm counting sheep: to enjoy my dressage school on Redmond tomorrow. And add more vodka to the grocery list.

September 28

As I'm grooming Redmond, I find bumps all over his haunches. I bathe him in Equitaine shampoo, an antifungal agent, and call Vet. "Could be the onset of systemic ringworm," she warns me. I tell her I'm competing at Morven this weekend, so I'm restricted in the medications I can give. "Give him 5cc of Banamine in the vein. It will be out of his system by tomorrow. And rub him down with alcohol. And don't worry—he'll be fine." The hives are a long way from his heart, so I take a deep breath. I'm getting way too neurotic. I can feel the illness that feeds on itself and every little minor thing brewing within and about to consume me.

Nonetheless, I enjoy my dressage school on Redmond with his bumpy ass and work hard to master the difficulty of Advanced Test D. Later, I notice on Morven Park's Web page that they've scratched the D division, a result of too few entries. My week's work of learning the more difficult test D down the toilet. If I'm lucky, maybe Test C will feel like a breeze— that is, if I can rememorize it on such short notice. Hang in there, Redmond. Show me how to do it.

Leesburg, Virginia

Our impromptu dressage test at Morven Park is well schooled and obedient, especially the trot and lateral work, until we get to the flying changes. Redmond pins his ears and bucks, until he finally gives them to me, albeit late behind. We won't get a great cumulative score on submission today. So many of our dressage efforts are like asking a big biker dude with tattoos and piercings to wear a tutu. I'm bugged for the rest of the day. I'd worked hard all week, and all I have to show for it is a lukewarm score for all of our misguided efforts. That's eventing.

Home means a meal of chicken pad Thai cooked by Barrett, and then a movie about a young ice skater who gets pushed by her insistent mother toward Harvard when all she wants to do is follow her dream and ice skate. Substitute any endeavor for ice skating and you have the recipe for a happy life. Except when your horse doesn't give you clean flying changes.

We made it to Benares! The city is packed, maybe more so than Delhi. Cows, people, monkeys, rickshaws, cars, beggars, and sadhus are everywhere. Our program house is very cool. Ganga ji (the Ganges) can be seen from our balcony. There are books, musical instruments, and a couple of soon-to-be-functional computers in the building. Our plans for the day consist of exploring the city a bit and attending a concert at an ashram and orphanage across the water in the evening. In a few days my homestay begins. Take care of yourselves at home. I'm thinking of you all on the other side of the world. Love, John

Did he say monkeys?

September 30

On our way to gallop at Pimlico with Huey and Redmond, Barrett calls up trainer J. W. "The Big Cheese and I are on our way," Barrett warns him. "Hey, look at this," Barrett says, handing me his new cell phone displaying his caller ID list with "The Big Cheese" as header.

Redmond is an angel on the track, despite any itchiness from the bumps dotting his haunches. We hook up with Mark O'Dwyer, the exercise rider, on Sylvia Plath. "How's Johnny doin'?" he asks in his roadhouse brogue, eyeing Redmond's bumpy ass. It takes me a second to remember—ah yes, of course, he knows John. I tell him about India, as we jog around the track the wrong way, which is the right way when you're trotting on a racetrack. Redmond is enjoying Sylvia's company—

who wouldn't? She is drop-dead gorgeous. He extends his trot to show off as Sylvia canters in place, bursting with energy. Wish I could get this trot in the dressage ring. "She can't keep up with his trot," Mark compliments my pony, with a wink, not having a clue what a mediocre trot Redmond has by eventing standards. None of these racehorses can trot a lick. Mark has been instructed to jog Sylvia the wrong way, then turn around and gallop easy for a mile. How does a frantic canter in place measure up to a mile's worth of trotting? Maybe she'll blast off ahead of us when we turn the "right" way, or counterclockwise, and start to "gallop." But she sets an easy pace, and Redmond keeps up just fine. After a mile, I tell Mark I'm going to drop back and turn around and trot some more, and he finishes with Sylvia soon after. He's ending on his third horse when I'm finally through with Redmond's trot sets and canter bursts a half hour later. "How long have you been out here?" Mark asks, surprised that we're still at it.

"Oh, not all that long. I cut it short today," I say. "He may be slow," I say to my Irish friend, "but he can go on forever."

Next is Huey, who is quivering and pawing with anticipation in the trailer. He remembers all too well what this is about. J.W. wanders over to our trailer to see what's going on. "You're looking at seventy race starts and seventy horse shows," Barrett brags to J.W. Every time my husband mentions Huey's career, the numbers increase.

"Events," I quickly correct. "And he's almost eighteen." This fact will undoubtedly impress our race trainer, who works with two- and three-year-olds.

I can hardly hold Huey on the track, particularly when I start to canter him. When three horses breeze by us on the rail, Huey takes off, and no amount of muscle can rate him. I yank him in the mouth a few to get him stopped, turn him around, and cancel any ideas I might have of galloping—trotting will have to suffice. He arches his swan's neck and struts his stuff. He, too, gives me more step in his trot on the track than he ever does in the ring. Maybe I should come to Pimlico to practice my dressage tests. A half hour later, even from trotting, my shoulders feel like they're going to fall out of their sockets. Huey, jigging all the way back to the barns, is in a lather and all washed out. Barrett takes him from me to untack and cool out, and starts walking him in the shed row. The horse is still so fired up that Barrett has to borrow a chain shank from J.W. He gladly lets the hot walker take him and admits that he can't hold the horse. I can't tell if he's serious or just showing off. How many events was that? A hundred? I must admit, it's pretty cool to see my big, athletic, almost-eighteen-year-old event horse this keen, strutting around the shed row with a hot walker in tow, just like the good old days.

October 1

Subcontinental Johnny calls before I head up to the barn for the morning. He's filled with life in Benares: a boat ride on the Ganges, life with his host family, his excitement about learning the sitar. "By the way, what's a *patouage?*" I ask him.

"That's p-a-k-a-w-a-j," he corrects. "You know tabla, right? That's two drums, pakawaj is one." His host father is a famous pakawaj player. The delay across the miles is longer this time, and John admits that he's homesick. But he is happy to be in India. John, unlike most people I know, is happy to be wherever he is.

I'm worried about Redmond's hives. I give Vet a jingle. She suggests a hit of dexamethasone. I bathe him once more in Equitaine, and Barrett suggests first baby oil, then baking soda rubbed into the bumps. A farm he once worked at did that for broodmares with skin disease who had to bear the weight of twelve hundred pounds thrashing away on their itchy, sore skin. We rub the powdery stuff onto the worst spots: Redmond's neck and rump. If this doesn't help, we'll try athlete's foot powder. A friend suggests the sheath cleaner Excaliber—just give him a bath in it. I hesitate to go to the tack store and ask for a twelve pack. Would I like any latex gloves with that? Nah, thanks, I'll just use a scrubby sponge.

Huey is a star show jumping today, which is especially gratifying after his 32-furlong blowout at Pimlico yesterday. Jerry is an even bigger hit in a cross-country school. I let him take a look and then pop over our very scary ditch in the grob, as well as the water ditch. He doesn't seem to mind and does everything I ask of him—as long as I let him take a look to see that the boogeyman doesn't live underneath the fences or in the ditches. The school is a reminder to myself about taking time to absorb what I'm about to do when it is new to me.

I help Katie with a Novice show jump lesson on her new horse. She recently bought Rusty Rudder off the track from J.W., after selling her other horse Boy as a dressage horse to someone who could take a heart-murmur horse Prix St. George. Rusty was sweet but too slow to win a third time. J.W. offered him to Katie for $5,000 and the promise she'd fix him up on a blind date. "The blind date is the easy part," she said. He dropped the price to $3,000 and two blind dates. Rusty is forward and does just fine in his very first jump school.

All is well, except for Redmond's hives, which have become my current torment. At least they're no longer hot to the touch and his skin not so sensitive. I consider scratching him from show jumping at Morven. Barrett's grocery list today is Perrier, tonic, popcorn, and 15 pounds of athlete's foot powder.

Leesburg (Again)

I see 3:30 A.M., leave by 4:30, spot a possum in the drive carrying something limp in its mouth, which necessitates a quick call to Barrett. "I hope it wasn't one of the kittens," I think he mumbles from half-sleep.

"Oh my God! Go round them up," I say. The Big Cheese, that's me, always manned with an order, no matter the time of day. There's a roadblock 3 miles down the pike on curvy Falls Road in the little town of Butler.

"Just turn around and head down Stringtown," the cop says to me nonchalantly from the mouth of his flashlight.

"How am I supposed to do that?" I ask, pointing at my mile-long rig as if it needed pointing out—I'm the only horse trailer or only vehicle period on Falls Road at this hour. The officer helps me back up someone's drive that parallels the side of a rocky cliff. Somehow I manage not to back the trailer into the ditch that lines the nine-foot-wide driveway, and I get us turned around to take the cop's suggested detour. Halfway to Leesburg, I stop for gas and notice that I've lost the running lights on my trailer. It's still pitch black outside. I do have turn signals and (I hope) brake lights, so I damn the torpedoes and keep going, hoping that I won't have another encounter with a police officer this morning as a result. I should have walked up the stairs backward when I had the chance.

Coach meets me at show jumping to walk the course frontward. She's not jumping her Advanced horse today, which translates that I'm on my own for warm-up. I start worrying about whom I can ask to help set fences for me. Once I'm tacked up, I ask Bonnie Mosser if I can follow her lead in warm-up, and she obliges. Redmond seems fine, maybe a tick quiet, so I rev him up with crop and spurs, which I find out soon enough is an unnecessary tactic. Bonnie points out that he's jumping to the right—his favorite trick, which I've never been able to correct. He crashes through one warm-up fence. "That's because of the right lean!" Bonnie calls out. I can't seem to do anything about that in the five minutes or so before I have to go in the ring. Instead, I glance back at his haunches, where the athlete's foot powder Barrett rubbed all over his ass has risen to the surface of his sweat. I frantically try to rub away the big powdery patches of white on his butt as Phillip Dutton, Adrienne Iorio Borden, Bonnie Mosser, Jane Sleeper, and other fearless leaders in my sport are warming up around my rabid Clown-Ass.

Redmond gets electrified as we enter the ring. He jumps well, but snuggles up too close to a couple of fences and has two rails—not his usual clean round. Must have been that right lean. Or his itchy ass. Or the speeding bullet syndrome.

Ten days before the Fair Hill jog. All my plans for Redmond in the process of coming to fruition. The five-and-a-half events since his comeback have been completed, and relatively well. He seems solid, physically, despite the fungus. There's nothing getting in our way.

. I hunt down the FEI vets while I'm at Morven to ask them about the withdrawal time for dexamethasone, the drug of choice for hives and other allergic skin reactions in horses. At international events that are run under FEI rules, like the Three Star at Fair Hill, horses are not permitted to have most medicinal assistance, with the exception of some antibiotics, so that their performance cannot be artificially enhanced by drugs, nor can the horses be put in harm's way by masking a medical problem. The vets at Morven assure me that the withdrawal time for dex is only two or three days, that I have plenty of time between now and Fair Hill to give Redmond a few doses of the drug. When I tell them that we've switched Redmond's bedding, his turnout paddock, and are now using a milder detergent for his pj's, they seem satisfied that we've covered our bases.

Over saag paneer, prawn masala, and veggie samosas, Barrett scans the pages of *Eventing Magazine*. "Bonnie Mosser is the year's third-best woman rider in the country," he says, with eyebrows raised.

"Who are first and second?" I ask, as if I didn't know: Kim Severson and Karen O'Conner. Barrett knows better than to tell me I'm tied for forty-sixth.

October 3

The little bit of rain we got the other day was just spit, so the ground remains rock hard and the pastures dried to a crisp. I don't think I've ever seen it this dry in Maryland. Every day the skies are relentlessly blue, including today, when I have it on my schedule to take Huey for a conditioning hack. We spend more time walking than anything else. The dogs canter on ahead and then stop and turn back to wait for us with quizzical looks. They're not used to me being a slowpoke. I take Huey to the Menzies' low woods, where in normal conditions, it's usually boggy. I'm hoping that the ground will have more moisture there and we might be able to trot for a stretch. I haven't been in these woods for some time. They meander on and go off in different directions. I take a fork in the trail I've never taken before, despite Huey's protests. Before I know it, we're coming out on a farm that is unfamiliar to me. I'm lost. A man is working on the outside of his house, and there's a pond to which the dogs make a beeline. The man is dressed like a slightly older Tarzan. No shirt. Even his nipples are tanned. I call up to the King of the Jungle that I hope he doesn't mind. He stares at me. "Dogs," I explain. "Water. Swim." Now he gets me. Gruffly responds that it's all right. Good thing, too, because no way can I call my Labs off water—they're already swimming circles around each other by the time permission is granted. After the dip, we turn around and head back the way we came, and I give Huey his head. He'll pick the right turns in the trail toward home. He always does, better than any compass. By the time we wander slowly home, I note that we've been gone for almost two hours, and the dogs are exhausted. They instantly pass out for the rest of the afternoon in the tack room.

The good news is that Redmond's bumps are better. I give him another antifungal bath for good measure, plus another packet of dexamethasone in his snack at night check. Ungowah!

October 4

I haven't had my period in two months. I'm grateful, after having spent the past year in more or less continuous menstruation. The shocker that Chandler is unexpectedly pregnant a week before her wedding curls the hair on the back of my neck. This hot-off-the-press item Katie has sworn me to secrecy for knowing is exactly the sort of man-bites-dog story that could wreck my chances at Fair Hill. I picture big-faced teenage boys with ball caps and wads of gum screaming, "Extra! Extra! Woman pregnant at 5-0!"

I'm distracted through my barn work and rides, have to run out for a haircut in the afternoon. Afterward, I go out of my way to stop at a pharmacy off the beaten track where I can be sure I won't run into anyone I know. Even so, I look right and left over my shoulder several times to make sure I don't recognize anyone in adjacent aisles, as I search for an EPT, hoping I won't have to ask a clerk where I might find an EARLY PREGNANCY TEST. How ridiculous must I look, a fifty-year-old buying a pregnancy test for her— what?—daughter, sister, friend?—certainly not for *herself*.

I find the item in question all by my embarrassed self, grab it off the shelf, race to the checkout, plucking an antibacterial soap along the way. Okay, so we need it in the barn, but it also covers up the *other* box I'm holding and makes it seem that I needed to come here for a variety of things, and not just for an EARLY PREGNANCY TEST. I'm behind a young, gum-chewing woman in the checkout line, who is buying ChapStick, complains about its price, doesn't have enough money for it, leaves the ChapStick on the counter. Then, as I'm putting my purchase down, she cuts in front of me to buy the ChapStick anyway when her boyfriend hands her an additional dollar. She continues to make a fuss about how expensive the ChapStick is, digging into her change purse for the thirty-five cents she still needs to square the exchange. Eyeing the EPT on the counter, she glances up doubtfully my way. Oh please, dear God, please let her not ask me anything. All I want is for the clerk to cover up the damn thing in a bag and ring me up. "Would you like a bag for this?" she asks, when it's finally my turn. Surely she must be joking.

In my early twenties, I had to have an ovary removed, and my ex, owing to a bout with childhood testicular cancer, only had one testicle, so we were batting only 500 before we even got started. Six pregnancies and two kids later, I've gotten used to the impossible becoming possible.

I dash home to pee on a stick before an ecstatic Barrett returns from his race with Poetry in Motion's Chapbook—the bastard of a horse and Johnny's favorite. I study the stick for the interminable two minutes it takes for the little negative sign to show its lovely design in the plastic window. Thank a merciful lord; I am restored, even as I'm on my way to becoming an old lady.

Chapbook won his race today at Delaware Park. That's where Barrett's heart is, and he's jubilant. It was a solid race for a horse he didn't think was ready to win at the $16,000 claiming level, or ready to win at all, so we both get what we want—no news and big news—and settle in to a night's celebration over citron vodka for him, Anapamu for me, and huge plates of clam spaghetti. After years of making it one way, we decide to make it another, leaving the clams in their shells and adding a gentle clatter to our big nightly eat. We carry the sweet buzz upstairs but he falls asleep before I have a chance to ask him to use a condom and maybe put on a second one in case the first one breaks.

October 5

My student Dan and I trailer two hours to Berryville, Virginia, for a cross-country school at Gordondale Schooling course. Jerry has his first Beginner Novice event this weekend at Olney Horse Trials, and I'd like to get him off the farm one more time before his big day. Dan wants to bring his horse along for my help over cross-country fences. It's the first time I've been to the schooling facility designed by Olympic event rider Nina Fout. There are considerable options for schooling Novice and Training level, with fewer possibilities for Beginner Novice. Dan has stopping issues with his horse, which I try to coach him through, while Jerry eats up all of the Beginner Novice and some of the Novice fences like they're candy.

Toward the end of the school, I cruise around the course and re-jump the smaller fences I've already introduced Jerry to. I have confidence in my pony, but when we trot up to the ditch again, he stops at the last second. I flip him around and am too aggressive presenting. He wheels, I slip off and land on my butt at the edge of the ditch. Jerry runs toward the other horse, and Dan reaches down and grabs one of Jerry's reins. He's trying unsuccessfully not to laugh. It must be pretty funny to see his coach plopped on her ass. Maybe he's even a little relieved that I finally have a problem, as up till this point green-bean Jerry has been perfect, while his horse has had multiple stops and run-outs.

I get back on, take Dan's lead over the ditch, and on we go. I use my mishap as a point of instruction. "I did exactly what I've been telling you not to do," I say. "I got in a hurry. Young horses and horses not sure of themselves, like yours and Jerry, need a moment to process what you're asking them to do." I hope it sinks in, to both Dan and me.

I get home to a call from Kim Meier, asking about the transportation of two yearlings Barrett is sending her to break. "I wouldn't take Jerry to Olney on Sunday," she says.

"Why not?" I say.

"I wouldn't ride any horse except the ones you trust implicitly a week out from a three-day." She tells me stories of riders getting hurt doing something stupid right before a big event and not being able to ride. "It would be bad enough if Redmond had a problem, but think how you'd feel if you got hurt and weren't able to ride at Fair Hill." She's got a point, and Barrett agrees with her.

"It's not worth the risk," he says. "I'd bag Olney, if you know what's good for you." I brace myself for being sore again—you can't even land on your feet when you're fifty and not be bound up the next day. Which I guess is a good enough reason to pare down before Fair Hill. Maybe I should ask Kim to ride Jerry for me on Sunday.

Barking and wagging my tail—that's how Barrett describes my conflicted state. I call Hans. He wants to know if I get hurt, can he ride

Redmond? Then he encourages me to take Jerry, Rusty, Pruitt, and the unbroken yearling, Rein Dance, to Olney, too.

Before bed, I'm surprised when my old red friend comes knocking on my door.

October 6

I'm a little neurotic jumping Redmond—not only am I by myself, but as we get closer to Fair Hill, I want things to go perfectly, and I worry that something will get in our way at the last minute. Every day seems to bring more stress with it.

I set up three different gymnastic lines, and Redmond pops through them as if he's got tennis balls in his feet. He's happy to have yet another opportunity to do what he loves and does so well. I take a long time cooling him out and soaping him up with the antifungal shampoo, even though his bumps are nearly all gone. Katie just clipped him yesterday, so he'll have an easier time staying cool during his monumental effort at Fair Hill. She has clipped and left hair in the pattern of two side-by-side diamonds on the right rump, and three on the left—our logo is five diamonds touching. No one clips or braids like Katie. We get compliments everywhere we go, and she's especially proud of the job she's done on Redmond's face this time. You can't tell where the clip lines begin and end, and that's hard to do with all the bones and angles in a horse's face. If I got as many compliments on my riding as Katie gets on her grooming, I'd be in the money.

I have a heart-to-heart with my student Audrey about her horse, who's too much for her and scares her. Because I haven't been teaching all that long, this is a hard conversation for me to have, one that some instructors might not even broach, more concerned about keeping horses and students in their loop. If I can't ride the horse successfully—which I can't—it's doubtful that Audrey will learn to do it. Audrey has been on the fence about the horse for some time, and my remarks seem to bring her relief as she decides on the spot to donate the horse to Garrison Forrest School's riding program. My honesty means we'll have a stall opening up, as well as a hole in our accounts receivable.

I finish my rides and lessons and office work and check off another day till Fair Hill. Six till the jog, only five till we leave. As I move around the sprinkler in the backyard, I notice that we've gotten a surge of end-of-season ripe tomatoes. I pluck them, along with a handful of basil, with plans for pesto and sliced tomatoes for dinner. Our tomatoes and basil apparently thrive on dry weather. The skies threaten all day but only deliver sprinkles. Our pastures look like yellowing scrub grass, with a few ugly, greedy, thriving, spidery weeds poking up. None of Barrett's tricks for making it rain seems to be working, such as leaving the car windows down or storing bags of grain outside the barn. It will be another day at Pimlico for Redmond tomorrow to accomplish his last conditioning workout, unless we get a few inches between now and then.

October 7

"It rained all night, so I turned off the sprinkler!" Barrett alarm-clocks up the stairs at 5:30 A.M. Which translates: Oops, I forgot the sprinklers, but yay!!! It's raining!!!

We bag the idea of taking Huey and Redmond to Pimlico, and instead I head out on Redmond for his last conditioning hack before Fair Hill. Despite the precipitation, the ground is still too firm, so I'm cautious where I take him, canter very little, then cut it short and head back to end our work by trotting fifteen more minutes on the rubber footing in the jump ring. I'm dodging raindrops, and by the time I get on Huey, I'm soaked. But it's warm and it's rain, and we all seem to love its foreign feel today. Huey is game and forward, and the ground is softening as we go, so I let him trot, practicing our lengthenings and shortenings of the gait. I feel something a little different in him—a willingness to lengthen his stride without quickening it. So I let the trot out a little farther, and for the first time in the ten years I've owned him, I feel a semblance of an extended trot happening underneath me. Both Huey and Redmond have struggled with their lengthened gaits for years, and I've worked nearly fruitlessly to produce the effect of longer strides within the boundaries of their limited movement. I am amazed by this different gear in my old man Huey. To think that he's been keeping this secret from me all these years. Then again, maybe it's because his hocks are responding to their injections.

I put both horses away, spend time in my office. Then back up to the barn through the pouring blessed rain to wrap Huey and Redmond's legs, pack their feet, and start the organizing process for Fair Hill. I resolve to keep my focus on Redmond and the momentous Fair Hill Three Star, to let nothing get in the way. Just my luck to get hurt riding a baby at his first competition. I take the cautious route and scratch Jerry from Olney Horse Trials, returning to the perfect footing of less personal risk over the ensuing days before Fair Hill.

We're invited to Chandler's rehearsal dinner at noisy Nick's Fish House, somewhere in off-the-beaten-track Baltimore, which takes us a solid hour through rainy, bumper-to-bumper rush hour to find. We're not supposed to know that Chandler's already pregnant, so Barrett and I put on our best blank faces, and then our most surprised and congratulatory ones when she confides her whispered news to the two of us.

"I want to talk to you about Smarty," she says. "I want to put him on training board and for you to take him Training level before the season's out."

Why not lease him to Audrey and save the money? I'll try and nudge her in that direction after the wedding.

It pours on our way home, and through the night. I listen to its music on our tin roof. "That ought to sweeten up the ground for Fair Hill," my just-as-sweet husband lullabies me to sleep.

October 8

Cats and dogs plummet from the sky. I get a call from Walter Reynolds at Radnor—"Don't bother coming up today; I'm not running." I've promised to be there for my neighbor, who had planned on running Stonehenge at the Radnor International Two Star this weekend. Then, a few minutes later, Walter's wife, Linda, calls to say that they've now switched show jumping and cross country, so cross country will run Sunday. The weather fiasco also happened three years ago when Walter was there last. It always seems to pour at Radnor. Except when Redmond and I were competing there in 2001, when it was 80 degrees and sunny. And then again in 2003, when I can't remember what the weather was, I was so upset not to make it out of the ten-minute box because of a stone bruise.

But I'm not complaining about the weather now. We get reports from our resident weatherman—whose pastime is studying radar screens on his big-screen TV in our barn apartment—that 5 inches have already fallen, with predictions of 3 more to come before it ends. Bring it on.

I hunker down for a day of rides and packing for Fair Hill before we leave for Chandler's wedding. Then it's "Jesu Joy of Man's Desiring" and lifelong vows in an Episcopal service that reminds me of my own upbringing. It also reminds me of the last time I was in a church, at my father's funeral just a year and a half ago. My father refused to go to church after my mother died, his faith shaken by the God who would let his lifelong companion suffer so at the end of her life and die by inches. Seven months later, he went in a blink, getting his own unconscious revenge and what he wished for.

No matter that I no longer attend church, Episcopal ones always feel like home to me. I know all the prayers by heart, and tonight I follow along in the *Book of Common Prayer* as if I recite them every week still, and sing the assigned hymns, joining Chandler and her Tom together in what we hope will be a happy and fruitful marriage—apparently they're already on that track. There's a heavy harvest theme—cornucopias on every pew and the groomsmen are wearing bright orange ties, reminiscent of pumpkins or road construction workers. Then it's lots of white wine and more orange and brown paraphernalia, and dancing in a country club ballroom to big band music, until Barrett and I slither out before the cake is cut, anxious to get out of the furor and home to put our ponies to bed. Daisy and Simon hate it when we leave them for the night, and now we've done just that two evenings in a row. Both dogs come wiggling their whole bodies to the front door to greet us, then shoot off into the night as we walk up to the barn through what is now only a drizzle. There goes the White Rocket. And her dark accomplice. Run Mr. and Mrs. Rabbit. Run for your lives.

October 9

Huey walks in from the paddock today with a fat leg—it's the same left front that blew up with cellulitis in Aiken. He's got a temp of 101, and I find a scabby rub on his fetlock. It's probably the same old cellulitis he's prone to getting, the bacteria having entered at the fetlock rub. Barrett calls Vet, who advises us to start him on a course of antibiotics.

My husband is upset. Huey is Barrett's favorite, the one he works so hard for, although he'd never admit it. "We've got three weeks, it's no big deal," I say, meaning the three seemingly long weeks between now and Huey's attempt to complete the Virginia Two Star. "We've got all the time in the world," I add. I clean and cold-water hose the leg and wrap it—we'll sweat it with a Fura-Zone sweat later at night check. Our attempt to get Huey through a Two Star becomes an even longer shot.

Redmond is my only ride today. I plan on practicing the Three-Star dressage test and then taking him on a long walk hack. The dogs are looking eager and expectant as usual as I tack up Redmond—they're hoping for a trail ride and aren't quite savvy enough to recognize my dressage saddle when they see it. They'll follow me to the indoor arena and mope by the door as I ride, critiquing my every move, until I say it's time to walk over to the Halles' pond for a dip. Redmond would rather return to his stall when we're done with the flatwork, and he pokes along as we walk away from the barn. But a hack will do him good and clear his mind. I'm thinking of all the mental energy and focus he'll need over the next several days at Fair Hill. He picks up his step as we go, as if he knows that it will be a while before he sees these hills again, this pond, this stream.

I give a lesson in the afternoon, then spend the rest of my day organizing and packing for Fair Hill. I toss and turn in bed all night. Barrett does too, sharing my sleeplessness. "I'm so excited," I say several times, midtoss.

"It's pretty amazing, considering where you started," my husband says, contracting my excitement.

"You mean Ann McKay's?"

"Yep," he confirms.

"I know. Beginner Novice at Ann McKay's. Twelve years ago. I remember it well."

My first little unsanctioned event was shortly after I'd met Barrett at a poetry reading. I was married unevenly at the time. Barrett and I were the featured poets. We became close friends, and my husband became jealous, afraid of the passion for horses and stanzas that Barrett and I shared and that he didn't understand. Horses had again become my true love, after a long hiatus that involved careers and families and kids. My attention when I met Barrett was turning back to them. My husband had already lost me.

"I wish it were tomorrow," I say, wanting to get up and start my new day. I feel like a kid on Christmas Eve, listening for the sound of hooves on the rooftop. My own sleigh bells are the Fair Hill ground jury's announcement: *Redmond has been accepted.*

Rain after 90 Days of None

It ceases
its tapping on our tin roof.
Then teases us all morning
with a maze of mist.
By late afternoon its applause
becomes the pelting of rice
or pebbles, thrown at us brides, us beggars,
even as it brings new life
and the colors deepen before our eyes.
Tonight, it will penetrate my dreams,
drench my pillow and my night clothes,
and when you leave our marriage bed again,
I'll throw my arms around that soothing sound,
as if it were enough, almost enough,
this bit of sugar sprinkled on my sleep.

This poem first appeared in *Pearl*.

Kim and Redmond at Fair Hill

CHAPTER SIXTEEN

Rose of Jericho

⁜ October 10

Cooper comes to shock wave Huey's hocks. He diagnoses Huey's problem as cellulitis and tells us we're on the right track with the Gentocin, alternating icing and sweating. The leg is already down when we take the wrap off. Cooper watches Redmond jog, goes over his legs and back, and pronounces him sound and ready to roll. Another big hurdle. Four years ago, with the trailer packed and ready to head out for the Two Star at Camino Real in Texas, Redmond got pulled up by Vet during his last jog before loading. He'd torn his hind origin suspensory, which is a career-ending injury for sport horses more often than not. Every small step is a milestone, right up to the bitter end.

I ride Redmond on the flat. We struggle with our flying changes, but the other movements ride well. I spend the rest of the day packing and organizing for Fair Hill. My excitement is mounting.

I head over to Grace's, armed with the tapes I got from Millbrook, as well as the one of show jumping at Morven. I want to show her a positional blooper I've noticed on the tape, namely my tendency to weight the right stirrup so that it looks as though I'm always falling off the right side of my horse, particularly when galloping cross country. "I've never really noticed it before," Grace admits.

"You should see the seat on my exercise bike, it's permanently tilted right," I say, holding both hands up parallel to her living room floor and veering them sharply right and downward as if I were imitating a banking airplane wing. "It's no wonder Redmond tends to jump right," I say.

"Or why you have problems getting your left flying change," she adds. Horses tend to go toward the weight of their rider, so if the rider is weighting one seat bone or the other, that's the directional tendency of the horse. Therefore, with my "right problem," Redmond is more likely to jump right and have difficulty getting his left lead change.

"We'll have our homework for the winter months ahead," I say. It's obvious that my crookedness is a function of my screwed-up back, scoliosis, and facet disease.

"Why don't you notch up your right stirrup a hole or two?" says Grace What a genius.

"I'll try it," I say, hoping for the quick fix, which is assuredly not the answer but my only alternative between now and Saturday.

I come home to finish packing and get on my very tilted exercise bike. By cocktail hour, I'm jumping out of my skin with anticipation.

Fair Hill, Maryland

I have my last jump school with Grace before shipping out to Fair Hill. It's short but sweet: I run Redmond through a couple of gymnastics and then pop him through a bounce at our water jump. "You're ready to go," Grace says to me, once Redmond effortlessly bounces into the water. I hop off and give her a big hug of thanks. My eyes well up. Hers do, too.

Katie and Barrett and I load the bags and the feed and the shadbelly and the passport, the hay and shavings, saddles, bridles, oh my lord, you name it, the pitchforks and shovels and wheelbarrows. Don't forget the nice clothes to jog in and the ice boots, towels and shampoos, poultices and leg wraps, the sheets and blankets, hat for dressage, helmet for cross country, and the velvet one for stadium. Don't forget the dog food and dog beds and doggie toys. Don't forget the doggies, either, nor Redmond's favorite treats, nor any of the hundreds of items we'll need to make this weekend successful and complete.

One more day till the much-awaited jog at the Fair Hill Three Star. I erase the reminder on our whiteboard—I won't need to cue myself anymore for the countdown of days because there aren't any.

We make the hour-and-a-half trip to Fair Hill, Maryland, without incident, pull in as it starts to rain again, and have to put the truck into four-wheel drive to negotiate the ravaged pasture that's already been created by the traffic of heavy trucks and trailers.

The first obstacle is the in-barn inspection. A team of vets go over Redmond from tip to toe and examine the passport, checking on his compliance with the necessary vaccinations. There's a hitch: an error in our math in the spacing of vaccinations. I can never seem to get the passport right. At Radnor one year, I got a warning for a noncompliance on a vaccination rule. The next three-day, when the passport was still in error because of a misspacing of yet another set of vaccinations, I was fined 100 Swiss francs. If they didn't think I could handle the passport paperwork, how did they expect me to find some francs lying around to send to the FEI headquarters in Zurich? Apparently, I'll get another warning this time, because they've changed the rules so that we have to get flu-rhino boosters every six months rather than every year. Plus, my passport has expired for the first time since Redmond's was originally issued—every four years the USEF, which is the United States' daughter to the FEI, wants more money for a revalidation of the supposedly lifelong equine passport that costs $500 to get in the first place. It's tense for a few minutes, and I try to add some levity and casualness to my exchange with the vets, even though I'm dying inside. I'm so worried about the passport fiasco that I miss the vets' actual examination of the horse, which goes without incident. Now, because we've goofed again, I'll have to start all over with Redmond's vaccinations: he will have to get his initial shots so many days apart, and only so far out from the next three-day. I'll be sure to bring out my abacus to get it right next time. The vets, nevertheless, let us pass into the inner sanctum of the stabling area. We've gotten past Cerberus.

The rain continues as we get Redmond settled in his temporary digs. We head out to buy some sort of tent or awning to rig outside Redmond's end stall of the stabling tent so our stuff doesn't get wet. I've been chintzy and neglected to rent a tack stall, and so the voluminous number of goods we have carefully packed have nowhere to go except right outside Redmond's stall, or around the corner, outside in the rain.

We find a tarp at Wal-Mart. Katie rigs it up, using a tree and a small stake. We walk and wrap and feed Redmond, and all is well and at least partially dry for the night.

We leave the show grounds to find our Motel 6. "Horse show?" the clerk at the front desk asks.

"Yep," I say, "Fair Hill."

"It won't get rained out?" she asks again.

"Rained out?" I say. "Is there more rain in the forecast?"

"All week," she says, with what I think is a mean gleam in her eye, "and right through the weekend."

"Rained out?" I say again.

I dream that I'm at the Rolex Four Star, too exhausted to walk the cross-country course in preparation for my ride. Nor can I get organized in time for my dressage test. When I finally hoist myself up into the saddle, my hair falls out in chunks, so that I'm left with a jagged pixie. The hat will cover it, I say to myself, before waking to the welcome weight of my thick braid and no chance to ride the dream test. No Samson here.

October 12

I've been waiting all year to hear the words: "Redmond has been accepted." It's the swiftest affirmation from a ground jury I've ever experienced. It is particularly sweet this time around, considering the year I've been through nursing Redmond's tendon back to health. "His leg looks really good," Coach compliments, as I'm waiting for my turn to jog. Damn straight. A lot of months, swine fetal bladders, and miles of careful rehab went into that leg. I'm surprised how confident I feel jogging down the lane, Redmond's soundness on display to a crowd of discerners. Redmond has come back from not one, but two potentially career-ending injuries since I've owned him—a fact I'm proud of. It helps that he looks better than ever. Katie has done her usual best with his braids and clip job and baby oil rubbed into his coat until he's gleaming. Thanks to a slow and steady conditioning program, Redmond also looks fitter than he has ever looked before.

It alternates misting and raining all day, but I don't care—I am happy to be where I am, and how often do we feel that in a lifetime? I walk the cross-country course. Every jump is a demon, but instead of the demons chasing me, I'll be chasing them. It looks manageable, except for one gigantic right corner. This may be an issue, reconsidering Redmond's right bulge and my crooked back. Toward the end of the course, a steeplechase fence drops enormously into the last water jump, which makes my eyes pop. But Redmond will be galloping toward home at this point and—I hope—won't care about the size of the fence, nor the fact that there's water on the other side, more eager to get back to where he started and finish. I am daunted by how long the course is. I cross my fingers that my pony will be fit enough to cope with the distance and the maybe forty jumping efforts that will be required of him.

I ride him a second time later in the day. It's a more rigorous dressage school with the double bridle. Redmond is unfazed by the hoopla of tents and flags, tense horses and riders galloping toward him, flying changes galore, dogs and trainers and loudspeakers blasting away. Despite all the goings-on, Redmond focuses on what I'm asking of him, keen pony that he is.

I run into Coach, who's also schooling her horses. As she's changing mounts, I trot up beside her, "Just so you know, Coach, Grace is coming tomorrow to warm me up for dressage." Her eyes get a little big, as if I'm a maximum fence.

"Does she know about us?" she asks. Coach knows I haven't told Grace that I've gone back to Coach for a couple of lessons, though she does know that I've continued taking dressage from Grace. Grace, to the best of my knowledge, doesn't know about my moonlighting with Coach. So I'm surprised by Coach's further remark, "Well, she's your neighbor, you're the one that has to live with her. As for myself, I don't really care." But I can tell from her tone that she does.

"I don't think Fair Hill is the time to have that discussion," I say, a little defensively. She shrugs her shoulders and mounts her next horse. "I hope you're not mad at me," I say, sounding like a kid. I table the issue—nothing is going to get in my way this weekend.

October 13

I hack Redmond and stretch him down at all three gaits. I pass him off to Katie and walk the cross-country course, which seems to shrink a bit on my second go-round. Then I get ready for my dressage test. Barrett and Grace show up right before it's time to get on, which rattles me. So far, all week, I've been in a focused, happy zone, and I feel the bubble start to break as I fret over how they'll both get through the front gate without a car pass.

But here they are. I pull on my shadbelly, wipe off my boots and get on, walk down the lane and through the echoey tunnel, and come out into the trade-fair area with the tents and dressage rings and all the goings-on. When I start to warm him up, Redmond is relaxed. He's stretching down nicely, and he's forward. I pick up the reins and manage to keep his relaxation as we practice the movements for Grace, who gives a few pointers. I do a bit of canter work, possibly too much, certainly too many attempts at the flying change, which Redmond is too eager to give me now. He tenses up, starts to make mistakes, and loses the quality of his gaits. I stretch him down again to get the relaxation back, but way too soon it's time for number 31 to canter down center line.

The first part of the test is okay. The shoulder ins to medium trots, the extended trots, even the walk work feel improved. But Redmond stiffens up when it's time to canter. In the first counter-canter serpentine, he breaks to a trot. I get the counter canter back and do my flying change. The judge's horn honks, signaling that I've gone off course—oh, shit!—forgetting the medium canter circle at S. I find where I'm going and try not to get flustered by my error. I do the circle, the other serpentine, the other flying change, the extended canter, and make it back down center line for my salute. I'm beating myself up over my error when I look up at the scoreboard to see that we've gotten creamed with a 76.5, including the two error points for going off course. I don't understand the severity of the marks. It wasn't the greatest test, but it was quiet and relatively obedient, and steady, which is what I was trying to produce. My elation of the past two days turns into disappointment and embarrassment. There are eighty-two participants and my score is higher—meaning worse—than eighty of them. Is it possible that I'm out of my league? Katie turns to Barrett with a devastated, Goth expression. "She screwed the pooch," he says, shaking his head.

I walk the cross-country course with Grace My heart isn't in it because I haven't had enough time to process what just happened in the dressage ring. At one point, Coach and her group walk by Grace and me. Neither Grace nor Coach greets the other, though they've known each other for years. I try not to read anything into their lack of exchange. "That must be fun," Grace says ironically, meaning my close stabling proximity to Coach, which translates to me that she doesn't have a clue about my new relationship with my old coach.

Fuck dressage. I've got to find the courage to keep going so I'll be able to attack those monster fences on Saturday. I decide the best way to do that is over dinner with Barrett and Katie and two huge margaritas, doctored with extra shots of tequila. Katie recommends Cuervo. Before she was my lifelong groom, Katie was a lifelong bartender at Champs in Columbia, Maryland. Good thing I'm not riding cross-country tomorrow: I'd be nursing a hangover for sure. "So what's with the stirrups?" Barrett loosens up enough to ask.

"What do you mean?" I say.

"You looked like Lester Piggott out there," he explains.

"So I wouldn't fall off the right side of my saddle, or something like that," I say, "which certainly would have been more entertaining."

October 14

I walk the course by myself in the morning, because that's who I really need to walk it with. I take my notepad with me and start jotting down thoughts on how to ride the jumps—specific lines and distances between fences, speeds to take the various jumping efforts, noting options, changes of terrain, and so on. Kim shows up, and Katie and Kim and I wheel it to locate my minute markers, and Kim gives me her two cents' worth, which ends up being more like several hundred dollars' worth. She asks what bit I'm using. When I tell her it's some twisted wire thing, she warns me to have someone bring a bottle of water to the finish line. "I guarantee, there will be blood," she says. I give her a hug and she's off toward home.

I wander over to the dressage rings to watch Coach's ride on her second horse. Her horse is restive and disobedient in the test and scores poorly. As she exits the ring, she stops next to me. "So, did you have a good course walk with Kim?"

"Yeah," I say, not knowing she knew that Kim was here.

"Did you have a good walk with Grace?"

"Yeah," I say.

"What is this," she goes on, "course walk by committee?"

"Of course I walked it with Kim," I reply. "Kim is my friend." She walks away with her horse. I don't have a chance to say anything about her test. She doesn't care about my moonlighting or getting information from others or not having her as my be-all-end-all coach, like I have a hole in my head. I head back to the stabling area, because it's time for the course walk with Coach, who has clearly put me on her *liste de merde*.

Coach chats with her two other students and ignores me, except when I ask a question, and even then, she won't look me in the eye. She gives us valuable information, which I add to my notepad. I'm feeling lousy about the way the last two days have unfolded, just as I'm about to face one of the biggest challenges of my life. I'll have to find the positive energy somewhere. Get in that zone where nothing else matters, not a bad dressage test or coaches mad at me, not the trepidation I still feel as I walk up to those massive 4-foot fences. Although I've walked the course six times, the jumps haven't shrunk all that much.

Barrett rejoins Katie and me for dinner. He's the only one in Wesley's Restaurant wearing a suit, although he's usually in jeans and T-shirt, smelling like the barn. First he tries to convince me that I'm the special occasion. But I know better. "You went to the racetrack today, didn't you?" I say.

"Ten-four," he says.

"Well?"

"Sylvia Plath won an allowance race. That's $35,000 for two months' worth of work." Barrett adds that he's brought one of J.W.'s missiles . . . a 2-foot-long, 4-inch-diameter tube of electrolytes for Redmond's run tomorrow. Sylvia's win and the missile are good enough to try and sleep on.

Cross-Country Day

I walk the course yet one more time in the morning and still have hours to stew before my ride at 1:23. I walk it alone for my last go, which is my usual custom, to create the bubble of focus and solitude I'll need to get the job done. Which are the exact words Caitlin uses when she gives me a good-luck call. "Fair Hill is your Broadway," she says cleverly. "Like Kim used to tell me before I'd go out on course with Sunny, 'Just get the job done!'"

No one seems to have a clear picture of the proper preparation for cross country without roads and tracks and steeplechase. Those other elements were used primarily as warm-up phases for the huge long effort of a Three-Star cross country. Some say interval sprints the night before, some say sprints on the morning of cross country. Others say speed bursts are entirely unnecessary, but attempting to recreate the phases A–C before leaving the start box is vital. I ask Coach what she does. "I just warm up like I do for a horse trial," she quips.

To break up the tension, Barrett and I take The White Rocket and Mr. Simon Sad Eyes on a walk. Three furlongs away from stabling, we see a half-dozen competitors galloping in sets, working their horses in thirty-second, quarter-mile bursts. "Should we be out here with Redmond?" I ask, ever the second-guesser.

"Nah," he says. In the distance we see Coach's groom lunging one of her horses on a 60-foot line: a forty-five-minute cardio without the hazard of a rider's weight. Well, of course she's not going to give away all her secrets.

I end up using Coach's system, with a little extra trotting thrown in. My plans get blown when there are not two, but three holds on course while I'm preparing to go out of the start box. Nothing like hanging around in warm-up for an extra half hour while they haul bodies off the course and repair jumps. Somehow I manage to keep my cool. It helps to have Kim there telling me exactly what to do to best prepare Redmond before he leaves the box.

"This horse has answered every question you've ever asked of him," Kim reminds me. "There's no reason to think he'll stop now."

We're off. There goes jump 1, then 2, and 3. There goes the first water that includes the skinny carved turtle. There goes the humongous corner that terrifies me, numbers 6, 7, 8. The bounce into water where so many have already had trouble. Redmond puts one stride in the bounce and splashes through and up the bank to the skinny oxer brush out. Another tough combination and a couple of fliers over the long gallop to where the crowds are gathered by the trade fair, the bank turning to the corner, to the third water, and the narrow carved loon (which has already seen its share of stops and falls), through the water to the skinny out. I hear whoops and whistles from the spectators as I gallop up the hill to attack the back loop, where the jumps get even more complicated. The aqueduct that involves the angled walls and ditches where I take the straight route through and feel my pony use all of himself to get the second element done. Jumps 20, 21, to 22 A and B, the turning corners, where we get the three strides in between, though Redmond has to reach and reach. Jumps 23, to 24, the coffin, where so many have had stops and run-outs. Jumps 25, 26, the huge steeplechase into the water, to the skinny house out, and a long gallop toward home. Jump 28, and through the finish flags. Kim shows up with the squeegee bottle of water and instantly squirts it into Redmond's bloody mouth.

I babble in the vet box, where my team of assistants helps me cool Redmond out. "That was hard!" I say over and over again, alternating with, "Is he all right?" and "I can't believe we did it!" I repeat myself, as if I had a concussion. Dan and his wife show up, armed with ice boots that they immediately slap on Redmond's front legs. People whom I haven't seen in a long time give me a congratulatory hug. Event riders I have never spoken to compliment me on my ride. Olympic veteran Bruce Davidson asks me what my plans for Redmond are. "Rolex in the spring?" he asks. I laugh it off. "He's a fabulous horse," Bruce says, "absolutely dreamy." Walter and Linda Reynolds stop by the barn with a bottle of champagne, which we immediately uncork and toast to Redmond.

Our work has just begun. We walk and ice, walk and ice, pack Redmond's feet, graze, poultice, walk him at night check, turn out his light. Sleep tight, my little almost-Three-Star pony. Then we hit the hay ourselves. Barrett tries to toast our success with a hint of romance. I want to celebrate with a hint of Percocet, dreams of tomorrow and beyond.

October 16

Up by 4:15 A.M., to the barn by 5:00. Barrett, Katie, and I get down to business to get Redmond ready for the final vet inspection. We walk, ice, ride, walk, laser his back, braid, lots of spit and polish, jog to test for soundness. "Maybe ever so slightly off on the right front," warns Coach. "But I think he'll pass," she adds.

My heart stops. I walk him and walk him, run into Bruce Davidson again. "Any more thoughts on Rolex?" he asks.

"Don't you think that's a little quick?" I say tentatively. He shakes his head decisively from side to side.

I step into a skirt, climb into a clingy top, best boots, and blazer, and walk Redmond over to the final vet inspection at the main arena, where the trade fair is, and the crowds, and the flags flying from all the countries represented. My turn comes up. The announcer, Brian O'Connor, approaches. "Great ride yesterday, Julia," he says. Redmond is accepted one more time, without hesitation, from the ground jury.

It's time for me to tack Redmond up and dress myself, get Barrett's help to tie the lucky silk tie my mother wore sixty years ago at Madison Square Garden, where she won on her three-gaited saddlebred, Noble Knight, whose very image is silk-screened onto the tie. We enter the arena with the crowds and the flags and the huge Three-Star stadium fences, and wait for the timer to beep, signaling the start of our round. Redmond catapults himself over the fences, picking them off one by one, and puts in the stadium round of his career. Cheers from the crowd as Brian announces, "That's the horse we'd all like to have, ladies and gentlemen. That's Redmond with a double clear, no jumping penalties, and well within the time." Redmond and I are one of seven horse-and-rider combinations to have a double-clear round in stadium, moving up from eightieth place after dressage, to thirty-second after cross country, and finishing in twenty-fifth place after our clear stadium round.

I call everyone from the road on our short trip home. I'm pinching myself to make sure that I'm feeling what I'm feeling. If I live to be a hundred, I'm quite sure I will never feel this way again.

October 17

6:30 A.M. The phone rings from India with around-the-block reception. John is eager to tell me about his new sitar and his sitar guru, and how sore his body is from endless hours playing the instrument lotus style. He tells me about witnessing cremations on the Ganges and about his community-service project, which involves vaccinating a population of under-privileged children against typhoid. He lights up when he describes his new interest in Kathak, a kind of Indian dance that includes a percussive rhythmic beat with bare feet and lots of expressive arm movements. He is taking Kathak dance lessons, along with his studies of Hindi and Buddhism. Finally, he tells me how homesick he's been the last few days. "We're almost halfway through the program," he reminds me.

"You'll be home before you know it," I say, "In the meantime, soak it up. We're on parallel tracks, you and I." After we hang up, I realize I hardly said anything about Fair Hill, as if I were hording my small personal triumph, trying not to be too selfish in the face of my son's stories of his own adventures on the other side of the world.

My phone rings with congratulatory calls from friends and neighbors and fellow event riders, some of whom have never called me before. I have seventy-six e-mails waiting for me, ranging from products to enlarge my penis to Williams-Sonoma and Victoria's Secret specials, to the more personal, "You Go, Girl!" and "Rolex, 2006!" and "Whoooooooooah!" My favorite is from Caitlin: . . . *Remember how a short time ago your biggest dream was to do Training Level at Jackson Hole?? Look at you now! If that isn't an example of how, if you put your mind to something, you can do anything, then I don't know what is!!*

All her teenage years spent guilting myself because I was always so busy with the horses now come back to pat me on the back.

Barrett takes me out for dinner at the Manor Tavern in Monkton, a favorite haunt, where we eat very alliteratively with sicilienne and spinach salads and Savannah shrimp. We toast to Redmond. Then Barrett gets down to business, with pen and pad. He writes down the names of our

event horses, along with their goals for the spring. He offers to be the
salesman for Jerry and Pruitt, while I take Redmond and Calvin south in
order to get a jump-start on Redmond's spring season toward either
Rolex or Jersey Fresh. The decision about which spring Three or Four Star
does not need to be made until later. Either way, I must make another trip
south, which I swore I wouldn't do this coming winter, or ever again, for
that matter. Suddenly, I find myself looking ahead and in another planning
mode. No sooner do I get the one goal accomplished than I'm on to the
next—my modus operandi for my fifty years on this sweet and sour planet
of successes and failures, jumps to jump and poems to write. We're home.
"Come on doggies, let's do night check"—then to dreams of Rolex.
Instead, I have my disturbing Samson dream of losing all my hair before I
ride. Only I know where my strength resides. It's fluttering just under my
rib cage, wanting out.

October 18

Huey is supple and sound and feeling good in a flat lesson with Grace. She
gives me pointers on trying to kick him up into the bridle to get him to
lighten his front end, while encouraging him to stay as pliable as possible
by bending him right and left and manipulating him through the lateral
movements. We talk about Fair Hill. I tell her what Bruce Davidson said
to me about Rolex. "Those big guys always want to go straight to Rolex
after only one Three Star," she says. Something tells me I will have to feel
my way toward this decision and listen to no one but myself, which will
be hard for me.

I get back to basics with Pruitt and Jerry, spending time bathing them
and scrubbing off the rain rot that has accumulated in my absence, pulling
their manes, lunging Pruitt and taking Jerry on a long hack with the dogs
on this brilliant fall afternoon. This is my favorite time of year in
Maryland—the air is crisp in the morning and sweetens up by afternoon,
the leaves are fluttering around us, and the sun is shining hard. These
October days seem to go on forever and invite me to reminisce about my
fall hacks fifteen years ago when I was falling back in love with riding on
my leased school pony, Peanut, three years before I completed my first
Baby Novice event.

Photographer Beth Collier calls—she's working on an article on Fair Hill for the local equine rag, *The Equiery*, and would like to interview me. I'm eager to talk about my experience at Fair Hill. Normally, I'm not so chatty on the phone, but before I know it, a half hour has gone by, during which I've given my long-winded scoop on my first Three-Star experience.

Chandler shows up in the afternoon with a bundle of pictures she took at Fair Hill. Shots of Redmond and me circling nervously in warm-up, then charging out of the start box and attacking the first fence. Then the last fence, and crossing the finish line, followed by pictures of an elated me and my puffing pony in the vet box. My favorite shot is right after I've dismounted and am leading Redmond over to the box—we are pumped and happy with ourselves. Except for the red foam emanating from his mouth, it's a winner—taken seconds before Kim squirts the squeegee bottle of water into his mouth.

October 19

Two days ago, Katie asked me if I felt different. I looked at her as though I didn't understand the question. Today I feel it for the first time. Somewhere within me, beating like a second heart, in a place that no one can touch, I feel stronger, more assured with my place in the world. Who knows whether it will last, but it's in there; I can feel it taking up residence, and its soundness and satisfaction carry me through this day.

I literally get my feet wet, coaxing a student's disobedient horse into our water jump. Huey looks confused when I tack him up for the second time today with plans to use him as a lead horse. "Hold on, Old Man, this will be an easy one," I say. Marrakesh couldn't care less about his buddy splashing through first. We're asking "Kesh" to drop down an 18-inch drop into the water. He'll canter through the water without the drop. He'll even jump up the little bank once he's in the water. But damned if he won't balk, rear, spin, kick out, and gallop sideways rather than get his feet wet by dropping over the bank into the water. I tell Jennifer to get off and unbuckle the reins on one side and lead him through. "I hope you don't mind getting your feet wet," I say. Kesh rears back and she lets go, and he gallops across the field to the broodmares at the gate. I gallop off on Huey, round up the naughty horse, call for Barrett's assistance in putting Huey away, and fetch a lunge line and whip.

"Do you think we'll get him in?" Jennifer asks skeptically. She ought to know better: Jennifer is an obstetrics resident at Johns Hopkins Hospital, a day job based on miracles.

"Oh, we'll get him in, all right," I say. As sure as those babies that she delivers will slip through the birth canal, her horse is going to jump into my water jump. "If I can do it, he can."

Kesh fusses and fumes at the end of the lunge line. I get in front and hold my nose and plop into the water. The horse decides to rear, hurling me back up the bank. I think quick and sit down on the lunge line, which gives me just enough leverage to stop his backward momentum. We get it sorted with the assistance of Jennifer behind him tickling the lunge whip at his hocks. Kesh finally takes the plunge. I manage to roll out of the way just in time so as not to get trampled. We do it again about fifty times, until he plops in pleasantly. At which point Jennifer gets on his back, and I lead him to the edge of the bank and let go. Success at last.

October 20

I take Huey on a long conditioning hack, Simon and Daisy trotting madly to keep up. As the hack lengthens, they start to lag, but they do their best. They know that water somewhere along the ride is in store for them, and they'll trot a lifetime if there's water at the end of that rainbow. I got to the other side of one just a few days ago, and now I've got my sights already zeroed in on another. I hope I won't anger the gods by my never-ending ambition. I have horses to ride and three-days to finish, and this is my life, every last delicious repetitious second of it. I lull to the rhythm of Huey's one-two, one-two, one-two underneath me, on this ride with no end in sight.

October 21

I rev myself up for Waredaca Horse Trials, where Crustacean will be going Intermediate this weekend. I get four rides done in the morning and head over to Waredaca in the afternoon to walk the course in an overcast drizzle. I have a couple of questions about lines to jump. As I'm finishing my second spin around the course, I run into a student of Coach's who's hooking up with her for a course walk. I have to get back home, because Caitlin is arriving for the weekend. I give Coach a call with hopes of getting my questions resolved. I leave a message, and then a couple of minutes later, she calls me back. "From the sounds of your message, I guess you didn't get the one I left earlier in the week for you," she says.

"No," I say, thinking of how I never check my cell messages, except when I'm on the road. "I no longer want to help you with your horses," she says. Silence. The long moment as I register what she is saying goes on forever in the confines of my car.

"What did I do?" I manage to squeak out.

"I really don't want to go into it," she says. "I hope we can remain friends."

On the way home, the high I've been riding on all week since Fair Hill is replaced with sobs.

Sunshine, Maryland

It pours all night and is still bucketing when I wake at 3:30 A.M. to get ready for Waredaca. The usual bags under my eyes could each carry about a cup of sand this morning. I don't want to ride in the worst way. "You should go," Barrett says, "Huey-Lou is depending on you." Katie and I leave at 5:30. It rains the whole way, and we have to put the truck in four-wheel drive just to pull into Waredaca's parking pasture.

"I really don't want to ride today," I confess again to Katie, as we plop our way around in ankle-high mud. "I guess I'll dig down, find the focus somewhere." I can't stop thinking about Coach.

"You're the master of that," Katie says. "Remember Plantation, remember Fair Hill." I manage to put in a fairly focused dressage test. The announcer confirms that because of the rain and bad footing, they've cancelled cross country and have changed the event to a combined test.

"Let's just go home," I say. But Katie looks at me with a combination of sympathy and go-get-'em.

"You don't want to show jump?" she says.

So I dig down again, and we show jump, and Huey jumps well, bless his old beating, murmured heart, despite two rails in the primordial slop. Why on earth would Coach have fired me?

Now we can go home, where I hope I can turn away from my own sad blood muscle and horses and the thing with Coach and tune into Caitlin. My daughter wants to bake bread this rainy afternoon—nothing like baking bread to take away the blues. We get down to culinary business by trying our mutual hands and elbows at sourdough biscuits. Dig, dig, dig we go. Pound, pound, pound. Rub it around until it feels just right. Get the old fingers working. Knead until they ache. Roll it out as thin as it will go. Smell the sweet and musty aroma wafting up, the poignant sweet and sour scents commingling: this bread, my life.

Rose of Jericho

Maybe everyone had a Rose of Jericho hidden somewhere, Jack thought. Perhaps it wasn't always the kind of tattoo you could see, but another kind —like a free tattoo. No less a mark for life, just one not visible on the skin.

—John Irving

If each of us has one,
a bud opening its small fist
to reveal some fluttery secret at its core,
well then, I never wanted a tattoo
until I realized I already had one
hidden just under my panty line—

probably a lot like yours—
a scar that sealed up
everything I've never said,
that fifty years of hiding
prevent me from describing
any further to you now.

Huey's 'Final' Salute

CHAPTER SEVENTEEN

The Art Project

///

✕ October 23

I write a letter to Coach but don't send it. I mope through my barn work and rides, then head out with Caitlin for some shopping and then to watch her dance lesson at the Towson Dance Studio. We park in the back alley off a side street in Towson and ride up in the snail-paced creaky elevator to the third floor, where we pass through a door into Arthur Murray's era with the studio's long, rectangular parquet dance floor, wood paneling on the dark walls, and mirrors running the length of one. I watch Caitlin dance Argentine tango and then her specialty, salsa, with her dance teacher, Dimitri. Caitlin is as fluid as ever. Dimitri compliments her dancing in his thick Russian accent, "With—how do you say it?—such energy, work . . ."

"Dedication?" I interrupt.

"Yes! dedication," he says brightly, "You could be good."

"Boy, are you nuts," I tell her later on the drive home. "When you have a talent like that, you're crazy not to go for it." But I question myself as soon as I say it, thinking of the poem by Milton that my father introduced me to maybe thirty-five years ago, "On His Blindness."

"Does God exact day labor, light denied?" the poet asks, struggling with the concept of his newfound blindness and what he is to do now that he can no longer best use his god-given talent. "He best serves those who only stand and wait," the poem concludes. Patience is everything. Be patient, Julia.

"No one my age is into international dance," Caitlin says. Which is one of the reasons I suspect she loves international in the first place—it is all hers. Lucky girl, to have found this passion. Same for John, wanting to play Sufi chord progressions on western instruments. He won't have too many rivals out there.

October 24

Caitlin doesn't like my letter to Coach, and neither does Barrett. They think it's too "you" oriented and will put her on the defensive. So I try again, but don't send this one either.

I call up Hans and talk with him about the situation. He's as perplexed about Coach's reactions as I am but doesn't say much. Instead, he dives into my other topic. "What about your dressage score?' he asks. "It wasn't a qualifying one." He's referring to the score—no higher than 75 points—that's required at the Three-Star level to qualify for a Four Star.

"That was with an error," I do my own bit of qualifying, reminding us both of how I went off course in the Three-Star dressage test.

"Then that should be all right," he says. "I don't think they count errors." Which would get my bad score down to 74.5, just under the mark. "But *if* you want to go to Rolex," he continues, "which I think is entirely realistic after your go at Fair Hill, then I think you have to work with a Four-Star rider who's out there currently doing it." I start to check them off in my mind. "And there are only a handful of them," he adds. Phillip Dutton, the O'Connors, Stephen Bradley, Kim Meier, Sally Cousins, Bonnie Mosser. Grace is not on the list. "And you'll have to devote your time from January 1 on exclusively to Rolex. You can't be divided." Hans has hit the nail on the head. He may be young, but he's a heck of a carpenter, having made a careful study of the sport. He has zoomed to the heart of what gets in my way as a rider—and what has intruded on my relationship with Coach.

Whole hog. No division of heart and mind. No splitting hairs or working with multiple instructors. I crawl in bed next to Barrett. I've not handled the last six months well. I've made an art out of keeping secrets in an effort to save feelings and face. But it has backfired. I can't imagine that Coach's decision is about anything other than my divided loyalties. I've divvied up my instructors among several superior riders so that I can manage my tendency to become overwhelmed by a controlling, exclusive student-teacher relationship. In the end, I've become my own Hitler. Keeping secrets is one way of controlling what might otherwise be out of control—an abusive relationship, a bad tendon, a rocky marriage, a sad childhood. But of course, in the end it's a lie, this power of secrets. Deceiving others deceives yourself. True control is found through revelation and honesty. These are my reins.

I consider the challenges that lie ahead of me. I pick up the phone, the sweet recorded voice already makes me feel a little better. I leave a message for Bonnie Mosser.

October 25

Bonnie is heading back to Unionville, Pennsylvania, through a snowstorm outside of her hometown Buffalo. I gulp to her my new plan toward Rolex, then ask about her availability for lessons. "Was this your second Three Star?" she asks. When I admit it was my first, I hear her pause.

"I know it's a stretch," I say. "Considering Redmond's past soundness issues, I'm thinking that time is of the essence, and maybe I should shoot for Rolex sooner rather than later." What I don't admit is what I hear at my back: time's winged chariot.

"Are you qualified?" she asks.

"Well, there's the rub," I say. I explain the awful dressage test. Quite a number of the horse-and-rider teams that finished behind us at Fair Hill are now qualified to go on to Rolex, all because their dressage scores were better than ours was. "I'm hoping they won't count the error," I say, sounding more like an impatient eighteen-year-old than a hopeful middle-aged woman.

"Don't count on it," Bonnie says. "They're getting pretty strict about that. I know it's ridiculous that dressage would keep a horse like Redmond from competing at Rolex, but . . . well, maybe if you did well at the CIC Three Star at Red Hills, the USEF would consider you."

"That's exactly my thought!" I say. We mark Friday on our respective calendars as the day that I'll come see her for a lesson. After we hang up, I get agitated about the potential hitch to my plan, about leaving Grace, about complicating my life even further with a new instructor whom I'll have to travel two hours to hook up with.

I call my brother, who is still suffering from atrial fibrillation. He's in the middle of a twenty-four-hour "episode," and I catch him at a fearful time. Though his problem is not life-threatening, it's enough to get in the way of a normal life, leaving his heart pounding out of his chest, and making him dizzy and out of breath after climbing a set of stairs. And this in a man who up to two months ago was a rigorous weight lifter with a sculpted, hairless, baby-oiled body to show for it. I encourage him to get some sleep and call his doctor in the morning if the symptoms persist. I turn out my own light, and repeat to myself *one carpe diems, two carpe diems, three carpe diems . . .*

October 26

Katie and I tack up Smarty and Pruitt for what will be Pruitt's first trail ride since his most recent comeback from his second splint bone popping. I slip the Segunda bit into his mouth for correction and control. We head out, with Simon leading the way—Daisy remains crashed on her pillow back at the ranch. Pruitt is surprisingly well behaved. I'm just about to give him a gold star for his day's efforts when we hear a distant chorus of foxhounds and the blaring of the hunt master's horn.

Two whips gallop down the hillside, right toward us. Pruitt is unglued by the advancing pair. We swiftly decide to go against hunt etiquette and exit stage left—without waiting to see which way the hunt will go. Who cares where the fox is? I'm on a young horse and don't want to get killed. We trot as fast as we can away from the pursuing hunt, Simon—tail between his legs, scared as shit—trailing right behind us. We cross streams and pick up a rocky trail toward home. The huntsman's horn and the speaking hounds get unnervingly close. I look back, and there's Simon again. Pruitt starts to lose it down another rocky slope, hopping and spinning, and thinking about rearing, but definitely not wanting to go forward. I put all of my energy and attention into staying on until I can get him home and settled. When I look back again, Simon's gone. Katie and I

call for him, but we have to keep moving. I won't survive if the hunt
catches us. We call and call but keep pressing toward home, down
Millender Mill and past the terrifying alpaca herd with their comical,
cartoonish faces, who gallop over to the fence to meet Pruitt and Smarty.
Pruitt's ready to explode, but manages to keep it somewhat together until
we reach our farm driveway, where he takes a deep breath of relief and
snorts the air out. I feel his whole body relax with the realization that he's
home. But no Simon Sad Eyes. Not a sign of him.

We throw the horses in their stalls and head out on the Gator, calling
and calling until our throats hurt. I start walking, backtracking on our trail
ride. The hunt horn is a distant monotonous note, calling the hounds in.
I'm wondering if my brown dog has joined their pack. What a silly sight
that would be, him bounding around all the businesslike hounds, trying to
make friends. We search for a good hour until my throat is killing me and
I've walked a few miles. Katie returns home on the Gator to fetch
Barrett. I walk and walk, and finally head back as the light starts to change,
hoping that home will bring news of Simon's whereabouts As I'm cresting
the hill at the top of our far paddock, Barrett spots me and cruises the
Gator up to get me, so expressionless, I'm sure he's about to deliver bad
news. He raises his index finger as he gets closer, that's all, but I read in
that gesture that Simon's been found. "An off-duty policeman picked him
up," he says, over the din of the Gator's motor. "He was across Blackrock,
roaming about in the Martins' woods." No doubt, he'd become scared and
confused by the hubbub of the hunt and gotten lost, and crossed the
dangerous road where too many of our animals, including a horse years
ago, have met their maker.

October 27

I wake with a raging sore throat from screaming for Simon, only to have
to scream some more. I have a lesson first thing with an older man who
has been eventing probably four times as long as I have and who is still
going around Training-level events—and who happens to be as deaf as a
post, or so he warns me before the lesson begins. I scream at the top of my
lungs through horse number one, then two and three. After two-and-a-
half hours of screeching, my voice is shot.

Off to Waredaca with Katie to school Huey cross country. It's hard to get the blood up to school Intermediate fences. There's a lack of adrenaline unless you come out of the start box under the pressure of competition, and that go-juice is an essential ingredient when jumping the bigger fences. My stirrups are tied because Huey needs this semblance of a run before his go at Virginia, as he hasn't run cross country in two months. The footing is still gooey from all the rain we've had, and as I feel him slipping in the turns to our warm-up fences, I realize that we haven't put big enough studs in. There goes any hope for speed, and maybe even of schooling the tougher turning combinations, unless we give him more traction. But I don't want to stop once I've started. Even bad momentum is better than no momentum.

I rely on impulsion to get me through life—it's a legacy of my struggle with the inertia of depression. At least I don't have to talk, only dodge herds of horses turned out in the cross-country fields and herds of Novice schooling horses and riders. I have to be cautious where I let Huey put his feet. My blood may not start to boil, but Huey's does—he pulls between fences and shakes his head and throws his tongue out the side of his mouth—his newest old-man trick—when I check him and won't let him run full blast. Katie follows close behind—running across fields to open gates and shooing grazing horses away from the jumps—and we manage to have a successful school.

Huey and I run on ahead to finish the course, including the toughest combination that involves a corner, then a turning four strides to a wide oxer, two strides straight ahead to another corner, and then we trot back around to find Katie. "You lost a bell boot," she says when we pull up, "and—oh-oh—you lost a shoe, too." A front shoe. Probably nothing, just a shoe that will need to be tacked back on tomorrow. Nonetheless, I hop off Huey's back to pick up the foot and start fretting about the outcome. Last time a horse threw a shoe when I was going cross country was when Redmond blew off both fronts at Millbrook and bowed a tendon in the process. Huey's foot isn't torn up, the ground is soft, and he's fairly sound without it except when we walk back to the trailer over a gravel drive. He's clearly ouchy. We kick some rocks at Waredaca as we wait for Huey's front legs all snugged up in ice boots to get good and cool before we head home. I spend the afternoon wrapping and soaking, soaking and wrapping the new bare foot, calling the farrier and begging him to come out first thing in the morning, which he promises to do. The fretting never stops, not with kids, not with horses, not when you're downright obsessive about goals and attaining them; the road is always chock-full of gravel that will get in your bare feet and hurt when you step on it on your way from Point Y and determined, full speed ahead, to get there. I suck on a couple of throat lozenges, take three Tylenol PMs, and cross my fingers under the covers while counting the cross-country fences I jumped today before sleep finds me.

October 28

I have been secretly corresponding with Jimmy Wofford.

hi jim, so sorry i'm going to miss you when you come through my place next—i'll be at virginia, trying to get huey through a two star one last time before i retire him (again). i'm in search of a new coach, in my endless quest to learn as much as i can from the best. i'd still like to hook up with you again, sometime in the future —i was thinking about you this A.M. of all the best i've worked with, i've learned the most valuable from you, hands down. just wanted to tell you that. it was good seeing you at fair hill, sharing my excitement with you. take care. see you out there. hope things are well with you, julia

j . . . your next coach should be someone who sees the horse, rather than the rider . . . phillip, lucinda green, etc. best of luck at VaHT, jim

jim, I'm curious . . . why the horse rather than the rider? funny you should say this, i was just thinking about that dichotomy today . . . same wavelength. how would bonnie mosser fit into that scheme?—jw

coaches fall into two general categories . . . see the horse, or see the rider . . . legoff, de nemethy, morris see the rider . . . phillip, sederhom (spelling?), green see the horse . . . both types want the same thing . . . express it differently . . . both refer to the other part often, but tend to find the answer in their instinctive area . . . bonnie would be good.

———————

Katie notices swelling in Huey's pastern of the shoeless foot when she takes off the wrap before soaking him. The ankle and pastern are warm to the touch, and the foot is hot. The farrier slaps a shoe on, and we jog Huey up and down the driveway and pronounce him lame. Back in the stall he goes. We give him some bute and call Vet, who tells us to put him on antibiotics right away, to ice him and alternate icing with a Panalog sweat. "Whatever you do, don't give him any bute," she warns. I suppose she's worried that giving him pain relief will mask the problem and only make it worse before we can identify its source.

"I wouldn't consider it," I say.

I spend my day nursing Huey instead of jumping him with Bonnie Mosser.

By afternoon, Huey is shifting and turning on the leg in his stall. I call Vet to get some more feedback. Her plane has just landed in St. Louis, where she's gone to attend what I think she says is a concert. Why the hell is she at a concert in St. Louis when Huey is lame? I later find out it's a conference, a word that gets garbled over the cell phone miles between us.

Vet encourages me to hand walk Huey and to get her associate to hoof test him. He walks out of his stall fine and is sound during the twenty turns we take around the indoor. When Associate arrives to examine him, he jogs sound for her, albeit with the verboten bute still floating around in his system, hiding whatever problem he might have. She's fairly sure we've dodged the bullet and diagnoses his ailment as a skin infection on his pastern area, which we hope to keep in check with massive amounts of Naxel antibiotic so it doesn't turn into lymphangitis, as it is prone to do in Huey's old legs.

We're invited to dinner on the fourteenth floor of a Baltimore high-rise. It still strikes me as miraculous, being able to go from our dark country hills to the lights of busy Baltimore in a short forty-minute commute. It gets late quick, but the dinner is an extended Thai affair, broken up by a game that our host wants his guests to play before indulging in dessert. We're all handed a stack of blank paper and a pencil. Our job is to answer the questions posed of us, crinkle up our responses, and throw them in a bowl, then guess who wrote which responses. This is only the second time I've met our host, although the other invited couple I've known for almost twenty years, since John and Caitlin were infants. Who would you most like to have dinner with, of anyone past, present, or future? What is the saddest thought you've had in the last six months? What is your earliest childhood memory? Though I'm irritated by having to play a party game when all I really want to do is go to sleep, my answers come from some subconscious place I'm able to tap into, with the help of a little Napa Valley nectar. Abraham Lincoln, I write, because he reminds me of my father. That I never got to know my father before he died, I write again. And then: waiting for my father to come pick me up out of my crib. The smell of his Vitalis and the muskiness that infused his being, hovering over my outstretched arms.

Unionville, Pennsylvania

It's Jerry's big day. I'm finally taking him to his first event at Plantation Field. Jerry is calm hanging out on the trailer by himself and in warm-up. He even manages to keep his head down in dressage. He zips around his stadium course, goey and a little strong, but he leaves all the rails up. Denis Glaccum is acting as cross-country starter today. "What a sport," he says. "How is it that 2 feet on a green bean can look just as big as the 4-foot fences you jumped at Fair Hill? Good going, Julia! You've had quite a season," he adds. "Where did you end up at Fair Hill?" When I tell him twenty-fifth, he seems a little disappointed, as if he were hoping for an even better finish.

"Never in a million years did I think I'd be running around Fair Hill," I say. That seems to satisfy his curiosity. Jerry the Racehorse and I are off, and he cruises around his Pre-Novice course. We head out before the final results are posted. I need to get home and organized before my next engagement.

Katie's father is cooking a crown pork roast for us—his excuse to get us to partake of the Patterson Park Halloween Lantern Parade. We walk down to the park with our go-cups of booze and wait for the parade's arrival. We walk up the spiral staircase to the top of the Pagoda to get another high-up view of Baltimore, our second in two days. Then back down when we see the distant lights beginning to appear. All of Baltimore's school kids have made their own lanterns, and just after dark they begin their march, starting a mile away at the Pulaski Monument and snaking their way up to the park and the crowd awaiting them. They've got stilters and middle-school bands, they've got lantern sailboats and snakes and skeletons and fish. Thousands of kids and their handmade lights fill up the park. It feels like New Orleans with the costumes and hubbub of crowds and lights. We absorb as much of the celebration as we can before heading back to the pork and booze.

October 30

Back down to Baltimore for my publication reading of *Dark Track*. My brother John and his partner, Mark, have driven from New York City. My brother has never heard me read my poems before. The reading takes place at a small gallery/book shop/gift store in Hampden, just up the block from where son John lived over the summer. Before we head out the door, Mark tells me about yesterday's terrorist bombing in New Delhi, along with a train derailment killing hundreds in the same city, where John stayed for the first few days of his trip. This, along with the earthquake killing thousands in the mountains along the Pakistan border where John's group trekked for two weeks following their arrival in New Delhi, make me paranoid that danger is following my son on his trip.

I have to put this out of my mind for the reading. About thirty people show up in the small upstairs room above the gallery. I read the poems from the new book, and I see my work again through the audience's eyes, through their reactions, their sighs and expressions. I pick out a couple of faces in the crowd, including my host, Rosemary Klein, who heads up the Maryland State Poetry and Literary Society. I can tell how my poems are being received by the look on her face as I'm reading. I end up reading almost every poem I'd chosen. Usually I skip ahead several poems in, worried that my audience is getting antsy while I'm anxious to get to the end of my spotlight. I sell a few books and donate the money to MSP&LS. This brings another smile to Rosemary's very reactive face. It's kind of a good feeling when you make someone use their face that much in a day.

Halloween

Cooper comes to shock wave Huey's hocks and ankles and to watch him jog. He pronounces him "solid" at the jog. That's the good news. "The bad news," I say, "is that we can't give him any drugs for the shock wave." Too close to the three-day. Out comes the twitch. Huey's eyes get enormous. He starts fussing, backing up and shying away from our attempts to put the endorphin-releasing instrument on his nose. Into the stall he goes. We have to pin him against the wall to get the twitch on, then drag him back out of his stall and into the shed row. Cooper's assistant, Wilson, holds him, while I man the shock-wave pedal.

Cooper begins the first of two thousand electrical pulses on Huey's hocks. All is well for about fifty pulses, when suddenly Huey lunges forward, knocking everyone back. He plows into the open hatch of Cooper's truck with his head, then tries to exit the unexitable gap between the truck and barn door. When that doesn't work, he rears back, the shock-wave cord now wrapped around his hind leg and the shock-wave machine bouncing off its ledge and flying across the shed row toward the horse.

We count to ten and manage to settle him just enough to rescue the machine and get the twitch off his nose. We're all saying our Hail Marys. I'm thinking *Shit! There goes the three-day,* and Cooper's seeing motherfucking dollar signs flashing in his head. "Let's see how tough this baby really is," Cooper says, righting the instrument, checking the damage to the cords, twisting some dials. The lights are still on, all systems go. Huey's still got two eyes left—and a completely unscratched head. He's got a tiny boo-boo where the cord was wrapped around his leg, but otherwise he's unscathed from the incident. We put a simple chain over his nose and pick up a leg to steady him the old-fashioned way, and he stands like a lamb for the rest of the procedure.

Bonnie Mosser's jump pattern incorporates cross-country–type obstacles in a stadium-jumping format. She's got a bounce that involves a skinny, a corner-to-corner one stride. She even has a couple of actual cross-country jumps on the edges of her ring, including a bank drop into the ring to a turning three-stride skinny. Huey's on fire today, and Bonnie is impressed by what a good soldier he is and how well he looks, considering his age. She offers apt criticisms of my position, commenting on my tendency to fold too much over fences, thereby adding to Huey's inclination to catch rails. She tells me to imagine a beach ball between me and my horse as he takes off before a fence, an image meant to keep my upper body a little more upright. She tells me to find a line and hold that line through the point of takeoff and over the tops of the fences. I tend to give the horse a little too much freedom a couple strides out, which allows him to wander with his body. She's seen this in my jumping of Redmond at the shows. It's not so much a problem with Huey, who's a lot straighter in his body and in his overall way of going than Redmond, but she still wants to change my tendency to turn my horses too loose at the fences. Find a line and keep it, find a line and keep it. Think beach ball, beach ball. I try hard to add the new mantra into my old repertoire. I'm grateful to have some new things to think about, another approach, and a different sort of feedback to keyboard into my system.

I talk to Bonnie about my desire to also continue working with Grace and my lack of interest in studying exclusively with one person, even though this "sleeping around" is exactly what has gotten me in trouble with my instructors in the last year. "I'm not the possessive type. I encourage my students to take lessons from others," Bonnie says, with that characteristic twinkle in her eye that makes me think of free love—if it feels good, learn it.

Maybe this will work out. Bonnie and I make plans to get together at the Two Star, then I begin the process of cooling Huey out and icing his front legs in the early dark before heading home. The days are so short now that we've lost an hour to standard time. Fall back, spring forward. Make a wish before sleep, and walk down the stairs backward tomorrow.

Coach tried to warn me. Maybe she was doing me a favor, after all. Maybe a student's loyalty to her instructor is necessary in order to become one of the best—and maybe one of the safest, too. If only I could find a coach with whom I am that compatible. I feel like a fifty-year-old new divorcée who craves to find love, but is too jaded to surrender to that delicious and vulnerable process of falling all over again. Maybe that is what awaits me in my fifties—developing the ability to let go, to trust completely in my coach, whomever it turns out to be.

I've forgotten the pumpkins this year. I make a note to pick some up tomorrow—maybe they'll be on sale.

November 1

Dear Coach, Who would you most like to have dinner with, of anyone past, present, or future? What is the saddest thought you've had in the last six months? What is your earliest childhood memory?

But of course I don't send it.

November 2

This is the first time in my twelve-year career as an event rider that I've gotten to two three-day events in the same season. For several years, I never even made it to one. I finally got through my first One Star with Redmond just five years ago, in 2000, after several failed attempts with Huey. At the time, that was my goal, a One Star, but after accomplishing that so quickly with Redmond, we went on. After Radnor, the One Stars got easier. Huey made it through, then Surf Guitar. Actually, I've been blessed with two horses of a lifetime, in Redmond and Huey, although Huey has seen too many miles and injuries and years to make it to the top. I think he probably could have, if I'd known several years ago that the main ingredient in an event horse is heart, not talent or soundness. And that the main characteristic of a successful event rider is stubborn perseverance. And if I'd believed in my own ability to get to the Advanced level. Redmond showed me the way, and now it is probably too late for Huey.

Before we put him on the trailer to his last event, the Two Star in Lexington, Barrett and I make plans for Huey's retirement party, designing the invitation, which will consist of an eventing picture and a racing win photo, Huey's long list of stats, and the poem "Catching Huey" on the back flap. We even start to compose a guest list of everyone who has put their hands on Huey over the years, from race trainers to vets and farriers and well-wishing friends. Huey's quivering in the cross ties. He knows what's up as we put on the shipping boots and the tail wrap. All the years I've spent with him come crashing down around me as we prepare to leave the farm for what I hope will be the event of Huey's life. It's time to march him onto the trailer.

Huey's story won't end in Lexington this weekend. I hope it will go on for several lush years of running around our 83 acres as if he owns the joint. I imagine him and Redmond ten years from now, when I'm sixty and they're almost twenty-eight and twenty-three, sharing racing and event stories, and tales of the road, of the Fair Hill Three Star and the Virginia Two Star, of Rolex and Canada and beyond, over rich blades of orchard grass. I hope it goes on and on, until they join my mother, who would have loved this tale of the creatures she adored most in the world.

I turn the truck key and rev up the diesel. The doggies in the backseat and Katie beside me are excited for the big weekend ahead. It's a brilliant day of sunshine at An Otherwise Perfect Farm. I look from right to left, surveying the farm that Barrett and I made and now work so hard to keep, then pull down the long driveway only to leave it one more time.

The Art Project

She hauled it home
in her brother's VW,
scratched the hatch paint
when she pried it out,

carted it up the stone steps
and into the mud room
of our farm house.

"We had to show movement
and light," she informed us.
"Everyone else made kaleidoscopes,
but I had my heart set on a chair."

She hammered for hours in her art class
the seat of the old metal stool
where she glimpsed
splintered versions of herself.

"Downright dangerous," we joked
around the dinner table,
wincing at the shards
of mirror glued on top

of our dented images,
concertina wire
wound helter-skelter
around the stainless legs

until we imagined
a kind of movement there,

a two-step forming
at the edge of our minds,

a debutante in her stiff
hoop skirt swooping
over a gleaming dance floor,
and balanced on the arm

of some tantalizing stranger
who might become our daughter's future,
which she has crafted in movement
& light. We still keep it at our entrance,

daring us to sit, or dance,
or look more closely at the painful
puzzle of ourselves.
Sometimes, we even like what we see.

This poem first appeared in *Willow Review*.

Calvin and Barrett and J. W.

Last Light

Finish Flags

※ I never find the perfect distance—at least not this year. Finding it would mean losing the need to look for it. The best I can do is find a better distance.

Huey makes it through the Two Star in Lexington—respectable in dressage, brilliant in cross country, but a brute the last day in show jumping, taking several rails down with his cocky, flustered attitude, conjuring up just enough of a disappointment within me to not give up on the horse, after all, in hopes of improving his show jumping in the spring and maybe even becoming competitive with him at another Two Star. We'll have to postpone that retirement party for at least another season.

Thanksgiving comes and goes without either John or Caitlin at home. Barrett and I return soon after to my hometown of Warren, Pennsylvania, where Barrett delivers the paper on Sylvia Plath—the paper that my father had committed to write for the Shakespeare Club in Warren before his untimely death in early 2004—while I give another poetry reading at the Warren Public Library. A couple of hours before my reading, we get a phone call from Katie, who has just gotten a call from Boulder, Colorado, who has received a call from a hospital in Benares. The miles between us are the longest they've been since John's departure. "They're running tests for malaria and typhoid," the program staff member tells me when I call from somewhere on the snowy highway between Erie and Warren. I pace and stew and have to put a lid on my hysteria to give the reading. Finally, around midnight, I get another phone call from Boulder, giving me John's hospital room telephone number in India. I call and actually get through to him, and as soon as I hear his voice, my fears dissolve. He's okay.

Even so, he is a sick puppy from food poisoning and has to stay in the hospital a couple more days, pumped up on electrolytes and antibiotics. The next day, however, he's not too sick to make a special request, via long distance. "Do you know what a mala is?" he asks me weakly. And when I tell him no, he explains: "It's like a Hawaiian lei, only it's made with marigolds. Indians give it as a token of well wishing and respect, and often to teachers and family members." There's a pause from across the world. "Could you have two malas made," he asks me, "and put them on Grandmother and Ba's graves?"

The local florist can't get marigolds this time of year. But they're able to make the malas with lilies and carnations. The florist's parents-in-law are East Indian, and she knows exactly how to string the flowers together. Barrett and I make a last stop at the cemetery on our way out of town. My parents' graves are littered with fallen oak and maple leaves, so we have to rake away the brown leavings with our fingers before placing the flower necklaces on the headstones. The smokestacks of my father's refinery, to which he gave forty years of his life, are still huffing and puffing just over the cemetery's horizon, forming an appropriate backdrop for his Eternity.

A few days later, we wait for John to walk off the plane from Calcutta via Bangkok and L.A. I obsessively watch the board flash from ON TIME to LANDING to ARRIVED and finally to AT THE GATE, but still no sign of John. I'm worried after a stream of passengers passes us, that he might have missed the flight or come down with another bout of food poisoning, compliments this time of Southwest Airlines. I finally see his characteristic lanky saunter from the farthest end of the terminal. I start running, and as I get closer, I spot the new beard, then the expression of calm and happiness on his face before our bodies collide in greeting. I stretch out the hug as long as I dare, between two weary travelers who have both trekked long and hard in search of something it might take a lifetime to articulate. John had to go to the ends of the earth, while I barely had to leave the state of Maryland. Now, and in subsequent conversations over the next few days, we feel the difference and change between us, because for both, the journey was inward as much as outward, and that passage is always more difficult to describe. "Just so you know," he says when I finally let go of his shoulders, "arrival is downstairs."

We spend days catching up. At first he is still in India, eating with his hands, having trouble with the quiet of the farm, with the excesses of life in the West, as he now calls America. He freely admits that he wants to return to India as soon as he's able. But as the days lapse into a week, and we drive up to see Caitlin's performance as a German soldier in a production of Maria Irene Fornes's absurdist musical, *Promenade*, John has settled back into his life, jokes easily with his sister, who is clearly thrilled that we, but especially her big brother, have come to see her performance. She will be home, too, for winter break, as soon as she finishes her semester.

"So how are things at the farm?" she asks me over brunch, before Barrett and John and I head back home. "How's Sunny? How's Huey? And Fuzzy? How are Redmond and Calvin and Jerry and Pruitt?" She reels the names off.

"Pruitt's gone," I say, referring to the four-year-old's recent sale. "It looks like they may throw out the dressage qualification for the three-days," I say, which would be my immediate ticket to Rolex.

"That's great!" she says, her attention already having wandered away from her polite inquiries about her life as she used to know it and back to her busy schedule this week of papers and tests and auditions. As it should be.

She circles back to the topic over dessert. "Why so fast?" she asks, the very same question the judge asked of her when she had to go to traffic court the second time. "They have those qualifications for a reason, you know, Mom."

"Because," I tell her, "I have to make it to Rolex before my curfew."

My daughter, for all of her turmoil and discontents, her outbursts and questionings, is still the one who best understands my ambition and is ever the voice of caution and reserve. She wants me to do well, but above all she wants me to be safe.

"There's a reason it's so hard to qualify and usually takes more time. They want riders to have more experience before they're able to move up to a Four Star," she explains.

I am relieved that Caitlin no longer pushes 75 in a 55 miles-per-hour speed zone.

"And Mom," she adds, glancing at her wristwatch, "it's already twenty minutes past your curfew."

But I continue to think of Rolex, of my planned trip south with my four event ponies, and of all the pages and miles and jumps and dressage tests that have gotten me to this point, when I can actually say, *No harm in trying*—words rooted in my attachment to the process of getting there and rubbing up against the Beautiful along the way. In other words, I'm still looking for it.

GLOSSARY OF TERMS

ACell—A treatment called UBM, made by the company ACell Vet, which promotes and stimulates healing in tendons and ligaments in the lower legs of horses.

Acepromazine—A tranquilizer.

Aids—Prompts that a rider uses to signal to his horse what he wants the animal to do. Aids are applied with the hands, legs, heels, balance, and weight of the rider's seat, and so on.

Allowance race—A horse race at a higher level than a claiming race.

Azium—A steroid used in the treatment of skin disorders and systemic inflammations.

Back at the knee—A conformational flaw in a horse. Ideally, there should be a straight line from a horse's shoulder to knee to ankle. In a horse that's back at the knee, the knee joint is set back too much and has a hollowed-out appearance, which causes undue pressures and strains on a horse's foreleg.

Banamine—A nonsteroidal, anti-inflammatory, often used as a soft-tissue relaxant.

Bascule—The roundness of a horse's back when he jumps. A good jumping horse is often admired for his degree of bascule.

Baytril—A powerful antibiotic used for horses.

Behind the leg—A horse is said to be behind the rider's leg when he is not listening to the rider's aids to go forward. The horse often appears sluggish and doesn't jump well as a consequence.

Behind the vertical—In dressage terms, when a horse is correctly on the bit, his head is perpendicular to the ground. If the horse is traveling behind the vertical, then his head is tucked closer to his chest, and the 90-

degree angle the head makes with the ground is closed up; therefore, the horse's head is behind the vertical.

Bell boot—Protective covering for the hooves to help prevent the horse from wrenching off a shoe.

Block—To numb; often used in equine medicine in order to diagnose the source of a horse's lameness. If a horse blocks sound to a foot, for instance, then the source of lameness is most likely in the foot; i.e., numbness in that area took away the pain and hence made the horse sound.

Bounce—A kind of jump in which the horse doesn't take a stride between efforts—his landing is also his takeoff.

Bowed tendon—An injury to a horse's foreleg in which the tendon is torn, causing a bowed appearance.

Breezing—Refers to a horse galloping at a high rate of speed (900 meters per minute or more).

Broodmare—A mare used for breeding.

Bute—A common medicine (nonsteroidal anti-inflammatory) used in horse care to alleviate pain; similar to aspirin.

Cannon bone—On a horse, the bone situated between the knee and the ankle. The shaft of the cannon bone is slender but capable of carrying a great deal of weight.

Cavaletti—An adjustable low wooden jump used in the jump training of a horse.

Cellulitis—A localized infection of the cells, usually in a horse's leg.

Center line—An invisible line that bisects a dressage arena. When entering the ring for a dressage test, horses enter by turning down center line and trotting or cantering directly at the judge, who sits at the opposite end of the ring.

Check ligament—A ligament in a horse's lower leg that is commonly injured through exertion, particularly when jumping. Slight to moderate lameness often occurs as well as swelling, and then thickening, at the back of the leg below the knee. It is a serious injury requiring careful rehabilitation.

Claiming race—A horse race, usually at the lower level, in which all the horses entered are for sale. A horse entered in such a race may be claimed, or purchased, at the beginning of the race and will go to his new owner regardless of the race's outcome.

Coffin—A type of cross-country obstacle that involves three jumps set at related distances, usually a vertical to a ditch to another vertical.

Colic—A stomach disorder of the horse; the number-one natural killer of horses.

Connection—A dressage term to describe the desired result of a rider's aids. When a horse is connected, or on the bridle, they are balanced, moving forward freely, and there is a direct relationship, or connection, between the horse's hindquarters, or engine, and the head and mouth, or steering. As in a boat, the engine propels the boat and the steering wheel steers it, and there is a distinct connection, or relationship, between the two. The better the connection, the better the control.

Corner—A kind of jump that is shaped like a triangle: on one side it comes to a point, and on the opposite it can get quite wide, depending on the level. The shape encourages the horse and rider to "dare the point," or to jump as close to the point as possible to avoid jumping the wide side; however, it's very easy for the horse to run out at the point. Corners are difficult fences and only seen at the upper levels of eventing.

Coronary band—Area where the hair stops and hoof growth begins at the bottom of the pastern on a horse's leg. Extends around the top rim of the hoof from one bulb of the heel to the other and is thickest and roundest at the toe.

Cosequin—Joint supplement.

Counter canter—Cantering intentionally on the wrong, or outside, lead.

Course walk—In eventing, riders are allowed to walk on foot the stadium and cross-country courses before the event in order to plan their strategy.

The horses, however, will be seeing the jumps for the first time when they go out on course.

Crest—The top portion of a horse's neck, just under the mane.

Cross rail—A small jump that forms an "x" with the rails that the horse jumps.

Cross ties—Two long lines that attach to barn or trailer walls used for tying horses.

Croup—The highest point of a horse's rump.

Dexamethasone—Anti-inflammatory, steroidal agent.

DMSO—Or dimethyl sulfoxide, derived from wood pulp. A chelating agent which penetrates skin easily. Used as a topical analgesic.

Dressage—A kind of riding in which the horse performs various movements and figures within the confines of a ring, often to display the quality of the horse's gaits, as well as the horse's suppleness, obedience, and relaxation.

Elephant trap oxer—A type of wide, airy cross-country fence.

Engagement—The degree to which the horse is utilizing his hind end within his overall movement. A horse is said to be engaged if his hocks are bending and working and he is pushing with his hind legs in order to create energy and momentum from behind.

Equitaine—Antifungal shampoo.

Ermine sock—A black and white sock having a mottled appearance on a horse's front or hind pasterns and ankles.

Extended trot—In dressage terms, an extended trot is usually a trained exaggeration, or extension, of a horse's normal trot that involves a longer, or lengthened, stride. An extended trot often takes years to develop.

Farrier—A rider's best friend. He's the one who makes, shapes, fires, and nails a horse's shoes to his hooves and helps keep the horse sound and able to run over all manner of terrain. Also good for woodstove repair.

Farrier's Formula—Hoof supplement.

FEI—Fédération Equestre Internationale.

Fetlock—The projection of a horse's leg, behind the joint between the cannon bone and pastern, which has a tuft of hair.

Fetlock joint—The joint at this point.

Flatwork—Another term for dressage (see "Start Box" section). The rider practices the horse's gaits and movements of a dressage test, focusing on the horse's suppleness, fluidity, forwardness, and obedience.

Flexion—When a horse has proper flexion, his head and neck are flexed, or bent, at the poll (the highest point of a horse's head, between the ears) so that the horse's head is carried perpendicular to the ground. When the horse is overflexed, the horse's head is bent at more than a 90-degree angle to the ground, and the nose appears tucked in toward the chest. This is an undesirable state (see *Behind the vertical*).

Flexion test—A test used to determine a horse's soundness and/or to diagnose the source of lameness that involves flexing or bending each leg at an extreme angle for a set period of time—between one and one-and-a-half minutes—and then having the horse jog off. The number of lame steps the horse takes after the flexion helps the vet to diagnose the lameness.

Flying change—The point in a horse's canter stride at which he changes canter leads midstride.

Footing—Used to describe the ground that a horse must work or run on. Footing is said to be good or bad, depending on its softness, hardness, depth, consistency, and amount of moisture resulting from rainfall or lack thereof.

On the forehand—A horse is said to be on the forehand when he is balancing his weight primarily on the front of his body, rather than on his hind end, which is the more desirable condition. A horse on the forehand often feels heavy in the rider's hands.

Founder—A potentially fatal effect of overeating that strikes the horse's hooves, causing him to go lame. Too much blood flows to the laminae of a horse's feet, resulting in a rotation and lowering of the coffin bone.

In front of the leg—Used to describe a desired result when the horse is listening to his rider's leg. When the rider puts his lower leg on, the horse responds by moving forward. If a horse is being disobedient, then he is not listening to the leg, and nothing happens when the rider applies the leg. The horse will often appear sluggish and not moving forward freely. That horse is said to be behind the leg. Conversely, when the horse is in front of the leg, he is responding to the rider's aids and is moving freely and fluidly.

Full pass, half pass—A dressage movement that involves lateral movement on the horse's part and a specific inside bend of the horse's body in the direction in which he is traveling.

Fura-Zone—Antibiotic ointment.

Galloping boots—Protective covering for a horse's lower limbs, often made of leather or nylon; either Velcroed or buckled closed.

Gentocin—An intravenous antibiotic used for horses.

Getting spun—An elimination at a competition, usually as a result of lameness.

Girth—The piece of leather or nylon or cotton that goes around a horse's barrel and attaches on both sides to the saddle. The girth is what keeps the saddle on the horse.

Grob—A cross-country jump that is situated in a depression in the earth that the horse and rider gallop down into, often sided with banks and a ditch in the middle for jumping. Grobs have a tunneling, claustrophobic effect on the horse and are therefore a test of a horse's bravery.

Ground line—A pole placed on the ground under a jump so that a horse can better gauge his take-off point.

Gymnastic (i.e., grid, or grid work)—Jumps set in a row at related distances that teach a horse how to better use himself over fences and provide the rider the opportunity to work on her position.

Hack—Or trail ride, or riding a horse in the countryside out of the confines of a ring.

Half halt— Or half a halt. Signals that a rider gives a horse to rebalance his gaits. The aids are the same as when asking for a horse to halt, but not as strong, so instead of halting, the horse momentarily slows and rebalances himself.

Handicapping—The process of assigning weights to the different horses in a race with the aim of each horse winning simultaneously. For example, one horse is said to be 3 pounds better than another horse.

Hock—The joint in the hind leg of a horse, above the fetlock joint, corresponding anatomically to a human ankle. If a horse is said to be hockey, then he is moving irregularly in such a way that indicates that his hocks are bothering him.

Hoof abscess—An infection in the hoof that can make the horse appear very lame but is easily remedied with proper care. It is one of the most common causes of lameness in horses; this diagnosis is often a relief to owners fearing a more major problem.

Hot walker—The person who walks a hot racehorse right after the jockey has dismounted. Walking a horse after work helps the horse's breathing return to normal and helps the horse to more easily cool out without stiffening up. It also relaxes the horse's diaphragm after galloping or jumping.

Hunt seat—A type of riding that takes place in a ring and focuses on the form of the horse's jump as well as the rider's position.

Ice boots—Boots placed on horses' legs at the end of a big exertion that are filled with ice in order to reduce inflammation caused by the stress of work.

Isoxsuprine—A drug commonly administered in order to improve circulation.

Jump cup—A metal cup that attaches to a jump standard and holds the poles that straddle the standards. The horse jumps the pole between the standards.

Laser—A therapeutic light-wave treatment used for chronic and acute bony and soft-tissue problems in horses.

Layup—A horse that is recovering from an injury and not in work is often referred to as a layup.

Leg yield—Lateral movement of a horse who, by the rider applying particular aids, is moving sideways with his front and hind legs crossing over in a specific pattern.

Lunging—A form of riderless exercise for the horse in which the horse is attached to a long line and circles at all three gaits around the person in the center who holds the other end of the line.

Lymphangitis—Inflammation of the lymph nodes.

Martingale—A leather strap that goes around a horse's neck and attaches to the reins, which prevents the horse from getting his head too high over the fences.

Naquasone—Diuretic and anti-inflammatory steroid used to reduce swelling.

Off—To be lame.

Oiling—A procedure that involves introducing a quantity of oil into the horse's stomach in order to relieve certain kinds of colic. The oil tends to get the intestinal system going again.

Orvus—A type of shampoo for horses.

Oxer—A wide jump. In the show ring, it is constructed of two rails set parallel to each other. In cross-country jumping over immovable obstacles, it denotes a jump that emphasizes width (a table, for instance) and can measure anywhere from 1 or 2 feet to 9 or 10 feet wide, depending on the level of competition.

Paddock—A fenced-in, open-air space used for turning out horses.

Panalog—A mild steroidal cream often used to treat dermatitis.

Pastern—The area of a horse's leg below the fetlock joint and above the hoof.

Platinum Plus—A type of supplement that is added to a horse's grain, much like a multi-vitamin.

Post—An up-down movement the rider makes in the saddle to coincide with the rhythm of a horse's trot. Posting to the trot (rather than sitting) is more comfortable for the rider, as well as kinder to the horse's back.

Poultice—A cool substance, usually made of clay, used to draw heat out of a horse's leg.

Prix St. George—The first international level of dressage.

Prostin—A hormone used to short cycle a mare—to make her come into season and ovulate before her natural cycle.

Pull a rail—Used to describe what happens when a horse knocks a rail in stadium jumping and the rail falls to the ground. Jumping penalties are assigned to the horse and rider as a consequence of the mistake.

Rack—A learned gait common among saddlebreds in which no two feet of the horse hit the ground at the same time. The hooves strike the ground one at a time in a clockwise rotation.

Rail Sitter—A bettor at the race track who hangs out at the rail.

Rate—To control a horse's speed.

Revolution—A substance that controls fleas, ticks, and heartworms in dogs and cats.

Robert Jones bandage—A large bandage that spirals up a horse's entire leg, used to immobilize it, named after its creator.

Rotococcus—A potentially fatal virus.

Run-in shed—A small, three-sided building placed inside a paddock, where the turned-out horse can run in to find shelter from bad weather.

Run-out—A disobedience when jumping in which the horse runs around the jump rather than jumping it.

Scope—A term used to signify the talent of a jumping horse. A horse said to have scope or be scopey is a good jumper who can easily jump a big fence.

Scratch—To withdraw.

Segunda bit—A type of bit used for correction and control.

Serpentine—A dressage movement that draws an S in the dressage ring. A serpentine can be executed at all three gaits.

Shadbelly—A rider's formal coat with tails used at the upper levels of dressage and eventing, as well as at all three-day events.

Shed row—Or barn aisle.

Shock-wave therapy—A series of electromagnetic pulses used in the healing of a horse's damaged bones, tendons, and ligaments.

Shoulder in—A dressage movement in which, by the use of the correct aids, the rider brings the horse's shoulder to the inside of the track of a riding ring while the hind legs are traveling straight down the track. It is a movement used to supple a horse and make him freer with his body and movement.

Show jumping (stadium jumping)—A jumping course that takes place in a ring over jumps that knock down if hit (see "Start Box" section).

Skinny fence (narrow fence)—A jump that is narrower than a regular 10- or 12-foot-wide jump, often only 4 or 6 feet wide, which increases the difficulty of the horse's jumping effort.

Splint—The splint bone on a horse is a non–weight-bearing bone that runs parallel to the tibia. When a horse "pops a splint," the splint bone becomes separated from its periosteal lining.

Stack wrap—A kind of multiple leg wrap for horses that wraps around the entire leg. Several layers of wraps are stacked on top of each other up the length of the leg.

Stakes—The highest level of flat racing, in which the owners stake the horses or put up entry fees.

Standard—The lumber on each side of a show jump that holds up the rail that the horses jump.

Steeplechase—A horse race over brush fences at a high rate of speed. Steeplechase horses are trained to brush through their fences rather than jump over them. Traditional steeplechase races are run in a pack, but in three-day eventing, the horse jumps the steeplechase course solo, within a set period of time and faster than the speed set for cross country.

Stifle—The joint between the femur and tibia on a horse, corresponding anatomically to a human knee.

Stocked up—Or swollen; used to describe a horse's swollen legs, usually a result of standing too long in a stall.

Strangles—A potentially fatal virus that attacks the lymph nodes in horses; strep throat for horses.

Studs—Blocks, caulks and cleats of various sizes and shapes that can be screwed in and out of a horse's shoes to improve the horse's traction in different kinds of footing.

Suspensory—Ligaments in a horse's legs that connect the long bones to the joints.

Sweat—A type of leg wrap on a horse that induces moist heat to promote the lessening of swelling that is due to an injury.

Teaser—A gelding or stallion used to determine if a broodmare is receptive to breeding. The teaser excites, or teases, the mare, and depending on her reaction, the handler can surmise if it is time to breed her to the stallion of choice.

Technical delegate—The official at each event who enforces the rules as set by the United States Equestrian Federation (USEF), United States Eventing Association (USEA), and the Fédération Equestre Nationale (FEI).

Timber knee, timber shin, etc.—A raised area on a bone or joint that is due to repeated trauma.

Trakkener—A type of cross-country jump that involves a log hung over a ditch. The horse jumps the log as well as the ditch as one jump.

Triple—In show jumping, a triple is a combination of three jumps set in a row at related distances.

Triple bar—A type of oxer that involves not one (as in vertical), not two (as in oxer), but three rails set parallel to each other, usually placed in ascending heights from front to back.

Turf race—A flat race run on grass.

Turn on the haunches—A dressage movement in which the hind legs step in the same spot while the shoulders turn around the haunches in order to face the horse in the opposite directions. Turn on the haunches is a trained movement used to gain better control of a horse's shoulders.

Twitch—Instrument that wraps tightly around the horse's nose and releases endorphins, which promote a horse's submission in difficult situations, such as veterinary treatments, that require a horse to stand still.

Two-point position—Used when galloping or jumping. The rider's seat comes slightly out of the saddle, and the rider has the appearance of standing up in her stirrups and/or bending slightly at the waist over fences. Moving the rider's weight forward and out of the saddle helps the horse's balance when galloping or jumping.

Verticals—Show jumps that are composed of one rail hung between two standards.

Vet box (ten-minute box)—At a traditional three-day event, the vet box is the mandatory place where horse and rider teams must congregate (for ten minutes) before and after they go out on cross country. Vets check over the horse in the ten-minute box to make sure the horse is fit, healthy, and sound enough to start the course, hence its name. The horses and riders must then return to the vet box upon completion of the course for a similar veterinary evaluation.

Whip—or, more correctly, a whipper-in, is a staff member of a foxhunt club who assists the huntsman. He helps keep the hounds in a pack when hacking to a meet and when hunting occurs. Whips ride out from the huntsman and hounds, on the edges of the hunted covert, to try and view a fox breaking cover. In this day and age, whips ride the roads a lot to prevent hounds from getting hit by traffic.

THE AUTHOR

Julia Wendell was born and raised in Warren, Pennsylvania. She received degrees from Cornell University, Boston University, and The University of Iowa Writers' Workshop. After making careers as an editor and teacher and mom, she turned her attention back to her childhood passion for horses. Since 1995, she has been engaged in the sport of three-day eventing. She is the author of three full-length collections of poems and three chapbooks. She lives in northern Baltimore County on a horse farm with her husband, Barrett Warner.

PHOTO CREDITS

Shannon Brinkman	*88, 198, 239, 253, 316*
Colonial Downs Race Track	*214*
GRC Photography, Inc.	18, *282*
Jerry Henery	*171, 172, 298*
Chandler Willett Lowing	*x, 2, 32, 51, 52, 315, 346, 381, 382*
Sport Horse Studio	*150, 254, 364*
Barrett Warner	*106, 240*